Sports Ground Management

A Complete Guide

Stewart Brown

Foreword by Alan Penn

Lincoln College

2004801

D1585770

First published in 2009 by
The Crowood Press Ltd
Ramsbury, Marlborough
Wiltshire SN8 2HR

www.crowood.com

British Library Cataloguing-in-Publication Data
A catalogue record for this book is available from the British Library.

ISBN 978 1 84797 094 7

Disclaimer
All tools and equipment used in turf management and in sports ground
management in general should be used in strict accordance with both the
current health and safety regulations and the manufacturer's instructions. The
author and the publisher do not accept responsibility or liability of any kind in
any manner whatsoever for any error or omission, or any loss, damage, injury
or adverse outcome incurred as a result of the use of the information
contained in this book, or reliance upon it. If in doubt about any aspect of
sports ground management, readers are advised to seek professional advice.

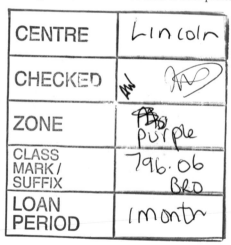
Typeset by Exeter Premedia Services Pvt Ltd., Chennai, India

Printed and bound in Malaysia by Times Offset (M) Sdn Bhd

Contents

Foreword

When first starting out in groundsmanship more than twenty-five years ago, there were very few books about the turf grass industry or that would give an insight into the world of the groundsman. This has changed to a degree with the introduction of the Internet, but there is still a general lack of information easily available in book form, whether for those persons starting out in groundsmanship or those interested in sports turf, right through to the professional at a large sporting facility or a stadium environment. This book follows on from the author's earlier *Sports Turf and Amenity Grassland Management*. This was intended to fill the void left since Frank Hope's *Turf Culture*, which has long been out of print, is now dated. *Turf Culture* was the original 'bible' of grounds staff countrywide – at least for those who are now thirty-five or over. With this new publication Stewart continues to provide good technical information, based on years of practical experience, for today's grounds managers and personnel.

The book has been designed to bring the art of groundsmanship and turf management to all, including the inexperienced. Good turf culture and management is becoming increasingly important as grounds staff often have to provide good quality facilities on a lower budget, with fewer staff and less machinery. Having recently completed a Master of Science degree in Sports Surface Technology, I know that this book will be of immense use to all those interested in Sports Ground Management, covering many of the subjects that I studied during my course. The book covers a vast array of subjects. Sports turf is no longer just about getting the grass to grow but extends to such aspects as management, budgeting, health and safety and environmental issues. All of these now have a bearing on our industry and are covered in detail here.

I believe this book will find its place, not only with experienced grounds staff, but also with students, such as those Stewart currently teaches, and those studying for qualifications. I am sure it will be regarded as a standard work of reference in the years to come. I attended several colleges in my early days looking for a suitable career. Tree surgery came to mind, but did I want to be climbing trees in my late forties? I looked at sports turf and thought there cannot be much to growing grass. Well, you live and learn and learn some more – and with this industry you never stop learning. This book will certainly be in my hand until the learning is over or I have gone to the great sports ground in the sky. I hope you enjoy the book and benefit from the wealth of information now available in the one volume.

Alan Penn BSc MSc

Independent Turf Grass Agronomist (Formerly Technical Manager for the National Playing Fields Association)

apgrassman@yahoo.co.uk

Introduction

We live in a society where many people enjoy sport and outdoor recreation. Many sports are considered to be 'national' pastimes and the fortunes or otherwise of our teams and professional players, for example in football and cricket, are followed with enthusiasm and often great passion by many fans and spectators. While some are content to spectate, many others play competitively in sports grounds at all levels throughout the country. All players, at whatever level, need surfaces on which to play, but it is often overlooked that the quality of the playing surface can have a significant impact on the game and even its result. Constructing, preparing and maintaining surfaces for play are the task of the professional grounds person. For players at all levels to give their best performance and enjoy their sport, surfaces must be provided to high standards. There are many pressures facing the grounds staff employed to manage an array of diverse sporting surfaces. To be fully effective, grounds staff must be trained, qualified and experienced in many aspects of surface construction, preparing them for play and then repairing them, often in the very brief time allowed, before they can be played on again. The grounds person or manager often has to cope with the complexities of more than one surface and the different seasons this often involves. Sports surfaces are not always at their best if resources are limited or, as often still happens, fixtures take place when ground conditions are not wholly suitable.

The condition of the surface is the responsibility of the turf manager, but it is not always their fault if it is not in its best state. Even non-turf surfaces, such as synthetic turf carpets used for hockey and other sports, or the polyurethane tracks used for athletics, need maintenance. A tangible benefit of these surfaces is that they often take the pressure off the grass pitches used for training purposes, which often suffer from overuse. For most sports, though, grass is still the surface of choice. Nothing looks as good and arguably plays as well as a well-constructed and maintained grass pitch or court. Looking after a sports surface is a demanding and sometimes frustrating job that requires coping with the vagaries of nature, the weather and the demands of players. Despite that, however, it can be the best job in the world for those who enjoy sport and working outdoors. Preparing a surface and seeing it in top condition as players enjoy the results of one's hard work is very satisfying. Grounds staff and managers are technically highly skilled, motivated, multi-skilled and resourceful and, given the pressures under which they work, they need to be.

Sports Ground Management, though, is a lot more than just preparing and looking after the playing surfaces. This book reflects the vast range of skills and knowledge required to manage sports surfaces today. There are resources to manage, events to run and a myriad of legislative and regulatory requirements to cope with. Environmental issues are ever more a concern for the grounds professional too. This book attempts to bring together many of the diverse disciplines that congregate in contemporary sports ground management and offer the reader an accessible reference source for the main information required for a range of surfaces and management tasks. Sports grounds are as diverse as sports themselves, from the village cricket ground to international sporting stadia. There are differences, too, in terms of the sports catered for, ranging from multiple sports fields in schools or under local authority care to private sports clubs. Some enterprises may only cater for one sport or surface, such as bowls, cricket, hockey, rugby, football or horse racing. Not all have the same issues or requirements. Despite this there are often, surprisingly, many common factors. Goods and services must be procured – whether you need 50 bags of topdressing or 500 – and the processes involved can often be the same. Grass sports surfaces, regardless of the level of game being played, still need to be mown and repaired. There are often some differences according to fixtures, standards of play and resources available, but these are often mere details or questions of scale.

This book is aimed at those concerned with the maintenance and management of sports surfaces and grounds. It will have relevance to those responsible for smaller private sports clubs and grounds as well as those working on larger scale local authority, school, college and university sites. It also has much for those managing larger scale facilities for such as professional football, rugby, cricket and horse racing. It will be of most value to those directly involved with the maintenance and management of the actual surfaces, such as professional grounds staff and managers at all levels. I hope it will also help to inform the many others engaged with sports grounds and surfaces, including club officials and secretaries, committee members, council officials, governors and players. For many clubs voluntary and part-time staff are the 'life blood' of the organization. This is especially so at smaller clubs, where they are often employed in pitch maintenance or other essential activities. These people should also gain much valuable information and insight to help them with their work. The last, but probably most important, group comprises the many young people entering the profession of what is often referred to as Groundsmanship: the many students of sports turf, trainees and apprentices. These will be the custodians of our sports grounds and facilities in the future and it is hoped that this book will assist their learning and professional development throughout their career. No single book can cover every situation and requirement, but I hope the content here gives the more useful and commonly needed information for the diversity of provision it attempts to cover. This book does not cover the fundamental principles of turf culture as that is covered in its sister publication, *Sports Turf and Amenity Grassland Management*. Together they offer a complete guide to all facets of turf management for sports grounds.

Acknowledgements

The author is indebted to the following companies for kindly supplying pictures for this book: Autoguide Equipment Ltd; Bernhard and Company Ltd; Dennis; Fleet Linemarkers Ltd; Harrod UK Limited; J Mallinson (Ormskirk) Ltd; John Deere; Ransomes Jacobsen; SISIS Equipment (Macclesfield) Ltd; Toro; and Waste2Water Europe Ltd.

Special thanks to my wife (Dawn) and children (Harry, Hannah and Hayley) for their continuing love and support in all my endeavours.

PART I

Management

1 Sports Ground Management and Administration

Much of a Sports Ground Manager's time and effort will be taken up in managing resources, including staff and finance. The context and scale can vary hugely, depending on the type of organization and its size. Sports grounds are owned and managed by organizations within the public sector (for example local authorities), private and commercial sports clubs and even registered charities. The organization may employ many staff or few, have a large financial resource or a limited budget. Whatever the individual sports ground's circumstance and resource availability, there will be common factors to manage. This chapter aims to provide guidelines that can be applied to resource management for all levels of club and organization. The first section will look at some of the many types of sports club encountered (particularly within the private, commercial and charitable sectors), before progressing to aspects of personnel and financial management relevant to the sports ground manager. The efficiency of service provision and ultimately the viability of the organization is dependent upon the management team achieving resource allocation targets, particularly regarding the budget.

Types of Sports Clubs

The law does not define a club, and indeed it would be very difficult to pen a definition that embraces all the different groups calling themselves clubs. They have one thing in common: they all consist of people drawn together by a common interest or link. Unless the group becomes what is known in law as a body corporate, it has no legal status of its own in the eyes of the law, but consists merely of, and is represented by, all the individual members. There are a number of types of club, depending on legal status or lack of it, and on whether alcohol is served.

Members' Club
A members' club is the simplest form of arrangement for a voluntary organization. The club does not have a legal existence of its own and it cannot sue or be sued, nor can it prosecute in its own name. Any

actions against the club would be through one or more of its officers.

Members' Club with Trustees

The appointment of trustees overcomes the problems associated with the ownership of major investments. A solicitor would normally draw up a trust deed, which appoints the first trustees and outlines the method by which they should be replaced. There should be a minimum of three trustees. The deed must also state that the trustees will at all times act on the wishes of the management committee and in the best interests of the club, and that the assets of the club must be held on behalf of and for the benefit of the club. Trustees must not be able to dispose of these assets without the agreement of the members.

Registered Club

A registered club obtains its name through its registration under the Licensing Act 1964 section 39, which authorizes the supply of alcoholic drinks to members and possibly the sale to guests (permissible for clubs with at least twenty-five members). Examples of this type of club are working men's clubs, sports clubs, social clubs and industrial sports and social clubs. The Registered Club is a form of cooperative in which all the paid-up ordinary members of that club jointly own the land, buildings and any other assets. (Non-voting members do not have the same rights.) The fact that all the members own a registered club in equal shares has certain consequences: in law, for example, the service of drink to a member is classed in law as a 'supply' rather than a sale; the club is exempt from taxation on its internal profit (but not investment income); and if the club is dissolved, the assets must be divided equally between the members.

Most registered clubs are run by an elected committee, but no member of the committee has any more rights than an ordinary member. The club is a financial democracy, regulated by a constitution and governed by the consent of the members. The constitution must be submitted to the Licensing Justices when applying for a Registration Certificate and the annual accounts should be audited by an independent person.

Proprietary Club

As the name implies, a proprietary club is owned by a proprietor and is usually run as a commercial business with the profits going to the owner(s), who will have to pay tax. Club 'members' have very few rights and no personal right to any of the club assets; they are only members in the sense that the proprietor, for commercial reasons, has agreed to allow the member access to the club. In some instances, members' committees may be formed to represent the interests of the 'members'. Proprietary clubs may not necessarily be profit making. For instance, many church social clubs are run as proprietary clubs, thus ensuring that the assets of the club remain the property of the club. Because the assets are not jointly owned by all members, a proprietary club cannot be registered under section 39 of the Act, so must apply for one of the various Justices' Licences, depending on how it wishes to operate. Even if the proprietor seeks a Full On licence, the statement that the licence is required to run a club, the justices are likely to impose a condition limiting sales to members and guests.

Registration as a Company

Many clubs have also registered as companies under the Companies Act 1985. This process enables the members club to acquire a legal status of its own, making it liable to be sued and sue in its own right. The major gain is that of limited liability. This gives the proprietor protection against personal ruin if the enterprise should fail financially. It should be appreciated that a members' club can avoid individual members being sued for the financial debts of the club by appointing trustees. Although there are obvious advantages, the owners and managers of companies have numerous duties and obligations, including the filing of annual accounts and the holding of statutory meetings and a Memorandum, which contains the Articles of Association. The implications are such that it is important that advice is taken from an accountant before setting up a company. Registration can take one of two forms:

FORMING A COMPANY LIMITED BY SHARES
This form of incorporation involves the organization issuing shares to individuals whose liability as shareholders will be limited to the value of the share that they hold. It is important that no dividends are paid to shareholders in a voluntary organization, because it may restrict the ability of that organization to receive grants or rate relief.

FORMING A COMPANY LIMITED BY GUARANTEE AND NOT HAVING SHARE CAPITAL
This form of incorporation is useful for a voluntary organization because, as no shares have been issued, there is no requirement to distribute profits and thus the requirements of the grant aiding agencies are met.

Registration under the Industrial and Provident Societies Act
Registration under this Act is available to clubs that exist with the object of benefiting the community, but which are not suitable for registration under the Companies Act. Clubs registered with the Registrar of Industrial and Provident Societies acquire the advantages of corporate persona and limited liability for its members for all club debts but are then supervised by the registrar, having to comply with rules relating to the club rules, the submission of accounts and annual returns and the issuing of shares.

Registration as a Friendly Society
Clubs that exist for purposes of social intercourse, mutual helpfulness, mental and moral improvement and rational recreation may register as a Friendly Society under the Friendly Societies Act 1974. In this instance, the assets of the club are vested in trustees who are given a certain amount of protection in the matter of club debts. As before, the club has to submit annual returns and ensure other administrative duties are carried out.

Registration as a Charity
A charity normally takes the form of an unincorporated association, such as a members' club with trustees, or an incorporated company limited by a guarantee. Registration as a Charity is through the Charity Commissioners and the club must comply with the rules and regulations laid down by the Charities Act 1960. Although there are many thousands of registered charities, the Charities Commission is currently examining the status of many of them and it is difficult to register new ones. As a charity gains various tax reliefs, the Charity Commissioners submit applications to the Inland Revenue, which considers the charity's eligibility for tax relief. If both are satisfied that the organization meets the requirements of registration, a charitable registration number will be given. A charity is also entitled to relief on business rates, which may save the organization considerable sums of money. Since 1 April 1990, registered charities in England and Wales receive 80 per cent mandatory relief. (The 1988 Local Government Act allows local authorities to award up to 100 per cent discretionary rate relief to non-profit-making sports clubs.)

The Club Constitution and Officials

The constitution of a club is the collection of rules and agreements that govern its day-to-day running. A members' club will usually have a comprehensive set of rules, especially if it holds a Registration Certificate. As identified earlier, these rules are vitally important for a number of the different club structures identified.

In a members' club, each member accepted enters into a contract with the other members, the terms of which are laid down in the rules of that club. This contract may be legally enforceable. A precise and comprehensive set of rules is necessary; this need not be issued to all members, but must be prominently displayed in the club. Every member is taken to have read, understood and agreed to abide by the rules when he/she applies for and is granted membership.

Depending upon the type of club, parent company or organization, the type and number of club officials will vary. The most significant positions in most 'sports clubs' are those described below.

Chairperson

The chairperson is one of the most influential people within the club and management hierarchy. His or her main task is to guide and direct club business and meetings, holding the casting vote at meetings. As well as this strategic role, they will often oversee the appointment of other club officials and thus control the daily business of the club, since these people report to the chairperson. The chairperson should be democratic and allow members to have their say, but should also be prepared to lead and direct, taking decisions for and on behalf of the club and its membership.

Secretary

The club secretary is the key figure in the management of the club, often responsible for both day-to-day operational matters and the organization of the various committees and their respective personnel and officers. This is often the most demanding role and, depending upon the scale of the organization, may be a full-time paid position. The secretary is usually answerable to the chairperson and the management board or committee. The secretary will direct other full-time staff, such as grounds staff and bar stewards, as well as controlling budgets and other resources. They will deal with membership issues and be involved in competition and sports activities and events. This is truly a multi-functional role that requires a strong leader who can communicate effectively, together with strategic organization, planning and vision.

Employment of Staff

The employment of staff in a club situation is no different to that in any other operation, although a number of points of a practical nature should be considered.

Firstly, all staff should initially be directly under the control of one person. In club situations where there is a number of staff, a line management system should operate. In a private members sports club, for example, the position of Head Grounds-man would be untenable if members of the Grounds Committee were able to give direct instructions to the grounds staff, countermanding the instructions of their line manager.

Bar Committees have the most difficult job because there are many rules governing the employment of staff. They should not employ staff under the age of eighteen to serve behind the bar, even though as a member that individual can legally be supplied with alcohol. Some clubs have a rule that strictly precludes staff from being members of the club.

Steward and Stewardess

Where a club has a joint appointment, it is usual to include in the contract that the dismissal of one will automatically lead to the dismissal of the partner. It would be impossible to continue to employ one if the other had been dismissed.

The person in daily charge of the bar must be fully aware of the licensing laws, especially those relating to opening hours. It is also usual to give the bar steward the authority to refuse service to members or require them to vacate the premises if they are causing problems. Any such action should be reported to the Bar Committee as soon as possible.

Legislation requires any person offering a catering service to have attended a course on food hygiene and be fully conversant with current legislation. This may be vitally important for the financial viability of the club. If food poisoning was to occur or the kitchens fail an inspection, the loss of income from that facility may be crucial. Again, it is important that the Committee member responsible for overseeing that area is also conversant with current legislation. Local authority environmental health departments usually have free leaflets on the subject.

Grounds Staff

It is important to appreciate that there are a number of regulations governing the work activities completed by ground staff: a member of staff spraying pitches to kill weeds, for instance, will be required to hold the appropriate FEPA Certificate. Similarly, if tree work is being carried out using chainsaws, the individual should be fully trained in the appropriate skills.

HEAD GROUNDSMAN/ GROUNDS MANAGER

The person managing a sports ground and estates complex should be qualified to fulfil the range of duties of a Head Groundsman/ Manager, together with the management of the estate and associated personnel. These could include the ability to:

- Design basic sports ground features and specify materials.
- Evaluate and develop sports grounds.
- Develop, negotiate and agree proposals.
- Commission projects.
- Promote the values and characteristics of the club.
- Develop teams of grounds staff to enhance performance.
- Allocate work to teams and individuals.
- Evaluate performance of teams and individuals.
- Develop trust with managers and subordinates.
- Make presentations to staff, managers, customers and public.
- Communicate with the media and general public.
- Make decisions and recommendations in accordance with Employment Law, the Health and Safety Act, and Accountancy Law.

All staff should be trained and appropriately qualified. (TORO)

In addition, the Grounds Manager could:

- Provide guidance to all grounds and estates staff on the purchase and control of all equipment and machinery.
- Manage and monitor the condition of the sports ground(s) and estate.
- Manage the development of all personnel.
- Manage the estate and sports ground environment.
- Manage human resources.
- Develop standard operating procedures.
- Control expenditure and costs.
- Negotiate with suppliers.
- Prepare and manage budgets.

GROUNDS PERSON

A grounds person's duty is to carry out routine sports ground maintenance tasks as directed in accordance with the club's Maintenance Policy, while working within its Health and Safety Policy.

The position's key responsibilities and accountabilities may require the grounds person to:

- Mow playing surfaces and ancillary areas of the sports ground.
- Set up areas for play, including marking out such areas as pitches, courts and wickets, as appropriate.
- Maintain playing surfaces and allied landscape areas.
- Identify and control pests and diseases.
- Renovate worn and damaged turf.
- Prepare and maintain machinery.

Organizational Behaviour and Staff Management

In both the work and leisure situation, individuals are involved with organizations, their members and groups. As a manager, one needs to know how your organization functions and what influences, both good and bad, it exercises over the members and their reaction to these influences. Organizational behaviour is concerned with the study of the behaviour of people in the organizational setting, the understanding, prediction and control of human behaviour and the factors influencing the performance of members. There are four areas to consider:

The Individual

Organizations are made up of individuals and it is necessary to study the behaviour of individuals in order to examine the organization as a whole.

- Do people work in isolation or in groups?
- How do they respond to the needs of the organization?
- How do external pressures affect the performance of individuals?

These are vital questions that need answering because, if the needs of the individual and the demands of the organization are incompatible, the result will be frustration and conflict.

The Group

Groups comprise diverse people, and in the organization may be created as formal or informal groups. Groups have defined or developed hierarchies and leaders, and the members can influence how individuals will perform through the setting of levels of behaviour or norms.

The Organization

Both individuals and groups will interact within the structure of the organization, hence the importance of that structure. The structure is developed to create distinct relationships between individuals and groups in order to provide a means of ensuring the objectives of the business are achieved. Behaviour will be influenced by the patterns of organizational structure, technology, leadership styles and management systems.

The Environment

People and organizations function within the wider external environment. Techno-logical development, economic activity, social, cultural and government actions all influence how the organization func-tions. Overall these factors influence the degree by which the organization manages opportunities and risks.

The Organization

A manager wishing to study staff and the organization must consider a multitude of factors including goals and objectives, organizational structure, management systems, the process of delegation, motiva-tion, leadership style, group behaviour and communications.

Aims and Objectives

All organizations serve some purpose so they should all have goals or objectives. It is vital that every business sets out a policy statement and the detailed aims and objectives. These aims and objectives should be known to all staff and translated into targets and standards for each member to achieve.

Structure and Systems

Organizations will have a structure. That structure may be detailed and in writing, or in other cases it may be through mutual agreement.

In the work situation the purpose is:

* To divide work between members.
* To coordinate activities.
* To provide channels of communi-cation.
* To define tasks and responsibilities.
* To identify work roles, authority and accountability.
* To create a framework of order and command.
* To enable work to be planned, orga-nized, directed and controlled.

There are a number of organizational struc-tures detailed in numerous management texts, ranging from T charts to circles to matrices. All structures must clearly identify the grouping of activities, the responsibili-ties of individuals, the levels of hierarchal authority, spans of control and formal organizational relationships. Whatever the structure, its operation will be influenced by the style of management. Finally, formal and informal relationships are formed.

The formal relationships are:

* Line relationship: showing the authority flowing vertically through the organization.
* Functional relationship: involving specialists within the organization, such as the personnel manager.
* Staff relationship: where an individual has no direct authority.
* Lateral relationship: existing across one level of a department or departments.

A number of informal relationships occur because of the formal structure; a line bypass occurs, for instance, when a superior blocks the access of a subordinate to a higher authority.

Motivation

Motivation is typified as an individual phenomenon and therefore must take into account people's individuality. Motivation is described as intentional, as it is assumed to be under the control of the individual's control. Behaviours that are influenced by motivation, such as effort expended, are seen as choices of action. Motivation is multi-faceted. There are two major factors: what gets people activated (arousal) and the force of an individual to engage in desired behaviour.

The purpose of motivational theories is to predict behaviour. Motivation is not behaviour itself, nor is its performance.

Motivation concerns the action of individuals and the internal and external forces that influence their choice of action. Motivation is seen as a driving force from within that helps us achieve some goal in order to satisfy a need or expectation. People's behaviour is determined by what motivates them, but their performance is a product of motivation plus ability.

Performance = Function (Ability
+ Motivation)

How Do You Use This in the Work Situation?

You need to identify the level of motivation of the staff, in other words the degree of their driving force, and then be able to channel that motivation into achieving the aims and objectives of the organization. What is this driving force? What are people's needs and expectations, and how do they influence behaviour and performance? Individuals have a variety of ever changing needs and expectations, which they endeavour to satisfy in a variety of ways.

This can be illustrated in a simple form, as shown by Figure 1.

What are People's Needs and Expectations?

People's needs start with physiological needs and extend through to social expectations. Some of these relate to the work situation

and others to non-work, while many relate to both. A three-way classification for motivation at work has been suggested:

- Economic rewards (this is not a motivational force).
- Intrinsic satisfaction (derived from the job and related to the personal growth and development of the individual).
- Social relationships (concerned with other people and including friendships, group working, and desire for affiliation, status and dependency).

A person's motivation, job satisfaction and work performance is determined by the composition of these needs, how much that person wishes to achieve them and the extent to which they have been fulfilled. Some people, in the work situation, may be happy with lower economic rewards, provided good social relationships and friendships are formed and they derive satisfaction from the job, while others seek high economic rewards only.

Frustration

In the workforce, or any other situation, frustration can block a person's driving force before they can reach their desired goal. When this happens, two outcomes may occur: they may change their

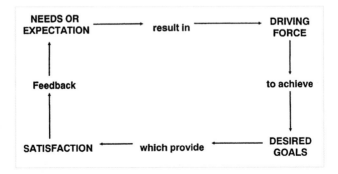

Figure 1   Individual needs.

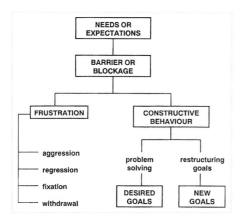

Figure 2   Frustration.

behaviour in a constructive way, in order to achieve the desired goal or change their goals, or they may become frustrated and cause difficulties at work.

Constructive Behaviour

Positive ways of reacting to barriers that stop the person achieving their desired goals. As shown on Figure 2, there are two main forms:

- Problem solving (the removal of the barrier).
- Restructuring (where the person changes their goals, usually to a lower target).

Negative Behaviour

When some people cannot obtain what they want, their response is negative. They become frustrated. This frustration may appear in a number of ways and it is important that you, as a manager, spot negative reactions in your staff and deal with them before they become a major problem that may ultimately necessitate disciplinary action. The accompanying diagram shows four categories of frustration, although reactions may often include more than one of these categories.

Aggression: Physical or verbal abuse of superiors and damage to property are two examples of aggression. Aggression is usually directed at the perceived source of the barrier in these instances. If it is not possible to react to a superior in this way, the person may take the frustration out on someone or something else. This is displaced aggression.

Regression: Resorting to childish behaviour, such as crying or sulking.

Fixation: Where the person continues to repeat actions or complaints where it is obvious there will be no positive results from these actions. It may be that the source of the problem is not that to which the individual continually refers.

Withdrawal: Arriving late all the time, absenteeism, sickness or eventually resignation are all signs of withdrawal.

In summary, the individual's reaction to not achieving needs or goals will be influenced by:

- The level of need (real or perceived)
- The degree of attachment to the goal
- The strength of motivation
- The perceived nature of the barrier
- The personal characteristics of the individual

The manager must try to reduce potential frustration problems by:

- Ensuring the right person is in the right job.
- The job is designed properly and work organized appropriately.
- The operation of equitable personnel policies correct recognition and reward for work done.
- The use of a suitable communication system to ensure all members of staff is fully aware of their responsibilities and what they can achieve.
- Using a participative style of leadership, which enables subordinates to be involved in making management decisions.

15

Leadership

Leadership can be defined in a number of ways:

- Getting others to follow.
- Getting people to do things willingly.
- The use of authority in decision making.

Leadership and Management

There is a difference between leadership and management. Leadership takes place anywhere and deals with interpersonal behaviour. It does not necessarily occur because of the organizational structure. Management is getting things done through other people in order to achieve the objectives of the organization. As a manager one has the authority to ensure people work, but as the soccer team captain, you try to get the best out of your team by leadership skills, not management practices. Leadership does not require the hierarchical structure of an organization to work. Managers often see their role as ensuring that the aims, objectives and targets set for the organization are achieved and do not consider the psychological and social implications for the staff involved.

The Leader

A leader may be imposed, appointed, elected, chosen informally or may emerge through the situation. Each of these will evoke a different response from the group members. An imposed leader may find it more difficult to motivate a group and get the necessary amount of work from them. A leader chosen by the group should have an easier time because the group has already accepted them.

There are three identified ways to examine leadership:

- The qualities or traits approach.
- The situational approach.
- The functional approach.

Researchers have tried, but failed, to produce a valid theory listing the qualities of a good leader. There is, however, a relationship between leadership effectiveness and the traits of intelligence, supervisory ability, initiative, self-assurance and individuality. In the situational approach, the person who emerges as leader of the work group is the person who knows best what to do and is seen by the group as the most suitable leader in the particular situation. In this case, professional knowledge and technical expertise rather than personality are seen to be important. The third group focuses on the functions of leadership, how the leader's behaviour affects and is affected by the group. It considers the group and its needs and how the leader can develop those group characteristics in order to succeed.

Delegation

Delegation is not the giving out of work to subordinates. They already have their duties assigned to them under the rules of the organization. It is possible to have delegation upwards, laterally or downwards. The text here will concentrate on downward delegation. Delegation means the conferring of a specified authority by a higher authority. In its essence, it involves a dual responsibility. The one to whom authority is delegated becomes responsible to the superior for doing the job, but the superior remains responsible for getting the job done. The principle of delegation is the centre of all processes in formal organization.

Delegation is founded on the concepts of authority, responsibility and accountability.

Authority: The power or right to make decisions and take action, to enable this responsibility to be successfully discharged. Authority legitimizes the exercise of power within the structure and rules of the organization. When authority is given to the subordinate, it enables them to issue valid instructions for others to follow.

Responsibility: The obligation of any member of the organization to perform duties or make decisions, and to have to accept the consequences for tasks not achieved correctly. Delegation embraces both authority and responsibility. It is not practical to delegate one without the other. To hold subordinates responsible for certain areas of performance without also conferring on them the necessary authority to take action and make decisions within the limits of that responsibility is an abuse of delegation.

Accountability: Means carrying the can, being ultimately held to account for success or failure. This ultimate responsibility cannot be delegated. As the late American President, Harry S. Truman, said: 'The Buck Stops Here'. It is important that a manager fully appreciates this. One cannot blame a subordinate for mistakes if one has delegated tasks that the subordinate is not capable of carrying out. A general problem managers have is when they are held accountable for the performance of their departmental staff when they may not have been involved in the recruitment, training or development of the staff.

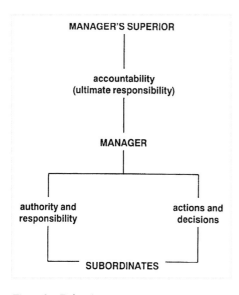

Figure 3   Delegation.

The Benefits of Delegation

USE OF TIME
Time is a limited resource that is very valuable to you as a manager. By delegating some of your tasks that your subordinates can carry out, you can release some of your valuable time to do things that are more important. This process will reduce the time spent on programmed activities and give you more time for the non-programmed activities from which come many ideas to improve output or performance. One will have more time to manage, that is, plan and organize, rather than supervise and control. One should also be more available to staff for consultation and discussion. If one is not planning, one will have to keep reacting to events instead of anticipating them, and your scope for initiative and enterprise will be severely limited.

STRENGTH OF WORKFORCE
Subordinates, if delegated work, will have the opportunity to develop their aptitudes and abilities and increase their commitment to the goals of the organization. They are likely to exhibit improved morale through increased motivation and job satisfaction. One should ensure delegation focuses on motivators and growth factors, so that subordinates can become more involved in the planning and decision-making processes. By delegating to various members of your team, one can encourage a team effort and reduce problems associated with job frustration.

TRAINING
Delegation is a good form of training and testing a subordinate's suitability for promotion. It tests the person's capabilities at higher levels of authority and responsibility, thus helping to avoid the Peter Principle – 'In hierarchy, all staff tend to be promoted to their level of incompetence'. Training subordinates to a competent level so they can replace you will both improve the organizational efficiency and enhance your own prospects for advancement.

SPECIALIST SKILLS

Organizations often need staff with specialist skills. It is important to have a backup to ensure availability should the specialist manager be unavailable.

ECONOMICS

Successful delegation enables both you and your subordinates to perform more efficiently within the organization. Decisions can be made at a lower level, thus saving time and money (decisions made at a higher level than necessary are made at a cost higher than appropriate).

Implementing Delegation

While the list above highlights the advantages of delegation, one must appreciate that delegation is not something that occurs overnight and there are problems that must be overcome before you delegate. All delegation involves risk, but that risk is minimized if you do things correctly. The first time you ask a subordinate to carry out a new duty, you may be as concerned as they are about the likely outcome. It is therefore vital to plan your delegation programme carefully, train the subordinate, and then encourage them by showing you have faith in their ability. What are you going to delegate? There may be duties you enjoy, but are not central to achieving your departmental goals. These tasks are known as vocational hobbies and take up time. Delegate them.

The process of delegation is slow in the early stages and not without setbacks. Results will not be immediate, indeed in the short term you will have to work harder because of the training activities and supervision added to your workload. Do not panic and step in to do the work because of the time factor. You must not be reluctant to delegate because you feel that you will lose power and not be on top of all departmental work. Delegate and communicate. If the subordinate knows exactly what is expected, leave them to make decisions, carry out spot checks, and

hold regular progress meetings – not too often mind, otherwise the subordinate will say you have given them the job but do not trust them to carry it out properly. All managers need time in the day to sit and think. Constructive thought about the future operation of a department is vital, so delegate the lesser jobs, trust your staff and concentrate on your role as a manager.

The greatest problem of all is the natural feeling that 'he/she will not do the job as well as I do'. This may well be true at first, but expertise will be gained after experience. You must not delegate recklessly, but if a subordinate can do a job well enough and has the capacity to learn, they should be given tasks that stretch them. Remember also that they might achieve the same results by using a different method. Delegate, do not abdicate. Ensure that you retain effective management control over the subordinates by maintaining good channels of communication both to and from the subordinate and with others with whom the subordinate will deal when carrying out delegated work. A control system is vital because you as the manager are still accountable for your actions and the actions of your staff.

Delegation Plan

All managers must delegate, but you need a starting point to help judge whether you could delegate more than at present, or more effectively. Write down the main objectives of your job, or read your job description if it is up to date. Go over your diary for the past month and note how you actually spent your time. Jot down roughly how much time was spent on different groups of activities. Draw up a simple chart based on the information revealed. This provides a comparison between stage one (your objective) and stage two (your actual activities). From this, you are now ready to decide what to delegate. There will be limitations that narrow your choice. These must be recognized and it is best to list those features of your responsibilities that cannot be delegated:

• Tasks beyond the skills and experience of any of your work team.
• Confidential, security and policy matters that are restricted to your own level of security.
• Matters involving exercising discipline over a subordinate's own colleagues.

Having ruled out any items that clash with the criteria above, you will be left with a range of possible tasks to delegate. The first two areas to look at are routine tasks and tasks consuming a lot of your time. Routine tasks are good delegation material. What is routine to you will be new to your subordinate and by delegating it you will, at the same time, be stretching the subordinate's ability and thus developing them. Tasks consuming a lot of your time provide obvious delegation opportunities, particularly if you have run out of new ways to try to reduce the time. You are now ready to produce a detailed delegation plan for one or more of your staff. You have identified the opportunities for subordinate staff to learn and develop by undertaking delegated tasks and responsibilities. You now have to decide how these increased responsibilities should be implemented and to whom they should be given. You then have to train staff and decide what control system should be adopted.

CHOOSING STAFF
Having carried out the above you now have to decide to whom the work will be delegated. This can be done by analysing each subordinate in turn thinking through these questions:

• What skills, qualifications and experience does each have?
• Which are currently being used and which are not?
• What type of work has each person shown an interest in?
• What type of work could an individual not cope with, even with training?

The correct answers to these questions help you decide who is most suitable for each delegated activity.

IMPLEMENTATION STAGES
You have identified the what and the who. Now you must ensure that the individual knows exactly what is expected.

(a) Clarify objectives of task.
(b) Agree terms of reference.
(c) Ensure subordinate agrees acceptance of authority and responsibility.
(d) Properly brief, guide and train the subordinate.
(e) Agree time limits, check points and performance standards.
(f) Confirm freedom of action within agreed terms of reference.

Most of the information identified in (a) should be written as part of your (manager's) specification and it should only be necessary to extract and give the appropriate information to your subordinate. Stages (b) and (c) are linked in that your subordinate must agree with the terms and fully understand the limitations of delegated authority and responsibility. Stage (d) is very important. Guidance and training are vital to the success of the exercise. It is also important that other people know of the delegation. Make allowance for (e) because it will take time to train your subordinate; the targets you set should get higher as time progresses. It is also important to note that delegation is not permanent and can be withdrawn if the work is not satisfactory. Finally (f) leave your subordinate to get on with work once you have completed the training programme. Nobody likes someone breathing down his or her neck all the time.

Groups

For most of the time individuals work together; few people like to work alone or in some form of isolation. The working of groups and the influence each group has over their membership is an important part of achieving organizational goals. The main feature of a group is that its members think of themselves as members of a group. A group consists of a number of people with a common objective, a group identity and 'boundary' and a set of values to which they work. An alternative psychological definition suggests a group is a number of people who interact with each other, are psychologically aware of one another and see themselves as a group. Organizations must have groups in order for them to function properly. Using researchers' results, we shall examine make-up, operation, conflict and factors influencing performance. In the work situation, if members of the group do not cooperate, then it is unlikely work targets will be met. People in groups influence each other through a variety of mechanisms and groups may develop their own hierarchies and leaders. Group pressures will influence the behaviour of individual members and subsequently their work performance.

Organization and Groups

The shape of organizations influences the number and size of both formal and informal groups. As one would expect, it is suggested that organizations function most efficiently when staff work not as individuals, but as members of highly effective groups. For this to work there needs to be overlap. This could work both vertically and horizontally. The groups themselves would depend on the technical needs and production system in any given organization and how management decided to organize the staff. Beside these formal groups, organizations have within them informal groups, which develop according to the needs of the workforce.

FORMAL GROUPS

Formal groups are created to achieve organizational aims and objectives and are either production groups or management groups. People have specific tasks or roles within the organization and group. Management will set rules, relationships and norms of behaviour. In the work situation, formal groups are likely to remain permanent, but the actual members change.

Three groups have been identified:

- Team groups (autonomous groups with broad terms of reference and limited supervision, e.g. maintenance teams).
- Task groups (jobs and individuals clearly defined, but some flexibility over pace and method of work, e.g. office staff).
- Technological groups (normal work groups in which individuals have fixed methods and targets of work. There is little scope for individual discretion and often limited group interaction, e.g. production lines).

INFORMAL GROUPS

There are always informal groups forming within a formal organization. Their size and composition depend on the complexity of the organization and the needs of the individuals. They will often cut across the formal structures and barriers. These groups serve to satisfy psychological and social needs as well as their technical needs. They may introduce ways of satisfying social needs, which the organization structure fails to do. The hierarchy of the informal group will set itself up and the leader will come through the consent of the members themselves. The informal leader may be the person who best reflects the attitudes and values of the group, is good at resolving conflict, and shows ability when dealing with management or others outside the group.

Why Groups?

The reason for group formation is the same in both industry and social situations. The combined efforts of a team may be required in order to achieve certain tasks. Groups provide companionship, mutual understanding and support from colleagues. The group provides guidelines on the generally acceptable behaviour of its members. The group may provide an opportunity to circumvent organization rules or to share unpleasant tasks. Finally, groups act as protectors of their members. It is important that managers foster groups, because by doing so they can ultimately improve the effectiveness of the whole workforce. It is important to ensure group cohesiveness of the right sort because if a group is close knit, the reward to the individual is greater and group morale is higher. Being part of the team often leads to lower absenteeism and a lower turnover. This cohesion and subsequent performance is influenced by factors such as membership, work environment, organization and development. What pointers are relevant to you as a manager in dealing with your own work groups?

The size of the group: If it is too large, it may become fragmented and friction occurs. The compatibility of members is also important. Personality, skills and competitive nature will all have an effect on the personal relationships and hierarchy.
The work environment influences cohesiveness: People often stick together in the face of adversity. Because they do the same job, people who work apart may be drawn into a group by virtue of that work. Physical closeness creates interesting reactions. Open plan offices suddenly become territorial cells through the positioning of filing cabinets, large plants and other barriers.
Communication: Plays a vital part in ensuring group cohesiveness. When people work on a production line, it is vital they are encouraged to mix during breaks.
Management and leadership: The activities of both informal and formal groups are influenced by management and leadership styles, as discussed above. If the manager is supportive, then the group will

support the manager. Successful completion of work to a given target often gives the manager an opportunity to increase that target and the group accept the challenge.
External threat: Finally, an external threat from the manager, the organization or outside is likely to cause the group to become more cohesive and they may create problems.

Group Performance and Behaviour
Communication plays a vital role in the success or otherwise of the group. Poor communication leads to problems. Often it leads to the reliance on the 'grapevine' as the source of all valid information, which, of course, is very wrong. The systems identified are used within groups and can be a source of aggravation to some group members if they do not receive information at the same time as their peers. One should choose the most suitable communication method to fit the groups and the individual situation.

AN EFFECTIVE GROUP
For a group to be effective there are two main sets of functions that must be achieved.
Task function: This function is directed towards problem solving, carrying out group tasks and achieving organizational objectives. Group members help each other carry out these processes through effective group behaviour.
Maintenance function: This function is concerned with the social and emotional life of a group by building and maintaining the group as an effective working unit. This is done by encouragement, giving support, maintaining cohesiveness and reducing conflict.

Both the group leader and the group members can perform both the task and maintenance functions. In some cases, the input of the group members is vital, since that of the leader is weak. All members of a group can be identified according to the way they react in particular situations.

GROUP BUILDING AND
MAINTENANCE ROLES

In this case, the analysis of member functions is directed towards those activities, which help build group centred attitudes or maintain group centred behaviour. These roles are identified as:

- The encourager
- The harmonizer
- The compromiser
- The gate-keeper/expediter
- The standard setter
- The group observer/commentator
- The follower

INDIVIDUAL ROLES

These are directed towards the satisfaction of personal needs. Their purpose is not related to either group task or to the group functioning. These roles are:

- The aggressor
- The blocker
- The recognition seeker
- The self-confessor
- The playboy
- The dominator
- The help seeker
- The special-interest pleader

From this information a leader can observe what happens within the group under the two function headings or, if they are involved, must ensure the following occur. Look for the following six task functions:

Initiating: Who proposes or identifies the task or problem and then suggests a procedure or the initial ideas to solve the problem. If you, the leader, are in charge it is important that you carry out the first parts of the process efficiently.

Information or opinion seeking: The group will need additional facts and someone will seek that information and ask for ideas. Again, you as the leader should initiate this if you are involved.

Information or opinion giving: As leader, you can offer ideas and information

to the group. When others of the group give suggestions, it is important to appreciate whether their opinions are their own or those of the group.

Clarifying or elaborating: As the process develops, it will become necessary for the leader to interpret suggestions, clear up confusion and indicate alternatives.

Summarizing: Now is the time to pull together all the ideas, restate proposals and offer a decision or conclusion for the group to accept or reject.

Consensus testing: Checking with the group to see if a decision has been reached. This function will not occur if the final decision is yours as leader, rather than a group decision.

The six group building and maintenance functions are:

Encouraging: Be friendly, warm and responsive to the group members, always accept the contributions of others, and ensure you give them an opportunity for recognition.

Expressing group feelings: You must sense the feeling and mood of the rest of the group and try to influence it by changing your mood.

Harmonizing: Attempt to reconcile disagreements and reduce tension by suggesting compromise or getting them to examine their differences.

Compromising: If you make a mistake you must, for the sake of the group, admit that mistake in order to maintain group cohesion.

Gate-keeping: Ensure that communication channels are kept open so that the group can participate at all times.

Setting standards: You must ensure your group knows the standards they must perform to and identify the mechanisms by which performance will be monitored.

Communication Skills

'I know that you believe you understand what I think I said, but I am not sure you realize that what you heard is not what I meant.'

Good communication skills are vital pieces in the armoury of any good manager. Whatever form of communication the manager uses to address staff, peers, superiors, customers or others, it is vital that the correct message is received.

What is the Objective of Communication?

Whether you are writing or speaking, trying to persuade, instruct, inform, convince or educate, there are four basic objectives:

- To be received.
- To be understood.
- To be accepted.
- To change other people's behaviour.

When you fail to achieve your objective, you have failed to communicate properly and it is important to identify why problems occur because frustration and resentment may occur. You use language to express the thoughts you have. This language is a form of code: unless the receiver can understand your code, they will not correctly identify your message. An important part of communications is the ability to understand the words being used. Because all people are individuals with different backgrounds, individuality is the main barrier to effective communications.

The Management plan emphasizes the importance of communications.

Different levels of staff are affected by the various points in the plan and it is important that the right skills are used to communicate information to staff if the aims and objectives of the business are to be met.

Why do People Communicate?

There are a number of reasons why people wish to communicate. Let us look at some of the major reasons.

To satisfy personal needs: By making requests or issuing commands, you are using communications to satisfy personal needs. However, this can be taken too far and people may say you talk for the sake of talking. Be aware of other peoples' needs in relation to speaking and listening.

To establish relationships with others: You spend much of your time developing and maintaining relationships through verbal and non-verbal communications. Saying 'Hello' or nodding your head serves to recognize the other person. This is vital in many job situations. For instance, the receptionist at the leisure centre has an important role to play. The way in which

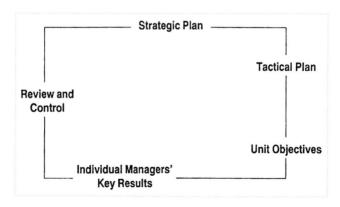

Figure 4   Communication cycle.

the customer is received will influence whether that customer returns or not.

To create understanding between yourself and others: Communication is used to share information and gain from others. The effects are twofold: the information may satisfy your need to know and it may be the first stage in the process of persuasion.

To persuade people and create change: Many communications are used to persuade people to change their behaviour, beliefs and attitudes.

To entertain: Although much communication may appear simply to entertain, it does have significant effects and sometimes intentions.

Verbal Communications

Verbal communication is regarded as getting the message across. You must consider what the message is, and whether it has been communicated properly. In other words, does the receiver actually understand what has been said?

'You tell him what you want him to know': This concept implies that communication is one-way traffic, with a message being transferred from the sender to the receiver.

Monologue: The passing of verbal information by one person without response from the listener.

Dialogue: A conversation between two or more people. Dialogue can create good conversation and understanding.

- It is a two way process.
- It may be formal or informal.
- It should be sincere and open.
- It is adapted to the situation in which it occurs.
- It constitutes a means to an end.
- It is often desired and enjoyable.

An important facet of dialogue is that it involves feedback from the receiver and the sender can modify the approach if it is obvious the receiver does not understand the original communication. Verbal communications are used in a multitude of situations and, without exception, we all develop styles to use in specific situations.

Non-Verbal Communications

If you are communicating face to face or over the telephone, other messages are sent in all sorts of ways.

- Facial expression (a smile, a frown).
- Gestures (movements of hands and body to emphasize a message).
- Body posture (how you stand or sit).
- Orientation (whether you face the person or turn away).
- Eye contact (whether you look at a person and for how long).
- Body contact (whether you make physical contact and for how long).
- Proximity (the distance you stand from a person).
- Head nods (indicating agreement or disagreement).
- Appearance (choice of clothes, length of hair, etc).
- Non-verbal aspects of speech (variations in pitch, stress and timing, voice quality and tone).
- Non-verbal aspects of writing (handwriting, layout, visual appearance).

All these non-verbal communications are a vital part of the communication process.

The Context

People may attribute different meanings to the same words at different times and in different contexts. Communication relates to a situation that will have a history and particular characteristics will make it different to other situations. In order to communicate, people learn to recognize similarities in situations, so they learn from them. This can create a problem because people will assume a situation is familiar, and therefore assume they know what to say and do.

Communication Barriers

There are a number of barriers to communications, which you should recognize and, where appropriate, take action to overcome.

Differences in perception: How do you look at the world? Your view is determined by experiences: age, culture, education, occupation, sex and status all colour the way in which you perceive situations and communications. Selective perception occurs here. Consciously or unconsciously, you receive what you want to receive or experience.

Jumping to conclusions: You often see what you want to see and hear what you want to hear, rather than what is actually said. People's attitudes and beliefs cause difficulties.

Stereotyping: Because you learn from previous experiences, you will most likely treat different people in the same way because of their common job or situation.

Lack of knowledge: It is difficult to communicate with others who have a very different background to you. This is especially so if you are trying to discuss technical or managerial matters.

Personality: This can create major barriers when communicating. One or both parties may be at fault. You must always consider your personality and approach to others and the way they are likely to react.

Emotions: These can be a barrier. Strong emotions block out logic and common sense. A lecturer speaking with little or no enthusiasm or emotion becomes dull and the audience does not take in what is being said.

Lack of interest: A barrier is created by the receiver's lack of interest in the communication. You must realize that not everyone is enthused by your pet project.

Selective attention: Your brain automatically receives all types of stimuli at once but reacts to only a few. When receiving a message your brain will filter some of the information. You attend to messages either voluntarily or involuntarily. Involuntary attention is given when you feel threatened. A shout of 'fore' on the golf course will cause an automatic reaction from a golfer. When the attention is voluntary, you must create an interest and then maintain that person's interest.

Communications Check List

This simple check list, based on the 'Five Ws and How', should be used when planning important communications.

Why
> Are you communicating?
> What is the reason for communicating?
> What are you trying to achieve in terms of the behaviour of the receiver?

What
> Is the purpose of the communication?

Who
> Is the audience?
> What sort of personality, education, background etc?
> How does the person react to the content of your message?
> What does the person know about the subject of the message?

Where and When
> Where is the message being transmitted?
> Is the place suitable or likely to create difficulties?
> At what point in the total situation does the communication occur?
> What is your relationship to the receiver?
> Is the communication likely to cause controversy?

How
> How are you going to communicate?
> Which medium is appropriate?
> How will you organize the points you wish to make?
> How are you going to achieve the right effect?

Difficulties with self-expression: An ability to express yourself both verbally and in writing is critical to your success as a communicator.

These are the main causes of poor communications. There are many others that you will come across. Not the least is the wrong choice of communication media. You cannot ask a notice a question. It is easy to misunderstand a notice if it is read in the first place.

Simple Dos and Don'ts of Effective Speaking

Whatever the situation there are certain rules to follow when using verbal communications.

Be prepared: Jot down some notes in advance. Anticipate questions and prepare your answers. Make sure you are carrying out the communication in the right place.

Be clear and simple: Use your own words but ensure people will understand them. Use sensible illustrations that people can relate to.

Handle questions firmly: Try to stick to the subject being briefed. Do not let the audience sidetrack the main purpose. If someone is not happy, talk to him or her alone afterwards.

Check understanding: Pause to allow questions and ask pointed questions to ensure your audience does understand what you have said. It is of little comfort if a gang spends hours doing a job in the wrong place and their excuse is that they thought they knew where to go.

Check your timing: Try to avoid talking for longer than is necessary. Allow time for questions. Always split up a long communication into parts if people are not going to absorb all you wish to say. Alternatively, prepare a written summary for them to take away.

Giving Orders

Orders are given for a variety of reasons in a variety of ways:

OBJECTIVES
* To stir people into action to achieve an objective – by giving them the information on a situation that demands attention.
* To indicate a particular person is held responsible for performing a task.
* To give the superior the opportunity of contacting the subordinate and issuing instructions in the most suitable way.
* To give the subordinate the maximum opportunity for consulting and participating in the situation.

TYPES OF ORDERS
Various factors influence the six types of orders. These include the selection of words, the tone of voice, facial expressions and gestures. Further factors may depend on such as the job to be carried out, the personalities involved, the type of subordinate receiving the order, and the relationship between subordinates and supervisors in that work situation.

The Command: A one-way direct autocratic order that will get something done quickly, provided it receives an acceptable response. Commands can cause antagonism owing to their directness. They are useful to jolt a worker into action or in the case of emergency.

The Request: The request is a more personal and tactful way, creating a friendly atmosphere of cooperation. It is very useful for dealing with subordinates who have made mistakes they are aware of.

The Suggestion: This is the mildest form of request. Mentioning the subject is sufficient to the reliable experienced who immediately sees the implication and acts accordingly. You should always remember the importance of the follow up in case the remark is not fully understood.

The Open Order: The supervisor gives information on what is required but leaves an adequate allowance for the operator to work out how to perform the task. This enables the subordinate to develop his capabilities.

Mutual Effort: This only works where morale is high and active participation is the norm. The order takes the form of discussing the situation with operatives. The result takes longer to achieve but is more effective.

Volunteers: Asking volunteers to carry out an unpleasant task.

Management Techniques

Programming and Scheduling Work
Before examining the types of work programming and scheduling that may be applied to ensure work is successfully completed, it is important to understand fully the importance of work planning and how it helps to achieve the aims and objectives of the organization. Any series of purposeful actions must follow a definite and logical sequence if they are to achieve the best results. This is particularly true in relation to processes in which material and human resources are involved and where different objectives may be linked. It follows that special techniques must be used to coordinate the use of these resources in the best way possible to achieve the set objectives. These special techniques come under the broad heading of planning. Planning can be defined as 'a formal process by which specific objectives are set and detailed ways of accomplishing these objectives are established'. A plan is 'a visual method of putting actions into a logical order or sequence in order to achieve that result'. Individual plans and objectives must relate to the organization's goals. Organization plans are developed by senior management based on broad objectives, expressed in general terms. Often today, an organization will prepare a Mission Statement to which all the aims, objectives and targets must relate. The aims and objectives will be set for each department or section within the organization and targets will be set for either staff output or production levels. At each stage through the process, the time span will reduce in length. The Mission Statement may be set for a number of years, while the targets for an individual member of staff may be for one day.

This section deals with the practical processes and techniques involved in the detailed planning and scheduling of work.

An Organization at Work
Purpose
Mission
Policy

Strategy and long-term objectives
Policies and medium-term objectives
Programme of work
Budgets
Short-term planning
Products and services

PEOPLE AS RESOURCES
Skills
Knowledge
Experience
Attitudes
Motivation
Development
Expertise

OTHER RESOURCES
Money
Materials
Methods of work
Machinery
Technology
Systems of work
Systems of evaluation
Management information systems
Organizational structure

The management process involves:

- Planning
- Organizing
- Directing
- Controlling
- Monitoring the resources used (time, staff, machinery and materials)

The planning process determines:

- What needs to be done
- When it has to be done
- How it will be done
- Who will do it
- What should be done if plans go wrong

The results of bad planning are obvious to all. It may be seen as a loss in production, failure to meet targets, dissatisfaction among staff, higher unit costs of work, misunderstanding and confusion, and a higher rate of accidents. Managers who do not plan have to manage by crisis management rather than anticipating problems and developing suitable alternative systems. This is known as 'management by exception'.

Policy Objectives

Policy objectives should be set for the business, identifying what it is seeking to achieve in the medium to long term. The modern approach is the development of a Mission Statement that details the overall direction in which the business is going to progress. From this, detailed objectives should be set. To achieve both, management of an organization should ask itself a number of questions (*see* box below) before deciding its objectives:

DEPARTMENTAL OBJECTIVES
From the Mission Statement and overall business objectives, a set of more detailed departmental objectives can be prepared.

OPERATIONAL OBJECTIVES
Finely detailed operational objectives are prepared. These can be identified in one of three ways:

- Operational methods
- Production targets
- Work schedules

As the objectives are set downward through an organization, they become more specific and consequently the derivative plans become more detailed.

Work Organization

Work organization starts at the primary objectives of the business, namely to produce goods and make a profit, if it is a commercial business, or, if a local authority, to provide a determined level of services within a specified budget. Once these objectives and others pertinent to that business are identified, then the various processes relating to the work organization can be developed. The first stage of the

Policy Objectives	
Business	What business are we in?
	What is our distinctive competence?
Profitability	What return are we getting on our assets?
Market standing	What is our share of our market?
	How good is our name?
	Who are our customers?
Problems	What current problems are so critical that failure to solve them would threaten our future?
Opportunities	What should we be going for?
Future	How do we visualize our future?

process is to identify the organizational structure for the business using a formal process such as a T chart. This will identify the formal line structure, which indicates the paths of communication in all directions. It also identifies levels of authority, responsibility and accountability. From this come the formal and informal relationships that are developed – be they staff, line or ad hoc – each playing an important role in the successful operation of the organization. To enable work to be correctly planned at all levels, organizational objectives and key results must be identified as well as targets. These key areas could include profitability, finance, marketing and sales, employment relations, new developments, physical assets and public relations. The aims of these objectives are that they should make people stretch themselves but be realistic, for example regarding the availability of adequate resources, and be sufficiently flexible to allow creativity, be understood by everybody and be updated periodically. This information will enable work to be channelled in the right direction and efforts can be coordinated. Good planning enables better coordination, more effective control of operations, easier delegation, and more economic use of resources, increased personal effectiveness, and a more involved workforce who have greater staff motivation.

Managers and supervisors will be involved in the:

- Setting of goals
- Scheduling of work
- Personnel management
- Communication of information
- Monitoring of work
- Control process

Using the example of a Head Groundsperson, he or she will be involved in the following:

- The completion of scheduled tasks, using specified methods within time parameters.

- Achieving the maximum productivity from the workforce within the time allowed.

From the specifications and work schedules, the manager can:

- Define the activities to be achieved.
- Establish work times.
- Review the resources available.
- Allocate resources to locations.
- Control and monitor work.

Good planning will result in more cooperative staff, as they will have a far better idea of what is happening and why. When something begins to go wrong, they will appreciate that no plan is perfect and will assist in changing the plans. It will include responsibility for the day-to-day activities of the workforce and the use of other resources to be carried out within the time span and involve the efficient use of staff, equipment and materials.

Planning Process

The planning process consists of three logical steps:

- Deciding what you want to accomplish, or Setting Objectives.
- Deciding how to accomplish the objectives through Outlining Procedures.
- Deciding what people and skills are necessary to meet objectives or Assigning Responsibilities.

SETTING OBJECTIVES

The first step in the planning process is setting objectives. Management objectives usually concern themselves with quantity, quality and cost. However, they are not limited to these three areas. They could relocate equipment, improve working conditions, introduce new products and so on. Objectives should always be specific, consistent and attainable. Care should be taken that the objectives do not conflict with higher-level policies or plans. To be specific, an objective must clearly state what is to be accomplished and how it will be measured. To be consistent, an objective must agree with the organization's overall objectives and policies. Such agreements must be in terms of both subject and priority. For example, a plant with a policy of providing maximum employee comfort cannot accept a cash-saving objective from the service department manager not to use the air conditioning during the summer. Attainable objectives mean realistic objectives. They may not always be met, but employees must know that it is possible to meet them. If an objective can never be reached, employees will soon become discouraged, and the results may be worse than if no objective exists at all.

OUTLINING PROCEDURES

The process of outlining procedures means deciding how the objective of the plan will be accomplished. This is a four-step process:

- Defining activities.
- Establishing times.
- Reviewing resources.
- Determining locations.

To define activities it is necessary to identify the individual components or stages necessary to achieve the objective and place them in a logical order. Once the activities have been defined and placed in a proper sequence, it is then necessary to establish times for the activities. After defining activities and establishing times, it is necessary to review resources. This means determining whether or not the equipment, materials, money and skills are available to perform the activities. The final step in outlining procedures is to determine the location, or where the activities are to take place. Having defined activities, established times, reviewed resources and determined locations, the second stage of the planning process, outlining procedures, is completed.

ASSIGNING RESPONSIBILITIES

This is the third step in the planning process. In assigning responsibilities, the employee(s) who can best provide the needed skills must be chosen. If staff are not competent then a suitable training programme must be completed before the work commences.

Planning Methods

GANTT CHARTS

GANTT charts can be either very simple or very complicated. They contain certain common parts with a vertical and horizontal axis; where these cross, each cell contains information.

NETWORK ANALYSIS

Network Analysis is a planning method that enables you to plan projects that contain a number of activities in their logical sequence. With any project, some activities are completed before others start and other activities can be carried on at the same time. The resulting diagram enables you to identify the Critical Path Analysis, which is the line of activities that must be completed in their allocated times in order to complete the whole task within its allotted time.

Resource Allocation

TIME MANAGEMENT

Time is an irreplaceable resource; once passed it cannot be reclaimed. In the work situation, the overworked manager may attempt to do so by burning the midnight oil. A good manager will always have more tasks to do than can be coped with, therefore it is essential for a supervisor to learn the art of delegation.

How often have you said or heard such comments as:

- The day is too short.
- It's quicker to do the job myself.
- I could cope if there weren't so many interruptions.
- If I want a job done properly, I do it myself.
- I find it hard to say no and then end up with too many tasks to complete.

- I do not have the right staff to support me.
- I do not delegate enough and do many simple jobs that my subordinates could easily do.

These are familiar statements from over-worked managers. Have you stopped to think why these managers (yourself included) are overworked? Is it due to lack of organization? Being an unorganized manager can have a number of side effects:

- Staff do not know what is happening.
- There is never time to talk about the problems or work properly.
- Colleagues find the unorganized manager unreliable.
- Relationships at work and home become strained.

A further, even more important result of poor time management is stress. It has been suggested that stress is a necessary part of work. This is so to a certain extent. The runner whose adrenalin is flowing will run that bit faster in the race. If in the work situation you become overstressed, you will be unable to achieve the work you have to do. Have you ever calculated how much your time is worth?

One suggestion is that you should not simply add your gross wage to the costs of your employment, but add the overheads associated with your office, the cost of employing the staff you control, and any special costs associated with your work. You should be able to calculate the cost per minute and then estimate just how much you are costing the business every time you waste a minute through needless interruption, unimportant tasks, unnecessary meetings, unnecessary jour-neys, the over-long telephone calls and the administration work that someone else could do.

PLANNING YOUR TIME
Having a finite amount of time means that it is crucial to plan how to spend it most effectively. This involves clarifying the main purpose of your job, which should relate to the objectives of the organization. Once this has been done, the key tasks essential to achieving the purpose can be identified. Tasks normally fall into two categories:

Active: The positive tasks you must do to achieve the objectives of your job and help build your business.

Reactive: The day to day tasks that have to be dealt with to keep things running. They are the tasks that some managers spend all their available time on.

Work can be identified in another way:

Routine Work: These are administrative tasks that are minor but essential. Since they can eat up time, however, they must be kept under control.

Regular Duties: These are the main areas of work, including directing and checking employees, giving work assign-ments, checking work quality and providing training and counselling.

Special Assignments: These are unpredictable and take time away from usual duties.

Creative Work: This involves the use of initiative to make improvements for oneself and the group through planning improve-ments in work methods to overcome pro-blems. One is likely to waste time through lack of focus, failure to delegate, failure to look ahead, failure to communicate, inter-ruptions, fatigue and related problems.

SCHEDULING YOUR WORK
The first step in scheduling your work is to make a list of all the jobs that need to be done, from the long-term tasks and priori-ties to the short-term tasks. You are then in a position to schedule your work in the time available, thus leaving your free time to yourself. This involves determining:

- The importance of the task and how long you want to spend on it.

• The urgency of the task and how soon it needs to be completed.

Urgency and importance is not the same thing. An urgent task may be trivial and should be dealt with straight away in the minimum time. An urgent and important task should take priority in your schedule and sufficient time allocated. These are usually the active tasks and the reactive tasks can then be slotted in. The list and schedule need updating as priorities change. This can be done in the form of a diary updating session, by you, or with colleagues or subordinates.

There are various aids to effective scheduling:

Diaries: These should be used to schedule chunks of time on active tasks, with time to carry out reactive ones. You can also schedule time for departmental visits and chats to staff.

Visual planners: Updated charts and planners can help schedule and monitor work, holidays and other activities. The visual presentation of information can alert you to potential crises and planning gaps.

Bring forward files: Useful as a memory aid if used properly. They can be used to act as reminders to take action or chase up queries and collect data for your positive tasks.

There are many ways by which you are able to improve your time management. These will depend on the job you have, your responsibilities, your duties and the number of staff reporting to you. The most important thing is to plan. Plan your month, your week and most of all your day. Try to divide your day into sections leaving at least part of the time to deal with the unexpected.

DEPARTMENTAL TIME MANAGEMENT

Just as time is a personal resource, it is also a departmental resource. In both instances,

getting more work done in less time will rapidly increase productivity. This does not happen, it must be managed. A manager will feel time pressure applied by production schedules, promised delivery dates and project completion deadlines. Often all three of these will occur together, putting pressure on you. Production schedules specify a given amount of output to be produced during a certain period. These schedules are made in advance and it is not possible to anticipate the problems and holdups that are likely to interfere with the smooth running of the department. Delivery dates are of vital importance, whether it is the delivery of manufactured goods or the delivery of a leisure programme. The scheduled delivery date becomes a vital deadline for the manager. In addition to routine production and promised deliveries, there are a range of deadlines that have to be met. These include equipment changes, renovations, special studies, budget preparation, method improvement and collecting information. These all have completion dates to be met. Managers, when dealing with these time pressures, use the same general principles as used for personal time management. One must eliminate waste time and plan the effective use of time.

TIME PLANNING

Scheduling of work is the planning of time, because the process involves allocating the available time to the jobs that have to be done. If this is done properly, resources will be effectively and efficiently used. Planning techniques such as GANTT charts and PERT charts help you to plan long blocks of time. It must not be forgotten that it is very important to manage short blocks of time, which will not usually receive detailed and formal scheduling. Daily or weekly time plans are important because small jobs arise that may not have been included in the grand plan. It is important that you manage these short time-frame decisions as the changes can rapidly eat away at the available time.

Organization and Method Techniques

The key elements for success for a commercial business making a product are:

- Producing a marketable product.
- Maintaining an acceptable quality standard.
- Manufacturing to enable a sale at an acceptable price.
- Ensuring adequate sales.

With a private or commercial sports ground or club the list is somewhat different, since it is providing a service rather than a tangible product. The key elements are in this instance:

- Supplying the service required.
- Maintaining an acceptable quality standard.
- Achieving the objectives at the least cost.

Two key words are identified that are critical to the development and use of organizational methods.

Standard: Is a point of reference provided to the people concerned as a guide to a range of activities or aspects? One of the prime functions of work-study is the setting of accurate standards in as many areas of the business as possible.

Labour standards, for instance, relate to the time it takes for a piece of work to be completed. This is not as simple as it might seem and in many industries has caused problems where unqualified personnel attempt to set accurate rates. The time for a job involves asking a series of questions:

- What is the best method to use?
- What type of worker is required to do it?

- What should be the precise nature of the available environment?
- What training should be given to the worker?
- What incentive should be given to the worker?

Although the setting of standards is difficult, it is important that they are set as the effort will be rewarded.

The main reasons for using standards are:

- To ensure the most efficient use of labour and materials.
- To enable management to plan the future work programmes accurately.
- To enable management to balance the workload across the workforce.
- To provide a sound basis for estimating and price fixing.

Performance: Is the required level of work achieved?

Management by Objectives

A participative approach to the activities involved in planning, organization, direction and control is the system known as Management by Objectives (MBO). This system or style of management seeks to relate organizational goals to individual performance and development of the organization through the involvement of all levels of management.

The basis of MBO is:

- The setting of objectives and targets.
- Participation by individual managers in agreeing unit objectives and criteria of performance.
- The continual review and appraisal of results.

The introduction of MBO should, it is claimed, provide the following advantages:

- Concentration on the main areas where it is important for the organization to be effective.

- Identification of problem areas during the progression towards the achievement of the objectives.
- Improvement of management control information and the level of performance standards.
- Development of a sound organizational structure, clarification of responsibilities and aiding delegation and coordination.
- Easy identification of areas where changes are needed and allowing continual improvement in results.
- An improvement in management succession planning.
- Identification of training needs and the provision of an environment that encourages personal growth and self-discipline.
- Improvement of appraisal systems, and the provision of a more equitable procedure for determining rewards and promotional plans.
- Improvement in communications and interpersonal relationships.
- The encouragement of motivation, thus improving individual performance.

To be successful it will require:

- The commitment and active support of top management.
- Specialist advice on implementation of the system and a thorough understanding by all staff concerned.
- Careful attention to the setting of key tasks, target figures and performance standards.
- Objectives that are profitable to the organization, clearly defined, realistically attainable and capable of measurement.
- Genuine participation by staff in agreeing objectives and targets.
- The right spirit and interest from staff concerned and effective teamwork.
- Avoidance of excessive paperwork and forms that lead to a mechanistic approach.
- Maintaining the impetus of the system.

SWOT Analysis

This management tool enables one to examine a product, facility or business so that one can make decisions as to the development of the business in the future. Although used primarily for marketing purposes, it can be used to examine various management situations within a business.

Strengths
Weaknesses
Opportunities
Threats

This analysis looks at the past, present and future of the business.

To carry out a SWOT analysis does not take long, but must involve a critical and honest view of the situation. The first stage is to list the internal strengths of the business or facility and its internal weaknesses. Secondly, list the opportunities that exist now or in the future and the threats to the business from the external environment.

This list covers the sort of areas one could identify for a facility. They may of course be either *strengths or weaknesses*, depending on the business being examined.

- Resources, location of facility, catchments area, transport structure, car park, pitches, landscaping, reception, decor, changing areas, activity facilities, refreshment facilities and a range of products.
- Activities, composition of programme, range of activities, timing of activities, coaching programme, membership.
- Staffs, quality of customer care, range of abilities, coaching abilities.
- Marketing, types of promotions, range, pricing structures, target market penetration, range of products, facility image.

Again, the list might include reference to some or all of the following; these may be *threats or opportunities* or both, depending on time or circumstances:

- Finance, restrictions imposed by budget, client, influence on price, disposable income of customers, capital for future developments.
- Competitors, their image, marketing, customer range, impact on your catchment area, programmed development, new facilities opened.
- Finance, reductions of external funding/lending, changes in standards of living.
- People, changes in living styles, changes in activity needs, mobility changes, working week changes, group/club development.

Having produced a comprehensive list for each of the four areas, the next stage is to examine them in detail. One should first examine your strengths. Obviously, these are the things you are good at. These strengths should be maximized. It is important to relate them to your future goals, however, and indeed the current objectives. You may have a well-designed facility with well-motivated staff, but if your programme is not good you will not attract the customers you seek. Secondly, examine your weaknesses. It is easy to identify strengths, but you must be truthful when listing weaknesses. Again, list them in order of importance, and then prepare ways of removing them or at least reducing their significance. Thirdly, look at the threats. This involves examining your local competitors to see how they are doing. Check also other leisure activities in the area, as people only have so much time and money available for leisure. Look to the wider horizons, especially national economic and employment trends. Again it is important to quantify the effect of each on the future of your facility. Finally, look at the opportunities. These opportunities may range from finance availability to improve the decor of the building, to the television publicity given to a national sports team, which will often attract short-term interest in participation, especially from juniors. Having completed your analysis, you are in

a position to select the most important items from each section and implement action plans to maximize or minimize effect.

Financial Management

Record Keeping and Financial Statements

Every organization, irrespective of size or type, has moral or legal requirements to keep adequate records of its financial transactions and then to prepare summary accounts. There are a variety of reasons for keeping financial records and account summaries:

- For inland revenue taxation purposes. The Inland Revenue uses the Trading, Profit and Loss Account as the base figure when calculating the tax liability of a sole trader, partnership or company.
- For the Customs and Excise (VAT, duty). The financial recording system is used to record the VAT paid and collected. The Customs and Excise regularly examines these documents to check that a business has made the correct VAT declarations.
- To provide information for members of a club. A club is a non-profit making organization and as such has no legal requirements to produce accounts. These should always be produced, however, both to show the members the state of the club's finances and to prove the trustworthiness of the Honorary Treasurer.
- To comply with the Companies Act 1985. The Companies Act requires that companies produce annual accounts. Those of public companies are available to the public.
- To satisfy the District Audit. The District Auditor is the watchdog over Local Authorities' financial competence and probity. The Auditor examines the financial summaries at the end of each year.

- To provide management information. In order to budget for the future, managers require base information of past performance.
- To collate with authorized budgeted expenditure. Local Government finance departments need to place all expenditure and income against the appropriate budget heads to ensure that no overspending occurs. At the end of the year a summary is produced and presented to the Councillors.

Accounting Systems

A variety of accounting systems are available to leisure operators. Whichever of the mechanical or computer financial recording systems is used, the end requirement in terms of financial summaries is the same, and hence whatever the system it must allow the construction of trading and capital statements at the end of a financial period. The complexity of a financial recording system will depend upon the type of business and the amount of transaction taking place during an account period. For instance, a local authority department working to a budget will have a very complex system because all purchases will be made using a section order book and the recording of the invoice must be allocated to a particular vote head. This is then further complicated by the need to keep a running total of the balance left in individual expenditure head. Conversely, the treasurer of a local football club will only have a limited number of financial transactions to record, so a simple system would be quite adequate. In this case, the important part is the reconciliation to enable the treasurer to prove to the other members that all the funds can be accounted for.

- *Bookkeeping* is the actual record-making process.
- *Accounting* deals with the use of the bookkeeping records, their analysis and interpretation.

A manager must study the relationship between results and the business events that lead to them and be able to understand what the accountant is telling him. Investors and lenders need the knowledge so they can make decisions about continued investment or lending.

The two main concerns for all are:

- Whether or not the business has made a profit (or loss).
- Whether the business has sufficient funds to meet its commitments.

BOOKKEEPING BACKGROUND

An appreciation of the basic bookkeeping process can be gained by looking at the basic financial transactions of the business, their classification and their purpose.

A sports sector business is likely to conduct five main groups of transactions:

- Revenue (entry charges, sales, subscriptions).
- Cost of sales (cost of buying trading goods, which are resold).
- Expenses (associated with running the business).
- Acquisition of funds:
  ○ Internal funding through ownership
  ○ External funding through borrowing
- Accumulation of assets (fixed and current).

ACCOUNTANCY SUMMARIES

This section outlines each of the accountancy summaries prepared and identifies the information necessary for the preparation of each. There are two fundamental answers to be found in the summary accounts. One relates to the profits or losses made by the business and the other changes in the level of assets or liabilities from the beginning to the end of that period. The final accounts, drawn up from financial records, which are normally presented in the annual reports of commercial, voluntary and local authority organizations, include:

- Trading, profit and loss account
- Balance sheet

- Sources and application of funds
- Gross profit statement
- Director's report
- Auditor's report
- Notes to the accounts

Understanding the final accounts is not difficult once the basic principles of how they were constructed are understood. First, it is necessary to define each of the accounts identified and outline its purpose and contents.

TRADING, PROFIT AND LOSS ACCOUNT

This account summarizes the results of the organization's operations for a period in time, usually a year. It identifies the types of income and the cost of obtaining that income during the year. Its main function will be to identify the level of profit or loss made, which the business proprietor will want to know for a variety of reasons, including:

- The ability to compare actual with budget.
- To assist future planning.
- To help obtain finance.
- To provide an income tax assessment.

This account is, in theory, divided into two sections:

- Trading
- Profit and loss

Two important calculations included within the account are:

Gross Profit: The excess of sales over the cost of goods sold in that period. This is the trading account portion.

Net Profit: The remainder after all costs is deducted. This is the result on the profit and loss portion.

It is necessary to understand what is and what is not included in the account.

Stock in hand: Because the operation of a business is continuous, it always has a stock of goods unsold. In order to consider this, it might be said that these goods are 'sold' at the end of each year to the next. Thus, the value at the beginning of the year is added to the expenses for that year and the end of year value is added to the receipts. The value placed on some classes of stock can influence the level of profitability. For instance, a tree in a garden centre may have a sale price of £10, but the owner is not going to value that tree at £10 in the end of year valuation because it has not yet been sold and the profit taken.

Capital purchases: In many businesses, buildings and machinery play an important part in the operation. The initial cost of these items is classified as capital purchases, so cannot be included in the expenses. Conversely, the sale of machinery cannot be included as income. What happens is that a percentage of the cost can be set against income in any year depending on a formula prepared by the Inland Revenue. This amount is known as the depreciation.

Debtors and creditors: It must be fully appreciated that the income and expenditure shown in the trading, profit and loss account is that actually incurred during the account year and not just that paid. Therefore, it is necessary to adjust the figures for the debtors and creditors at both the beginning and end of the year. Debtors and creditors from the previous year paid in the current year will be included in the bookkeeping totals and will have to be removed from the totals. Debtors and creditors outstanding at the end of the year have to be added onto the totals.

There are different layouts used to produce the trading, profit and loss account.

The headings for the receipts and expenses will depend on the business in question. With sole traders (single owner) and partnerships, no private drawings or

Simple Example of a Trading Profit and Loss Account	
Opening Valuation	Receipts
Stores	Goods sold
Stock for resale	Fees
Wages and salaries	Subscriptions
	Sponsorship
Expenses	
Rent and rates	Closing Valuation
Insurances	Stores
Office charges	Stock for resale
Miscellaneous	
Fuel and electricity	
Stock	
Building repairs	
Building depreciation	
Machinery depreciation	
Interest on loans	
Bank charges	
NET PROFIT	NET LOSS ( )
TOTAL	TOTAL

the value of own labour provided can be included. In a company, Directors are paid for the work they do.

RECEIPTS AND PAYMENTS ACCOUNTS
Clubs, associations and other non-profit-making organizations do not have to prepare full Trading, Profit and Loss Accounts, but Treasurers of such organizations will have to prepare some form of annual summary account. These accounts are known as Receipts and Payments Accounts, or Income and Expenditure Accounts. The Receipt and Payments Account is simply a summary of the cashbook.

BALANCE SHEET
The balance sheet takes a photograph of the capital source and disposition of the organization. It lists, with values, all the assets, liabilities and capital worth of the business. It is part of the end of year accounts but may be drawn up at regular intervals to give a snapshot of the organization's capital and the way in which it is dispersed.

THE ACCOUNTING EQUATION
A business needs resources in order to operate. These resources need to be supplied to the business by someone – the owner(s), investors or lenders. Resources owned by the business are *Assets*. Those assets are supplied by the *Owner*, the amount is known as *Capital* (often known as *Owner's Equity* or *Net Worth*).

$$Assets = Capital$$

Example of a Balance Sheet in Full	
Assets	**Liabilities**
Long-term	*Long-term*
Land at cost	Loans – brewery
Land development	Loans – governing body
Pavilion	Loans – bank
Bar and kitchen equipment	
Tractor	
Other machinery	
Office equipment	
Furnishings and fittings	
Current	*Current*
Shop stock	Creditors
Bar stock	Income tax
Sundry stock	Hire purchase
Debtors and pre-payments	
Cash at bank	
Cash on hand	
Building Society deposits	
	Net Assets
Total	*Total*

Example of a Bar Trading Account	
Sales	£163,840
Cost of sales	£100,764
Gross Profit	£63,076
Less:	
Employment costs	£21,047
Equipment hire and repair	£91
Glassware, stocktaking, cleaning	£1,571
Net Profit	£24,709

Some items such as bank balances and stores have a real value, while others are not easily valued and may be left at their original purchase price (land) or depreciated at a set rate (machinery).

If the balance sheet is being provided to aid further borrowings, it is vital that the assets are not over-valued. If they are, a false picture of the financial viability of the business is produced.

Liabilities: These are the items owned by the organization and claims on the assets by third parties. This includes creditors awaiting payment for goods supplied and those who have loaned the business money, including banks and shareholders, and debts such as tax.

GROSS PROFIT STATEMENT

This was referred to earlier concerning the trading profit and loss account. The statement shows the difference between what the business paid for its inputs and what it sold the products for. It is an expansion of the revenue and cost of sales section of the profit and loss accounts. It identifies how

Some of the assets will have been provided by others. The indebtedness of the business for these resources is known as *Liabilities*.

Assets = Capital + Liabilities

The two sides of the equation must balance. (This is a basic principle of all accounts.)

Assets: Assets comprise all the items of value owned by or owed to the organization.

individual costs have generated particular levels of income.

This information is very useful. The gross profit margin percentage, for instance, can be calculated and the employment costs related to turnover to see if they are similar to accepted levels.

DIRECTORS' REPORT

It is a legal requirement that directors of companies present reports for specific financial periods. This may be half-year interim reports or full-year audited accounts.

AUDITORS' REPORT

This is the validation of a set of accounts by an independent accountant. This is a legal requirement for a company, but a sole trader will need only to provide a statement of accounts from an account based on information supplied.

NOTES TO THE ACCOUNTS

These are included to explain methods, calculations, compositions and any problems.

Bookkeeping Systems

This book does not set out to enable readers to become competent at completing book-keeping activities, but for them to be able to decide which system would be suitable for a situation and what information can be extracted from the records.

SOURCES OF FINANCIAL INFORMATION

- VAT invoices from suppliers
- Credit notes given or received
- Monthly trading statements
- Cheque book stubs
- Paying in book stubs
- VAT sales invoices
- Bank statements
- Petty cash vouchers

Income and expenditure transacts through a business in three ways: as cash, as cheques or non-cash, or as direct debits.

Cash: Income is usually recorded in a day book or ledger and is then paid into the bank. It is important that some mechanism be used to ensure correct recording and to avoid the problem of fraud. In a retail situation where money is going into a cash register, the till roll is checked against the money in the till. If possible, money should not be taken out of the till to pay petty cash items. Where money is used to pay expenses, a separate petty cash system should be operated.

Cheques/non cash: Today's modern banking and credit facilities create additional bookkeeping problems. Income from cheques is easy to deal with because all cheques should be paid into the bank. More complicated is payment for goods sold using credit cards or Switch. In these cases, information may be recorded via the cash register and later the amount will be paid directly into the bank account or sent in the form of a cheque.

Direct to bank: This is in the form of either a direct debit or standing order. Organizations may set up this facility to pay suppliers in order to gain additional discounts. Standing orders are used to pay monthly repayments or annual subscriptions. The same applies in reverse when payments are being made.

Recording Systems

CASH ANALYSIS SYSTEM

The simplest system used is that known as cash analysis. This name is incorrect because

---

Sample expenditure column headings

Date
Reference number
Detail
Item and supplier
Amount
Cheque number
Contra
Analysis columns
VAT paid
Value of inputs (VATable items)

Sample arrangement of Analysis Book headings								
Date	Ref no.	Detail	Amount	Chq no.	Contra	Analysis*	VAT	Value input

*The headings will suit the type of business

it actually records monies as they pass through the bank account, thus if cash income is then spent as expenditure it must be recorded separately. Small commercial businesses and voluntary clubs often use cash analysis. The expenditure and receipts are recorded in different parts of the analysis book. This book contains cash analysis paper, which enables the transactions to be analysed into between fourteen and thirty-two columns. This is very useful as the financial controllers can see how much income or expenditure has accrued in particular columns. This system can also act as the VAT record.

DOUBLE-ENTRY BOOKKEEPING

Double-entry bookkeeping originated in Italy in the Middle Ages and is still used by a large number of businesses today. The documentation used is as listed above but, unlike cash analysis, entries are made through a number of ledgers or books.

For every transaction there is an original document, which is entered into one of the Books of Original Entry. Because these books are often used every day, with records used in chronological order as they happen, they are often called Journals.

The ledger is the main book of account and it is this that is recorded using the true double-entry principle. Every page in the ledger is called an Account and only items relating to that heading are recorded on that page.

Personal Accounts are those for the other companies the business deals with. Real accounts are the accounts kept for all the things the business owns, including land and buildings, stock and cash at bank.

Nominal accounts are those accounts where money is there in name only, and a record only is being kept.

From the ledger, it is usual to take a trial balance, usually on a monthly basis. Since every ledger entry has a debit entry and a matching credit entry, the total balances on all the accounts with debit balances should match the total of those with credit balances.

The final accounts for the business can be complied from these balances, as is shown in the accompanying diagram.

In summary, you can see that there is a variety of ways of keeping books. Whichever system is used, it is vital the records are kept in order so that the correct final accounts are produced at the end of the year and that no fraud is being perpetrated. Many businesses now employ computerized systems, which require operatives who have knowledge of both bookkeeping and computers. By coding every item, the computer will allocate every entry to the appropriate heading and the results should balance.

Marginal Costings

Marginal costings recognize that some cost items increase or decrease according to the level of sales. These costs are known as Variable Costs, since they vary in direct proportion to the sales.

Costs that do not come into this group are known as the Fixed or Common Costs. This category covers costs necessary for the operation of the business and that are incurred irrespective of output.

A simple example to understand is that of a retail shop. The fixed costs would

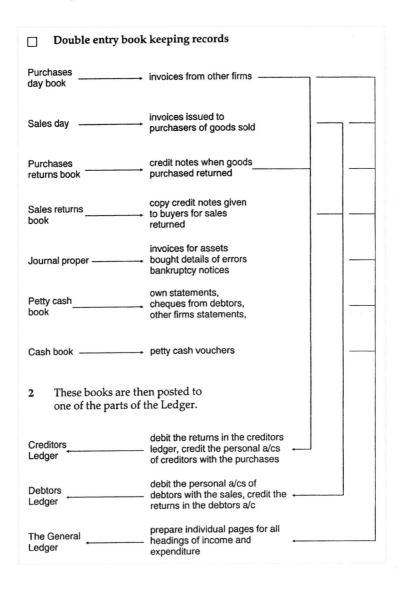

☐ **Double entry book keeping records**

Purchases day book	→ invoices from other firms
Sales day	→ invoices issued to purchasers of goods sold
Purchases returns book	→ credit notes when goods purchased returned
Sales returns book	→ copy credit notes given to buyers for sales returned
Journal proper	→ invoices for assets bought details of errors bankruptcy notices
Petty cash book	→ own statements, cheques from debtors, other firms statements,
Cash book	→ petty cash vouchers

2   These books are then posted to one of the parts of the Ledger.

Creditors Ledger	debit the returns in the creditors ledger, credit the personal a/cs of creditors with the purchases
Debtors Ledger	debit the personal a/cs of debtors with the sales, credit the returns in the debtors a/c
The General Ledger	prepare individual pages for all headings of income and expenditure

include rent, wages, heating and so on, all of which have to be paid before any sales are made. The variable cost might simply be the unit cost of buying goods for resale. The important calculation necessary is to find out how many units of sales are necessary in order to cover the variable and fixed costs and then the sales levels necessary to make particular profit levels.

Breakeven Analysis

The breakeven analysis makes use of the information in the marginal costing statement. It is used to calculate the level of sales necessary to cover both the variable and fixed costs without leaving a profit or incurring a loss.

This is useful, for example, when considering changes in sale prices. A lower sale

Sales	_____
Less variable costs	_____
Less fixed costs	_____
Profit or Loss	

Sale price	£1.45
Variable costs	£0.63
Contribution to fixed costs	£0.82
Fixed costs	£1,500.00

$$Breakeven\ Point = \frac{fixed\ costs}{contribution\ per\ unit}$$

$$Breakeven\ Point = \frac{£1,500.00}{£0.82}$$

$$= 1,829\ units\ of\ sale$$

Sale price	£1.99
Variable costs	£0.63
Contribution to fixed costs	£1.36
Fixed costs	£1,500.00

$$Breakeven\ Point = \frac{fixed\ costs}{contribution\ per\ unit}$$

$$\frac{£1,500.00}{£1.36}$$

$$= 1,103\ units\ of\ sale$$

price might increase the total sale income, but the unit contribution to the fixed costs is reduced, thus raising the breakeven sales point. Conversely, an increase in sale price will increase the unit contribution towards fixed costs, but the demand/price factor may reduce the overall level of sales,

even though the breakeven number is reduced.

The following examples show how the minimum level of sales can be calculated, and then how estimates of profit levels at different sale prices and guestimates of sales levels may be made. In each case the fixed costs are set at £1,500 and there is a potential sales level of 2,500 units.

If all 2,500 units of sale are completed, 671 units will contribute 82p each towards profit, giving a total profit of £550.22.

If, because of the increased price, 2,000 units of sale are completed, 897 units will contribute 1.36p each towards profit, giving a total profit of £1,219.92.

Budgeting

One of the most important responsibilities of the Sports Ground Manager is the preparation and development of the grounds maintenance budget. The purpose of a budget is to analyse, cost and apply financial control to all activities carried out on the sports ground within a complete financial year. In the UK the financial year is currently between April and March, although some sports grounds or clubs will operate their internal budgets to follow the calendar year. Whichever is used, each department will submit its section budget to go towards the overall company budget. The budget statement should be presented in a manner that is easily understood by the Club Committee, Management Team, Manager and interested parties, and does not have to be a highly technical and detailed manuscript.

The budget document will be an outline and guide of expected expenditure and the detailed analysis will be available later. A detailed explanation and justification for each of the budget areas, along with accurate estimates, will greatly enhance the probability of receiving adequate funding to maintain the sports ground in accordance with the stated objectives and standards for that facility. A properly prepared budget will also be a live document that can be referred to throughout the year as a reference guide to the original objectives that had been set out.

A budget can also function as an aid in ensuring that funds have been allocated in an orderly manner. Unusual or unexpected demands on funds to meet a maintenance crisis are more likely to occur if the budget procedure is haphazard. The properly prepared budget will allow for the identification and control of:

- All expenses incurred.
- Means and methods for cost reduction.
- Human factors that can be manipulated to improve efficiency.

The sports ground budget is developed in a systematic manner in a series of stages and will be presented in two forms, containing different types of information.

Capital Budget
The capital budget is prepared and will cover expenditure for equipment and materials with a life expectancy of more than one year. The capital budget plan may also be further divided into two smaller areas.

CAPITAL IMPROVEMENTS
This covers expenditures that will improve the overall value of the sports ground as a business, such as:

- Construction – additions, pumphouses, shelters, paths, parking areas.
- Ground improvements and developments – new pitches or surfaces.
- Landscaping projects, tree plantings.

CAPITAL EXPENSES
Equipment, including machinery, plant and vehicles, will make up the major portion of this budget area. Lockers,

permanent tools, and office furniture are also included.

Operating Budget
This budget covers the expected expenditure and requirements for materials in the short term. Operating budgets can be split into two categories:

- An amount that changes year to year as the circumstances dictate, for example if dry summers require the unforeseen replacement of plant material and/or turf.
- An amount that remains constant from year to year, such as the herbicide and fertilizer requirements.

The categories listed below should be considered for inclusion in the operating budget. Some of them will be obvious, some you may not have thought of, and it may be necessary to revise your budget planning to incorporate them.

PERSONNEL
Salaries: Grounds Manager, Head Groundsperson.
Wages: Permanent employees, seasonal employees, and extra workers.
Benefits: Include holiday time, sick leave, social security, National Insurance, private medical schemes, life insurance, retirement, uniforms, meals and Grounds Manager expense allowance.

MATERIALS AND SERVICES
Fertilizer: Specific types and quantities based on a pre-planned programme, with fertilizer in stock taken into account. An effort should be made to not store fertilizer beyond a year.
Water (if purchased): Approximate cost established by averaging gallonage from past five years and adding any anticipated rate increase.
Irrigation: Age of system and the costs for past repair for piping, controllers, control lines, valves and sprinkler heads are considered. Allowing a contingency sum

for possible major pump repairs during the year is wise.

Chemicals: Includes herbicides, fungicides, insecticides, and wetting agents. Present inventory should be included to keep chemicals revolving in storage.

Drainage: Projected costs for repair of drain lines, French drains, ditches, stream banks, ponds, and surface contours.

Topdressing: Based on pre-planned maintenance for year ahead.

Seed and turfing: Any planned construction or renovation projects, as well as routine overseeding and returfing needs, should be considered.

Fuel: Petrol, diesel fuel, oil and lubricant use records should be kept for accurate cost projections. Purchase of any additional new equipment should be taken into account, along with anticipated rate increases.

Equipment parts and services: Cost projected for mechanical repairs from past cost records with consideration for new or different equipment. Equipment rentals and leasing would be covered in this category.

Landscaping: Amount for annual flowers, bulbs, border edging, ornamental shrubs, tree pruning and tree replacement programme.

Sports ground equipment: Corner flags, flagsticks, nets, goalposts, scoreboards. Past records of vandalism may give an estimate of how much should be budgeted in this category.

Maintenance of buildings: Amount for painting, repair, window replacement, plumbing and heating facilities.

Electricity/gas: Costs projected from past records and anticipated rate increases.

Equipment depreciation: A detailed depreciation schedule to fund the purchase of new equipment.

Contract services: Based on past records and projected plans, and any anticipated cost increase. Services may include turfgrass consultant, architect, engineer, surveyor, repair specialist and tree maintenance contractor.

Staff development: College education/ training costs, pesticide applicators' licences, association subscriptions, educational exhibition/conference/field day expenses.

Insurance: Includes fire, property loss and liability insurance.

Miscellaneous: May include office supplies and printing, telephone, vehicle licences.

Contingency: An amount to cover unanticipated expenses for replacement of turf and trees caused by flooding, extended droughts, vandalism, winterkill and so on.

Budget Preparation

The sports ground budget is developed systematically in a series of stages. The starting point in preparing an operating budget is to review both the club and department objectives for the coming year.

TIMETABLING

Budget preparation is like planning a tournament, and plenty of time should be allocated to prepare for the budget to be researched and presented to the relevant officials in the organization. In fact, planning for the next one should start as soon

Typical Budgeting Timetable

Corporate strategy approved	September
Budget priorities agreed	October
Budgets submitted and evaluated	November/December
Draft budget plans	January
Business plan and budget finalized	February
Presented to the Committee	March

as the current one starts. Reference should be made to the budget document that may have been referred to throughout the current budget year, taking into consideration any changes of plan or projection that may have been noted.

PLANNING STAGE 1

This information will provide you with a starting point from which to establish priorities in the maintenance plan for those items needed to meet the overall projections. Long-range objectives should be reviewed at regular intervals to ensure that the current plan being followed is up to date and everyone is aware of any changes that may have been made. Every major capital budget item should be clearly explained with emphasis on the positive. Factors that can influence the changes and capital requirements include:

- Member objectives
- Overall aim and goal
- Economic trends
- Labour requirements versus labour availability
- Time scales

The establishment of time scales for both the start and completion of specific projects, such as construction and the purchase of large-scale machinery or equipment, is an effective way to help determine the impact of the project in relation to ongoing maintenance practices.

PLANNING STAGE 2

The next stage is to conduct a complete evaluation of the present maintenance practices and techniques that are carried out with the aim to establish possible improvements to both efficiency and effectiveness of that operation or application. The secondary objectives are those that originate within the sports ground maintenance team and are required to accomplish the prime objective, that is to produce, manage and deliver a sports ground on behalf of the client. Information is required

to help plan the second objectives and to realize their realistic potential. Past records, meeting minutes, past budgets and records or routine maintenance and management practices are invaluable in planning this part of the budget.

A comprehensive collection of current distributor information, stock and price lists will assist in determining the level of costs projected for the operational (and capital) budget requirements in the coming year.

The Grounds Manager should not hesitate to request help and advice in determining costs for stage 2 and should aim to obtain realistic costs, since budget estimates that reflect an accurate appraisal of these factors are more likely to be approved.

PLANNING STAGE 3

The final stage at this level is the preparation of a budget statement that, in the final document, will set out the budget objectives in relation to the preceding budget success:

- Whether the current year's standards of operation and resources/equipment will be sufficient to meet the following year's needs.
- The specific improvements that the sports ground will undertake (in relation to the club type, members' needs, and so on).
- The current financial status and the outlook for the following year.
- Any local or central legislation that will have an effect on the cost of implementation of operations.

Throughout all the stages that you embark upon, consistent record-keeping is of immense value when preparing budget presentations. Good record-keeping makes the overall task much easier, since this supplies a sound basis on which to reference and base expected costs and increases. For example, equipment and plant costs can be derived from past records and adjusted in accordance with:

- Projected inflation rates
- Adjustments in the maintenance programme
- Specific projects' application and proposal

Projected needs for equipment will become apparent from these records and the level of maintenance and repair that has been carried out on existing machinery types, along with running costs and other factors, can help to decide whether the same equipment should be replaced like for like when the current unit needs replacing. Good record management will help to portray this information to the relevant officials when arguing the case for new equipment.

Budget Presentation
The presentation of a budget to the club committee, owner or governing authority at the sports ground is often the responsibility of the Grounds Manager, and after much hard work. The Grounds Manager is often the most informed person to carry out the presentation of the documented information, able to reply to questions from the committee that may often arise from the presentation. Just as much planning is needed in the successful presentation and defence of a proposed budget as there is in the planning of the document. One approach to the presentation is to summarize the highlights of the budget and then give appropriate supporting information. This is often the best approach as the people that you are presenting to have no technical knowledge of the budget content and will be primarily interested in the bottom line figures. The information is then available to them in detail to peruse at their leisure later.

A copy of the proposed budget should be sent to each committee member prior to the budget meeting. The presentation should be as short and concise as possible, yet must effectively communicate the budget proposal and justification. Simple language is better than trade jargon and scientific terms, since club officials are usually unfamiliar with these. Use of visual aids to communicate concepts and plans is always desirable. These aids may range from a marking pencil and scratch pad to drawings, charts, models, pictures or a slide presentation. During the verbal assessment of certain capital improvements, both the advantages and disadvantages of the concept should be presented. It is also helpful if the major features of the budget are discussed with key members of the club management team and green committee before the actual budget meeting. Finally, it is important that sufficient time be allocated following the budget presentation for discussion and questions.

Adjusting to a Tight Budget
Budgets are not always going to show growth and development in both the long-term and the short-term projection. Often there are influencing factors, both internal and external, that will influence the budget. These can include:

- Reduction in new members.
- Reduced visiting parties and functions.
- Competition from new or existing local sports clubs.
- Increased legislative requirements.
- Crisis requirements to other areas of the organization.

Often budgets have to be 'nipped and tucked' to consolidate costs in this period of financial reflection. Ways to control what can often be perceived as spiralling maintenance and operating costs, within the framework of a reasonable budget, may involve carrying out and executing efficient labour operations and improved maintenance practices. A limited budget often calls for superior management. For this reason, a well-trained, experienced Grounds Manager will more than recover a somewhat higher salary through management efficiency. Certain categories of the sports ground budget offer the most potential for economies. Since 65–70 per cent of the budget is allocated to labour costs, economies in this area will have a substantial impact.

Budget costs can be reduced by:

Machinery and equipment: Using the proper labour-saving equipment will quickly pay for itself through reduced labour expenditures. A well-planned and executed equipment maintenance programme requires expenditures in the present but may produce future savings. Well-maintained machinery often lasts beyond the anticipated depreciation period. In addition, proper storage of equipment, chemicals, fertilizer and top-dressing can prevent deterioration and thus save money.

Staff and personnel: Two-way radio communication facilities allow more efficient utilization of staff and equipment, which in turn produces economies in maintenance. Skilful management strategies include carefully hiring the right staff, such as experienced casuals and students, during times of increased demand. Year-round staff members should be recognized and encouraged, since their experience, cooperation and loyalty can facilitate budget economies. Club members or managers should be aware that providing funds or defraying expenses for these loyal employees to attend colleges, conferences, seminars and field days is a good investment.

Maintenance operations: Strategies related to maintenance practices and programmes should be judiciously evaluated for possible budgetary savings. Costly hand trimming around poles, trees and buildings often can be eliminated by use of an appropriate contact herbicide or growth regulator. Consideration should also be given to the feasibility of rescheduling certain turfgrass maintenance practices. Many hours are lost annually by interruptions due to intense play. Thus, scheduling of projects at times when they can be completed without undue interruption is advisable. Similarly, projects should be planned throughout the year, not just during the playing season. A number of work projects on a sports ground can be

planned as off-season winter tasks to provide year-round employment.

The Grounds Manager's efforts to economize within a constrained budget should be communicated to the club members and Club Manager. Priorities should be carefully honed and established in preparing and executing an alternate budget to deal with reduced funds. The aid of club members and officials should be enlisted when adhering to there priorities. A tight budget demands sound management strategies and more efficient utilization of machinery and manpower resources.

Budget Preparation Summary

The method of organizing a budget will vary with each type of facility and the requirements of the roles within that organization.

- The budget should be prepared well in advance of the fiscal year.
- The budget activity is a team effort involving the turf maintenance staff and key figures such as the mechanic. Grounds staff can provide alternative viewpoints and help to focus course maintenance objectives. The involvement of other staff members will also help to improve staff morale and reinforce the team effort. Final decisions, however, must rest with the Grounds Manager.
- Involvement of club officials and management helps to plan, present and ultimately approve the budget.
- The operating and capital budgets should be prepared jointly as one will influence the other. Budgeting of one phase of the course maintenance programme must be coordinated with and relate to the budgeting of other phases as well as the overall course budget proposal.
- Accurate records, procedures and expenditure controls are necessary in preparing and executing the budget.

- Budget requests should be realistic without padding or across the board percentage increases.
- Once the primary objectives have been established and approved for both ongoing course maintenance and long-range improvements and construction, they should be adhered to during the budget year. This will ensure that no unexpected catastrophic events will occur.
- In some situations, an alternative budget for supporting unanticipated contingencies may be advisable. In these cases, a plan for higher than anticipated, as well as less than anticipated, income should serve as the base.

2 Procurement and Contract Management

It is accepted that throughout history 'man' has often had to rely on other people for goods and services. The management of any facility today relies upon the constant interaction of both individuals and organizations and it is often necessary to formalize these arrangements for either economic or legal reasons. Such 'arrangements' or 'agreements' have become generically known as 'contracts'. Sports Ground Managers, grounds persons, agronomists, landscape architects and designers frequently use varying forms of contract for the efficient provision of sports turf and other playing surfaces. Contracts are used to procure new constructions and installations, specialist works or services, maintenance work, products and materials, labour, and machinery and equipment. Today the use of contracts in the sports ground industry is well established and has become an accepted method for service, product or goods procurement. In the public sector, particularly, the introduction of Compulsory Competitive Tendering (CCT) in 1988 led to a rapid increase in the use of contractors as local authorities had to tender works such as sports ground maintenance to the private sector. Although CCT has now been replaced, many of the contractors formed at that time to take advantage of this work remain in business and the use of contractors is still very prominent in both public and private sectors.

What is Involved in a Contract?

The fundamental principle of a contract is that both parties seek benefit from such an agreement. The buyer (Employer or Client) wants to procure goods and/or services, while the supplier (Contractor) is interested in the business for the income it will bring. The concept is that of fair exchange between two (or more) parties in a mutually beneficial transaction. Because things often go wrong in human relationships and business dealings, or increasingly due to the distances involved between the relevant parties, it has become necessary to have proper written administrative arrangements in place in order that any disputes that arise can be effectively dealt with within an agreed contractual framework. The following points have become the basis of contract law and practice:

- Procurement or exchange
- Reward or payment
- Performance related to quality, quantity and time
- Administration regarding disputes, claims, sanctions and the like

A contract can be defined as 'an agreement between two parties for the exchange of goods and services of value for a reward of value'.

The Stages of a Contract

1	Employer decision to contract out work
2	Preparation of contract documentation
3	Identify contractors and invite tenders
4	Preparation and submission of tenders by contractors
5	Tender evaluation and contractor selection
6	Award contract
7	Contact works and management
8	Contractor payment
9	Contract review

The Elements of a Contract

Contract law is complex. It is based upon three basic principles or elements that must all be present if a contract is to be valid:

Agreement: Agreement is effected, and a contract brought into being, through a process of offer and acceptance. This process forms the basis of most contract tender procedures. To become legally binding, the offer from one party must be accepted clearly and without condition by the other party.

Exchange: The law presumes that parties enter into a contract on the understanding that they will be legally bound by it and that they intend to effect a contractual exchange. The exchange must transfer ownership of the subject of the contract from one party to another. In entering into the contract this implies that all parties involved agree to comply with the principles and rules of the contract.

Value or consideration: Consideration must have a defined and recognizable value. The most common form of consideration is that of monetary reward, that is the contractor or supplier is paid a sum of money for the goods or services that they have provided. Such 'value' does not have to be proportionate as the contract is freely entered into. It is up to the individual parties themselves to decide whether they are receiving value for the benefit they gain from the contract.

The above factors have meant that the written 'agreement' or contract has evolved to include clauses that:

* Identify the parties involved.
* Determine the specific rights of each party.
* Define the extent and duration of the contract.
* Quantify and qualify the subject of the contract.
* Value the payment that results from the contract.

Best Value

The Local Government Act of 1999 introduced the concept 'Best Value' for the provision of local authority services, including those of parks and sports grounds management and maintenance. This new regime marked the end of the previous system of Compulsory Competitive Tendering (CCT), which had been in place since its introduction in 1988. CCT required local authorities to offer their services to tender and the private sector. As a result much grounds maintenance and related provision was conducted and managed by commercial contractors. Many have argued that this system and its emphasis on sourcing the cheapest price for service provision led to the rapid decline in the quality and range of local authority parks

51

and sports grounds. Best Value legislation challenged councils to look at the way they deliver services to the public and the communities they serve. The Act states that 'a best value authority must make arrangements to secure continuous improvement in the way in which its functions are exercised, having due regard to a combination of economy, efficiency and effectiveness'. These three factors may be defined as:

- Economy (obtaining given services, supplies or work, of given quantity and quality, at the lowest cost)
- Efficiency (the ratio of quality or effectiveness to cost, for given services or work)
- Effectiveness (the extent to which inputs secure the ultimate purpose of given services or work)

The Act requires local authorities to review all their service provision over a five-year period. These reviews require answers to basic questions under four headings: Challenge, Compare, Consult and Compete (colloquially known as the 'four Cs').

While the Local Government Act 1999 does not require authorities to put everything out to tender, the government has stated that fair and open competition is the best way to demonstrate that a function is being carried out competitively. Increasingly local authorities and other public sector organizations are moving away from traditional contracts and forms of contract management, which tended to keep the contractor at arm's length and were often adversarial, and towards building constructive relationships with contractors and suppliers.

Basic Principles of Procurement

A company or organization has three basic options when sourcing services, goods or products:

From within its own organization: In large organizations this is commonplace and one part or department of the organization may often be used to supply goods or services to another. This is especially the case for generic services such as Finance, Personnel or IT.

From the marketplace: Usually by competitive selection, whereby specialist goods or services are procured from an external supplier or contractor offering the most favourable deal.

Through some form of merger: Normally two or more organizations join

Challenge	Why do we provide the service?
	How do we provide it?
	What benefit does the community get from it?
Compare	Are other authorities giving a better service than we are?
	Does the private sector or voluntary service also offer the service and, if so, do they offer a better service than we do?
	Do other public organizations do better than we do?
Consult	What do others think of our service?
	Do they have any suggestions on how we can improve the service?
	Can we set ourselves some challenging targets for improving the service?
Compete	Will our users get better value through competition?
	Would it be better to use different approaches to delivering services, such as partnerships or private finance?

permanently but continue to trade 'independently' while cooperating in delivering services to each other.

In the management of sports grounds and allied facilities, the second option is the most common, but local authorities, particularly, will use the first method also.

The Decision to Outsource and Enter into a Contract or Agreement

The decision to obtain goods and services is clearly a very important business decision and should only be taken after due consideration of the relevant options and of the work or services required. The decision must relate to the wider objectives of both parties who might wish to enter into and be legally bound by such a contractual agreement. Clients must decide whether to contract work and contractors need to decide if they should tender or bid for such.

The client will need to consider:

- If they have the necessary staff skills and expertise to do the work.
- If they have the capacity (time and physical resources).
- Whether or not it may be cheaper to 'employ' a contractor.
- That there are contractors that can provide the services or goods.

On the other side of the fence, the prospective contractor or supplier will need to determine:

- Do they want to work for or supply the client in question?
- What are the consequences of not bidding for or undertaking this work?
- Do they have the necessary capacity to undertake this work?
- Will it be a profitable venture?
- Do they want all the work themselves? Will subcontracting be an option?

Employer Requirement or Product of a Contractor?

When formulating procurement agreements or contracts both parties need to recognize whether they are working towards the employer's specified requirements or in accordance with the product or service of the contractor/supplier.

Employer-specified requirements enable them to control precisely all aspects of the service or product required. The emphasis is on compliant performance from the contractor. The employer specifies the work or service to be undertaken in detail and determines the necessary standards of quality, timing and duration of the works and the way in which it is to be conducted. These types of contract are particularly suited to and used for works of a unique or specialized nature, such as for new constructions or specialist surface renovation treatments. The employer retains a degree of managerial control over some parts of the delivery process. Various alternatives are available and include:

- Competitive contracts
- Partnering agreements
- Preferred contractor agreements
- Framework agreements

Often the employer or client wishes to purchase or acquire a particular brand of product or item. This could be for a particular piece of machinery or equipment or patented construction system. In such cases, the contractor or supplier determines and defines specifications and delivery timescales. These systems are also used for particular services, such as for computer and IT equipment. The employer needs only to ascertain the ability of the contractor or supplier to deliver the 'goods' by comparison to other providers and through negotiation. In practice, the employer relinquishes responsibility for the delivery process and only controls final acceptance or rejection of the goods or services. These types of contract are most useful for the supply of specific products or services and include:

- Service level agreements (SLA)
- Preferred supplier arrangements (PSA)

Many procurement arrangements, such as management type packages and trust agreements, often utilize elements of both employer requirement and product of the contractor or supplier.

Works and Service Procurement

The process of procurement involves two interrelated but distinctly separate elements that deal with the administrative arrangement between the parties to effect an agreement and the technical processes used to achieve the arrangement. The administrative arrangements are enacted either through a formal contracting arrangement or by some form of constituted agreement.

CONTRACTS

The employer, who sets out their requirements in documents in order to invite an offer from one or more contractor, normally formulates these arrangements. The contractor is selected via one of the following methods:

Competitive Tendering: Using open, closed or restricted tendering processes.
Selected Contractor: The employer chooses to appoint directly a contractor to conduct the work or service. This is useful where the work demand may be intermittent and can be useful in arranging 'framework agreements'.
Negotiated Contract: Useful where there is some flexibility in requirements and where aspects such as costs and quality can be negotiated to some extent. These may also be used to extend existing contract arrangements.

AGREEMENTS

These are jointly constituted between the employer and the contractor. The end contract price is still important, but wider

aspects of the agreement, such as packages of mutual benefit and risk sharing, will also be important features. The employer will normally determine the outcome requirements. Agreements can be formulated by any of the following methods:

Service Level Agreement: These are arranged with a specific provider for a particular service that can be either internal or external to the organization concerned. The service is normally provided under the terms of the provider with, perhaps, some modifications to suit the employer.
Trust Venture: Where the service is entrusted to a charitable or cooperative trust.
Joint Venture: Here the partners enter into a 'partnering arrangement' with the aim of sharing costs or resources. These can also be formed around public or private finance initiatives (PFI).

Procurement Considerations

The above systems do not cover all of the possible options and permutations found in procurement practice, but they are the most common in sports ground and landscape construction, maintenance and management. There is considerable potential for overlap in the main procurement options.

The technical processes used to achieve these procurement options are varied but can be categorized as being related to:

Employer requirements

- Specifications: as related to tasks and physical properties.
- Performance statements: based on performance indicators and quality outcome statements.
- Facility outcomes: based on end-user requirements.

Economic considerations

- Disclosed budget statements: require the contractor to specify quantity and quality of service against a set budget figure.

- Unit Price statement: employer sets specification and unit price, with the contractor accepting with a percentage variation on the overall package.

Service management

- Based on statements of how a service or a facility is to be managed to achieve defined outcomes.

Contract Documentation

Contracts used for sports ground construction, maintenance or renovation will typically comprise the following documents, which together make up the actual contract: terms and conditions; quantity documents; specifications; and drawings and plans.

Terms and Conditions

These constitute the legal framework of the contract and will vary with contract formats, but all contracts need to have the basic elements that enact a contract. These typically will include:

- Articles of agreement, which identify the parties, state the contract works and location, and identify the contract sum, nominated employer and contractor representatives.
- General conditions that describe contract administration procedures, contract conduct and party obligations. Work control and variation, payments and communications.
- Nomination of subcontractors and suppliers (if this is allowed) and the procedures to be followed, with the payment and obligations of such parties.
- Fluctuations where the contract is not for a fixed price, and how the contract sum is to be varied to allow for cost fluctuations.
- Arbitration procedures in the case of dispute and the process to be adopted.

Quantity Documents

The purpose of these documents is to quantify all the identified and defined elements of the works to be undertaken within the contract. These allow all contractors to have the same information and therefore an equitable basis for pricing. This should ensure that such contract pricing is fully competitive. There are several names for such documents in common usage including:

- Bills of Quantity
- Schedules of Work
- Work Schedules
- Contract Bills
- Cost Schedules
- Pricing Documents

Specifications

This is the 'quality statement' of the contract and has two major functions:

- To describe all works to be carried out in a manner that enables contractors to cost the works and submit a realistic offer.
- It determines the standards of performance, delivery and outcome that are required by the employer.

Specifications can be grouped into two broad types:

Descriptive specifications: written as 'statements of attributes', so that the employer can establish what the outcomes of the contract are going to be.

Requirement specifications: detailing the works in such a way that the actions of the contractor conform to the stated detail.

Various forms of specification are in use but in landscape construction or maintenance, which generally includes sports surfaces and facilities, the following types have been identified:

Technical specifications: These give detailed descriptions of materials, work processes, methods and workmanship, together with methods and verifying

Features of the Main Procurement Options

Type	Concept	Structure	Core Features	Arrangement	Strengths	Weaknesses
Competitive contract	Direct competition, market forces, best price.	Separate roles for employer and contractor. Employer inspects for satisfactory completion.	Contractor complies with employer specified requirements.	Employer produces contract documents that are priced by the contractor in an open, closed or restricted tender system.	Best price is achieved. Contract design and control remains with employer.	Minimizes contractor input. Maximizes employer involvement in contract control. Requirements need to be fully determined before contractor input.
Selected contractor	Working with a contractor of proven performance. The 'preferred' contractor.	Employer and contractor have an understanding of each other's systems and work.	Same as for competitive contract.	Contractor prices employer produced documents, which are assessed against budget. Single tender process and often some negotiation.	Saves tender selection and often pre-/ post-tender appraisals. Contract design and control with employer. Contractor tender risk eliminated and potential for continuous employment.	Contractor input to contract design still minimal. Reliant upon employer appraisal for value for money. No comparative price available.

Negotiated contract	Contract price negotiated around employer stated requirements.	Employer and contractor interaction at pricing and work detailing stages. Limits number of contractors involved.	Negotiation skills required from both parties. Degree of openness for contract design.	Negotiation to maximize advantage to both parties. Early discussions to formulate requirements desirable. Possible form of shared management.	Replaces the need for the contractor to 'win' and fosters collaboration.	No competitive benchmark to assess value for money for the agreed sum. Assumes both parties have equal understanding of contract requirements.
Joint venture	Parties unite for mutually accepted aims and work to enhance each other's success.	Some form of 'partnering' agreement. Often involves a joint management board and in some cases sharing the financial risk.	Strong desire for successful completion of project. Full openness from initial negotiation to conclusion. Joint management for problem resolution.	Full negotiation on financial and technical requirements. Both parties are stakeholders in developing and improving service to end-user.	Maximizes strengths of both parties. Promotes cooperation and desire to succeed.	Managers on both sides may lose sight of their responsibility. Project may also become more important than the principal organizations.

(*Continued*)

Features of the Main Procurement Options (Continued)

Type	Concept	Structure	Core Features	Arrangement	Strengths	Weaknesses
Trust	Parties concerned institute and invest in a 'not-for-profit' Trust organization, which then works to deliver the service for these parties.	Separately constituted organization acting on behalf of the principal organizations. Board members may include end-user representation. Trust can employ staff directly or second them form the principal organizations.	Separate organization with single purpose of fulfilling project requirements. Joint staffing assumes interests of all parties are protected.	Trust organization is very dependent upon the project for its existence.	Full integration of principal parties' interests. Trust must succeed to survive. Principal parties minimize operational involvement and costs.	Can become remote from original organizations. Economy of scale can become difficult to manage with small specialist organizations.
Service level agreement	The provider has a service or product that the employer 'buys' into through agreement.	Service provider delivers to agreed standards or benchmarks with employer specifying outcome requirements.	Contractor designs systems, service and delivery. Adaptations can be made for the employer.	Formal supply contract often based on contractor's terms, conditions and specification. Any amendments presented as a separate memorandum of agreement.	Maximizes contract special abilities. Allows employer to gain a specialist service with no direct capital cost. Contractor has direct control over service.	Employer can become reliant on service provider. Split priorities may have an effect on response relationships and employer often has no say in service development or improvement.

standards. They are commonly used in construction contracts and also known as frequency specifications when used in maintenance works.

Performance specifications (based on physical attributes of tasks): These are written in a similar way to the technical type but without determining work methods or frequency of activities. Tasks specified in terms of the lowest and highest required performance parameters.

Performance specifications (based on physical outcomes): Here the prime concern is to determine the performance afforded by the facility or component rather than the quality of individual components or tasks. Enables progressive development to be specified and is useful for quality sports surfaces.

Facility management specifications: This option is the preferred choice for many leisure and sports facility managers in the public sector and has been termed 'minimum documentation' or 'no quantities' contracts. Essentially these are package type agreements that provide detailed management descriptions about how a facility is to be controlled and administered. The specification details the parameters of end-user and employee relationships, specifying the desired quantitative output required from a facility. The land, facility or asset's management is fully ceded to the contractor.

Drawings, Plans and Maps

These documents are provided to show the location(s) of the works and details of the different construction or maintenance details. They should be professionally drawn to show all salient dimensions and details of features and/or site characteristics, and be to a recognized scale.

Additional Documentation

In addition to the above, the Preliminary section of the contract documentation will often provide details of:

- General scope and conditions of the contract statements and definitions and terms.

- Conditions relating to the tendering process.
- General commentary on the conditions of contract.
- Specific requirements of the employer.

Contracts often feature other documents depending upon the nature and scope of the works or services. These may include:

- Instructions to tender
- Accommodation leasing arrangements
- Vehicle and equipment leasing arrangements
- Equal opportunities policy
- Health and safety policies
- Quality systems
- Customer care charters

Contract Specification: Selection and Design

The contract specification is the most important part of the contract as it dictates the work to be completed and the levels of quality required. It is the nucleus of the contract and will have the most influence upon the particular project or works and the success of the venture for both employing and contractor parties. It is therefore essential that great care and attention be given to its writing. Prior to writing the specification one needs to determine the type of specification to be written, which needs to consider a number of requirements. The principal basic requirements to consider comprise:

- The outcomes required from the employer.
- The contract management control system to be implemented.
- How the works or services are to be monitored and tested.
- The knowledge and ability of the specification writer.

Employer Outcomes

The employer naturally expects benefit from the contract agreement, but these

59

benefits can be assessed in a number of ways, including:

What is to be put into the work (Task Inputs): Here the tasks to be executed by the contractor are specified in terms of 'inputs' needed to complete such to a defined standard.

What is the output for the works (Physical Outputs): These are worded such that the physical properties required from the works are specified but the method of operation is ceded to the contractor. The emphasis is on contractor performance rather than compliance.

What is the value to the end-user (User Outcomes): Here end-user benefits are prescribed and the performance is detailed in terms of facility or asset management and administrative procedures.

Management Control System

In cases of land or facility management, it is necessary to determine which party (either employer or contractor) has responsibility for management and control, or whether this is to be shared. The traditional approach is that the contractor provides a service or conducts the work and the employer manages the outcomes.

Works Measurement and Testing

The common methods of works measurement include:

Visual inspection of the works operations, inputs and outcomes. This relies heavily on the judgement and opinion of the inspector.

Physical measurement of the completed works. Here the results can be equally assessed by both parties and are less likely to be challenged.

By comparative performance, whereby works (products) are assessed against predetermined indicators or benchmarks. The contractor is required to prove performance against the monitoring criteria.

Monitoring arrangements will be dependent upon:

- The monitoring and testing resources available.
- The monitoring skills and knowledge of the employer.
- The level of contract monitoring required.

Specifier Knowledge and Competence

Effective contract specification writing requires a high degree of technical and contract administrative knowledge, as well as a thorough understanding of the outcomes or product required from the contract arrangement or specific project.

Writing Contract Specifications

The works or services required are written as a series of clauses or statements that must convey accurately and specifically all the operations, services or products required by the employer. For a specification to be effectively implemented and adopted it must have due regard to quality requirements, be sufficiently detailed without being unduly verbose, be of appropriate size for the desired outcomes and always be specific to that project or works. Writing specifications is a skilled task in itself and must be undertaken by an appropriately qualified and knowledgeable person. The specifier needs considerable skill to make the required judgements and experience of the type of works will be invaluable. The ultimate quality of the finished works depends almost entirely upon the standard of the specification. Time spent preparing a good specification will save misunderstandings occurring and possible additional expenditure later. A good specification is essential for an effective employer/contractor working relationship. It should be written to protect the interests of both parties as well as facilitating a successful project or service outcome. Specification statements or clauses must be written carefully so that they are clear, concise, simple and unambiguous, clearly indicating the employer's desired outcomes.

Material selection is often an integral part of most maintenance or constructional contracts and these are most often specified in one of three ways:

- By type
- By British (or International) Standard
- By proprietary name

This last way is usually where a specific product is required, such as a patented construction system or a specific piece of machinery or equipment. The more freedom that a contactor has in selecting materials or products the more cost-effective will be the outcome for the employer. Obviously, a 'tight' specification is required to ensure that quality is achieved to the employer's specified standard.

Finally, it is imperative that the specification once written is carefully checked for both completeness and lack of ambiguity. A shrewd contractor may quickly notice omissions in the specification document and seek to exploit these by seeking 'day works', which will incur additional expense, often at premium rates, for the employer. Misunderstandings due to poor wording of contract phrases or clauses may result in works of a lesser standard.

Forms of Contract

Many employers draft and use their own contract forms, which they believe will be most suited to their own circumstances and requirements. There is a real danger that by taking such an approach some important details may be omitted, and this may later prove to be costly. Several off-the-peg standard forms of contract, suitable for use in sports ground construction or maintenance, are available and can be adapted to local specific conditions and requirements. These include the following forms:

- JCT Standard Forms of Contract, issued by the Joint Contracts Tribunal.

- JCLI Form of Contract, issued by the Joint Council for the Landscaping Industry.
- ICE Conditions of Contract, issued by the Institution of Civil Engineers and the Federation of Civil Engineering Contractors.

When used and amended to local criteria these forms offer several advantages to the user:

- They have been written by experts, including those in the legal profession, and will be written concisely and without ambiguity.
- They have been tried and tested in the industry and will be familiar to many practitioners and contactors who are used to using them.
- They have been subject to dispute and existing legal precedents will facilitate quicker resolution and settlement where differences arise.
- The rights and obligations of both parties are clearly set out. Using such forms will prove to be cheaper than legal fees when drawing up new or alternative forms of your own.

Tendering and Contractor Selection

Awarding contracts for capital or maintenance works can be a daunting prospect for the Sports Ground Manager or sports club, since it can often mean a substantial financial outlay. Getting the right contractor, value for money and a successful outcome for the contract is a process that must not be entered into lightly and demands substantial management input and specialist technical and administrative knowledge. Having established the need for the contract and that writing good documentation is obviously important, the selection of the contractor often proves to be just as or even more critical.

Obtaining an Offer for Work

In many instances, the process of obtaining an 'offer' for works simply involves asking the contractor for an estimate or quotation. This is especially the case where the employer has no or limited technical knowledge and where he or she is relying upon advice from the contractor. The employer provides often only basic details about their requirements with the contractor providing estimates or quotations that are more detailed but without detailed specifications or quantity documents. The contractor assumes responsibility for compiling the list of works, determining the contract terms, conditions and the contract sum. There is often confusion in using the two terms 'quotation' and 'estimate'. Many contractors use the term 'quotation' for a fixed price contract, whereas 'estimate' infers that the price is not fixed and can be adjusted to a final figure on completion of the works. It is generally held, however, that where a price is submitted for a 'known' amount of work it is an offer in the order of a 'lump-sum' contract, irrespective of the term used, and that no adjustment to this can be made unless there is a variation in the quantity of works. This is a very simple system of procurement that does not require any in-depth technical knowledge by the employer and minimizes pre-contract costs. The contractor is able to specify the works to be conducted, so minimizing the chances of them not being awarded the contact. The major disadvantage with this system is that it will not necessarily provide the most competitive price, as most employers will not usually seek more than two or three such offers. It is not unusual with specialist work for only one offer to be sought.

Tendering

Tendering is a formal process used by many organizations in obtaining offers for works or services. The process aims to provide the employer with one contractor who can deliver the goods or services required at a price offered by the contractor and accepted by the employer. Tendering is a sequential series of operations or stages that should, if properly managed, arrive at the selection of the 'best' contractor and the awarding of a contract to that successful contractor. Having already determined the need for such a contract, the employer must then determine the tendering procedures to be followed, including the selection of contractors who can tender for the works, designing and preparing contract documentation and deciding upon the timescale for such a process.

There are a number of options in deciding upon the contractors that will be invited to submit tenders for the works or services. These include using either a closed, open or restricted invitation procedure.

Closed tender: A simple process by which the employer selects one or a small number of contractors on a personal preference basis, perhaps on the philosophical basis that is 'better the devil you know' and electing to pursue what is perceived to be a 'safe' option. This method is often seen as uncompetitive and fails to give real 'best value', but its proponents like the concept of working with known contractors of proven ability and eliminating some of the risks inherent in contracting.

Open tendering: In principle this is an open invitation to all contractors to submit tenders for the works. It has the advantage of creating interest among the largest number of contractors, so increasing the competition. In theory this achieves the lowest price, but there is also the possibility that it will attract submissions from inquisitive and speculative contractors. This increases the work of the employer in evaluating tenders, which may be from contractors who have insufficient resources or technical knowledge for them to conduct the required works.

Restricted tendering: This practice overcomes the problem of being inundated with tender bids, many of which may not be appropriate and merely increase the time and expense of the tendering process. Many organizations have developed 'approved' contractor lists that are used for inviting tender bids. This system allows the employer to check upon the credentials of the contractor, with only those that meet specific criteria being placed on the approved list and being issued with contract documents for pricing. Most organizations regularly review such lists and may 'rank' such approved contractors so that they can further narrow the number who will be invited to tender. This approach means that only genuinely interested contractors and those that have the capacity for the desired works will be used in tendering.

Contractor Selection Criteria

When selecting tenderers for inclusion in a tender programme, there are a number of criteria that can be used to assess their eligibility and suitability for the contract works.

Contractor ability can be assessed by taking into account:

- Skills
- Efficiency
- Experience
- Reliability

Technical capacity can be assessed by reviewing:

- Contractor staff educational and professional qualifications.
- Past work undertaken and references from former clients.

- Numbers of staff, including managerial.
- Plant, equipment and other resources available.
- Conformity to Quality Assurance Standards, such as ISO9000.
- Membership or Affiliation to Professional or Trade Organizations.

Economic and financial standing needs to be carefully examined:

- Bank references
- Evidence of professional indemnity insurance
- Financial accounts
- Overall business turnover

The Tender Programme

The employer needs to consider the programme for the tendering process well in advance of the anticipated works schedule. Sufficient time must be allowed for the two parties to complete the work involved in inviting tenders and their appraisal to ensure that the contract is awarded in advance of the required start date for the contract. Dates should be set for commencement and completion of the tendering process. The accompanying table provides an example of a possible tender programme.

Tender Submission

It is the contractor's responsibility to complete all the necessary documentation and to ensure that it is submitted to the

Tender stage	Task for completion	No. of weeks
1	Production of contract documents	8
2	Invitation and selection of tenderers	6
3	Contractor pricing documents and completing required documents	4
4	Tender submission	1
5	Tender appraisal	2
6	Award contract	1
7	Commence work	3

employer (or their representative) by the specified date and time. Failure to meet this deadline should mean the exclusion of that tender from evaluation. The tender must be received in a sealed envelope. In order to ensure a fair and transparent process, a number of procedures should be followed, including:

- Issue of tender receipts (where required).
- Keep all tenders unopened until the appointed time.
- Tenders should be opened by the appointed person (with witnesses present).
- Tenders received are listed.
- The lowest two or three tenders are submitted for further analysis.

If the contractor has a query relating to any aspect of the contract documentation, for example if there are any discrepancies or errors present, the contactor must inform the employer in writing. The employer should provide a written response to all tenderers to ensure that all are pricing on the same information and the resulting tenders are fully competitive. This written information becomes part of the contract documentation. It is normal to make provision for site access to the contractors in order that they can fully evaluate the site conditions and constraints. It is best to organize a time for all contractors to visit the site at the same time, since then any questions arising can be answered to all, thus again ensuring equity of information.

Tender Evaluation and Analysis

The process of evaluation is designed to assess the contractual, technical and financial aspects of the tender and to make a recommendation leading to award of contract. The submitted tenders for evaluation must be carefully scrutinized in order that the 'best' offer can be arrived at and a contract then awarded to the successful contractor. It is good practice to have predetermined criteria against which tenders can be assessed. It is possible to have a number of criteria that are weighted and against which the tender is scored. Money should not be the sole criterion in this process: remember the maxim, 'You get what you pay for'. Nevertheless, cost will have a major effect upon the final selection and if the tender processes, including the initial selection of contractors, have been thorough, then the decision as to which contractor to choose can be difficult. Good technical documentation, including Specifications and Bills, should ensure that most submitted tenders fall within a narrow price range. Any falling wide of the average can be discounted, as often such tenders will be under- or overpriced. There is no merit in awarding the contract to the lowest tenderer if it is so low that the work cannot be done to standard. This is another reason why good technical documents are essential. The submitted tenders should be checked for mathematical accuracy, that all necessary items have been priced and that the contractor has made no changes in the submitted documents. This is important to avoid any possible acrimony later between contractor and employer. Normally contractors are allowed the opportunity to correct any errors in their submission before a final judgement is made. Finally, it is necessary to check if the contractor can indeed carry out the work. It may be desirable to check whether the contractor has allowed sufficient resources, including management, to efficiently execute the works to the schedule required. Programmes, work schedules, material deliveries and the like can be examined to determine contractor capacity and readiness. The principles of evaluation are that it should:

- Be non-discriminatory
- Not distort competition
- Be systematic and objective
- Be well documented

Three questions need to be addressed:

- Does the submitted tender comply with the requirements of the tender documents?
- Is the tender technically capable of meeting the specification?
- Is the tender viable?

Awarding the Contract

After due consideration and checking of the submitted tenders, a decision can be made as to which tenderer is to become the contractor. The acceptance of an offer creates a contract, so thorough attention to detail and process must be followed to ensure that both parties are in full agreement as to what has to be delivered and at what price. Only a person or persons properly authorized to accept the offer can make acceptance. Acceptance needs to be notified to the contractor and this notification becomes prima facie evidence that a contract exists between the two parties. There is no legal obligation to notify unsuccessful contractors, but it is considered courteous to do so and to name the successful contractor. The contract is ultimately confirmed by the signing of the contract by the two parties. This also represents the final act of the tendering stage and the first action of the contract implementation stage. Two sets of identical contract documents are signed, with each party keeping a copy.

Contract Management

Contract management is the process that enables both parties to a contract to meet their obligations in order to deliver the objectives required from the contract. It involves proactive management and developing a good working relationship between the employer and the contractor throughout the life of the contract. The following factors are essential for good contract management:

Good preparation: An initial accurate assessment of needs helps to create a good specification (better if output based). Effective evaluation procedures and selection will ensure that the contract is awarded to the right contractor.

The right contract: The contract is the foundation for the relationship. It should be comprehensive and include quality of service/product and procedures for communication and dispute resolution.

Single business focus: Each party needs to understand the objectives of the other. The employer must have clear business objectives, coupled with a clear understanding of why the contract will contribute to them; the contractor must be able to achieve their objectives, including making a reasonable profit.

Service delivery management and contract administration: Effective management will ensure that the employer gets what is agreed, to the level of quality required. The performance under the contract must be monitored to ensure that the employer gets value for money.

Relationship management: Mutual trust and understanding, openness and excellent communications are as important to the success of a contract as the fulfilment of the formal contract terms and conditions.

Continuous improvement: Improvements in price, quality or service should be sought and, where possible, built into the contract terms.

People skills and continuity: There must be people with the right interpersonal and management skills to manage these relationships on a peer-to-peer basis and at multiple levels in the organization. Clear roles and responsibilities should be defined, and continuity of key staff should be ensured as far as possible. A contract manager should be designated early in the procurement process.

Knowledge: Those involved in managing the contact must understand the business fully and know the contract documentation inside out. This is essential if they are to understand the implications of problems (or opportunities) over the life of the contract.

Flexibility: Management of contracts usually requires some flexibility on both sides and a willingness to adapt the terms of the contract to reflect a rapidly changing world. Problems are bound to arise that could not be foreseen when the contract was awarded.

Change management: Contracts should be capable of change (to terms, requirements and perhaps scope) and the relationship should be strong and flexible enough to facilitate it.

Proactive management: Good contract management is not reactive, but aims to anticipate and respond to business needs of the future.

What Can Go Wrong and Why

If contracts are not well managed by the employer any or all of the following may occur:

- The contractor may take control, resulting in decisions being taken that do not serve the employer's interest.
- Decisions may be taken at the wrong time or not at all.
- People in both contracted parties fail to understand their obligations and responsibilities.
- There are misunderstandings, disagreements and underestimations, and issues are escalated inappropriately.
- Progress is often slow; there is an inability to move things forward.
- The intended outcomes or benefits are not achieved.
- Opportunities to improve value for money and performance are lost.

Ultimately the contract may become unworkable. There are several reasons why organizations fail to manage contracts successfully. These often include:

- Poorly drafted contracts.
- Inadequate resources are assigned to contract management.
- The employer team does not match the contractor in terms of either skills or experience.
- The wrong people are put in place, leading to personality clashes.
- The context, complexities and dependencies of the contract are not well understood.
- There is a failure to check employer assumptions.
- Authorities or responsibilities relating to commercial decisions are not clear.
- There is a lack of performance measurement or benchmarking by the employer.
- There is a focus on current arrangements rather than what is possible or the potential for improvement.

Good contract management consists of a range of activities that are carried out together to keep the arrangement between employer and contractor running smoothly. They can be broadly grouped into three areas:

Service or product delivery management: This ensures that the service or product is being delivered to the required level of performance and quality.

Relationship management: This keeps the relationship between the two parties open and constructive, aiming to resolve or ease tensions and identify problems at an early stage.

Contract administration: This handles the formal governance of the contract and changes to the contract documentation.

All three areas must be managed effectively for the contract agreement to be a success. These areas of contract management may be handled by different personnel but should never be separated from each other, as a fully integrated approach is essential for success. When contract management experience is not available in-house, it will often be necessary to buy in advice from professional consultants, or even appoint a professional contract manager. Such arrangements must be clearly defined to ensure that ownership of the arrangement as a whole continues to rest with the employer organization; it is also important to safeguard commercial confidence when third parties are involved.

Consultants in Sports Ground Management

The use of independent consultants or agronomists has become an established management practice in contemporary sports ground management and there are many practising professional consultants who offer a range of services. Independent consultants can bring a range of benefits to their employers as they can:

- Provide technical and managerial advice and information.
- Manage or supervise projects such as new constructions.
- Manage change within the organization, such as staff recruitment.
- Develop learning capacity through training programmes and seminars.

The use of consultants has grown in recent years as the management of turf and other surfaces used for sport has become increasingly technical and more science-based, but also because consultants:

- Bring objectivity to the organization concerned – an independent or fresh view.
- Are usually low risk management as they mitigate the chances of works or projects failing.

- Bring with them a wealth of experience and knowledge that will benefit the employing organization.

Finding the Right Consultant

Seek recommendations. Ask colleagues and contacts who have appropriate experience for names of recommended consultants. Follow up on work that has impressed you and find out who was involved, scan the trade and technical press for projects and names in the same way. Approach professional bodies for the names and addresses of members in your area.

Contact several of these consultants or companies asking for details of the range and type of services offered, staff (qualifications and experience) and resources, fees and methods of charging and a client list. Ask for the names and contact details of clients willing to act as referees.

From the replies draw up a short list. Prepare a brief so that you are able to tell potential consultants exactly what you will expect from them. If you have a set or limited budget, make this clear. Ask them to submit a specimen report and check it against your brief.

Check the qualifications and experience of the individuals with whom you will be working. Qualifications vary enormously, but most importance should be placed on their sports ground or sports turf content. Experience within the sports turf industry is also essential.

Membership of professional bodies is a pointer to professionalism; in many cases membership means that members have to abide by codes of practice and professional ethics. Check carefully with the bodies concerned for any bogus claims. An important organization recently formed for such professional consultants is the Register of Independent Turfgrass Consultant Agronomists.

Make sure that the consultant is completely independent and not attached to another company (a materials or product supplier, for example, may retain a consultant).

Before you appoint anyone, meet him or her in person to see if you can actually work together. Make sure that the people you meet will be those that you will actually be working with.

If necessary, and appropriate, visit their offices to ensure that they have the staff or resources needed for the job. This will only be a factor for large contracts. Most independent turfgrass agronomists are self-employed and will work from home.

Check that the consultant has the necessary level of professional indemnity and third party insurance.

Discuss contract terms. It may be inadvisable to appoint new consultants on a long-term contract, but unfair to put them on a very short contract, since they have to put in a lot of work at the beginning of any contract. The best option maybe a renewal type contract after a trial period of six months. Take legal advice before signing any unfamiliar agreement.

Once you have appointed your consultant, communicate with him/her. A consultant cannot solve a problem if they do not know about it and could possibly have averted it if consulted at an early stage.

Arrange regular meetings, on site whenever possible, and ask for written progress reports.

Following the above procedure should ensure that things run smoothly and that no problems occur. If you have cause for complaint, you must notify the consultant immediately, preferably with a face-to-face meeting to discuss your issue. It is highly unlikely that you will need recourse to law to solve disputes as most reputable consultants and consultancy practices value their good name and integrity extremely highly. With good management and careful control, an external consultant can inject new impetus and thinking into your company. Finally, if you do not have confidence in the advice or information given to you by a particular consultant look elsewhere for another.

3 Strategy, Management Plans and Performance Standards for Sports Grounds

The term 'strategic' is derived from the French *stratégie*, and from the Greek *stratêgia*, meaning the office of a general (from *stratêgos*, 'general'). Strategy is therefore often linked to battle plans or game plans. In the increasingly complex and international environment in which businesses and service organizations operate, it is necessary for such organizations to plan effectively and have a long-term view of where they want to be and how they are to develop their market share or business activity if they are to continue to be successful. The way in which this is achieved is through effective strategic planning, subsequent implementation and continuous review. Strategy is about what the organization wants to do, what the organization needs or wants to be, and where it is going. Strategic planning provides an organization with a framework for:

• Understanding its position in the marketplace.
• Moving forward with a sense of direction, purpose and urgency.
• Focusing on the key issues of customers and markets and the skills needed to deliver to those customers and markets.

Strategy can be defined as a plan of action intended to accomplish a specific goal.

In our context, a strategy or strategic plan is used to set out an organization's vision for using its land resource (the sports ground or playing areas) and the goals it wants to achieve with the resources it has at its disposal and the methods and time needed to meet these goals. Strategic plans can be perceived as:

• Exploiting opportunities.
• The future 'shape' of the sports ground (or landscape).
• Assessing the effects of external variables.
• The responses of the senior managers.
• Developing overall objectives and strategy.

In developing a strategic plan, the first stage is to look at the organization and the environment in which it operates. It is only when these aspects have been critically reviewed and evaluated that strategic choices for the future of the organization can be formulated and implemented by managers and staff throughout the different levels of the organization and its operations. Many large organizations such as local authorities will formulate strategic plans as part of a whole suite of management policy documents written for all their landscape and other service areas. The strategy should provide a policy framework for more detailed site-based management plans or sometimes for other specific subjects such as environmental, ecological or sport development. Strategic planning is a continuous process and typically involves a continual cycle of research, issue identification, objective setting, policy formulation, implementation, evaluation, review and revision. The adoption of a strategic planning approach to planning and managing sports grounds and other recreational open spaces requires a study of demand or needs, an evaluation of current provision (specifically in terms of their quality and quantity) with an assessment of the resources required for their provision and management. The completed document will used by managers, but will also be available to planners and politicians in the context of local, regional and even national provision for sport and recreation.

Why Have a Strategic Plan?

Producing a strategic plan can be time-consuming and labour-intensive. The benefits, however, can be considerable. These will differ in importance and detail depending upon the size and nature of the organization, its scale of provision and business or social focus – in short, its *raison d'être* and scale of operation. These benefits may include:

- Ensuring a strategic approach to pitch provision that will provide overall direction and allow for priority setting for particular sports or other requirements to be met.
- The provision of strong evidence when seeking funding for capital projects from external agencies such as the Sport England Lottery Fund.
- It can help to meet government policies, such as those for social inclusion, healthy living or urban regeneration.
- For local authorities it can be used to demonstrate the value of such service

provision when competing with other services for increasingly restricted resources.
- It can assist in the 'Best Value' process and the achievement of the 'four Cs' and promoting continuous improvement.
- It can provide the basis for new pitches in response to changes in demand.
- It can provide a useful tool in the protection of recreational green space where threatened by potential developments.
- It can link to other strategies for sport and recreation provision as well as those for environmental or other landscape situations.
- The strategy will improve an organization's use of resources for management and promote greater efficiencies in operation.
- It can be used to highlight where quality of provision can be enhanced or strengthened.
- It can assist in determining community usage and demand for sports pitches.
- It will provide better information for users and local residents.
- It will promote sport development and the fostering of new sporting talent and players.

What is involved in Preparing a Strategic Plan?

A common strategy method deployed for sport and recreational areas has five stages, which are all part of a continuous process. The stages are:

- Survey
- Analysis
- Plan
- Monitor
- Review

Survey
The first task is to complete a survey to identify the two elements of supply and

demand. This is a relatively straightforward process involving the collection of quantitative information about the sports ground(s), such as the location and the site and its facilities. Qualitative data is also sought, such as the particular site management problems or issues, an assessment of the quality of the pitches and playing areas and of the opportunities for development. Research into demand seeks to quantify information about the users and non-users, the characteristics of the catchment area and qualitative information covering people's likes, dislikes and aspirations. It is important to identify the community's recreational demands. This may be achieved through a number of ways including market research, user forums and communications between users and managers. In order to develop a successful strategy from demand studies, it is important that the information obtained be correctly interpreted. For instance, cultural background, gender and age will influence responses, so it is necessary to use qualitative research methods to explore people's attitudes. Consider the correlation between the sports ground's users and the make-up of the surrounding population. This will give an indication of the groups that currently do not use facilities. From this information, it is necessary to contact non-users to identify latent demand. This is not an easy task but is one that it is vital to carry out. The benefit of the involvement of a wider set of people is the identification of a wider set of demands, which, if met, can make sports grounds more relevant to a wider population. The kind of information sought includes the requirement for sport, the identification of specific user groups, reasons why people may not use the facility, how far people are prepared to travel and what they may need or expect in the future.

Analysis
The analysis seeks to identify the major issues affecting provision and service. These can be examined under three headings:

policy context, political context and resources. Under the policy context, consideration should be given to the differences between the local scenario and the national or regional policy. The national policy is outlined in a government document, *Planning Policy Guidance (PPG) 17: Planning for Open Space, Sport and Recreation*, and its sister publication *Assessing Needs and Opportunities: A Companion Guide to PPG17*, both published by the Office of the Deputy Prime Minister in 2002. Local policy can be determined from county structure plans and local development plans, produced by County councils and City or Borough councils respectively. In the case of local authority provision, it is politically important that the councillors (elected members) are involved in the strategy, since if the issues identified within the strategy do not correspond with their own views they are unlikely to give their support to its implementation.

Objectives and targets to resolve the issues must be formulated within the realistic expectations of the availability of resources over the plan period. The use of a strategy document will help managers when bidding for additional resources necessary to achieve these strategy targets. The strategy should draw a distinction between the existing activities and the subsequent opportunities for income generation, reinvestment and the standards of maintenance.

Plan
The strategy contains a set of objectives covering standards of provision, maintenance and for programming (fixture planning and organization). Assessable targets must be set for each objective, including the identification of who is responsible for achieving these objectives, time scales and allocated resources. Having prepared these objectives and the associated work plan, it is sensible to allow those who were involved in the survey to see them and respond. After this stage, the final plan would be prepared.

Monitor

Having completed a planning exercise and implementing it, managers must ensure that adequate monitoring is carried out in order to continue the process. There needs to be a system for reporting the achievement of targets, thus a system of performance measurement must be included. This should be both quantitative and qualitative. Continuous consumer surveys will identify new demands arising from the strategy's implementation and will enable managers to assess the effects of policies.

Review

The final stage is that of review. The continuous monitoring system will allow constant review. This should be formalized into an annual reassessment of the strategy, with those areas where demand or supply have changed being altered appropriately.

The Playing Pitch Model

Sport England and the Central Council of Physical Recreation (CCPR) have produced their own guidance for producing playing pitch strategies. The guide is primarily aimed at local authority officers who are responsible for producing playing pitch strategies. However, many of its features are common to all areas used for sport and recreation and as such it is an eight-stage model that can be adapted for the private sports ground.

1 Identifying Teams/Team Equivalents

The basic task here is to count all the pitch sport teams for the sports ground or study area. Teams should be categorized as adult or junior teams and by gender. To determine the adequacy of provision, it will also be necessary to count the number of teams in the area that do not play at that site.

2 Calculating Home Games per Team per Week

In this stage one calculates the total number of home games played by each team per week at the sports ground (or within the study area). This variable is calculated in two stages:

- total number of home games played in a season by all teams/equivalents ÷ number of weeks in a season = *average number of home games per week*
- average number of home games per week ÷ total number of teams/equivalents = *average number of home games per team per week*

3 Assessing Total Home Games per Week

To determine this figure one must multiply the value found in Stage 1 by that of Stage 2. The total home games played each week for the facility or area can then be determined.

4 Establishing Temporal Demand for Games

This stage determines the proportion of home games played on each day of the week. Temporal demand is required to show:

- Time of peak demand.
- Use of the pitch throughout the week to assist in calculations of capacity.

5 Defining Pitches Used/Required on Each Day

This is calculated by multiplying Stage 3 by Stage 4. The resulting figures indicate the number of pitches currently used on/at each day/time during the week.

6 Establishing Pitches Available

This is an audit of adult pitches available on the site or in the study area. It should record sizes and pitch condition of grass and non-turf surfaces used for sport. In the absence of pitch capacity data, a figure of two games per week should be assumed.

7 *Assessing the Findings*
Here one compares the number of pitches required on each day (Stage 5) with the number of pitches available (Stage 6). This will reveal whether there are spare or underused pitches, excess demand or if supply matches demand.

8 *Identifying Policy*
Options and Solutions
When identifying policy options and solutions, issues that often occur and need specific attention can include:

- Current and potential capacity
- Key sites for multi-use or sport-specific outdoor use
- Geographical spread across a district or area
- Funding
- Needs of target groups
- Provision, upgrading and maintenance of facilities
- Drainage
- Role of artificial surfaces
- Quality of pitches and ancillary facilities
- Recommendations for standards of provision
- Community use of education sites
- Future of specific sites

This stage will require consultation with other organizations such as planning, leisure and recreation departments, sport governing bodies and Sport Development Officers.

Application of the Playing Pitch Model
The Playing Pitch Model is a management tool that can be used in three main ways:

- To reflect the existing situation, using data on existing teams and pitches.
- To test the adequacy of current provision by manipulating the variables in the model.

- To predict future requirements for pitches by incorporating planned pitches and projected changes in population.

The strategic approach is a continuous process of surveying, analysis, implementation, monitoring and review. Strategic planning and management can help to ensure that sports grounds and recreational areas are protected and managed to ensure continuity of use and quality of provision. A strategic approach will help in fulfilling customer and community needs, meet the demands of politicians and lead to more effective decision-making in the allocation of resources for management.

Management Plans

Every sports ground should have a management plan that embraces its management, maintenance and utilization. The management plan will ensure that there is continuity in management and maintenance practices, and that the needs of the user and the site are balanced for optimum usage and sustainability.

Specific reasons for having a site management plan will usually include several of the following:

Consultation, involvement and consensus: This can help to resolve conflicts of interests with user groups, encourage community involvement, promote particular sports or activities and ensure that all stakeholders have had their input for the site's management.

Continuity and capacity: This will ensure continuity and that future managers are guided to the formative principles of management as agreed initially by previous management and users. It will provide a framework for monitoring progress over successive years or changes in management.

Preparing for change: To monitor and assess changes on the site, identify

Worked Example of the Playing Pitch Model for Strategy Formulation*

Any Town Sports Ground

Stage 1: Identifying teams/team equivalents

Adult teams	74
Junior teams	40
Mini teams	10
Total teams	**124**

To assess the *adequacy of current provision*, add teams travelling outside study site/area/'virtual' teams, etc.

To *predict the future*, future total games required should be calculated, and targets from sports development plans applied.

Stage 2: Home games per team per week

= 0.5

(based on principle of one week home, one week away)

The exact figure can be calculated if data is collected on the number of home matches played by all teams for the study site/area.

Stage 3: Total home games per week

Adult	(74 × 0.5)	37
Junior	(40 × 0.5)	20
Mini	(10 × 0.5)	5
Total		**62**

This is calculated by multiplying Stage 1 by Stage 2.

Stage 4: Temporal demand for games

	Sat. a.m.	Sat. p.m.	Sun. a.m.	Sun. p.m.
Adult	40%	10%	40%	10%
Junior	0%	0%	60%	40%
Mini	0%	0%	100%	0%

To assess the *adequacy of current provision*, factors that influence the current pattern of play need to be considered, e.g. league structure/kick-off times.

To *predict the future*, predicted changes in the pattern of play need to be considered, e.g. the potential for more midweek games, future competitions, shifts in participation trends, etc.

Stage 5: Pitches required to meet demand on peak days

	Sat. a.m.	Sat. p.m.	Sun. a.m.	Sun. p.m.
Adult	14.8	3.7	**14.8**	3.7
Junior	0	0	**12.0**	8.0
Mini	0	0	**5.0**	0

This is calculated by multiplying Stage 3 by Stage 4. Carry the peak day data through to Stage 7.

Stage 6: Community pitches available to meet demand

	LA owned	LEA owned	Privately owned	Total
Adult	11	2	3	16
Junior	4	4	0	8
Mini	5	3	0	8
	20	9	3	**32**

To assess the *adequacy of current provision*, it is at this stage that weightings can be added to reflect the capacity/availability of existing pitches.

To *predict the future*, issues such as land available for the development of new pitches, changes in National Governing Body rules, potential improvements to quality/capacity should be considered.
Take total pitches through to Stage 7.

Stage 7: Underuse or shortfall of pitches

	Total pitches	Peak demand	Shortfall/Underuse
Adult	16	14.8	**+1.2**
Junior	8	12.0	**– 4.0**
Mini	8	5.0	**+ 3.0**

This is calculated by subtracting Stage 5 (peak day demand) from Stage 6 (total pitches available).

Reference: Towards a Level Playing Field: A Guide to the Production of Playing Pitch Strategies. SPORT ENGLAND/CCPR

Stages in Producing a Playing Pitch Strategy

Establish steering group

⇩

Define – objectives, study area/site, sports to be included, timescale

⇩

Appoint project team

⇩

Produce audit of teams and pitches – surveys, consultation, desk research

⇩

The Playing Pitch Model (8 Stages)

⇩

Formulate policy and strategy for the future

⇩

Produce action plan

⇩

Monitor and review

analysis and in comparison with other local or national information.

Framework for decisions: The management plan will facilitate more effective decision-making based upon clear information derived from defined objectives that have been laid down. It can help managers to react positively to changing external demands and constraints.

Setting standards: Standards need to be agreed by all interested parties and then used to set benchmarks against which service delivery and performance can be measured. This can often be in the context of national standards.

Strategic planning: As a contributor to the strategic planning process, a site management plan can be used to achieve comparability between sites and to achieve a balance or provision within a defined catchment area.

Action planning: To cost work, bid for funds or in programming and scheduling work. To develop cost management frameworks for site maintenance and development.

Content and Structure of the Management Plan

The management plan should ideally identify and describe the following aspects for the sports ground or site in question:

THE CURRENT SITUATION
This should be an appraisal of where the organization is in respect of the facility in question. The information base should include:

- The physical aspects of the sports ground.
- Details of the local community including user and non-user groups.
- The structure of the organization including the staff and other available resources.

Physical aspects of the sports ground: Information that could be included relating to the sports ground will include details of

future requirements and consider external factors that have an effect on the site and its use.

Information and recording: The site, its characteristics, features and facilities need to be accurately described. A management plan will also assist in the data the natural landscape, such as site geology, hydrology, soil types, topography and land types (woodland, heathland and so on). The ecological and natural conservation aspects such as site flora and fauna, noting particular species or areas of significance, should also be evaluated and included. The designed or manmade features present, including all playing surfaces (pitches, greens, courts) as well as the landscaped areas, car parks and paths, will need to be surveyed and assessed. These should be evaluated in terms of their condition, life expectancy and investment needs. Features of archaeological and heritage interest or value should be included within the survey.

Local community and user groups: Communities are often very diverse, containing many different ethnic, social and cultural groups. Local demographic information about communities within the catchment area of the sports ground will be needed, including details of population ages, gender and ethnicity, as well as socioeconomic status. Details of user groups (including any membership) will be needed and must include frequency of visits/ site use, duration of visits and activities for participation and facilities used. Details pertaining to where users come from and how far they travel to use the facilities are also required, together with any discernible patterns of use. Of greater significance, sometimes, can be information relating to non-users and why they do not visit or use the site's facilities; of greater interest will be information as to what would encourage these people to visit the facility and possibly join the club. This is obviously the goal of a market research initiative.

Management and resources: The attitudes and approaches of those who manage and maintain the site will have a major impact upon the quality of provision and the experience of users. It will be necessary to record the details of employees, including numbers, specific roles and responsibilities, together with their qualifications, knowledge and experience. It is particularly important here to note any skills gaps that may be constraining service delivery or the efficient utilization of resources. Finance must be considered and included, and will usually cover existing financial resources as well as opportunities for capital investment and income generation to improve the facilities and user satisfaction. The structures of financial accounting and management should be known. Of great importance for the grounds staff will be the nature and availability of machinery and equipment for the maintenance of the playing surfaces and landscape areas. Shortfalls should be identified for future procurement, where required for facility upkeep or improvement.

AMBITIONS OR EXPECTATIONS
OF MANAGEMENT
This category covers such areas as plans for increased usage or improvements to buildings or pitches. This is a view of what the organization hopes to accomplish.

The information gained from the audit should enable managers to define the main areas of concern or issues. The most significant aspects of the provision can be identified and analysed alongside the statistical and contextual information gathered. The focus is now to determine whether any aspects of the provision and management need to be amended or modified in any way. This can mean scaling down activities as well as increasing resources or provision in other areas. Most often such themes as pitch quality, number of pitches, environmental issues or player needs will emerge and will need to be considered separately within the final report. Managers can use the analysis and assessment of audit information to:

- Assess playing pitch performance against expected standards.
- Determine the most valuable features or aspects of the provision.
- Identify best options for management.

- Develop plans for facility and staff development.
- Identify any constraints to service delivery.
- Determine needs for finance and other resources.

A useful tool in the analysis of audit information is the use of the SWOT methodology (SWOT = Strengths, Weaknesses, Opportunities and Threats). This well-known management technique (*see* Chapter 1) can be used for the sports ground to quickly identify the most important features or aspects of the site and its management. This method can also be applied to any identified themes such as sports development or playing surface standards. Following such analyses, one can formulate specific aims and objectives for the facility. Aims and objectives are not the same, although objectives are born out of the identified aims. Aims are general statements of intent that provide a framework for management to pursue. Objectives describe more specifically how staff should achieve the aims; normally there will be several objectives for each aim. The aims and objectives represent the priority areas for those employed at, or responsible for, the sports ground in question. They will drive future management decisions and allocation of resources and should always be informed by site users and players. On a final point it is advisable that aims and objectives are linked to targets that satisfy the SMART criteria (that is, they are Specific, Measurable, Achievable, Realistic and Time-constrained).

WORK PLAN
The requirement here is to produce some form of plan or method by which the above objectives can be achieved. Put simply, this explains 'How will we get to where we want to be?' Such a work plan will specify the elements of work necessary to achieve the aims and objectives. Normally a management plan will be for a fixed period but usually for a number of years

(five is common), and there will need to be work plans or schedules for each year in a phased implementation programme. Priorities can be set in this way also, with the most important tasks set for year one and others planned as appropriate for future years. Work plans or schedules should identify:

- Who is responsible for completing the work.
- When the work should be completed by.
- Resources required (staff, finance, machinery and equipment etc).
- Reference to which objective the work or task applies.
- Reference to staff involved and/or users, as appropriate.
- Outputs required for effective completion.
- Means of work monitoring and achievement of requisite standard.

PROGRESS MONITORING
This covers the method or means by which progress can be assessed in order to determine the success or otherwise of the management's planned objectives. Monitoring and review is an integral part of management for continued improvement and the achievement of organizational aims and objectives. A comprehensive work plan that has been clearly linked to objectives, set with measurable targets, will allow staff to identify when these have been achieved. A timetable should be used to ensure effective monitoring under the jurisdiction of a named manager. The management plan itself should identify which components need to be updated and when. Regular meetings of staff and stakeholders should be a feature of monitoring. Annual meetings can be used to review progress, objectives to be achieved and the priorities for the year ahead. Aspects of the plan that should be updated at least annually are user surveys and user consultation, together with budget and cash flow forecasts.

The Roles of Strategic and Management Plans

There are obviously very close links between strategic plans and management plans. Ideally the latter should be a product of the former. Strategic planning is seen as a higher-level activity looking at the longer-term goals for the organization and broader strategic objectives. Management plans are for specific sites and must take into account detailed condition survey information, for instance the state of the pitches and how these can be improved, together with more local and immediate requirements. Management plans are therefore the operational aspect that will be used more by site managers and ground staff. When collating information for writing strategic and management plans much information will 'feed' into both documents, such as user information and local population demographics. This is not a problem as long as one remembers the contexts in which you will use it for the two different types of document. Formulating strategic and management plans is neither a small task nor one to be undertaken lightly, but nevertheless both will enhance the quality of the facility and allow goals to be achieved in an effective and efficient manner for the benefit of site users, managers and the wider community. Honesty and realism are critical to success, as is a degree of innovation and teamwork.

Quality and Performance Standards for Sports Turf Surfaces

It has become a common aspect of today's consumerist society, particularly within the service sector industries, that both producer and consumer have become more concerned about the quality of goods and services from their respective viewpoints. Consumers need to be certain that they are buying a quality product or service and are more discerning with their cash in a competitive marketplace, while producers need

to fulfil ever-increasing user expectations and requirements in order to prosper or survive. The sports turf industry has not escaped this phenomenon and in recent years there has been an increasing awareness, development and use of performance standards. Some of this has been prompted by the growth of contracting, especially in the public sector, firstly with Compulsory Competitive Tendering (CCT) and still today with Best Value. It has also arisen with developments in technology, media coverage and increasing demands of players and coaches for better quality surfaces, particularly in professional sport. The most basic requirement for any surface provided and maintained for sport is that it should fulfil the particular requirements for that sport. It must provide a surface that provides a fair test of all players' abilities, make for an enjoyable game and minimize any inherent possibility of player injury.

People working in the sports turf industries have developed performance or playing quality standards for different sports over many years. Early pioneers involved in academic and industrial research included Dr V. Stewart and Dr W. Adams, both formerly of the University of Aberystwyth, who conducted research into soils for cricket pitches and investigated properties of clay loams and ball pace and bounce in the 1960s. Another early exponent of playing surfaces standards was Peter L.K. Dury, who has conducted much research and written widely on standards for playing surfaces, particularly for cricket and winter games pitches, firstly at Nottinghamshire County Council and later as a consultant. Staffs at such institutions as the Sports Turf Research Institute have also conducted research into aspects of surface performance from which 'standards' have then been developed. Most recently the Institute of Groundsmanship has produced its own guidelines for different sports, based on the work of these earlier researchers and industry exponents.

Not everyone in the industry is agreed about the use of performance standards and there exist at least two 'schools of thought' regarding their value or even need in contemporary sports turf management. In essence, there are those who maintain that there should be more focus on minimum standards for materials and construction methods rather than an emphasis on playing surface standards when in use. The former belief is based on the assumption that if playing surfaces are built with quality materials to precise specifications, then surfaces will provide good playing conditions. An aspect of the latter case is that performance standards can be used to develop and maintain surfaces better when in use, and that their implementation will raise standards of management and subsequently playing surface quality. Today most people utilizing any form of performance standard are doing so from the standpoint of increasing the quality of playing surfaces in use, in an attempt to increase standards of provision or increases in surface 'carrying capacity'.

The Role of Performance Standards in the Industry

Performance standards provide a means of setting objectives and monitoring the condition of facilities so that management decisions can be made based on factual data rather than subjective observation. This is a more scientific approach and relies more on 'hard' measured data rather than the opinion of the players or grounds staff alone. This can only be a sound basis for management. Such standards can be used to identify any deterioration in surface quality and guide future actions. This in turn leads to more effective resource utilization and management. Specific uses for performance quality standards include:

- Monitoring the condition of surfaces.
- Determining the quality of surfaces.
- Identifying the work required to manage and maintain surfaces.
- Identifying defects in playing surfaces.
- Assisting in ensuring value for money is being obtained.

- Provide information on which to base resource requirements.
- Assisting in producing management and strategy plans.
- Assist in ensuring the best possible surfaces are provided with the resources available.

It can be seen that the introduction of performance quality standards can have a major impact upon any organization. They remove the possibility of personal prejudices and subjectivity, which can occur in the assessment of playing surfaces, and offer distinct and clear targets for improvement. Their use demands a level of technical knowledge and a professional approach, which leads to a culture of proactive management and responsible decision-making. They can be used to great effect in strategy and management planning for future works and development. Finally, they can play a vital role in the education of both users and maintenance personnel about surface preparation, renovation and management. Indeed, they can clarify for all just what can be achieved and how improvements can be made.

Categories of Performance Quality Standards

In the maintenance of a sports area or surface, performance standards are often grouped into three distinct sections or categories:

STRUCTURAL QUALITY
This is the physical make-up of the surface and includes the soil or rootzone properties, such as drainage and water infiltration rates, vegetation present and growth characteristics. This category might ask such questions as:

- How long is the herbage (grass)?
- How much Annual Meadow Grass is present in the turf?
- How much earthworm surface casting is present?
- How even is the playing surface?

PRESENTATIONAL QUALITY

The appearance of the surface and facility is very important, especially in the view of the user. Players often judge the quality of a sports turf surface by its visual presentation and this may be exacerbated by media coverage. This category might ask such questions as:

- Is there any debris on the playing surface?
- Can the line markings be seen from an appropriate distance?
- How uniform is the turf?

PLAYING QUALITY

Of prime importance for the sport itself is how the actual surface plays or performs when in actual use. Consistency of performance is as important as the actual levels of performance achieved with a surface used for sport. This category might ask such questions as:

- How much foot grip (traction) is provided by the surface?
- How hard is the surface?
- How fast is the surface?

There is a vast array of sports surfaces in existence for different sports, as also for different levels of sporting participation. There are obviously differences between the requirements for professional and amateur sport and even variances between levels in these categories. Local authorities, schools and universities, private clubs and commercial sport organizations provide sports surfaces. It is therefore apparent that performance standards for these surfaces need to be appropriate for the level of provision concerned and user expectations. There is a correlation between the level of game being catered for and the resources deployed to achieve these, although imbalances often exist. It is only sensible, therefore, that there should be different 'levels' of performance standard to cater for the different levels of sport. In their Performance Quality Standards the Institute of

Groundsmanship have adopted a three-tier approach for standard differentiation:

- High Quality Standard – where the surface is intended for professional and international use.
- Standard Quality Standard – where the surface is designed for general club use.
- Basic Quality Standard – where the surface is designed within tight financial limitations and for recreational level facilities.

Key Criteria Affecting Performance Levels for Sports Surfaces

The following list details the eight most significant criteria that have an effect on the performance levels of the majority of sports surfaces.

BALL ROLL

The main aspect of this criterion is that of speed. The speed at which a ball travels over a surface is important in most sports and is even critical with sports played on fine turf surfaces such as bowls. Many other surfaces, such as those used for hockey or the cricket outfield, are required to provide fast, true surfaces. True surfaces are required to ensure that the ball does not deviate from the path intended for it by the player. Judging and controlling the speed of the ball becomes an important part of the game and a real test of the players' skill in many sports. Surface smoothness, uniformity and speed place great demands on the level of groundsmanship required and exert particular stresses on the grass plant. It is often the case that cutting heights are reduced in an attempt to foster pace, but this is often at the expense of grass cover. The most common method for determining ball speed is to let it roll down a standard ramp and to measure the distance rolled. Ball deceleration can also be measured if the ball is set to roll through electronic timing gates. For lawn bowls, the green speed is often assessed by recording the time taken from the bowler's hand to a jack placed 27.4m from the front edge of the bowling mat.

BALL BOUNCE

This refers to the rebound height of the ball from the surface and is an important facet of any game where ball bounce affects the shots that a player can make. Tennis and cricket are the main sports where this factor can make the most impact on the game. Tennis and cricket surfaces must provide consistent ball rebound properties and are specially prepared to give this criterion for play. In other sports, such as football, this is still important and play can be adversely affected by wet pitches or hard, dry ones with little grass cover, thus creating unfavourable conditions. To assess this property of the playing surface, a ball is released from a given height and the height of ball rebound recorded. Such recording may be done simply by eye or, for greater accuracy, using video recording equipment; the latter method is favoured to get the most accurate measurements for ball bounce in sports such as cricket, where it is a critical component of the game. Ball release heights are most often at 3 or 5 metres.

BALL SPIN

This is the reaction of the ball to how it has been struck by the player or how it is affected by the surface mechanical properties. Players can impart topspin or backspin onto a ball with their shot-making to influence the flight, direction and bounce of the ball when it alights on the surface. True vertical bounce is rare in most sports as the ball is most often struck from another direction. Spin and angled ball behaviour is affected by the frictional properties of the ball itself, as well as how the ball reacts after hitting the playing surface. How the surface deforms or withstands ball impact can significantly influence the pace, spin and direction of the ball. Again judging these aspects becomes an important skill for the player and a tactical facet of the game between opposing players or teams. This

is a complex factor to assess, as specialized equipment is needed to project the ball, impart spin and record the ball's behaviour on impact. A number of research establishments have developed and used such methods and equipment.

TRACTION

It is important that in sports where players are running and turning on a surface, often at speed, the surface affords good levels of grip or traction for the player. Unduly slippery surfaces can often lead to player injury and poor playing conditions. It is also a feature of many sports that the surface should have some capacity for 'give', as is often seen in football with sliding tackles by players and in tennis as players stretch for the ball. A surface that creates too strong a grip for the player may increase the likelihood of knee or ankle injury, a property formerly associated with many non-turf playing surfaces. This can be assessed using a studded disc on the turf surface and measuring the rotational force or torque needed to move the disc, tearing the surface in the process.

HARDNESS

This is another feature of how the surface reacts for the player. The hardness of the surface will obviously have an effect on the players running or, sometimes more significantly, falling on it. Two aspects are important here: how the surface deforms under loading (stiffness) and its resilience for the player. A surface that is too stiff can cause player injury through the jarring of limbs, muscle soreness or from impact by falling onto a hard surface. Surfaces lacking in resilience often lead to player fatigue. This is an important property in any sport where there is running and falling on the surface (principally football and rugby), but this also significantly affects other properties such as ball bounce. Hardness can be measured using a penetrometer, which gives a numerical value for surface stiffness, or more frequently using a specialized piece of equipment based on the Clegg Impact Tester. This device measures the deceleration of a falling weight onto the surface.

SURFACE EVENNESS

A uniform surface that is relatively even over the whole playing area is an important factor for many sports. Such uniformity and surface evenness is critical in affording consistent playing conditions across the area for properties such as ball roll and bounce. Unexpected changes in surface levels will lead to adverse changes in playing conditions and can cause a player to stumble and fall, possibly with serious injury resulting. It is another skill of the player in being able to judge changes in surface levels, but sudden changes are unacceptable as this can cause a ball to bobble or deviate in an unpredictable manner that is inherently unfair for the player. This can be measured using a 3m straight edge on the surface to see where any deficiencies or differences occur in surface levels. One can also use a profile gauge, which consists of a frame with moving rods that are displaced by surface undulations. A more accurate method often used is to conduct a full levels assessment using surveying equipment with a grid system of recording. This can be useful in illustrating very effectively changes in levels over the whole playing surface.

INFILTRATION

This is a physical property of the surface and refers to the capacity of the surface to drain or permit water infiltration after rainfall or irrigation. Many games have been cancelled because of unduly wet surfaces that were unfit for play. The nature and properties of the soil or rootzone have a significant effect on this criterion. Surface moisture levels also influence dramatically most of the playing factors already mentioned above. It is a feature of many new constructions that precise specifications are followed with materials used to ensure given levels of water infiltration. It is also a feature of many older constructions or club

or recreational level facilities that this is a failing aspect to the surface and most in need of remediation. Infiltrometers, which can be purchased or constructed quite easily, measure the infiltration rates of water into the turf surface, usually arriving at a value in terms of millimetres per hour (mm/h).

GRADIENT

Surfaces are generally laid to prescribed gradients to enhance surface drainage properties perfectly acceptable for most sports. Governing bodies commonly allow for such and even prescribe specific falls or gradients within their guidelines. Extremes that affect safe play and surface performance, however, are unacceptable. Many club and local authority pitches have gradients that impede safe play. This factor will also adversely affect properties such as ball roll and speed, possibly favouring one team or player over the other, depending on the direction of play. These are best assessed using the same methods as for surface evenness and with surveying equipment for most accurate results.

Using Performance Quality Standards and Determining Overall Quality

The underlying principle of performance quality standards and their implementation is that of increasing standards of provision through raising the standards of construction and maintenance. This places greater expectations on the skills and knowledge of those maintaining surfaces for sport but also raises the standard of sport. What is most important is that one is realistic about what can be achieved with the available resources and that this is clearly understood by users, sports ground managers and ground staff. The process for using performance quality standards can be as shown below:

1. Assess the condition of the existing facility or surface.
2. Select appropriate quality standards for the facility to be managed to.

Principal Components of Playing Quality for Major Sports (adapted from S. W. Baker, 1999)*

	Football	Rugby	Hockey	Tennis	Cricket pitch	Cricket outfield	Bowls
Ball roll	***	*	***	*	*	***	***
Ball bounce	***	**	*	***	***	*	*
Ball spin	*	*	*	***	***	*	*
Traction	***	***	**	***	**	**	*
Hardness	***	***	**	**	**	**	*
Surface evenness	**	*	***	***	***	***	***
Infiltration	***	***	**	*	*	**	**

***Major importance   **Important   *Minor or no importance

*Reference: The Playing Quality of Turfgrass Sports Surfaces, S.W. Batler *in* International Turf Management Handbooks. Edited by D.E. Aldous, Butterworth Heineman 1999.

3. Draw up a specification for that facility detailing the performance standards.
4. Write a maintenance document (a management plan) to show how the surface or facility is to be managed.
5. Implement this plan and review performance periodically.

In determining overall quality, a common method is to formulate a grading or ranking system for the performance quality standards used. With any standards there are inevitably differences that need to be implemented depending upon the level of facility and the standard of sport being catered for. Points can be attributed to different levels of standard (for example, low–high) and the overall standard of provision determined.

Management can decide after consultation an appropriate level that the facility must achieve and maintain. The techniques used to measure and assess quality can also be used to determine the management and maintenance programmes and the levels of use facilities can sustain without a major deterioration in the structure of the land, which in turn will lead to reduced levels of use in the future if the deterioration is not diagnosed early enough. Performance quality standards provide a basis for determining the current condition of the land and this in turn influences the carrying capacity, which is just how much play the surface or facility can sustain. One frequently discovers that facilities are deteriorating because no quality assessment or evaluation is being undertaken and that both user and maintainer point the finger of blame at each other for the resulting poor surface.

Cost-Effective Management for Sports Grounds (Achieving Best Value)

It is important for the efficient utilization and maximization of resources that managers make decisions based on sound information and with clear targets or goals in mind. The term 'best value' has been used extensively in the grounds maintenance

Benchmarking

Benchmarking is a rigorous and consistent system of comparing and measuring an aspect of an organization's performance or service provision with another similar organization in order to ascertain how improvements can be designed and implemented to improve that organization's processes and outputs. Benchmarking requires the measurement of your own and another's systems and work processes. It has been a prominent feature of local authority management since the Best Value legislation was introduced. The aims of Benchmarking can be summarized as:

- Seeking improvement in performance and productivity.
- Striving for continuous improvement in work processes and output.
- Achieving 'best practice' in all activities.
- Advancing the cost-effectiveness of each organizational activity.

There is little point in entering into the benchmarking process unless there is a real desire by management to achieve these things. Benchmarking can be built into an organization's strategic planning as a mechanism for achieving continuous improvement. Organizations need to make resource and structural provision for implementing improvements that emerge from the benchmarking process. The philosophy of improvement needs to be owned throughout the organization and most of all by management for this process to have real effect.

industry since it was adopted by New Labour with its 1999 Local Government Act and the revision of public sector management and procurement (*see* Chapter 2). Aside from this timely political intervention and definition in a wider context, we can consider best value to mean obtaining the best results for our facilities for the inputs or resources deployed. Evaluating cost-effectiveness and value for money in sports ground management is not easy. In order to make judgements one needs to have a series of norms against which both the cost-effectiveness and value for money criteria can be monitored. This may be in the form of unit values, quality standards or benchmarks.

A manager needs to define precisely what the product is and what level of quality has to be achieved. Only when this has been determined can one identify norms or benchmarks against which the cost of provision can be monitored. The management of resource inputs is fundamental to quality. Where facilities are not cost-effective, profits or business surplus will be adversely affected. Management must provide value for money for their goods or services or otherwise the facility will not be used. No matter how cost-effective its production has been, if buyers are not sure of its value, they will reject it and go elsewhere. A manager must have a monitoring system to ensure that value is being provided to the end-user. What the user or customer considers to be good value for money must be determined and a series of norms or performance indicators identified against which the service or provision can be measured. These indicators can be many and varied, and include such aspects as number of games played, opinions of players or performance quality standards for the actual surfaces.

With all sports surfaces provision there are levels of quality that are unacceptable. What is acceptable at one level of sport will not invariably be appropriate at a higher level. Management must be clear about the level of provision required and the audience or client group to be catered for. In understanding the true costs of provision and assessing cost-effectiveness, there are many variables to identify and quantify. Broadly speaking, they can be divided into inputs and outputs. Remember that every input has an associated cost and every

Performance Indicators

Performance indicators are used for setting targets and measuring the performance of service provision. These indicators can be national or local, arising from a governmental source, a professional body or simply constructed in-house by the organization. Many organizations need to assess themselves in both local and national contexts, depending upon their business and scale of provision. It has been suggested that the benefits accruing from the use of performance indicators are:

- Organizational reviews of services or provision.
- Making judgements about service provision.
- Identifying benchmarking organizations.

- Setting targets for improvement.
- Monitoring progress.

Managers have a fundamental responsibility to achieve, and encourage others to achieve, required levels of operational performance. This is particularly so where the organization adopts a mission to create and sustain a quality operation for its provision of sporting facilities. Performance indicators have become an essential tool of management and can be used specifically for:

- Retrospectively measuring achievement.
- Prospectively setting targets for future performance.
- Describing key requirements in project specifications.

output should contribute directly or indirectly to a profit or return for the business. Inputs should be calculated, monitored and adjusted as necessary to ensure the provision remains cost-effective within a budgeted framework. Inputs include finance, labour, machinery, time and administration. Outputs can include sales and quality standards. Even where provision may be subsidized, as is the case for most local authority provision, the true costs of production must be identified and whenever possible minimized. Today in sports ground management there is far more emphasis on management control and effect utilization of often limited resources.

4   Event Management

Event management is an important activity for many involved in the management of sports grounds. It should always be remembered that sports grounds exist to provide turf and other surfaces for sport and recreation and that the needs of the end-user should be the focus of all managerial activity. The management of events at whatever level will often feature prominently in the running of sports clubs and grounds as a means of raising funds, business income from new members or simply raising local awareness of the facility. Sporting events often dominate the press, television and radio broadcasting. Many large sport events, such as the Wimbledon tennis championships, the British Open golf tournament and the Grand National horse race, have truly become a part of the national calendar of spectator events.

What Are Events and Why Hold Them?

Events are generally considered those 'occasions' when an activity is held that is outside the routine provision of management for a facility or venue. They are usually unique, sometimes being termed 'special', and have a specific management goal or objective. Events can obviously vary enormously in scale, from mega international events such as the Olympic Games and the Football World Cup to local events such as sports days and fetes. They can be serious tournaments and competitions,

fund-raising activities or simply fun days and social events. We are concerned here with 'local' events organized by private or municipal sports clubs and grounds. Factors that distinguish these local events from the routine provision organized by sporting facilities include:

- Events are distinctive and perceived as being special. They have fixed start and finish times or dates and certain deadlines. For management they are often an additional encumbrance to the normal workload.
- Events are often used for promotional or marketing purposes; they can be groundbreaking events that will present the organization concerned as a pioneer. They often require unified management from within the company calling on the work of more than one department or persons. They are resource intensive and may highlight internal strengths and weaknesses within that company or organization.
- Events have to comply with regulations set by external bodies, such as requirements for Health and Safety, and may require the attendance of police and first aid officials. Licensing issues can be complex and demanding, depending upon the nature of the event. Some events such as firework displays must be carefully planned and controlled.
- Events are often problematic and dealing with the unexpected or unforeseen

is par for the course in their staging and management. Advance planning is essential, as the event will be concentrated into a fixed period, often within the normal range of activities. Problems occurring can be dramatic and can have a significant impact on the organization concerned. Lack of coordination, resourcing, control or communication will have an adverse effect on the event.

- Events lend themselves to certain management styles and methods. Events need a coordinator, precision, tight administration, entrepreneurial skills and an authoritarian style of leadership and control.
- All events have similarities in terms of their management approach. The planning sequence of decision-making, planning and preparation, presentation and evaluation will be present for all well-managed events.

Well-organized events can provide a great boost to the organization, but badly managed ones will be detrimental. Being out of the ordinary, they lend themselves to promoting the facility to a 'new' audience and can be valuable in boosting community relations as well as attracting funds or new members. Large events are now usually managed and organized by event professionals, since event management has now become an industry in its own right. The public will expect professionalism at whatever level of event they attend, especially if they are paying good money to be there, and so good managerial organization and control are essential. There is no single best method of organizing and staging events as this depends upon the organization, scope and scale of the activity, but a methodical approach with due care and attention to detail is paramount for success. At the outset it is essential that there is a clear purpose or reason for holding the event in question. Events require a lot of concentrated effort from many individuals, often including volunteers who need to clearly understand the aims of the event and their roles in staging it. Commitment can only come out of genuine belief by all the staff, volunteers and others involved that they are doing something that is worthwhile and will be beneficial for all concerned.

The Process of Event Management

It is a fact that all events need good planning and organization, and that many are not well planned or organized. This is often the case with those organized by the public or voluntary sector. The essential consideration is that a methodical approach is taken to ensure event success and that the desired outcomes are achieved. The detail will obviously depend on local circumstances and requirements, but several key phases will be common to all and will include:

- Event feasibility
- Setting event objectives
- Planning and resourcing
- Organization
- Event management
- Evaluation

These phases can be seen as part of the life cycle of an event with all stages dependent upon the effective execution of the others for overall success. Breaking down an event into these key areas will allow detailed tasks to be identified and individual responsibilities to be clearly understood. A high degree of coordination and synchronization will be necessary and ultimate control must be vested with one person or authority, who must keep tight control over the discrete tasks and requirements and scrutinize closely the work of the team members as required. Effective resource allocation and efficiency will also result from such a managed approach to event organization. This is often a prime requirement for many organizations where resources are limited.

Event Feasibility

Many events have been unsuccessful and should probably never have been held in the first place. Before making the decision to hold an event, whatever the scope and scale, a thorough feasibility study should be undertaken to establish the viability of the event well in advance of the anticipated timing. The starting point will be the initial concept or idea, which may come from a group or an individual and may constitute a written proposal or merely a discussion point between colleagues. The feasibility study needs to review the initial proposal and will seek to provide answers to the many questions that will arise. Key questions will include those of what are the implications for the organization and the perceived benefits. Any event will cause disruption to routine work, have particular resource demands and require detailed planning and organization. The feasibility study needs to determine:

- The nature of the event (type, scale)
- Aims and objectives
- The resources required (human and equipment)
- Potential income
- Potential expenditure
- Likely issues or problems
- Potential/anticipated benefits
- Time scale for organization

The following fundamental questions need to be addressed by any organization proposing to hold an event:

Why Do You Need or Want to Hold an Event?

There must be a good reason to hold an event if you are going to spend time, money and energy that could be spent on other activities. Always ensure the event opportunity matches the purpose of the hosting organization, irrespective of the needs of the initiators. If the proposal comes from an outside body, you should examine the credibility of that organization, its standing, financial and administrative abilities.

What is the Nature of the Event?

It is vital that that you identify exactly what is being organized and for whom. If this is not done then later decisions may be difficult to make. It is also important to note the possible involvement of outside agencies, such as sport governing bodies, environmental health departments and licensing authorities.

When will it be Held?

The first point to consider is whether there is sufficient time between the event being suggested and the proposed date to organize everything to an acceptable standard. People who are very enthusiastic about their idea will often ignore or brush aside major problems. Always check local, regional and national diaries to see what other events are on. Do not organize an event reliant on spectators when there is a major televised event on the same day.

Where will it be Held?

This may not be a consideration if you have a sports ground of your own, but this may not always be an appropriate venue. Examine the needs of the event and see whether the appropriate facilities are available when the event is scheduled. Both the geographical location and the venue itself may be vital factors when determining the suitability of the location. Convenience of the transport links is likely to be vital when spectators or competitors are expected from a wide area. Similarly, the ease of finding the venue within its locality can create difficulties, as can a lack of local public transport. The fabric and quality of the venue is also important. If people are paying high prices for entry, they expect surroundings in keeping with their expectations.

How Can it be Achieved?

You must ensure that the personnel, administrative structures and support services are all available at a sufficient level.

WHAT IS THE COST?

Adequate funding is vital for the successful operation of any event. Initial budgets should be drawn up that include both estimates of the cost and possible sources of income.

WHO WILL ORGANIZE THE EVENT?

This is a key issue. The event takes time. Is sufficient staff available to organize it? Have they sufficient time to devote to the event when they may have a full programme of normal activities to carry out. The structure of the organizing group or committees is of vital importance, especially the role of the coordinator, who must be an effective leader.

WHO WILL ATTEND OR PARTICIPATE?

There must be a clear identification of the target audience because you are planning the event for them. Without competitors, paying spectators or visitors the event will be a flop.

It is essential to determine whether the proposal will achieve the aims or reasons for holding the event. If this proves to be the case, and if there is a positive commitment from all concerned with the event, a firm decision can be taken and communicated to all. Ample time must be allowed for forward and detailed planning. At this time the event can be publicly announced, organization committees formed and an overall coordinator appointed. This latter person will be the key figure in planning and controlling the event.

Setting Event Objectives

The event must have a clear purpose and set of objectives against which performance or outcomes can be measured. Event objectives should be SMART:

- Specific (to the particular event)
- Measurable (express objectives in quantifiable terms)
- Agreed (all team members must know and agree them)

- Realistic (targets that can actually be achieved)
- Timed (timescales must be set and adhered to)

For event success, it is critical that objectives be made explicit, clear and free from any conflict between individuals or organizations with an interest in the event. In formulating objectives, the event coordinator will consult and liaise with policy makers and key personnel involved in the event, whether as representatives of other organizations (partners) or as members of the team. The setting of dates, times and deadlines will also be a feature at this stage. The organization structure and discrete teams or units should also be finalized and a marketing plan formulated.

Objectives will vary according to the specific event but may include some of the following:

- To make an immediate financial profit.
- To establish longer term profitability by creating or occupying a market niche.
- To eradicate or diminish competition.
- To satisfy the needs of a the local community.
- To satisfy the needs of a target group or audience.
- To encourage participation in a particular sport or activity.
- To increase membership.

By determining specific aims and objectives and the means by which these can be measured, clear post-event evaluation will be possible and the subsequent consequences more fully realized. SMART objectives allow for objective rather than subjective evaluation.

Planning and Resourcing Events

Events are important for sport and can be very beneficial for the organization and the event participants. They do not just happen, however, but require professional, detailed and thorough planning. To make the event 'special' requires hard work and commitment from many people working together and following a dedicated plan. The planning of any event will be different but there are several stages common to all. These will include:

- Compile a budget.
- Identify personnel.
- Identify equipment and material resources.
- Specify event requirements.
- Identify team and individual tasks.
- Define event structure and disseminate.
- Detail plan and time-scales.
- Establish control and communication systems.
- Plan event presentation, implementation and recovery.
- Finalize accounts.
- Hold team debriefings and circulate final plans.

The length of time given to these tasks will obviously vary, as can the precise order in which they are conducted. Different activities will often be delegated to named persons or teams from the outset with some tasks being addressed consecutively.

Event resources can be considered under the four categories of Physical, Personnel, Legal and Financial. An event may require any of the following or, of course, other resources specific to that event:

Physical resources

- Land (car parking, pitches, access etc.)
- Buildings or cover (marquees etc.) for toilets, catering, staff, storage
- Equipment and tools as required by the specific activities
- Seating for spectators
- Staging
- Security (fences and barriers)
- Public address system
- Services (electricity, water etc.)

Personnel resources

- Staff including managerial, supervisory and operational
- Technicians and support staff
- Referees and sport officials
- Marshals, stewards, and security staff
- First aid and emergency services
- Specialists

Legal resources

- Permits from landowners, local authorities
- Licences (for example for alcohol and copyrights)
- Insurances

Financial resources

- Budgets for all items of expenditure
- Authorities and procedures for payments
- Safeguards for cash
- Income collection and banking

Detailed planning can be assisted greatly by using planning tools, such as work flow charts, critical path networks, checklists, targets and key dates. The event coordinator must lead the team and keep tight control over every aspect of the planning work. The planning stages will be far easier by following some simple procedures:

- Fix key meetings in the calendar well in advance.
- Each team should have its own leader and programme with target dates.
- Work backwards from the event date agreeing dates on an overall event flow chart.
- Keep people informed, circulate information frequently.
- Monitor progress and check detail meticulously.
- Check budgets systematically and review.

- Follow a detailed plan, anticipate problems and have contingency arrangements planned.
- Use checklists and keep up to date.
- Practise key activities, rehearse before the event.

Events can be planned and promoted either by individuals, specialist event management companies or by an internal or in-house team. Specialist event companies can be employed within the confines of contract, employment and licensing laws. Those organizing events for 'their' own company must abide by their own organizational frameworks and internal procedures, and utilize human and other resources from that company. With such scenarios, the organizing or management committee will largely be made up of professional colleagues. Events for the local community may often include steering groups of local stakeholders who are mainly volunteers. These can be more problematic as they are often reliant upon 'goodwill', but nonetheless often tap into large areas of particular and often highly relevant expertise. Whatever the event and its planning structures, care should be taken to ensure that:

- The appropriate 'vehicle' is selected, as overly large committees can be problematic.
- Identify clear roles and responsibilities on the basis of experience and expertise.
- Establish the duties and powers of all paid employees in job descriptions.
- Understand the overall process and the need for forward planning.

Once the planning methodology is established the process of detailing all the event requirements can be undertaken. This will be a time-consuming activity and should be conducted by a group who can think of every possible item and requirement needed for the event. Comprehensive lists can be compiled for each area of resource requirement. At this time, costs can be analysed and personnel identified for specific resource procurement. The next task is to fit these requirements into a time-scale for action. It is critical for all events that a time schedule with key dates for particular aspects is set. Every individual task should be allocated a period that must fit into the overall master plan. This is especially important for crucial stages such as procurement, resourcing and funding. A simple diagram illustrating this work can be used to great effect and can convey quite complex structures very effectively. A detailed implementation plan can be drawn up. This may range from a simple list for a small event to more complex flow diagrams for large events.

Funding and Sponsorship

For most events, funding is the crucial factor or determinant for the actual staging and eventual success. This will often require managerial time and input as well as often being most troublesome. For well-considered events that have been thoroughly researched and have good and specific objectives, external funding can usually be found. Many organizations are interested in events and in supporting them, especially where these support their own organizational missions or objectives. Many such funding bodies are very keen on partnership working in order to achieve wider objectives or reach specific target audiences. These can include:

- Local authorities
- Tourist associations and hoteliers
- Local Chambers of Commerce
- Regional agencies
- National agencies, such as Sport England
- Major local employers
- Local and national charities and trusts

Some people may believe that sponsorship is easily available for funding events but this is frequently not the case. It is true that sponsorship is vital to many sports events, tournaments and competitions, but it is often hard won and seeking sponsorship requires a high degree of professionalism. Many sponsors are found through personal contacts; this is a valuable avenue to pursue but cannot ever be relied upon. When developing a strategy to obtain sponsorship you should remember that:

- What is special to you is simply another request for money from your potential sponsors.
- You are often dealing with specialist marketing or promotion staff.
- Your attractive proposition may be of very specialist interest.
- No company owes you a favour.
- Sponsors usually work to an annual budget.
- You must always indicate the benefits to the potential sponsor of the event, not what the sponsor can do for the event.
- Each sponsor will have specific reasons for entering into a sponsorship arrangement.

In order to obtain sponsorship from a particular company you should:

- Prepare a detailed written proposal.
- Detail exactly what the event is for which you are seeking sponsorship.
- Highlight the unique opportunities and benefits to the sponsor.
- Detail the various opportunities available to the sponsor for publicity.
- Calculate the possible commercial value of the publicity and compare it with the amount of money or value of goods being asked for.
- Identify your likely audience or target group.
- From this, target possible compatible sponsors.
- Draw up a shortlist and then personalize your presentation to each.
- Obtain a contact name for each company.

- Present a comprehensive professional package to each company representative if possible.
- If you are turned down, try and find out why.
- Do not forget: if you do not succeed at first, keep trying.

Sponsorship is a partnership and both parties should work together for the success of the event. Working closely together and keeping each other informed is essential – communication is vital.

Event Organization, Structure and Rehearsal

Events need organization and structure if they are to achieve their objectives. The structure will show all the main elements and key personnel leading smaller units or teams. The structure may not follow the normal business structure of the organization because people with specific expertise may be included from outside the company or organizing department. The structure must cover all aspects of the event and may contain several units or teams that may include:

- Personnel and staffing, including volunteers
- Finance and budgets (accounts, payroll)
- Administration and support, such as secretarial support
- Ancillary services, such as parking
- Event programme and content
- Marketing and publicity
- Technical services, such as grounds staff
- Catering and social

For each section or team, there should be a leader who accepts responsibility for that team and its work and links with the main coordinator.

The Coordinator
The first person to be appointed should be the event coordinator. This is a dynamic

leadership role and should be filled by someone prepared to be autocratic when urgent decisions have to be made. This individual may act as the focal point both internally and externally. If the latter role is part of the function, then that individual must have experience of dealing with the media. The coordinator's role is to ensure that all strands of the event management progress at the correct rate and that all staff are kept fully briefed at all times.

The Organizing Group

Only the smallest of events can be organized and managed by one person. Most events will require the coordinated efforts of a group of people and a committee structure is often created for the event. This committee may utilize the skills, knowledge and experience of a diverse group of people, including full and part-time staff, representatives from other organizations and companies, volunteers and sponsors. However many people there are on a committee, all event staff need to be aware of event activities, progress and requirements. It is normal that each committee member may have devolved responsibility for a particular event function or team activity. Each should be fully aware of their roles and responsibilities and how their component links to the others in the event management structure. Written aims and objectives are best to ensure this is the case and to minimize duplication of effort, while ensuring all gaps are plugged and nothing is left uncovered. Effective administration systems are necessary for efficient execution of each team and in communicating with others. A central administration office where all records and progress details can be held is desirable for all large events. This will often also be the base for the event coordinator.

Good organization is paramount for the success of the event. Problems that are likely to have an adverse effect on the event should not be tolerated and must be dealt with quickly at source. Areas of poor organization in event management often include:

- Lack of clear objectives
- No Event Coordinator
- Inadequate administration
- Insufficient planning time
- Poor organizational structure
- Lack of unity and coordination
- Poor anticipation of problems
- Insufficient prior adherence to licensing and safety regulations
- Lacklustre, unprofessional event
- No event evaluation

In order to ensure the smooth running of the event it is always a good idea to rehearse or practise key activities beforehand, especially if new or complex ones are being held for the first time. This will allow any inherent problems to be found and resolved before the actual event, when they may occur and lead to a disastrous consequences. You can never prepare for every possible eventuality, but having well-drilled and efficient teams and staff should eliminate most potential problems. Staff can be trained, systems checked and contingencies put in place before the event. Go over the plan, follow checklists, make adjustments as necessary, prepare for emergencies, rehearse and practise components as is possible and double-check arrangements meticulously.

Event Publicity and Promotion

Telling people about the event is obviously critical if the event is to be well attended and a success. Marketing is a specialist activity and it may well be worthwhile employing, if even on a temporary basis, a marketing professional or company. Marketing and publicity needs long lead-in times to allow for design processes, preparation and printing of materials. There is a vast array of promotional outlets and opportunities available and the size and nature of the event, together with budgetary constraints, will obviously dictate which particular sources and methods are used and to what effect. The possibilities include the use of:

- Public sector and commercial television
- Public sector and commercial radio
- National and local press, including free newspapers
- Specialist magazines and periodicals
- Posters and leaflets
- Brochures and programmes
- Display boards and signs
- Event guides and publications
- Press and media events
- Internet and other electronic systems

Obviously printed materials can be distributed widely in public, commercial and educational establishments or directly via mail shots or leaflet drops in key areas. Advertisements can be placed in a wide range of media and press releases sent to relevant press organizations. An event usually will use as many as these options as possible to give the greatest coverage possible with the resources available.

Health and Safety

Health and Safety is an essential aspect of event management and must be given the highest priority by the event organizers. There is a requirement to comply with the Health and Safety Act. This Act sets basic standards of health and safety that all must achieve during events (including set-up and breakdown). It is designed for the benefit of employers and employees, as well as the safety and welfare of the public. The Act is an umbrella act that covers a great number of regulations, most of which apply to all companies and organizations operating in the sports and leisure sectors. Health and Safety in holding an event is far more complex than putting up safety rails and there is a wealth of literature and information available from the Health and Safety Executive (HSE). Large organizations or those promoting large events will most often have or seek the advice of a specialist

Health and Safety person or consultant in order that they know how to comply with the legislation and its requirements. Remember also that any company or business that employs (or is responsible for) five or more people is required under this legislation to have a written policy on health and safety and written risk assessments for the operations they carry out. There is every likelihood that insurance companies will drop you instantly for any signs of non-compliance to health and safety legislation and associated regulations or codes of practice. Local authorities who issue Public Entertainment Licences also have a duty to enforce the Health and Safety at Work Act and are much more concerned now with such work in the events market.

Insurance

Insurance protection for events may often be the last consideration, or worse still overlooked, but it is an essential requirement for all events. Specialist insurance companies can be sourced directly or via an insurance broker. Areas of cover that can be provided include:

Cancellation and abandonment: This type of cover is available to protect the organizers against cancellation or abandoned events due to causes beyond their control, such as bad weather, industrial action or power failures. It is not possible to insure against lack of support for an event or financial failure.

Equipment insurance: Organizers are responsible for equipment they own or hire and so adequate cover is required. Much equipment and small items can be lost or stolen at events or subject to accidental damage. Cover can usually be provided for all items. Although it is not normally essential to list everything for insurance purposes, it is only good practice to do so in order to check on losses during or after the event.

Public liability: This is a very common form of insurance and is well known to most who work with or for the public. It deals with the organizer's legal liability for damage to property and death or bodily injury to third party persons.

Employer's liability: When employing staff or even taking on unpaid volunteer helpers, it is important to make sure that they are covered in case of injury (or death) while working under the direction of the organizer.

Personal cover for participants: Accidents can occur even though there is no allegation of negligence. Organizers may therefore consider providing cover for participants so that they can claim individually should they need to.

There may be other areas to consider depending on the particular event; advice should be sought from event consultants or insurance companies.

Event Management and Presentation

Management has an important role to perform on the day of the event to ensure that everything runs smoothly and according to plan. They must ensure that activities are controlled and sites managed, make decisions in the event of unforeseen problems and implement contingencies as necessary so that the participants are not affected and get value for money. Outdoor events are obviously subject to the vagaries of the weather; planned contingencies in the event of adverse weather are required and may need to be enacted quickly. Management should ensure that:

- Last minute checks are made to the venue and all the facilities being used.
- Check weather forecasts and plan accordingly.
- Keep copies of all documents to hand to resolve any issues quickly.
- All internal communication systems are working.
- Staff are appropriately dressed and in their positions.

- Emergency services have unhindered access.
- Security measures have been taken as appropriate.
- Everything is in place for all visitors, guests and VIPs.

An event needs professional presentation to make it truly memorable. Open the event with style and present with flair and imagination. The event coordinator should remain free from other obligations in order to maintain overall control and decision-making. Close the event on a high with some form of display or presentation to create a long-lasting memory in the attendees. At the close of the event, remember to thank everybody, especially the visitors and guests but also the emergency services, special guests and sponsors. Clear the site, cash up, check stock and items and make good any damage.

Event Evaluation

Many events fail or struggle due to a lack of learning from previous mistakes following insufficient evaluation, monitoring and feedback from past events. Evaluation is not something that takes place solely after the event but should be a continual activity throughout the event planning and build-up. Evaluation of objectives and targets can occur when these are met. This is no more than good management practice. Post evaluation should be carried out not too long after the event, but long enough for the financial summaries to be produced. A date should be set for an evaluation meeting and event debriefing. The major question to be addressed is: 'Has the event fulfilled its objectives?' The work of the different teams or units should be examined together, with particular attention given to any unforeseen occurrences either during the build-up or during the event itself. A written report should be produced with full and detailed analysis of all aspects of the event included. Remember to learn from any mistakes and not repeat these with any future events.

Events Summary and Conclusion

Staging events can be a rewarding and exhilarating experience for both organizers and participants. They are a very useful method in promoting the work and activities of a sports club or ground and in securing greater patronage and financial income. They require detailed planning and organization, strong motivation and commitment from organizers and staff as well as effective coordination and control. Remember that each event is different and must be planned and managed accordingly. Even if you intend to hold the same or similar event again not everything will be the same and improvements can always be made. Good events have most, if not all, of the following:

- Definite purpose
- Market research
- Customer care
- Feasibility study
- Committed personnel
- Clear objectives
- Coordinated effort

- Quality leadership
- Appropriate structures
- Business planning
- Good communications
- Resources committed
- Appropriate management
- Political support
- Flexible systems
- Public support
- Accurate budgeting
- Financial control
- Detailed evaluation

In order to run a successful event:

- Have specific aims and objectives for the event.
- Examine all relevant questions and issues.
- Identify all event requirements.
- Recruit or utilize appropriate personnel.
- Seek specialist advice or guidance when required.

For any event, the key aspects are funding, people, forward planning and organization, structures and communication.

5 Health and Safety

Health and safety at work is a vital part of any modern management practice, whatever the business or rationale for the organization concerned. Employers and employees both have legal and moral obligations for their own and for the welfare of others who may be affected by their work and actions. The employer at a sports ground may be the local municipal authority, the committee of a private sports club, the management board of a commercial company or even the trustees of a charitable trust. Such 'managers' may be elected or appointed, paid or unpaid, but in all cases they have responsibilities for the effective management of health and safety, as do their employees, the people 'employed' to carry out operations and tasks at that place of work. Good health and safety practice at work depends upon a positive attitude, a level of staff awareness and guidance from management. The following chapter provides only general advice and does not attempt to give detailed interpretations of the legislation or regulations. In all cases, the proper legislation and regulations should always be consulted and advice sought from the Health and Safety Executive (HSE).

Managing Health and Safety

Managers of sports grounds utilize systems and methods to produce surfaces and associated facilities suitable for sport and recreational activities at a range of different levels and for a variety of public and commercial organizations. Turf professionals plan for maintenance activities and operational tasks, monitor surfaces and facilities under their control and make decisions in order to ensure continued successful provision and improvement. Managing health and safety is no different and, as well as being a legal requirement, it makes for good business practice. Management of health and safety will ensure good standards are maintained in the workplace and that the occurrence of costly accidents or other mishaps are minimized. Managers must have procedures in place that are compliant with legislation but also competent to ensure effective health and safety management. To manage health and safety in the workplace there must be a positive culture within and throughout the workforce, a dedicated policy for health and safety written by management in consultation with the staff, and appropriate systems in place for the implementation and review of working practices and methods.

Health and Safety Legislation, Roles and Responsibilities

The Health and Safety at Work Act of 1974 and its many additions, including the Management of Health and Safety at Work Regulations 1999, place duties on companies and individuals to ensure that adequate provision is made for health and safety at work. The employer must ensure as far as is reasonably practical the safety and welfare of their staff at work and consult staff on all matters relating to health and safety. The main requirements of the employer under the legislation are that they:

- Make the workplace safe and without risks to health.
- Implement safe systems of work.
- Ensure all plant, machinery and equipment are safe to use.
- Make sure that any chemicals, substances or other materials are stored and used correctly.
- Provide adequate staff welfare facilities.
- Train and supervise staff as necessary to comply with regulations and legislation.

All employees are required to:

- Take reasonable care of their own health and safety and that of others who might be affected by their actions.

- Work with and cooperate with the employer on all H & S matters.
- Use all items and equipment correctly in accordance with any training and instructions given.
- Not to misuse or abuse anything provided for their H & S.

The following list includes some of the major items of legislation and regulations covering aspects of Health and Safety relevant to the management of sports grounds:

- Health and Safety at Work Act 1974
- Food and Environment Protection Act 1985
- Management of Health and Safety at Work Regulations 1999
- Provision and Use of Work Equipment Regulations 1998
- Manual Handling Regulations 1998
- Control of Substances Hazardous to Health Regulations 2002
- Noise at Work Regulations 2006

Some Health and Safety Terminology

LAW

Acts of Parliament make Health and Safety Law. The main Act in the UK is the Health and Safety at Work Act of 1974. This is an enabling act, which has been updated and had many amendments and additions made to it since its introduction into UK Law. Any contravention of this Act (or indeed any Act of Parliament) by an organization or individual is deemed a criminal offence and can attract a fine or even imprisonment.

REGULATIONS

These are made by appropriate Ministers of State in consultation with the Health and Safety Commission and Executive. They are written instructions on safe practices for specific areas of work. Examples include the Control of Substances Hazardous to Health Regulations 2002 (COSHH) and the

Personal Protective Equipment at Work Regulations 1992.

APPROVED CODES OF PRACTICE

These are prepared and issued by the Health and Safety Commission and Executive in consultation with industry representatives. They are designed to give practical advice on the interpretation of and compliance with the various Acts and Regulations.

CODES OF PRACTICE

These are generally industry-specific guidelines issued by relevant organizations and professional bodies to assist their members in implementing and adhering to legislation and regulations. The Institute of Groundsmanship has issued its own Code of Practice for Grounds Maintenance Operatives, which covers many of the operations commonly encountered in the maintenance and management of sports grounds.

- Personal Protective Equipment Regulations 1992
- Reporting of Injuries, Diseases and Dangerous Occurrences Regulations 1995
- Supply of Machinery (Safety) Regulations 1992
- Electricity at Work Regulations 1989
- Fire Precautions (Workplace) Regulations 1997
- Workplace (Health, Safety and Welfare) Regulations 1992
- Health and Safety (First Aid) Regulations 1981
- Control of Pesticides Regulations 1986 (amended 1997)
- Lifting Operations and Lifting Equipment Regulations 1998
- Control of Vibration at Work Regulations 2005

The Costs of Accidents

Accidents obviously affect the individual personally, and sometimes for life, but they can also have a severe impact financially on the company or organization. Good employers recognize that accidents and ill health among their staff have an effect on their businesses and therefore take measures to maintain good standards of health and safety in the workplace. Costs to the organization can include:

- Sickness and compensation payments
- Loss of output/productivity through loss of staff
- Expenses of replacement or temporary labour
- Damage to equipment and machinery
- Loss of income (e.g. loss of fixtures or games)
- Increased administration costs
- Insurance and legal costs

In the period between 1993/94 and 2002/03, according to the HSE, there were 483 fatal injuries in the land-based industries (which include horticulture):

- 167 to employees

- 254 to self-employed
- 62 to members of the public (including 31 to children under 16 years old)

Common causes of such fatalities included falls from heights, being struck by moving vehicles and contact with machinery and electricity. Many more injuries, approximately 2,000 in land-based occupations, are reported to the HSE each year that result in costs to the injured person or business. (The HSE believe that many more go unreported and that this may be as high as 10,000 per annum). Common causes of such non-fatal injuries include those arising from lifting and carrying, slips or falls, or from machinery. In many cases where incidents or symptoms of ill health are not reported, the effects may become apparent only many years later and may even be fatal. This has been seen in the effects of substances and chemicals such as asbestos and pesticides after individuals have been exposed, often needlessly, to high levels of toxic materials.

Enforcement of Health and Safety

The enforcement of health and safety is the responsibility of the Health and Safety Executive (HSE) via its Inspectorate. Local authorities also employ inspectors whose remit it is to enforce the legislation. Inspectors have powers that allow them to visit and enter premises without notice, talk to employees and take samples and photographs as evidence. They can issue Improvement or Prohibition Notices on individuals and organizations as necessary or, if required, institute legal proceedings. Inspectors also have an advisory role in assisting businesses, especially small companies, about the legislation and the requirements.

Promoting Health and Safety

Paramount to the successful implementation and management of health and safety is the creation of a health and safety ethos or culture permeating throughout the organization. The key elements for this to happen are communication, cooperation,

Working in teams when moving large or heavy objects is always to be advised. These goalposts with a rear roller and wheels are easily moved by four people. (Harrod UK Ltd)

competence and control. Communication is necessary at all levels and between managers and staff to ensure everybody understands their responsibilities and the policies and systems adopted by that organization. There is a need for cooperation between management and staff in policing health, safety and implementing procedures. Employers have a legal obligation to consult employees on their health and safety at work. Matters that should involve such consultation include changes to work or systems, arrangements for staff training and development, any information required to execute work safely and any consequences of new technology or machinery. There should be nominated health and safety representatives and all should work together to safeguard everyone's health and safety. Staffs need to be competent to execute all their tasks safely and efficiently, thus they must be trained and, where necessary, certificated to ensure safe working practices are followed. They must know all the risks associated within their work and

the necessary precautions to be taken. Finally, it is important that people are accountable for their own areas of work as relevant to their job and that responsibilities are clear and known to all. All sites should have a competent person who is responsible for the overall promotion and coordination of health and safety. This person most often will be specifically trained in H&S legislation and its requirements in the workplace. It is important that this person has knowledge of safe working practices and procedures relevant to that workplace and environment. This role in no way relieves management of their responsibilities for health and safety, and the competent person must work with both management and staff to fulfil everyone's obligations.

Health and Safety Policy Documents
Employers with five or more employees must prepare a written safety policy. This is a working document that describes responsibilities for safety, explains procedures

such as accident reporting and gives information on operating methods that should be followed so that employees work safely. The policy may include information on dangerous equipment or hazardous chemicals. The employer must make sure that employees are aware of the policy and provided with any information that may be relevant to them. This should be included in the employer's training programme. As well as being a legal requirement, the H&S policy document shows a company's commitment to planning and managing health and safety. It is the key document in achieving acceptable standards, reducing accidents and cases of ill health and informing the workforce that management takes health and safety seriously. The H&S policy document may include:

- A Health and Safety policy statement
- Nominated staff responsibilities
- Employee consultation
- Risk assessments
- Machinery and equipment
- Safe handling of substances
- Information, instruction and supervision
- Staff training and competence
- Accidents, first aid and ill health
- Emergency procedures – fire and evacuation
- Monitoring and review

Reviews of the policy must be undertaken at least annually and take into account changes to working practices, equipment, machinery and materials. It is necessary to show that learning has taken place from previous experience and particularly with respect to any accidents or incidents that have occurred in the interim period from the creation of the policy and its initial implementation.

Risk Assessment

Risk assessments are a requirement of the Management of Health and Safety at Work Regulations 1992. Identifying hazards and assessing the risks they create is essential in managing health and safety. The process involves identifying what may cause harm to people and making judgements about whether you have taken sufficient precautions to minimize the risk. In this methodology, a 'hazard' can be defined as anything that has the potential to cause harm. 'Risk' is the chance of harm actually being done or, simply put, a measure of the potential danger associated with an activity. Risk assessment involves the following process:

- Appoint a person or team to conduct assessments.
- Assess the risks.
- Communicate the findings.
- Monitor and review the implementation.

For the risk assessment to be suitable and sufficient as demanded by law, the organization must be able to demonstrate:

- An understanding of the risk
- How the relative importance of each risk was determined
- The magnitude of the risk

Once documented the risk assessments should have:

- Identified hazards
- Eliminate hazards where practical
- Recommend remedial measures

The Health and Safety Executive promotes a five-step procedure in conducting risk assessments:

1. Look for hazards.
2. Decide who might be harmed and how.
3. Evaluate the risks and decide whether existing precautions are adequate or more should be done.
4. Record your findings.
5. Review your assessment and revise it if necessary.

Some authorities use a scoring system when evaluating hazards: a ranking system from 1 to 5 may be used, for instance, with 1 representing a low risk and 5 a high risk. This may help in prioritizing and in resourcing for risk management. It should be remembered that the overall aim of conducting such assessments is to eliminate the hazard altogether, if possible, or at least minimize any risk of injury or ill health to the absolute minimum practically possible.

The Workplace and Working Environment

The workplace may contain many dangers to employees and others who are exposed to working establishments and premises. It is important that workplaces are assessed for potential hazards and appropriate measures are taken for the health, safety and welfare of all who use or encounter such premises. In general, the employer should ensure that:

- Buildings are in good repair.
- Precautions are taken where people or materials may fall.
- Floor openings are securely covered when not in use.
- There is sufficient space for safe movement and access.
- Glazing is safe and protected if necessary.
- Floors, passage ways and steps are free from obstruction.
- In wet working areas there is good drainage.
- Windows can be opened safely and cleaned.
- Weather protection for outdoor workplaces is provided where practical.
- Outdoor routes are kept safe during icy conditions.

When creating a safe workplace and working environment for a typical sports ground we can consider three areas.

Staff/Player Accommodation

Buildings must provide comfortable conditions and sufficient space for rest and work. A reasonable working temperature of at least 16° Celsius is required with appropriate heating and cooling where a constant temperature cannot be maintained. Heating systems must not give off dangerous or offensive levels of fumes into rest or working areas. There should be adequate levels of ventilation and precautions against excessive noise levels. Lighting is very important and where possible natural light is often best. Artificial lighting is often required but consideration should also be given to room decor, using light colours to brighten walls and surfaces where possible. When moving around it may be necessary to separate pedestrian and vehicular traffic. Surfaces should be level and without holes or damage. Surfaces should be non-slip and, where necessary, handrails or ramps provided. Premises, furniture and fittings should be maintained in good order and in a clean condition. Walls, floors and ceilings should be kept clean. All waste materials and products should be removed and disposed of correctly. Workstations should be designed for the individual with seating, where appropriate, suited to the individual and equipment within the operator's reach and stored correctly. Workers using visual display units such as computer monitors need well-designed work areas with suitable lighting and comfortable, adjustable seating. This will help to reduce eyestrain, headaches and back or upper limb problems. Special attention must be given to fire and evacuation procedures and facilities. There must be sufficient exit routes for everyone to get out easily with fire doors and escape routes marked and free from obstruction. Fire alarms and extinguishers must be in place and checked regularly to ensure they work. The local fire authority can give specific advice on all matters regarding fire and fire safety and should be consulted. Provide safety signs where a significant risk to health and safety remains after all other control measures identified by risk assessment have been taken.

Workshops and Stores

Many sports grounds have maintenance facilities where machinery and equipment can be serviced and repaired as well as, most often, stored. Workshops can be dangerous places with plant, chemicals, gases, flammable materials and pressurized systems often present. Specialized equipment such as lifting gear, boilers and compressors need to be inspected regularly by a competent person. Manufacturers' instructions for maintenance schedules for items of plant, ventilation and electrical equipment should always be consulted and followed. Protective clothing, equipment and guards must be in place and used. The workshop area must be kept clean and tidy at all times with attention to potential hazards such as trailing cables given special consideration. Welding bottles must be kept upright and moved with trolleys when required. Battery charging must be done in a well-ventilated area away from any possible ignition sources. Welding areas should be separate and protected, as should equipment such as abrasive wheels and cylinder grinders. Inspection pits must have clear and easy access and exit with protected inspection lamps. Noise levels from plant such as compressors can be reduced by sitting these in a separate area or even outside in a lockable cage. Ventilation and extraction equipment should be provided where necessary. All hand tools should be stored away from floors in cabinets or racks on benches and maintained in good working order for easy access and safe use when required.

The Sports Field and Pitches

There may be many hazards present on the actual sports field or playing surfaces. The National Playing Fields Association (now known as Fields In Trust) has reported figures from the Department of Trade and Industry's Consumer Affairs Directorate that record 487,265 accidents serious enough to warrant hospital attention resulting from ball games, mainly football. Many of these accidents were associated with sports nets (1,627), goalposts (6,877) and natural or synthetic sports pitches (173,096). Playing surfaces themselves should be inspected as part of routine maintenance. On 'open' sites one may encounter problems from pest damage by such as rabbits, whose scrapes present a hazard to players, or even with dog fouling. Other physical features that may be present and warrant attention from a health and safety perspective include:

- Goalposts and playing equipment
- Field margins and boundaries
- Access routes for pedestrians and machinery
- Hedges and trees
- Ditches and other drainage facilities
- Banking and slopes
- Areas of wetland or poor drainage
- Lakes, ponds, reservoirs and other watercourses
- Areas of landfill
- Plants and wildlife
- Overhead power lines and cables

All of the above, where present, obviously need risk assessment and appropriate precautions put in place including warning signs and notices displayed. Staffs need to be made aware of all site features and their impact upon work practices, especially where this may involve machinery, for example using tractors on slopes or uneven ground. The NPFA recommends that risk assessments be conducted annually as part of an annual inspection process. It has issued a methodology for doing this with its own Technical Advisory Note No.107: *Risk Assessment Methodology, Checklist and Log Book for Playing Fields*. It is important to remember that children and youths may often abuse playing equipment and use it for purposes other than those for which it was intended. This may be more frequent where sports equipment is left *in situ* and not removed and locked away after use. Risk assessments therefore need to be carried out in this context.

Security

Attention to site and building security is an important aspect of managing health and safety and should be the concern of all staff. All employees have a responsibility to their employers for staff, building and equipment security. Security measures will vary with different organizations. Some like to use staff uniforms and name badges; this can be very useful on sports grounds to identify staff from the public or visitors to the site. Gates, doors and barriers should always be closed and secured when not in use. Perimeter boundaries and fencing should be inspected and maintained; consideration can also be given to anti-vandal measures and precautions for buildings and equipment. Machinery, hazardous materials and fuels must always be locked away under ventilated cover. Consideration should be given to security locking and alarm systems.

People

Employers must, 'as far as is reasonably practicable', provide adequate and appropriate welfare facilities for their staff while they are at work. Welfare facilities are those that are necessary for the well-being of employees, such as washing, toilet, rest and changing facilities, and somewhere clean to eat and drink during breaks. Staffs must also be provided with personal protective equipment (PPE) appropriate for their work and have received the necessary training to execute such work safely. Finally it is also a requirement that due precautions and procedures are undertaken to ensure the safety of the public, children and contractors working on your property. The following section describes basic requirements and procedures in respect of personal health, safety and welfare of employees and other persons who may enter the sports ground environment.

Welfare, Health and Hygiene at Work

Employees must be provided with adequate toilet and washing facilities with enough toilets and washbasins for those expected to use them. Where possible there should be separate facilities for men and women. There are many types of portable chemical toilets available for use in remote areas away from public sewers. Facilities should be maintained in a clean condition with supplies of washing and cleaning agents and both hot and cold running water. Where chemicals are routinely used and the work is dirty, showers should be provided. Drinking water that is free from contamination and preferably from the public supply is required; bottled water dispensers are an acceptable alternative. Sources of potable and non-potable water must be clearly labelled. Where work requires employees to wear specialist clothing, such as overalls and boiler suits, then it is necessary to have sufficient changing rooms or areas for the number of staff affected. Such areas should be designed to ensure individual privacy, have sufficient clothing and hanging storage, seating and separate sections for clean and dirty or contaminated clothing. Drying areas and good ventilation should also be a feature. A clean area is needed for meal breaks, which should have seating and a means of heating food or water for hot drinks. This should be sited away from possible sources of contamination and maintained to good levels of hygiene. There should be rest areas where smoking is prohibited.

Health problems in the sports turf industry can sometimes develop unnoticed, unlike physical injuries that are apparent immediately. Health problems are best prevented by being aware of the potential risks and reporting any symptoms of illness immediately to a doctor. Make sure that medical staffs are informed about the nature of work involved when reporting any symptoms of ill health, particularly where staff may have been exposed to substances, fumes or chemicals. There are many sources of ill health that may be present in the sports ground environment. Diseases passed to humans from animals are known as zoonoses and approximately 140 are

Goalposts

It is a sad fact but falling goalposts have killed several young children during the last few years. Some incidents have no doubt arisen when 'home-made' goalposts have been used or when goalposts have been tampered with. It is known that children often move and assemble goalposts themselves and all too often they are not aware of the inherent dangers arising from improper use and set-up of these goal posts. Where competent adults do not inspect these goalposts prior to their use then there is an enhanced risk of a potentially fatal accident occurring. During the 2001/2 playing season the Football Association conducted its own research programme investigating goalposts and their safety at a number of sites around the country. Their findings showed that, of all goalposts tested, 41 per cent of mini-soccer goals, 50 per cent of five-a-side goals and 22 per cent of junior goalposts failed stability tests. The FA also found that there was a general lack of training in the assembly, erection and handling of goalposts.

The innovative goalpost risk assessor developed by Harrod UK Ltd. (Harrod UK Ltd)

Since then the FA has been working with manufacturers and the British Standards Institution to set new standards in goalpost safety. A Football Association leaflet (*Goalpost Safety – Play Your Part*) offers four 'golden rules' for the safe use of goalposts:

1. Make sure that goalposts are in good condition and properly constructed. Homemade goalposts should not be used.

2. Goalposts of any size must be anchored securely to the ground as per the manufacturers' instructions. Portable goalposts must be pinned or weighted down to prevent them from overturning.

Portable goalposts should be removed from the pitch when not in use and stored securely.

3. Before use, adults should test the goalposts to make sure they are stable. If there is any doubt, they should be inspected and tested by a competent person.

4. Respect the equipment. Goalposts are not designed for gymnastic displays!

For guidance on this matter one should consult the British Standard (BS8461:2005): Football Goals – Code of Practice for their Procurement, Installation, Maintenance, Storage and Inspection.

The goalpost risk assessor conducting a strength test. (Harrod UK Ltd)

known. Microorganisms, such as bacteria, viruses, parasites and fungi, can cause illness by infecting the body when they are breathed in, swallowed or when they penetrate the skin through small cuts, for example. Of most significance in the sports ground situation are toxocariasis, caused by roundworms frequently found in dog faeces, and Weil's disease, which is a serious form of leptospirosis commonly encountered in the urine of rats and other rodents. The best prevention is being careful, using protective clothing and thoroughly washing hands before eating or drinking. In the latter case, the control of rats is also highly advisable. Skin problems such as dermatitis can be caused by repeated contact with substances such as pesticides, oils, chemical cleaning agents and cement. Again, being sensible and wearing appropriate protective clothing, and washing after use, will lessen any threat to health. Chest and breathing problems may arise from the inhalation of dust from fertilizers, soil conditioners and other materials unless appropriate protection is worn. Another potential agent for harm is that of sharp objects such as glass fragments, old metal objects and even hypodermic needles, all of which can be encountered on the sports ground. Diseases such as tetanus and septicaemia can gain access through punctured skin, as can Hepatitis B and HIV. Sharps need careful handling and disposal in order to prevent any serious health problem occurring.

An unseen but very real problem for many workers is that of stress and other mental health problems. Many workers in the sports turf industry have excessive pressure or other types of demand placed on them. Many such people work under pressure from conflicting demands, such as from players or management, with too much to do in too little time, or working with inadequately controlled hazards. This can be the cause of many absences from work or sometimes more serious problems for both individual and employer. Mental health problems must be taken seriously and it is a requirement of the law that employers do all that they can to manage the risks associated with work-related stress. Problems can often be compounded by alcohol or drug abuse, which must be carefully looked for in often already difficult situations. Obviously it is imperative in all such situations that specialist medical advice

and counselling be sought and the underlying reasons carefully investigated, and where possible eliminated.

Many health problems are best managed by careful scrutiny and taking appropriate health surveillance measures before they do real harm. Health surveillance means having a system to look for early signs of ill health caused by substances or other hazards at work. It includes keeping health records for individuals and may include medical examinations and testing of blood or urine samples, so that corrective action can be taken. Health surveillance is not required for most workers and it is best to take the advice of specialists for specific areas of work. In sports ground maintenance, problems may arise from use of pesticides and using vibrating equipment over extended periods, and both are worth screening staff for periodically. A key factor in all health and welfare matters is that of both personal and workplace hygiene. This cannot be emphasized too strongly and it is the responsibility of all to maintain a tidy and clean work environment. Clear up your own mess, do not leave it for others and report any occurrences of unhygienic or potential hazards.

Personal Protective Equipment (PPE)
Personal protective clothing is defined in the regulations as all equipment (including clothing affording protection against the weather) that is intended to be worn or held by a person at work and protects him or her against one or more risks to his or her health and safety. PPE should be considered as a last resort when all other engineering controls or safe systems of work have been implemented and a hazard remains. In many situations on the sports ground, though, it is an absolute must to be provided by the employer at no cost to the employee. PPE, where provided, must offer adequate protection for its intended use and be fit for purpose. Training must be given in its correct and safe use and it needs to be maintained and

Body part/area	Possible hazards	Example PPE
Eyes	Chemical splash, dust, projectiles, gases and vapours	Spectacles, goggles, face shields
Head and neck	Impact from falling or flying objects, risk of head bumping, hair entanglement	Helmets, hats, skull caps
Breathing	Dust, vapour, gas	Disposable filter masks, respirators, breathing apparatus
Torso	Temperature extremes, adverse weather, chemical splash, impact or penetration, contaminated dust	Conventional or disposable overalls, boiler suits, specialist protective clothing, high visibility clothing
Hands and arms	Abrasion, cuts and punctures, impact, chemicals, electric shock, skin infection and vibration	Gloves, gauntlets, mitts, wrist cuffs, armlets
Feet and legs	Wet, slipping, cuts and punctures, falling objects, chemical splash	Safety boots and shoes with steel toecaps, gaiters, leggings

stored in an appropriate place after its use. The accompanying table shows the most common PPE equipment likely to be needed for different parts of the body and different hazards.

When procuring PPE you should only buy 'CE' marked products, which means that it satisfies certain basic safety requirements, and in most cases it will have been tested and certified by an independent body.

Staff Training and Competence

People are a danger to themselves or others if they cannot do their jobs correctly. This can be because they are in jobs for which they are unsuited and/or are not competent. It is a legal requirement that people are adequately trained and competent to do their job safely. Workers engaged in sports ground maintenance are often exposed to many high-risk activities and skills. Workers are often required to work in remote areas with difficult terrain

and in all weathers. Training is a basic requirement for safe and efficient work. Accident statistics show that many accidents occur when employees use machinery, equipment or substances without proper training and instruction. All employees must receive health and safety training together with any specific training they need to do their job, for example using specific machinery or chemicals. New employees (including volunteers and casual staff) should receive induction training on health and safety, including using machinery safely, using pesticides, emergency procedures, fire and evacuation. Staff competence should be subject to continuous scrutiny and review. Update or refresher training should be provided and special attention given to staffs whose role changes, even if only for temporary cover in order to maintain competence and safe practice. Training can be conducted 'in-house' or sourced from specialist training companies and colleges. In many

109

Sun Protection Code

An often neglected area for people working outdoors maintaining sports grounds is that of sun protection. Exposure to ultraviolet (UV) radiation from the sun can cause skin damage including sunburn, blistering and skin ageing, and in the long term can lead to skin cancer. Skin cancer is the most common form of cancer in the UK, with more than 40,000 new cases diagnosed each year. UV radiation should be considered an occupational hazard for people who work outdoors.

- Keep your top on. Clothing forms a barrier to the sun's harmful rays – especially tightly woven fabrics.

- Wear a hat with a brim or a flap that covers the ears and the back of the neck – these areas can easily get sunburnt.
- Stay in the shade whenever possible, during your breaks and especially at lunchtime.
- Use a high factor sunscreen of at least SPF15 on any exposed skin. Apply as directed on the product.
- Drink plenty of water to avoid dehydration.
- Check your skin regularly for any unusual moles or spots. See a doctor promptly if you find anything that is changing in shape, size or colour, itching or bleeding.

---

cases, specific qualifications or certificates of competence are available.

Child and Public Safety

The controller of a sports ground is responsible for ensuring the safety of all persons while they are on the site. The controller may be the owner or, more likely, the owner's agent in day-to-day control of the site. In the management and maintenance of sports grounds contact with the public, either directly or because of operations being carried out, is a common occurrence. Grounds managers have a devolved duty of care to ensure that the maintenance operations for which they are responsible do not in any way cause harm to such as spectators, players or any members of the public. Risk assessments should consider public access and presence on the site and all appropriate safety procedures are followed. Many sports grounds may have public rights of way passing through them or are sited in public parks. Warning signs and operator vigilance are also necessary when executing maintenance operations in such areas. Children are especially vulnerable, as they will often get into places that are apparently inaccessible and often behave erratically. Potentially hazardous machin-

ery and chemicals, when not in use, must always be locked away in secure buildings or compounds that are resistant to child or public interference. Machinery and other equipment should never be left unattended in the presence of the public and especially children. There are specific regulations that make it illegal to allow a child under thirteen to ride on or drive tractors and other self-propelled machinery. There are also regulations requiring employers to make sure that their risk assessments for employed young people under the age of eighteen take full account of their inexperience, immaturity and lack of awareness of relevant risks.

Lone Working

Where possible this should be avoided, but with sports ground maintenance this is often unavoidable. Whenever possible work should be shared or at least done within the sight of another person. Lone working may be particularly dangerous on large or isolated sites. Ground staff should always inform a second person when and where they are going and when they should be expected to return. Mobile phones or two-way radios should be used to maintain contact with base or supervisory staff. Managers and supervisors should be aware of where all their staff are working and check on them periodically.

Contractors

In sports ground management contractors are often used for specialist tasks such as weed control, construction projects or arboricultural works. Such works are usually covered by a formal contract and it is good practice that health and safety requirements are written into contract documentation. It should be remembered, however, that health and safety responsibilities are defined by criminal law and cannot be passed on from one party to another by a contract. In such client and contractor relationships, both parties have duties under health and safety law. Employers (clients) have a duty of care to ensure that contractors they employ are competent to undertake the work required. Follow a simple process to complete any contractual works required:

- Identify the job or works required.
- Select a suitable contactor and check their competence.
- Complete risk assessments.
- Provide any necessary information to the contractor with respect to H&S.
- Manage and supervise the contractor.
- Evaluate contractor performance and the H&S of works.

Plant, Machinery, Equipment and Power

Sports turf and sports ground maintenance and management are today highly mechanized industries with a wide and diverse range of machinery and equipment used to maintain surfaces for play. Most maintenance operations require the use of either pedestrian or ride-on operated machines that are often specialized and sophisticated, requiring a high degree of operator competence for their efficient and safe use. It is a fact that most accidents occurring in sports turf management result from the incorrect or inappropriate use of machinery. It is absolutely imperative that all such plant, machinery and equipment is in safe working condition and used by trained operators in conditions for which it was intended. No machine should ever be engineered or used for purposes or in conditions for which it was not designed. Many accidents also occur in the handling and transportation of materials, whether by manual or mechanized means. Further hazards arise in the workplace when using power sources such as electricity. The following section describes some of the key areas of health and safety for using machinery and utilizing power sources.

Transport and Materials Handling

Moving materials mechanically can be very hazardous and many people are injured every year in the process, either being crushed or struck by materials or products falling from moving equipment and machinery, or when dislodged from storage stacks or storage facilities. In sports ground maintenance, tractors and trailers, turf utility trucks and all-terrain vehicles (ATVs) move many items of plant, equipment and materials. The mechanical handling of materials may also require the use of fore-end loaders or forklift trucks. Overturning tractors and other utility trucks are a major cause of injury. Serious and fatal injuries are common involving drivers, other workers and sometimes pedestrians in the vicinity. Transport movements in and around the workplace need to be controlled to protect pedestrians and to prevent damage to equipment and buildings. Other incidents occur when operators leave a vehicle without making sure that it cannot move or otherwise cause injury. Parking brakes must be applied, drive mechanisms left in neutral, engines turned off and ignition keys removed when leaving a vehicle. Any raised implements or attached equipment should be lowered to the ground. Where rollover protection is fitted, you should also have seatbelts fitted if a machine will be used in situations where there is a risk of overturning. It is imperative that ground conditions are fully assessed in risk assessments prior to using any vehicles on sloping or unstable ground.

All-terrain vehicles have been involved in many serious accidents and fatalities, involving vehicles overturning when driven by inexperienced or untrained persons. Training is available from training groups and colleges and is essential for all new users. Everyone driving an ATV should wear an appropriate safety helmet. When lifting with machinery, such plant must have been properly designed, manufactured and tested for such use with operators fully trained and competent in its use. Consider what you are lifting, its weight and centre of gravity together with how it is best secured to the lifting mechanism. One must also be aware of who is controlling the actual lift, all round visibility and the safe operating limits of the lifting equipment or machinery. Materials and objects should be stored and stacked on a firm and level base so that they are not likely to fall and cause injury.

Manual handling includes lifting, carrying and putting down loads or using other bodily force such as pushing and pulling or supporting objects and physical loads. Weight alone may not always be the sole cause of injury, since size, shape, available grip and the way in which loads are moved and carried are significant factors. More than a third of all injuries requiring more than three days' absence reported each year to the HSE and local authorities are caused by manual handling. Musculoskeletal problems, aches, sprains and strains may occur because of manual handling operations or other tasks that involve repetitive movements, force, unusual postures, prolonged pressures on a joint, badly organized working practices or work environment. When assessing manual lifting or moving operations you should endeavour to avoid manual handling whenever possible, for example by using appropriate equipment or machinery, and consider means of

Make sure machines are supported on correct and tested lifting equipment. (Stewart Brown)

reducing the risks. Make sure that everyone knows the correct lifting techniques and always train all staff in safe lifting and handling. Follow the safe lifting code:

- Think before lifting/handling.
- Keep the load close to the waist.
- Adopt a stable position.
- Get a good hold.
- Start in a good posture.
- Do not flex the back any further while lifting.
- Avoid twisting the back or leaning sideways.
- Keep the head up when handling.
- Move smoothly.
- Do not lift or handle more than can be easily managed.
- Put down, and then adjust.

When making assessments for manual handling operations there are four elements to be considered: the task, the load, the working environment and individual capability. For simple tasks, there is no requirement for assessments to be written down. Good handling techniques are no substitute for other risk reduction steps, such as improvements to the task, load or working environment. It is a valuable addition to other risk control measures and requires training and practice.

Machinery and Equipment Safety

Many serious accidents on sports grounds involve the use of machinery. Some occur because a machine has been used for a job for which it is unsuitable or because guards are missing or incorrectly set. In sports ground maintenance many operations are conducted using ride-on or tractor equipment where power-take-off (PTO) shafts can be particularly hazardous. Machines should be routinely checked to ensure that they are in safe working order with all ecessary safety guards and other features in place and operating correctly. Staff training is essential for every machine, as are thorough and comprehensive risk assessments. Make sure that all machines are:

- Suitable for the job.
- Maintained so that they can be used safely.
- Fitted with any safeguards required by law and the manufacturer.

Tractors, and indeed any powered vehicle, can be unstable on slopes, uneven ground and near ditches and watercourses. Incorrect loading, poor handling or turning too severely maximize the chances of them overturning. Grass slopes and banking can be slippery and require careful assessment of conditions when using such vehicles. Roll bars, safety frames and cabs, where fitted, will afford driver protection. Drivers must be adequately trained to know the limits of the tractor and the need for vigilance when in operation, especially concerning ground conditions, machine stability and forward speed. Brakes must be working efficiently and tyres inflated to proper working pressures. Tractor PTO shafts can be extremely dangerous and must have correctly fitted guards in place. They must never be approached when in motion or use.

Mowers vary in size and type and, as well as general safety features, particular attention needs to be given to the careful handling and setting of cutting parts. The power source should always be isolated when adjusting blades and cutting cylinders. Rotary type mowers can be particularly hazardous if they have blades rotating while stationary. Extreme caution needs to be taken when cleaning, clearing blockages and adjusting mower cutting units and parts. Steel toecapped boots are essential when using mowers, particularly pedestrian rotaries like the hover type, where it is relatively easy to pull the machine onto one's feet while mowing. Brush cutters and strimmers pose similar hazards and need the same operator safeguards and requirements for training as pedestrian-operated mowers. Petrol- or diesel-fuelled engines drive most machines employed in sports ground maintenance. Make sure that staffs are adequately instructed in the safe use, transport and storage of petrol and diesel to minimize any possible hazard or risk of fire.

When buying machinery and equipment, check that it is 'CE' marked. This is a legal requirement and represents the manufacturer's claim to have built the machine to legal safety requirements. Check that they supply you with a 'certificate of conformity', confirming the safety requirements to which the manufacturer has built the machine. The British Agricultural and Garden Machinery Association (BAGMA), in consultation with the HSE, has recently issued a National Code of Practice for Operator Training and Assessment. The aim of this code is to ensure that operators of tractors and machinery are competent to work with tractors and machinery in whatever area of work is undertaken within the boundaries of the manufacturer's handbook. The code provides a framework and guidelines for operator training from initial familiarization to assessment and competent use. The code has been endorsed by several organizations, including the Institute of Groundsmanship (IOG), and should be used as the basis for the training of all staff in sports ground and turf care machinery use.

Noise and Vibration

Noise at excessive levels can be a major health hazard. Exposure to high noise levels can cause permanent hearing damage, often without the sufferer becoming aware of it until too late, and may lead to tinnitus (ringing in the ears) or deafness. Noise is measured in decibels – usually written as dB(A). The noise level (the loudness) is measured on a scale from a silent 0dB(A) to 140dB(A) in the noisiest situations. In most jobs, the risk depends not just on the noise levels but also on how long people are exposed to them. Noise levels above 85dB(A) require the implementation of protective measures and action. Protection against noise is best achieved by controlling it at source. Get noise levels assessed by a competent person and keep a record. Buy machines and tools with low noise levels and maintain them correctly to lessen the chances of noise increase with age and wear. Reduce exposure times by limiting duration of operation per operator and rotating or scheduling work between operatives. Always ensure that silencers and other noise reduction devices are correctly in place and serviceable where fitted. Ear protection should be worn when using high-decibel equipment such as chainsaws and strimmers.

Repeated or prolonged use of vibrating tools such as chainsaws, brush cutters and strimmers can lead to hand-arm vibration syndrome (HAVS) – a group of conditions including vibration white finger, nerve, muscle or joint damage. Warning signs include tingling or numbness in the fingers, fingers turning white in cold or damp conditions, followed by throbbing and flushing. Driving tractors or other self-propelled machinery can subject the body to vibration or jolting, which is associated with chronic backache or pain in the hip and knee. Warning signs include pain and stiffness in the back, hip or knee after tractor work. Precautions similar to those for reducing noise can be taken. Noise and vibration often feature together when using ground care and turf machinery. Many machines are fitted with anti-vibration handles and seat devices. Travel at appropriate speed and maintaining smooth paths and roadways will help also in minimizing often unnecessary vibration when driving tractors and other machinery.

Electricity

Electricity can cause shocks and burns, start fires and kill. Many incidents and fatalities occur each year from contact with overhead power lines, poorly maintained hand-held equipment or extension cables. Electricity can flash over from overhead power lines to nearby objects with results that are sometimes lethal. Particular hazards result from the operation of tractor fore-end loaders or other equipment such as boom sprayers near to power lines or anyone working from ladders or using long-reach equipment such as pole pruners. Care is needed when conducting any work near such power lines. Care must also be exercised when using tipping trailers or other such machinery near to overhead power lines. An unseen, but still potentially lethal, hazard is that of the underground electricity or other service power line. It is imperative that the location of such cables is known and recorded or specialist equipment used to trace such underground cables where their presence is suspected. This is particularly important in sports turf surfaces where deep-penetrating equipment may be used in turf maintenance. Special care must be given where electricity is in close proximity to water, such as in the case of irrigation pump houses and where electrical cables are used in the operation of sprinklers. Check for such cables prior to any excavation works. If necessary, seek advice from the electricity or other service provider.

All fixed electrical installations should be designed, installed, operated and maintained to prevent electrical danger. Electrical tools used outdoors or where there is a lot of unearthed metalwork should be operated at reduced voltage from a safety-isolating transformer (for example 110 volts centre tapped to earth) or connected through a residual current device (RCD), which will cut off the power quickly if there is an earth fault. Check the RCD is working correctly by pressing the test button. RCDs must be used when using equipment with electrical extension leads. The use of pneumatic equipment may be a safer option in the workshop but will need to be checked for noise levels. A competent person must check plugs and electrical connections regularly. Visual assessments should be included in all checks to machinery and equipment prior to their use. Activities such as battery charging should be carried out in a well-ventilated area away from sparks and other sources of ignition. It is important that staff know what to do if someone receives an electrical shock.

Remember always to disconnect the power source first. If that is not possible, never touch the electrocuted person except with non-conducting items – never use metal. First aid training will ensure that your staff know what to do and how to resuscitate people if required.

Gas and Oil-Fired Equipment

There is a danger of fire and explosion from piped gas supplies and of toxic fumes (carbon monoxide) if appliances are not working properly. Explosions can occur in gas- and oil-fired plant, such as boilers. Any suspected leaks in supply of gas must be isolated and reported to the appropriate supplier or authority. All appliances must be installed, checked and serviced by competent persons registered with the Council for Registered Gas Installers (CORGI). Plant, including petrol-driven compressors and liquefied petroleum gas (LPG) fuelled equipment should be designed and operated to ensure there is enough air to burn the fuel properly. Explosions can be caused by the ignition of unburnt fuel or emitted flammable vapours from such plant. There should be sufficient ventilation to remove combustion products and solvents given off. Make sure that operators are fully trained – use a safe procedure for purging, lighting up and shutting down the plant.

Hazardous Substances

Using chemicals or other hazardous substances at work can put people's health at risk. The law requires employers to control exposure to hazardous substances to prevent ill health. They have to protect both employees and others who may be exposed by complying with the Control of Substances Hazardous to Health Regulations 2002 (COSHH). Hazardous substances include:

• Substances used directly in work activities (for example adhesives, cleaning agents and pesticides)

- Substances generated during work activities (such as fumes, vapours and smoke)
- Naturally occurring substances (including pollen and dusts)
- Biological agents such as bacteria and other microorganisms

The effects of hazardous substances obviously depend on the actual material, its properties and the period of exposure, but common complaints can include:

- Skin irritation or dermatitis because of skin contact
- Asthma because of developing an allergy to substances used at work
- Losing consciousness as a result of being overcome by toxic fumes
- Cancer, which may appear long after the exposure to the chemical that caused it
- Infection from bacteria and other microorganisms (biological agents)

To comply with COSHH the following eight steps need to be followed and any necessary precautions or measures implemented:

- Assess the risks.
- Decide what precautions are needed.
- Prevent or adequately control exposure.
- Ensure that control measures are used and maintained.
- Monitor the exposure.
- Carry out appropriate health surveillance.
- Prepare plans and procedures to deal with accidents, incidents and emergencies.
- Ensure employees are properly informed, trained and supervised.

The assessment of risks does not have to be written down, however it is useful to do so especially when control measures are more complex. Recording assessments will also provide evidence of compliance and will help to ensure good and thorough procedures have been adopted and followed. The process should be kept under review and subject to revision as and when required.

Use of Pesticides
Pesticide products are wide ranging and include fungicides, herbicides, insecticides, pest control products and wood preservatives. Their sale, supply, advertisement, storage and use is prohibited under the Control of Pesticides Regulations 1986 (amended 1997) (COPR), unless they have been approved. Only approved products can be used and manufacturer recommendations for use must be adhered to. Anyone working with pesticides must be competent and hold the necessary approved certificates in pesticide application and handling. The regulations also dictate how pesticides and old containers must be disposed of through approved waste regulation authorities and licensed contractors. All pesticides should be stored in a suitably constructed bin or cabinet that has a sump and is capable of resisting fire for at least thirty minutes. It needs to be robust enough to resist accidental damage or vandalism, and should be kept locked when not in actual use. Appropriate warning notices need to be displayed on the container or store. There are several proprietary containers and purpose-built pesticide stores on the market that comply with the legislation.

Flammable and Explosive Substances
Some gases, liquids and solids can cause explosions or fire. For a fire to start, fuel, air and a source of ignition are needed. Common materials may burn violently at high temperature in oxygen-rich conditions, for example when a gas cylinder is leaking. Some dusts form a cloud, which will explode when ignited. A small explosion can disturb dust and create a second explosion severe enough to destroy a building. Serious explosions can occur in work-

All pesticides should be stored securely in a purpose-constructed facility. (Waste2Water Europe Ltd)

shops and boiler rooms. Some materials are explosives that need special precautions and licensing arrangements. These include fireworks and cartridges, which are controlled by their own specific legislation. The advice of the HSE should be sought concerning licences and permits. Flammable liquids and substances may also be corrosive or toxic and pose very specific risks to health. The safest place to store any flammable liquids and substances is in a separate building or in a safe and secure place in the open air. If highly flammable liquids have to be stored inside workrooms you must not keep more than 50 litres and they should be kept on their own in a special metal cupboard or bin. Larger stocks should be held in a fire-resisting store with spillage retention and good ventilation. If you store even small quantities (for example 15 litres) of petrol or petroleum mixtures, you may need a licence under the Petroleum Acts. For the use and storage of any explosive and flammable substances, you should seek the advice of a competent authority such as the HSE or your local fire authority.

Procedures

Good health and safety management requires that there are procedures and systems in place for ensuring safe working practices and for responding appropriately to incidents and accidents whenever these occur. These should be written down and communicated to all staff and relevant personnel and agencies. Having clear procedures helps staff to ensure that tasks are conducted in a safe manner. When devising systems, do not forget routine work such as setting up, preparation and post-operative works such as cleaning and storage. Essential maintenance works should not be forgotten either, as these are often crucial to safe and efficient execution of works, especially when using machinery and equipment. One must also ensure that you have procedures for dealing with emergencies and the unexpected, such as plant or equipment failure. Each task (or series of tasks) can be broken down into their component operations and assessed for both efficiency of working and for hazards. A good way to achieve this is to ask staff to

117

Purpose-built fuel storage and pumping tank. (Waste2Water Europe Ltd)

do this for themselves, since they will have to think carefully about what they do, how they do it, possible hazards and possible alternatives to reduce such risks as are inherent in their daily work. Consider:

- Who is in charge of the job?
- Do any responsibilities overlap with any one else's?
- Is there anything for which no one is responsible?
- Who has checked that any tools, equipment or machinery are right for that job?
- Are safe ways of doing the job already in place?
- Could the job have an effect on the health and safety of others?
- Are safe working procedures laid down?
- Have operatives been trained?
- If the job cannot be finished at that time, can it be left safely?
- Are operatives familiar with the work and needs of maintenance personnel?
- What might go wrong?

Dealing with Emergencies

If things go wrong, people may be exposed to serious threat or danger. One should plan for reasonably foreseeable events, such as fire, chemical spillage, electrocution or vehicle accident. You may need a written emergency plan if a major incident at your premises could involve risk to the public. Consult with and liaise with the emergency services. Consider what could go wrong and inform staff what to do in the event of an incident or accident while at work. Staffs should know where to find safety, help and appropriate equipment such as fire extinguishers. In addition, the names of responsible persons and first aid staff and how to shut down operations and protect any site or persons from further harm should be known. Make sure that:

- The emergency services are familiar with your site and its structures and contents (especially where there may be explosive or flammable substances or other chemical hazards).

- There are sufficient signed and operable emergency exits.
- A nominated person has been appointed to take control.
- There are adequate first aid resources and first-aiders.
- People have been trained in emergency and evacuation procedures.

First Aid

Immediate and proper examination of persons following accidents and their treatment may save lives and is essential to reduce pain and maximize their recovery. Neglecting even minor injuries, such as small cuts and abrasions, may lead to future infection and subsequent ill health. At the place of work, you should have:

- A suitably stocked first-aid box or container that is easily accessible.
- Adequate information and signage for staff, informing them of arrangements, facilities and equipment.
- Someone in charge of first aid arrangements and qualified first-aiders.

Personal first-aid kits should be issued for lone workers and included in tractor cabs and other vehicles. Obviously these must have periodic inspection and refilling as required. Staff trained in first aid need to have their certificates checked and update training should be undertaken when required, normally every three years.

Reporting Accidents and Incidents

Reporting accidents and ill health at work is a legal requirement. All incidents and accidents including near misses must be reported to a supervisor or manager and entered into the company's accident book. Such occurrences should always be investigated and appropriate measures taken.

Deaths, major injuries, injuries more than three days' absence, diseases and dangerous occurrences must be reported to the Health and Safety Executive.

When an accident happens, take any action to deal with the immediate risks, assess the investigation requirements and find out what happened and why, record the facts and take photographs, descriptions and measurements where necessary. Take steps to prevent something similar happening again and look at near misses and property damage.

The Importance of Health and Safety

It is in everyone's interest to take health and safety matters seriously. We all have legal and moral obligations to protect ourselves and others who may be affected by our actions and decisions. The management of sports playing surfaces and facilities has many inherent hazards and risks to health and well-being. Good health and safety practice is integral to good management and proper and efficient execution of works. Systems and procedures must be in place, staff must be trained and all made familiar with health and safety requirements and obligations. Larger organizations may have a dedicated health and safety officer, but this in no way lessens an individual's obligations. There are many sources of advice and information regarding health and safety, its management and the many individual areas of works encountered on the sports ground. The Health and Safety Executive provides much specialist literature on health and safety topics, as do many professional organizations. The Institute of Groundsmanship has produced its own *Health and Safety Guidance for Sports Grounds Managers*, which covers in greater detail many of the topics discussed above.

PART II

Construction, Development and Resourcing

6 Sports Ground Construction and Development

The construction of a new sports ground is a major engineering and landscape undertaking. There are many factors to consider and the advice of specialist architects, engineers, agronomists and consultants should be procured at an early stage in any discussions pertaining to such a major project. An important factor, possibly the ultimate one, is that of business viability and the real financial feasibility of the project. There is always a need to satisfy business and economic criteria in the first instance, as without such any proposal is probably doomed to failure. The spirit of current developments is generally one of partnerships and community involvement, especially where there is public funding or grant aid. If funding is secured and business objectives agreed, the next major factor may often be finding a suitable site. This is a crucial factor as it has the most profound influence upon the construction details and

costs, and also potential for player access and use.

There is a need to compile basic information prior to any employment of contractors or even consultants for the proposed development. The sports to be catered for need to be identified as well as levels of user participation or perceived demand based on market research. The frequency of games and training activities need to be considered. Carrying capacity, that is how much play surfaces can take, is an important design factor. Other factors such as long-term resource implications and possible future extensions or other developments need also be considered. Potential non-sport use and requirements for ancillary services such as floodlighting must be evaluated. Finally the costs associated with both construction and future management must be determined and their implications for the business or organization recognized.

Project Management

There are four stages for the construction of a new sports facility or the extension of an existing one.

Preparation

This includes the formation of initial concepts or ideas through to the stage where the project is beginning to materialize as a definite plan of action. At this stage the client (or their appointed agent) will shoulder the bulk of the work, which will normally include a feasibility study and consultations with the 'stakeholders' or likely funding organizations or partners. Options for procurement will need to be evaluated and necessary legal frameworks followed. The advice of specialists should also be sought early in the development proposal stage; this can often limit costly mistakes or omissions that may otherwise occur later.

Design

This stage involves the input of designers and engineers up until the actual construction phase. The client will veto or agree to designs submitted. It is important that designers are clear about what the client wants and are aware of any specific criteria and limitations relevant to the proposal. Detailed drawings and models will be produced to illustrate the 'worked-up' concepts. At this stage planning permission is sought from the local planning authority. Plans and other documentation need rigorous checking if undesired or costly omissions are to be avoided. It is more costly to make alterations when construction begins!

Construct

Major project expenditure is now committed as the actual works commence on site. Funds for payments, usually in stages, must be made available by the client. Project decisions will have already been taken and changes now will only disrupt the construction process and add to the total costs. There may be further design aspects at this stage, which will be matters of detail not affecting the overall infrastructure to any extent. Arrangements must be

Examples of Approvals, Permits and Consents

Building in general	During construction	Particular building or site	Employer's and building owners	Public places
Planning Permission	Contract Law	Tree preservation orders	Health and Safety	Fire safety
Building Regulations	Health and Safety	Listed buildings Party walls	Light levels	Escape
	Construction, design and management regulations	Adjoining owners' rights	Disability Discrimination Act	Hygiene
			Property Law	Licences
		Archaeology		
		Utility companies	Facilities management	
		Highways	Insurance Sports governing bodies	

made for final check and handover from contractors.

Use

When the facility is ready for use the continual cycle of maintenance and management begins in order to ensure that it remains fit for purpose. Maintenance and management must be considered at the design stage and necessary resources budgeted for. Continued monitoring and user consultation should be included in management of the facility. Usually there will be some form of 'official opening'.

Finding Funding

Funding major projects such as the construction of a new sports ground is never easy and the greater the amount of partnership funding that can be attracted to your project the better. Funding organizations such as Sport England and the National Lottery are always keen to see evidence of wider community involvement or benefit before they commit to part funding of specific projects. There are numerous ways of raising money to fund new initiatives, such as sponsorship, grants and fund-raising events. Where an organization invests its own money, it also invests more of its own pride, energy and times, improving its position. There are numerous sources of potential financial support for sport:

- Within your own organization
- Loans (from members, supporters or financial institutions)
- Sports organizations (such as governing bodies of sport or local advisory sports councils)
- Charitable organizations
- Private sector organizations
- Football Foundation
- Local authorities
- Central government funding
- European funding programmes (e.g. the European Regional Development Fund)

- Foundation for Sport and the Arts
- Sports match
- Sponsorship
- New Opportunities Fund

Funding Strategy

Before you approach any organization for funding, consider the following points:

- Which are the best fundraising methods for your project (such as grant application, sponsorship or event)?
- How appropriate is the potential funder? Your project's aims and objectives must coincide with your potential funder's to be successful. Their criteria for funding will be listed in their application instructions.
- Does your proposal suit the aim of your potential funder? When applying for funding, it is helpful if you can demonstrate a connection with the plans of other organizations, for example a National Governing Body (NGB) or local authority. Most local authorities and NGBs have a funding strategy for sport enabling you to gauge whether your proposal shares any aspect of their agenda. If there is shared ground, potential funders will be reassured that their investment will enjoy widespread support and have a high impact.

Fund-Raising Schemes

Organizing an event can be an enjoyable method of raising funds. Profits from admission fees can boost an organization's revenue considerably. The following are just some of the smaller fund-raising events that can be encouraged:

- Quiz night
- Casino evening
- Race night
- Disco
- Sponsored marathon
- Coffee morning
- Jumble sale
- Auction
- Raffle

Project Briefs

Item	Administrative brief	Planning brief	Design and performance brief	Management brief	Programme brief
Aim	Sets the administrative ground rules for design/construction project	Specifies the planning context	Set objectives/ priorities for project scale / content / capital / revenue costs	Future management policy as it may affect design/ construction	Specify programme for design/ construction of project
Content	Project title Contact details Project Coordinator Details of client instructions/ procedures/ terms/conditions Status of the Brief (e.g. sketch, design or final etc.) Lists of individuals/ agencies to be consulted	Details of site boundaries/owners of adjoining land Existing/proposed access Parking requirements Mandatory specifications for roads/parking (highways authority) Underground services Overhead power lines Height restrictions Tree preservation orders Landscaping requirements Details of listed buildings SSSIs/ANOBs Townscape requirements Local Plan requirements General planning policies for the area Building lines Details of land liable to flooding/ underground watercourses Details of any contaminated land Details of made up ground	Objectives of proposed project Proposed philosophy of use/ management Range and scale of facilities required Key design features Priorities – in case the capital cost of the project exceeds the budget available The performance required from different elements of the project Approximate throughput anticipated /overall pattern of use Acceptable financial implications The 'building policy'	User control requirements, e.g. will spectators be allowed in without payment Pricing policies (this will guide quality of finish and space standards) Opening hours Programming, including sessions for clubs etc. Key target groups and how attracted Catering policy – nature/quality of food etc.	Timescale for project implementation Target dates – e.g. cash flow In time for major competitions?

- Bingo evening
- 100 Club (A typical format is for 100 people to pay £1 a month into a club account. Each participant is given a number and a draw is held each month for cash prizes of £10 or £20.)
- Club lotteries (Remember that a club must establish its eligibility and register with its local council.)

Fund-raising is important for any organization, so fund-raisers should be supported and thanked, and their efforts publicized.

Raising Sponsorship

All sponsorship is dependent on convincing potential sponsors they will benefit from the arrangement. Consequently a coherent project plan is essential for success.

- Prepare a sponsorship brief, which must be well thought out and professionally produced.
- Identify companies in your area that have an interest in your organization. Contact the individual who makes sponsorship decisions in the organization and research the company in advance of contact.
- A personalized, rather than duplicated, letter of introduction is best. Details should include the sum required, how it will be spent and what the company can expect in return for its investment. The audience for their product, where their logo will be displayed and how often should all be outlined. They should also be informed of events and competitions that will attract media attention.

Site Selection

When deciding to site a sports facility, and there is a choice of sites to consider, one needs to assess them using a number of considerations, many of which are identified below. At the end of the day the decision is often a compromise and down to professional judgement. There will never be a perfect site! The cost of land will always be a significant factor. Building land, greenfield sites, brownfield sites, school playing fields and others all have different costs. Joint ventures between educational authorities and the private sector can ease the costs of developments. Costs of land can vary from free for brownfield or reclaimed to over £200,000 per hectare for land with outline planning permission for development. Brownfield and reclaimed land may have hidden costs that are associated with existing and potential problems such as pollution. Specialist expert advice should be sought.

The total land areas available and the number of pitches, courts and so on required will also be important in determining site feasibility. The site needs to have access with good road links and other transport means, depending upon the scale of provision and the anticipated catchment area. There is little point in developing a facility that people cannot get to or access easily. Existing buildings are rarely wholly suitable and can have restrictions placed on their usage or even development (especially when seeking change of use). The siting of new buildings must consider vehicular access and disturbance to neighbours. Public consultation is often necessary and is always a factor when seeking planning permission

Developing Brownfield Sites

During the last century, and continuing to this day, our towns and cities have changed as industries and centres of population have moved, declined or evolved. Our large urban conurbations were once great centres of industry and the focus for community living. As these industries have either declined or moved to the urban fringe in recent times, so too have the main populations. Heavy industry has largely moved from urban centres and left as their legacy areas of dereliction, so-called 'brownfield' sites consisting of abandoned buildings and landscapes. Increases in domestic waste and landfill sites have also created many areas of contaminated land that is potentially harmful to the environment and human health. The Environment Agency estimates that there are some 300,000 hectares of land in the UK affected to some extent by contamination left by industrial activity. Brownfield sites are difficult to develop for housing because of the often high remediation costs and in the past have been converted to grassland and recreational use. For any proposed development on a particular site it is important that the environmental status of that site is fully investigated and understood prior to any commencement of works. Full surveys for site history, geology and geo-environmental factors including the laboratory testing of soils should be undertaken by qualified engineers/surveyors. Of particular significance will be the levels of any soil contaminants including heavy metals, chemicals, soil acidity or alkalinity (pH) and the leachate potential from groundwater. Often the remedial works may involve the importing of a 'clean' soil or 'rootzone' to cover the contaminated material below. Specialist advice should be sought in this instance. Typically such clean cover systems may range from 300mm to 400mm in depth. These systems often utilize a granular layer for venting of gases and/or the installation of a geotextile synthetic mesh. Site assessments need to consider potential risks to site end-users, construction and maintenance workers, groundwater contamination and toxicity to plants. Remedial works undertaken later in the development could be unduly disruptive and costly and therefore investigations need to be conducted in the feasibility study and design stage.

from the local planning control authority. Services are essential and need to include water, electricity and telephone; these should be considered at the outset and their costs budgeted for in the development. Site topography, geology (including soil types and depths), water table levels and site hydrology must be evaluated by an agronomist or land engineer/surveyor. Local archaeological and conservation interests may also restrict development and these aspects must be evaluated and reported. The site may be subject to tree preservation orders, be a site of special scientific interest (SSSI) or other legislative order. These all need careful consideration in the planning and developmental process. A final, but quite critical, factor is that of demand for sport in the locality. One needs to assess both demographics and the perceived demands for the sports in question. Local or regional competition will also be important to determine prior to any further development or capital outlay. Site feasibility and assessment can be complex and so a ranking method such as the one in the accompanying table is often a useful way of choosing the best option.

The list is by no means exhaustive and not all the factors given in the table will apply to all sites. One needs to exercise one's own judgement and common sense too in site evaluation. Using the identified criteria it is then necessary to assess its significance in the range 1 to 5, where 1 is not that important and 5 is very important. This is called a weighting factor and is used to make sure that highly important factors, such as soil type, are given a higher rank than lesser factors. For the particular site one will have to then assess the importance or score of each of the individual factors, again on a scale of 1 to 5. Then multiply this by the weighting.

Soil, for example, is an important factor in natural turf grass constructions so it may be given a weight of 3. If the site has good soil for pitch construction, then give it a score of 1×3, if some treatment is needed then give it 2×3, 3×3 or 4×3, depending on what needs doing. If the soil needs removing and replacing with fresh rootzone, give it a $3 \times 5 = 15$. Finally add all the scores up: if ten factors are used with weights of 5, then a score of 50 (all ones) means the site is very suitable and 250 (all fives) will mean rejection out of hand. Scores in between will need one to make a qualified judgement. Reasons will have to be given! This method can be used to decide between different sites or areas within sites. If assessing two or more sites make sure that the same factors appear for all sites, even if some or more are given a weight or rank of zero, as they do not apply. This makes comparisons easier and fairer. This method of site assessment can also be an indicator of major possibilities and problems. It may also suggest solutions to problems as well.

Factors that Influence the Actual Positioning of Sports Pitches on a Site

The two most critical or influential factors that will dictate the siting of a sports surface are orientation and the land area or space available.

ORIENTATION

Grounds that are incorrectly laid out, especially those with an east–west orientation, place significant restrictions on pitch and court usage. In certain circumstances this may result in inefficient use of the total land area. Good planning and siting of pitches can reduce the disadvantages and hazards presented by the setting sun. A north–south direction is desirable for most games and for those sports where the player may be looking into the air for the ball, such as tennis and cricket, it is essential: a player looking into the sun is placed at a serious disadvantage.

LAND AREA AND PITCH/COURT SIZE

The total area of land available will obviously dictate both the size of the pitch or court that can be laid out and probably its actual position or orientation; the shape of the land area available will also influence

Siting Sports Facilities – A Ranking Method

Factor	Comment	Factor	Comment
Area	Must have enough land for proposed use.	Access	Consider increases in traffic and any difficulties getting in and out of the site.
Historic structures or landscape	If present always weight and score highly.	Car parking	Expensive to provide from new.
Archaeology	If present always weight and score highly.	Views in and out	Screening may be needed.
Shape of land	Odd or eccentrically shaped parcels of land are difficult for most sports facilities.	Legal restrictions	These can block or severely restrict the whole proposal.
Conservation value	If present always weight highly, but the score will depend on rarity and value.	Existing amenities and facilities	Buildings, toilets, machinery storage etc.
Potential nuisance	If present always weight highly, but the score will depend on type and extent of nuisance.	Leisure potential	Consider local competition and facilities.
Existing vegetation	Shade, costs of removal etc.	Conflicts on site use	Sites may be needed for other activities.
Topography	Level sites are best.	Rainfall	Lots of water is needed for grass pitches but so is drainage!
Safety	Needs careful evaluation.	Services	Particularly electricity and water.
Aspect	Sun-shade and also pitch orientation.	Irrigation	Important for natural grass systems, less so for artificial surfaces.
Soil texture	Clay and chalk based soils are the most problematic.	Drainage	A crucial factor. Natural drainage is an advantage.
Soil depth	Grass needs a minimum of 450mm depth of top soil.	Soil contamination	Can be very difficult to deal with.

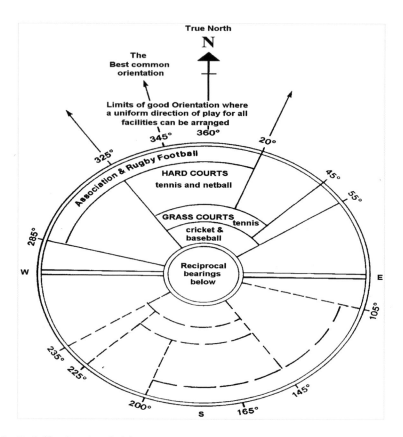

Figure 5 Desirable orientation of pitches.

pitch positioning. When planning a pitch or court position, remember that it is not just the area needed for the actual pitch itself but also for 'run-off' areas. The overall sizes of pitches and courts are laid down by the particular sports governing body, for example the Football Association. Many sports stipulate both minimum and maximum sizes, providing a degree of flexibility when selecting a final size of pitch depending upon the room available. Many governing bodies, however, do specify a fixed size for a particular level of play, such as International competition. For final verification regarding dimensions of a sport pitch or court, you should always consult with the governing body concerned. The area of land available may thus limit the standard of play or competition that can be catered for. National or International sized pitches/courts tend to be larger. (Further information can be found in the Sport England publication *Comparative Sizes: Pitches & Courts.*)

SEASONALITY OF USE

An area of turf may be used for different activities at differing times of year. The most common example of this is where cricket outfields are used for hockey or football during the winter after the cricket season has finished. This does cause some problems, particularly during the change-over period from one sport to another, but it does mean that a limited size of field can be successfully used for more than one sport.

Outdoor Pitch and Court Typical Dimensions and Areas
(* actual area of land required, and not the pitch or court makings)

Sport	Length (m)	Width (m)	Area (m²)
American Football	109.73	48.77	5,352
Outdoor target archery range	105	5 per lane	735 (6 lanes and 1 clear lane)
Athletics track *	179	106	1,8974
Long/triple jump *	49	2.75–3	135–147
Pole vault *	45	5	225
Baseball *	38.79	38.79	1,505
Cricket square	20	22	440
Cricket outfield *	160	142	22,720
Five-a-side football	36	18	648
Football	90–120	45–90	4,050–10,800
Soccer 7s pitch	64	45	2,880
Gaelic football	130–145	80–90	10,400–13,050
Hockey	91.4	55	5,027
Lacrosse – men	100	55–64	5,500–6,400
Lacrosse – women	100–110	60	6,000–6,600
Netball	30.5	15.25	466
Rounders *	17	17	289
Rugby League	112–122	68	7,616–8,296
Rugby Union	120–144	69	8,280–9,936
Shinty	128–155	64–73	8,192–11,315
Softball *	25.86	25.86	669
Tennis	23.77	10.97	261
Short tennis	13.4	6.1	82
Polo	274.3	182.8	50,143
Bowls – Crown	27.5–55	27.5–55	757– 3,052
Bowls – Flat	36.58–40.23	36.58–40.23	1,338–1,619

DUAL USE OF NON-TURF SURFACES

Many non-turf surfaces used for sport, such as synthetic grass pitches or macadam court areas, cater for more than one sport in order to increase usage and to satisfy a particular demand. This is achieved by using lines and markings of different colours on the surface. Usually two to three different colours are used to mark out the area for the same number of sports, for example hockey, tennis and netball. It is necessary to use strongly contrasting colours in order to avoid player confusion over which set of markings they are playing to. Obviously only one sport can be played on the same area at any one time, but the markings mean that the area is immediately ready for a different sport straight away.

WEAR AND TEAR
Many sports facilities 'move' their pitches from year to year in order to spread wear and tear and facilitate a period for the badly worn areas to recover. Football pitch goal-mouths and tennis court base-lines can be very badly worn after a playing season and recovery can often be enhanced by moving the pitch or court a few metres to the side or up the field. Obviously this can only be practised where there is sufficient land area for pitches/courts to be set out in a different area.

GRADIENTS
A uniform fall of 1:100 is ideal for most sports but gradients up to 1:50 are possible, if of even fall. The gradient of any area of land will influence pitch positioning to a certain degree, although in most cases will probably have to be 'lived' with. Steeper slopes may be used but players' fatigue will then have to be taken into account. Steep banks adjacent to pitches are dangerous.

To these principal factors should be added a number of practical considerations:

• The location of changing facilities, pavilions and spectator stands and so on in relation to the particular pitch/court.
• The accessibility for maintenance equipment and machinery, including the availability of water.
• The safety in terms of direction of play, for example cricket nets in relation to athletics activities such as jumping.
• The proximity to adjoining property and roads, and any need for protective netting or fencing.
• Emergency exits for spectators and players. Consider the health and safety implications at all times.

Earthworks and Grading

Frequently sites do not conform to desired levels or gradients necessary for the installation of sports pitches and playing surfaces. Most sites need grading, that is amending soil levels to the desired gradients. Moving soil is both complex, since it impacts directly on land stability and soil water movement, and expensive, as it involves time and labour and specialist machinery. Such works should only be planned by qualified engineers and undertaken by experienced and reputable contractors. Making an area level for the purposes of sports ground construction can be achieved in three ways:

By cutting into a bank: Grading by cut (earth removal) generally results in stable ground, minimizes erosion and causes the least disturbance to the landscape. One is left with material to dispose of, however.
By filling out from a bank: Grading by filling can be difficult as finding the appropriate quality soil is not always easy and areas of fill are generally not sufficiently stable for building works without installing elaborate foundations or compacting with special equipment. They can be subject to erosion as slippage and slides can occur, since there is little or no bondage between existing soil and the fill.
By a combination of cut and fill: This is the most popular method for levelling works. There is an appropriate balance of cut and fill, and expensive hauling and disposal fees are eliminated.

A number of initial constraints must be considered when preparing a grading plan:

• Determine whether existing vegetation is to be saved, transplanted or removed.
• The finish floor of existing structures is fixed, so proposed grading must meet it to ensure proper drainage.
• Finish grades of existing roadways form constraints and must be maintained and

Finished levels and gradients are important. Here a laser level is being used to achieve final tolerances.
(J Mallinson (Ormskirk) Ltd)

Typical Drawings Expected for a Major Sports Ground Construction

Description	Typical Scale
Site survey	1:500 to 1:2,500 with existing contours at 1m intervals and relevant site features
Proposed finished site plan	1:500 to 1:2,500 with details of finished sports ground layout, access, buildings, etc.
Site access and storage of materials	1:200 to 1:500 with details of site accommodation, storage of vehicles, no-access areas, etc.
Site levels and topsoil stripping	1:200 to 1:500 with details of storage of transported topsoil
Sequence of levelling	1:200 to 1:500 (for cut-and-fill excavations)
Subsoil levels	1:200 to 1:500 with spot heights relative to finished heights and natural contours
Finished heights plan	1:200 to 1:500 with finished spot heights
Field drainage plan	1:200 to 1:500 with details of cut-off drains, main carrier drains, lateral drains, and slit drains
Drain sections/outfalls	1:10 to 1:50 with details of drain depths, widths, pipe sizes, depth of permeable fill, etc.

Sports ground construction necessitates the use of heavy plant and equipment. (J Mallinson (Ormskirk) Ltd)

met by proposed grades. Grades of public roadways must not be changed by private developers.

- How much change is justifiable to the existing land form? Does the land have special qualities worth saving?
- The extent of the property forms a constraint. One must meet existing grades at the property line (generally before the property line, as fill has a tendency to slip and may cross the line). Excess drainage water must not be diverted across a property line.
- Existing utilities and underground structures should generally not be graded or changed. (Check on the rights of any easements as they usually affect grading.)
- Surface or subsurface geological factors, such as rock outcroppings, ground-water, bogs and difficult soil types, should be avoided unless explored as to technical feasibility.
- The existing drainage pattern, water channels and water bodies must be allowed to function naturally. Any change caused by grading must be carefully checked to assure continued operation of the natural drainage ways.

Practical Grading and Drainage Considerations

There are several factors that influence the cost of grading and drainage. It should especially be borne in mind that a balanced cut and fill proposal will always result in lower grading costs than an unbalanced solution.

Since removing soil from the site and disposing it elsewhere is expensive, you will save money by using it onsite. On the other hand, importing soil for filling can also be a problem as a suitable soil has to be sourced fairly nearby and this needs to be reasonably priced. On large projects this will also need to be stockpiled until it is needed.

The most economical procedure with grading involves removing and placing of soil in one motion. If it has to be unloaded and reloaded later, however, additional costs will be incurred.

The time of year when work is undertaken will have an effect on costs – in winter, for example, work will be difficult, wet and muddy. Levelling and grading works are best carried out between the months of March and August. Rock outcrops or any mechanical constraints can also increase grading costs.

Inexpensive grading requires considerable room for large equipment to operate. As a result small urban projects will be more expensive than large rural ones. Owing to the size of modern grading equipment, it often appears cheaper to remove everything from the site and rebuild later, but the following factors should be considered:

- The cost of rebuilding the landscape following grading (erosion control, replacing trees, topsoil and so on) should always be included.
- It is cheaper to remove trees than save them. Protect those trees that need to be saved.
- Topsoil is easily mixed with subsoil – and can save money. Ultimately, though, it is very expensive to replace the contaminated topsoil.

When not to Grade (Potential Problems Created by Grading)

Interruption of natural drainage patterns: This will result in a concentration of run-off elsewhere, which can cause erosion, sedimentation downstream, visual degradation of natural waterways, or flooding of neighbouring land.

Loss of topsoil, erosion, mixing of topsoil: It takes approximately a thousand years to build 25mm of topsoil, a precious commodity essential for plant life. All grading operations will disturb topsoil, leaving some eroded, some mixed with subsoil and some lost. Such loss must be minimized.

Loss of vegetation: Plants are climate moderators causing changes in air temperature, surface radiation and rainfall. They also help to control erosion. Destruction of vegetation is therefore a bad thing. To replace vegetation can be costly.

Natural disasters: The results of slides, slippages, floods and other disasters can be compounded by careless grading. Take into consideration the following:

- Steep banks are most likely to slip very easily.
- Layering of soils can cause slippage, especially if heavy loading is increased by grading.
- Many layered profiles include an impermeable layer that causes water to back up and can then create flooding.
- Some clays can shrink or swell, which then creates heave.
- Installing elaborate deep pile foundations into steep banks will diminish the danger of slippage – but this is expensive.
- Natural disasters can be triggered by grading work done hundreds of metres away.

Impossible conditions: Avoid areas that are too steep, areas where the soil is a problem (a bog, rock outcrop), and areas rich in wildlife.

Aesthetic degradation: Site plans are normally designed to serve utilitarian purposes, resulting in loss of site character and replacing it with an environment on a scale that is uncomfortable for most people's requirements.

Alternative Design Solutions to Major Mechanical Grading

Reduce the area to be graded: This can be achieved by cutting down the number of functional areas required, for example parking. In built environments you can also save space by considering buildings with two storeys instead of one.

Smaller areas: Break large level areas into a number of smaller ones using such means as terracing and linked areas.

Orientation: Building configurations that run perpendicular to contours require little grading.

Concentrate the development: Emphasize the 'maximum damage to a minimum amount of space rather than minimum damage to all the area'.

Impact evaluation of various design solutions: This should include short-term and long-term costs of various project solutions, contrasting those requiring extensive grading and those that minimize grading.

Forward planning: Pre-grading an area three or four months beforehand reduces damage from erosion, run-off and sedimentation that could occur once major grading has taken place.

Plant graded areas immediately following any disturbance: Use hydro-seeding and, if necessary, erosion control nets on steep banks.

Grading Procedure

Scrape off the true topsoil and place it in heaps positioned so as not to interfere with subsequent work.

Adjust the levels using subsoil, the surplus 'cut' off high areas being used to 'fill' the lower areas (cut and fill). This is the most common method of level adjustment. Using imported fill to raise lower levels is sometimes a better alternative.

Where filling is carried out, any large stones, boulders and rubble should be used to fill lower regions only, and kept at least 750mm below the finished surface to avoid difficulties when introducing drains. Imported filling, particularly on the upper levels, should be generally fine material, such as reasonable quality subsoil, crushed stone or ash.

All filling should be completed in consecutive layers 225mm deep and adequately firmed. Time may be needed for settlement, particularly with landfill sites or former refuse tips. The finished formation should be trimmed smooth to required levels before topsoil is returned.

Banks should then be formed with easy slopes, preferably not exceeding 1:3 to ease

maintenance and minimize any risk of slip. It is particularly important to ensure that there is adequate consolidation as the face of fill banks is built up.

The preserved topsoil is replaced to produce the finished surface and graded smooth to provide a uniform layer before work is done. Mixing topsoil and subsoil should be avoided during all stages of the work. Topsoil should be left in spoil heaps for as brief a time as possible.

Where level improvement is necessary in local areas only, it is often possible to carry out minor surface grading by spreading imported topsoil in minor depressions and marrying it to the surrounding ground levels using lutes.

Construction and Drainage Systems

An effective drainage system is desirable for most horticultural situations and is essential for areas of turf used for sports. An adequate supply of soil moisture is essential for plant growth but an excess will be both detrimental to growth and will often mean that any affected surface is unplayable. For sports turf situations, drainage is particularly important where they are played upon in the winter when wetter conditions usually prevail. Winter sports pitches are particularly susceptible as they receive heavy wear that damages the soil structure, impeding drainage at a time when they are receiving their greatest use.

Any installed drainage system, however, will only be as good as the maintenance and management to which it is subjected, particularly when a few years have elapsed since its installation. All too often the drainage system is forgotten about until a collapse or failure means that expensive excavations and repair works are necessary. A little attention to flow rates in ditches and at farms, together with a close watch on surface indicators and attention to maintenance works when needed, will avoid

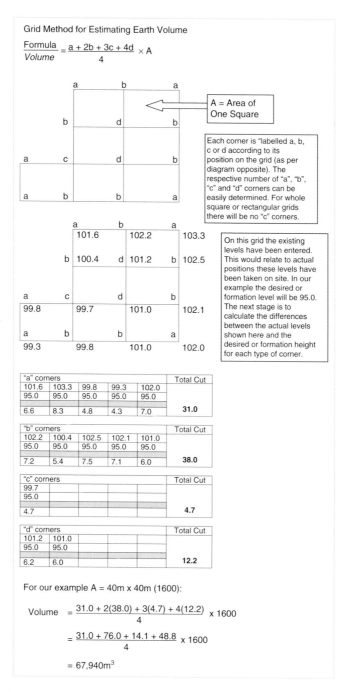

Grid Method for Estimating Earth Volume

$$\frac{Formula}{Volume} = \frac{a + 2b + 3c + 4d}{4} \times A$$

A = Area of One Square

Each corner is "labelled a, b, c or d according to its position on the grid (as per diagram opposite). The respective number of "a", "b", "c" and "d" corners can be easily determined. For whole square or rectangular grids there will be no "c" corners.

On this grid the existing levels have been entered. This would relate to actual positions these levels have been taken on site. In our example the desired or formation level will be 95.0. The next stage is to calculate the differences between the actual levels shown here and the desired or formation height for each type of corner.

"a" corners					Total Cut
101.6	103.3	99.8	99.3	102.0	
95.0	95.0	95.0	95.0	95.0	
6.6	8.3	4.8	4.3	7.0	**31.0**

"b" corners					Total Cut
102.2	100.4	102.5	102.1	101.0	
95.0	95.0	95.0	95.0	95.0	
7.2	5.4	7.5	7.1	6.0	**38.0**

"c" corners					Total Cut
99.7					
95.0					
4.7					**4.7**

"d" corners					Total Cut
101.2	101.0				
95.0	95.0				
6.2	6.0				**12.2**

For our example A = 40m x 40m (1600):

$$Volume = \frac{31.0 + 2(38.0) + 3(4.7) + 4(12.2)}{4} \times 1600$$

$$= \frac{31.0 + 76.0 + 14.1 + 48.8}{4} \times 1600$$

$$= 67,940m^3$$

Figure 6   Methods for calculating earthworks (cut and fill).

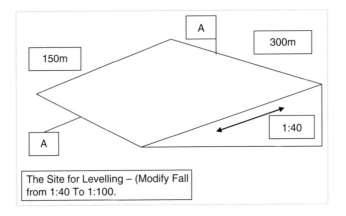

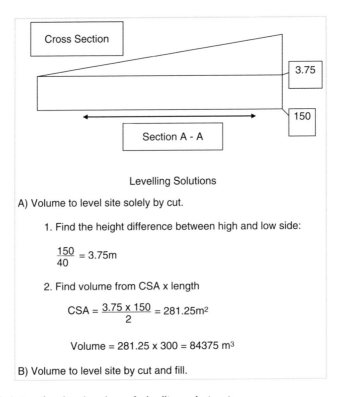

Figure 7   Calculation of earthworks volumes for levelling a sloping site.

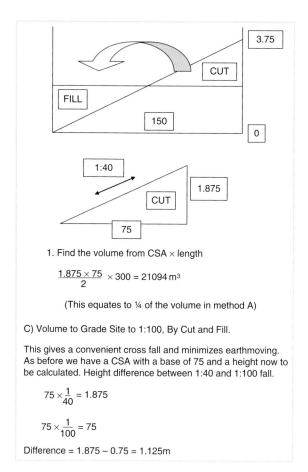

1. Find the volume from CSA × length

$$\frac{1.875 \times 75}{2} \times 300 = 21094\,\text{m}^3$$

(This equates to ¼ of the volume in method A)

C) Volume to Grade Site to 1:100, By Cut and Fill.

This gives a convenient cross fall and minimizes earthmoving. As before we have a CSA with a base of 75 and a height now to be calculated. Height difference between 1:40 and 1:100 fall.

$$75 \times \frac{1}{40} = 1.875$$

$$75 \times \frac{1}{100} = 75$$

Difference = 1.875 – 0.75 = 1.125m

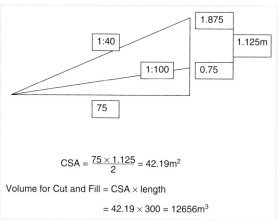

$$\text{CSA} = \frac{75 \times 1.125}{2} = 42.19\text{m}^2$$

Volume for Cut and Fill = CSA × length

$$= 42.19 \times 300 = 12656\text{m}^3$$

Figure 7   (Continued.)

Calculating Earth Volumes Using Contours
Where contour plans are available it is possible to calculate the volume of earth to be removed or added. The formula is:

$$V = \frac{A}{2} \times (B + C) + 2 \times (D) + E$$

Where:
- V = Volume of material (earth)
- A = Contour interval
- B = First area
- C = Last area
- D = Sum of all other areas
- E = Top part (where required)

---

such expensive work. Drainage is such a critical factor that more attention to its upkeep is well deserved. A good drainage system that has been installed correctly and had adequate maintenance and management has the potential to last indefinitely, so it is well worth implementing on effective management policy. Guidelines for sports turf drainage installation are available from the Land Drainage Contractors Association.

The purpose of field or land drainage is to ensure that excess soil water does not remain in the soil for long enough to:

- Inhibit the growth of the desirable vegetation.
- Prohibit access of maintenance on other essential machinery on site.
- Prevent a sports surface from being used when required.

Benefits of a Drainage System

Good drainage is essential for healthy plant growth and for allowing surfaces to withstand vehicular and pedestrian traffic and play. It is an essential prerequisite for any sports turf surface; for those that are played on during the wet winter months, it is absolutely vital if any amount of play is to be catered for. In sports turf, particularly, the following benefits may be accrued from an effective drainage system:

- Removal of excess moisture and lowering of the water table
- Improvement in quality, firmness and durability of turf, particularly in the case of winter games
- Quick drying of soil, thus extending possible playing time
- Prevention of erosion, so restricting surface run-off from newly constructed banks and steep slopes
- Prevention of soil 'heave' in winter
- Better air movement in the soil
- Increased root development
- Increased capillary moisture in dry weather
- Improved drought resistance (due primarily to increased root development)
- Better soil structure
- Higher soil temperature at certain seasons and therefore a longer growing season
- More efficient use of fertilizers, less leeching of nutrients, particularly nitrogen

Possible Causes of Field Drainage Problems

It is usual to think of drainage simply in terms of pipes and pipe systems. In many situations, however, pipes are irrelevant to the solution of a drainage problem, or are only part of the solution. Before any investment is made in expensive drainage systems the cause of the problem should be thoroughly investigated. Poor drainage will usually be found to occur as the result of one or more of the following six causes:

- Surface compaction
- Subsurface compaction
- Subsurface pans
- High water tables
- Impermeable soil texture
- Run-off from adjacent sites

Practical Determination of the Causes of Drainage Problems

Where water lies on the surface of the soil, spike the surface to a depth of 100–150mm. If the water starts to disappear from the surface only in the treated area, suspect surface compaction and seek the cause, such as vehicle tracks.

To confirm this diagnosis and determine any other causes, dig a trial hole at least 30cm wide and 100cm deep. Examine the soil in the exposed side of the pit for signs of:

Layers of compaction: Layers of soil of different texture, structure, colour or wetness.

Iron pans: Dark or reddish layers of hard material in a sandy profile.

Subsoil mottling (gleying): Blue and grey mottle in a brown or red profile. The top of the mottled area indicates the winter level of the water table.

Soil texture/structure: If none of the above are present, check the clay content of the soil and look for beneficial drainage cracks or wormholes running from the surface deep into the profile.

Observe water level: Leave the pit covered for twenty-four hours to prevent any rain getting in. Any free standing water after this period represents the level of the water table during the current season.

Rooting depth: The presence of active root growth is a good indication of adequate soil conditions.

Only if the water table is rising to within 750mm of the surface, and/or the soil is exceptionally heavy and poorly structured, is a pipe drainage system likely to offer any advantage. In the case of exceptionally heavy soil, weak, shallow-rooted grasses often suffer more than trees and shrubs. Unless the water table is exceptionally near the surface (300mm), topsoil amelioration coupled with subsoiling will often be of more benefit to herbaceous plants than installing pipe drainage systems.

In most landscape situations pipe drainage systems have more applications for amenity grassland than other planted areas, since:

- The excessively wet soil may encourage grass growth while denying access to maintenance machinery.
- Public access is liable to cause surface compaction and rapid wear of the grass.
- The surface becomes unusable for its intended purpose.

Practical Solutions to Drainage Problems

SURFACE COMPACTION

If the surface of otherwise permeable soil is compacted, then water will collect on the surface. In this situation, installing a pipe is of no use since water is unable to percolate through the soil to the pipe. It should be noted that a compaction layer only a few millimetres thick is sufficient to hold water on the surface for several days. The solution is simply to puncture or lift the compacted layer, and to take steps to avoid any re-compaction.

SUBSURFACE COMPACTION

This is commonly caused during the process of construction by the use of heavy machinery on wet soil. Again, if the soil is reasonably permeable, then breaking up the compacted layer with a subsoiler (preferably wing-tined) is all that is required.

SUBSURFACE PANS

Some soils naturally develop hard pans of iron-based substances below the surface of the soil. These 'iron pans' are common on sandy soils and should be suspected if winter drainage is poor on soils of this texture. Subsoiling to break the pan is again likely to be the most effective solution.

HIGH WATER TABLE

Where a permeable top soil overlies an impermeable soil, then rainwater percolating through the soil will collect on top of the impermeable layer. This water tends to find its own level and forms a (ground) water table at a certain depth in the soil. The water table rises nearer the surface in the winter and recedes in the summer. The soil below the water table is saturated and almost without oxygen, so it will not support plant growth. The solution to this problem is to install a pipe just into the impermeable layer to collect all the water as it accumulates and transport it away from the site. This is the traditional role of a pipe drainage system.

IMPERMEABLE SOIL TEXTURE

Some soils, mainly heavy clays, are naturally poor at transmitting water from the surface through the soil profile, even where the soil is not compacted. Placing a pipe deep in this type of soil will have little effect, because water cannot pass quickly to the pipe. Subsoiling on its own is also only a partial solution, since although it will remove water from the surface, the water will tend to collect in the impervious soil beneath the surface. In this case a multi-faceted approach may be required:

- Planting on ridges to run-off water.
- Improving soil structure with additions or organic matter.
- Subsoiling to create drainage cracks from the surface to lower in the soil profile or into drainage trenches.
- Primary and secondary drainage systems:
  - Mole ploughing to collect water from subsoil cracks.
  - Sand slitting to keep drainage channels open from the pipes to the surface.

- Pipes encased in gravel to transport away from the site any water collecting in the subsoil cracks, mole drains or sand slits.

Interceptor Drains

These are required where significant amounts of water may run into the drained area from surrounding land, either through surface run-off or by groundwater flow (seepage). The solution is the same in either case: install an interceptor drain at the relevant point.

INTERCEPTING RUN-OFF AND SEEPAGE

An open ditch, often called a 'French drain', is constructed at the foot of the slope to catch the surface and seepage water. The key points to note are:

- Width (W) must be sufficient to prevent water flooding across the top of the ditch in heavy rainfall (300–450mm minimum)
- Depth (D) must be sufficient to intercept any significant amounts of ground flow.
- Ditches must be stabilized by back-filling with clean granular material.
- Granular backfill must be continued to the surface and left soil-free.
- Pipes laid in the trench bottom will increase the effectiveness of the ditch providing they are of sufficient capacity; this is difficult to calculate, but a minimum of 150mm diameter is suggested.
- Where depths exceed 1.5m any pipes must be made of crush-resistant clay ware.

INTERCEPTING SPRINGS

A trench similar to the surface water interceptor is laid in the impermeable layer far enough back from the spring line to prevent waterlogging in the rootzone. The pipe is covered by gravel, which must be continued into the permeable layer. A blinding layer of sand can be used to prevent silting of the gravel.

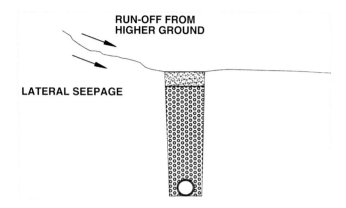

Figure 8   Interceptor drain.

MOLE DRAINS

Mole ploughing creates surface cracks that link to subsurface 'mole' channels. These channels cut across the gravel fill of the pipe drainage system so that water runs rapidly from the surface to the mole and then to the pipe. Forming the cracks also causes surface heave and mole ploughing may be inappropriate on very fine turf. The following points should be observed:

- Mole channels only work if there is an effective gravel-topped pipe drainage system already installed and the mole drain crosses this at approximately 90 degrees.
- Mole channels only work well in stable clay-rich soils, with a minimum clay content of 15 per cent (ideally more than 35 per cent).
- Moles should be formed to a depth of 450–600mm to lie 150–200mm above pipes.
- Spacing should be a maximum of four or five times the depth so that the cracks formed at the surface are continuous between the moles. Spacing of 1.2–3m is commonly used.
- The diameter is usually 50–75mm, but when fitted with an expander this can achieve 100mm.

- To avoid silting the gradient should never be less than 1 in 200, or more than 1 in 60 to avoid scouring and collapse.
- The effective length is the distance between lateral pipes: 30m pipe spacing avoids excessive water flow in moles and the risk of collapse.
- Avoid periods when the soil is saturated or dry and crumbly. A damp soil in a drying period is ideal.

Pipe Drainage

The principal effect of installing a pipe drainage system is to lower the water table. If the water table is maintained 500mm below the surface then the site is capable of:

- Supporting the growth of most types of vegetation.
- Allowing access of maintenance machinery throughout the year.
- Supporting maximum use of amenity grassland.

To allow for irregularities in the depth of the water table, most drainage designers prefer to design for a minimum water table depth of 750mm below the surface.

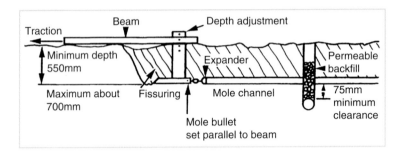

Figure 9   Mole plough.

In most situations there is little advantage in maintaining the water table below 750mm and it may 'over-drain' the site so that insufficient water is available during the growing season. Some authorities maintain that a water table depth of 1.0–1.3m is beneficial for trees and shrubs, but this depth is by no means commonly found in nature.

On heavy or compacted soil the main problem is getting the water from the surface quickly, while not necessarily altering the level of the water table. Secondary drainage in the form of mole ploughing or sand slitting may be required and the pipe system acts as a collector of water from the mole channel or from the sand slits.

Pipe Drainage Design and Specification

The design of pipe drainage systems is considered under ten headings:

- Determining a suitable discharge position for the pipes
- Determining that ditch design and capacity matches the pipe system
- Designing a layout for the system
- Pipe materials
- Pipe spacing and length
- Pipe depths
- Pipe gradients
- Pipe diameter
- Backfill materials and depths
- Trench sizes

The calculations used to determine values for some of these design parameters appear in Appendices 1 and 2, but guidance to suitable values is given in this section where appropriate.

Determine a Suitable Discharge Position

The usual situation for a field drainage system is to discharge the water from the main pipe into an adjacent ditch. The obvious and usual solution is to feed the water into the ditch adjacent to the lowest point on the site. This siting needs careful consideration on steeply sloping sites, however, where having the outfall at the lowest point may result in unacceptably steep gradients for the main pipe or overloading the ditch capacity in heavy rainfall. There is a strong relationship between the pipe system layout and the optimum discharge position, and they should not be considered independently.

Ditch Design and Capacity

For obvious reasons the ditches into which the system discharges must be made suitable before the pipes are installed. The main considerations are:

Soil type	Vertical units	Horizontal units	Width at top for ditch 1m deep
Clay	1	1	2.3m
Clay loam	1	1.5	3.3m
Loams	1	1.5	3.3m
Sandy loam	1	3	6.3m
Loose sand/peat	1	4	8.3m

BOTTOM WIDTH

If the bottom is too wide then water erodes a narrow channel in the base and choking weeds establish on the unused portion. Too narrow is less of a problem, as water tends to erode the sides, creating a wider channel. On steep batters, however, this can cause undercutting of the bank and danger of the sides collapsing. For catchments up to 10 hectares the usual range is 200–300mm width (*see* Appendix 2).

DEPTH

The sides of ditches more than 5m deep are prone to be dangerously unstable. This should be avoided by piping these sections. Ditches must be at least 1m deep. This allows for 450mm soil cover over the pipe, 150mm for the pipe itself, 150mm drop from the outlet to the winter water level, and 250mm depth of water in the ditch.

BATTER

Ditch banks are dug to a batter that must be less steep than the soil's natural angle of repose in order to be stable. In practical terms this gives the following ratios for different soil types:

A ditch 1m deep in clay will have a width at the top of about 2.3m, while the same ditch in sandy loam would need to be 6.3m wide. If the site cannot accommodate this width then the ditch walls must be stabilized, for example by a concrete channel, or the ditch must be piped. Piped ditches use concrete or stoneware pipes.

GRADIENT

The rate of flow of water through a ditch is determined largely by gradient (and bottom width). The aim is to create a flow rate fast enough to prevent silting up but not so fast that the ditch is eroded.

- The slowest acceptable rate is 0.5m/sec.
- The fastest acceptable rate is 1.5m/sec.
- A rate of 0.75m/sec is required to suppress the growth of weeds.

The correct gradient of the ditch can be obtained from tables relating the flow rate of the pipe discharge to the flow rate in the ditch (*see* Appendix 2). Gradients as low as 1 in 1,000 can be suitable for catchments up to 9 hectares.

OUTFALL DESIGN

To avoid premature silting up, a silt trap should be incorporated in the main pipe just before the outfall.

HEADWALL PIPE PROTECTION

Outfalls are prone to a number of problems: bank erosion, if the pipe is too near the bank or there is no splash plate; frost damage to the exposed pipe; physical damage or distortion of the exposed pipe; and vermin infestation blocking the pipe.

Culverts

These are short lengths of ditch that have been piped and covered over to allow vehicle access. Their design has to be such that adequate support is provided for crossing vehicles without damage to the pipe, and that the pipe size is adequate for the greatest possible flood flow.

FLOOD FLOW

This is taken to be thirty times the average daily rainfall. This will often produce figures in excess of 1,000mm/day or 40–60mm/hour, so providing flow rates of at least 7 litres/second per hectare served by the ditch. The practical implication of this is that pipe size must be at least 300mm and may need to be as much as 1m.

SUPPORT FOR VEHICLES AND PIPE

Strict guidelines must be followed for the installation of pipes, which must be concrete or glazed clayware.

- Pipes should be laid on a concrete foundation along their entire length to accommodate the pipe collars.
- Pipes must be laid to the same gradient as the ditch.
- Pipes should discharge onto a concrete or stone apron to avoid ditch erosion.
- Headwalls must be made of 200mm wide mortared brick, blocks or stone.
- Headwalls must be laid on a proper (concrete) foundation.
- Headwalls must be securely located into the bank by penetrating undisturbed soil by 450mm.
- Pipes must be packed on all sides and on top with stone-free sand (or concrete) to a width of 150mm.
- Fill must be brought up to road level by packed aggregates.

Pipe Layouts

There are four main types of pipe layout:

Natural: Used to drain irregular scattered wet spots in an otherwise dry site, and therefore has no regular pattern. Natural systems are the cheapest solution to draining scattered wet spots or odd hollows created on the undulating land forms common on some landscape sites. They should be used where draining the whole site would be inefficient.

Fan: A simple system where individual pipes drain into the adjacent stream or ditch. Pipes are often laid flat and rely on gravity drainage. Silt accumulation is readily removed because the pipes are accessible from either end for rodding. Fan systems are used on very flat sites or on sites vulnerable to silting, because each pipe is readily accessible for maintenance.

Grid: A composite system where regularly spaced lateral drains are connected to a leader at angles of about 90 degrees. Laterals often connect to one side of the leader only. Grid systems are the most economic and effective systems for flattish sites with small gradients. On undulating sites and steep slopes the fixed 90-degree angle can create undesirable gradients in the laterals, or create bends in the pipes. It is a system particularly suited to sports turf applications and where moling or sand slitting is to be carried out.

Herringbone: A composite system where the regularly spaced laterals connect to a leader at angles of less than 90 degrees, the angle being set to optimize the gradients of the laterals. Where the site undulates or is very steep, the flexibility of the angle of the laterals with the leader pipe allows optimum gradients to be achieved in all areas. However this can cause problems when secondary drainage, for example moles, must cross at right angles.

SLOPING SITES

Where the natural slopes exceed 1 in 50, the pipes must be aligned across the slope at gradients of about 1 in 60 to 1 in 100, often necessitating a herringbone layout. Where there is a natural slope of 1 in 200 (0.5 per cent) or less, the lateral pipes must run exactly on the down slope, lending itself to a grid system.

Pipe Materials

For laterals the choice is between:

- Clay laid to open joints
- Smooth plastic with slots in the wall

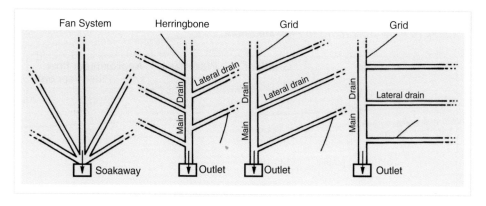

Figure 10   Drainage systems.

- Corrugated plastic with slots in the wall

If main pipes are to collect water from the laterals but not from the soil ('restricted inlet' pipes), the following may be added to this list:

- Concrete
- Vitrified clay
- Pitch fibre
- Ribbed plastic (smoothbore pipe ribbed externally for strength)

The important differences between these materials are shown in the accompanying table.

Trenchless drain-laying of lateral pipes by machine, using coils of corrugated plastic pipe, is so cheap it is nearly always to be preferred to other materials even if pipe sizes must be larger.

For main drains that require trenches smooth plastic of smaller diameter may be preferable, since excavation and backfill costs may be lower.

Clay pipes are out of fashion because they are prone to breakage, they are difficult to lay, have high transport and handling costs, and their superior performance is easily lost by misalignment. They also require larger trenches per unit diameter

because they are so thick-walled and require the larger grades of granular backfill.

Concrete (and cast iron) have specific uses where high strength is required, for example in the outfalls to ditches.

Pipe Spacing

If lateral pipes are too far apart, the water table in the area between the pipes will not be lowered to the required level. Pipe spacing can be calculated from a formula (*see* Appendix 1) and should not be altered from specification without permission. Typical spacing could be 5–10m in heavy clay soils and up to 40m in sandy loam soil. Designers usually specify a regular spacing for all laterals, 10m, 20m and 30m being commonplace. Other considerations come into play where the drainage above the pipe is being improved by subsoiling, moling or sand slitting. In heavy rain, water reaches the pipes more quickly and this may require the use of closer spacing to clear the peak flow water quickly enough to avoid the mole channels collapsing.

Sand slits transfer water only slowly along the line of the slit, and the centre of the slit should never be more than 3m from a lateral. This means a maximum spacing of 6m between laterals or, on

Rates of Flow According to Pipe Materials

	Material	Gradient	Pipe size in mm	Approximate flow rate in litres/second
Laterals	Smooth plastic	1 in 100	100	10.0
	Clay	1 in 100	100	8.5
	Corrugated plastic	1 in 100	100	6.0
Mains	Ribbed plastic (smooth bore)	1 in 100	150	22
	Clay	1 in 100	150	20
	Corrugated plastic	1 in 100	150	13
	Concrete	1 in 100	150	20

The table clearly demonstrates the dramatic effect that pipe materials can have on pipe performance: corrugated plastic, for example, has 30 per cent less capacity than clay pipe and 40 per cent less than smooth plastic. This lower flow rate can be useful on steeply sloping sites.

some sports turf applications, as little as 4m.

Pipe Length

Maximum lateral pipe length is determined by looking up tables to find the area that a pipe of that material and diameter can serve. Dividing this area by the drain spacing will give the maximum possible pipe length. Theoretically lateral pipes should not exceed about 400m; in practice 200m or less may be safer, since it will be easier for maintenance. Pipe lengths for different diameters and gradients can be determined quickly from a ready reckoner (*see* Appendices 1 and 2).

Pipe Depth

In many undisturbed soils in the UK there is an impervious (clay) layer within 1m of the surface. Traditionally pipes are laid in trenches cut into this impermeable layer to follow the natural fall of the land. This

Pedestrian/ride-on mower/no cultivation	450mm
Cultivation likely	600mm
Mole draining to be carried out	750mm
Frequent heavy traffic	900mm

system works well providing it achieves an even, adequate gradient and pipes have the following minimum depth of cover, depending on use:

It is a mistake to dig deeper than this unless the design and/or surface undulations require it. Lateral drains installed too deep in the soil are expensive and can over-drain an area. Where the depth of cover exceeds 1.5m plastic pipe is at risk of collapse under the weight of backfill.

Pipe Gradient

There is a practical limitation to pipe gradients in that it is extremely difficult to lay pipe accurately at a gradient of less than 1 in 500 (0.2 per cent), which is generally taken to be the absolute minimum gradient. Pipe gradients have an effect on the capacity of the pipe to transmit water (litres/second). As importantly, however, they have an effect on the speed at which water flows through the pipe. If water flows at less than 0.3m/sec (1ft/sec) then the drain pipe may be liable to silting up. If water flows at more than 1.5m/second (5ft/sec), then the joints in the drain are liable to scouring and erosion unless they are positively sealed. To achieve acceptable velocities the following rules should be used for laterals, irrespective of how difficult they are to achieve on site.

Maximum gradient	1 in 50	(2%)
Minimum gradient	1 in 300	(0.3%)
Practical optimum	approx. 1 in 100	(1%)

Through necessity, main carrier pipes are often laid to steeper gradients than laterals and carry more water at a greater velocity. Consequently continuous pipe or sealed joints may be essential.

AVOIDING UNEVEN GRADIENTS

It is important that the gradient does not alter over the length of a pipe. Dips in the pipe will cause the flow rate to slow down and encourage silting up. The decrease in velocity can cause water to build up behind the obstruction during peak flow. The build-up of pressure from this 'surcharging' may cause water to flow through the soil rather than to the drain and create a 'blow out' to the surface. The more severe the gradient of the pipe, the more likely is a 'blow out' if the drain becomes obstructed. Obstruction may also be caused by bends, kinks or misalignment of pipes. All the causes of 'blow out' may be avoided by careful construction (*see* below).

Pipe Diameter

When specifying drain pipe it is important to check whether the figures quoted are for internal diameter (ID) or external diameter (OD). All measurements given here are for ID, but pipe manufacturers commonly grade pipe by OD or quote both. As seen from the table opposite, pipe diameter has the greatest effect on the capacity of the pipe to transport water. Increasing the diameter of pipe selected by 50 per cent, for example from 100mm to 150mm, can more than double the flow rate.

Since the flow rate of the pipe determines how much water it can deal with, it therefore determines what area of soil the pipe can drain. Pipe diameter must therefore be considered in relation to pipe length, pipe spacing and gradient (*see* Appendix 1).

In practice it is found that, at the gradients commonly found in field drains (between 1 in 80 and 1 in 100), adequate flow rate can be achieved by corrugated plastic lateral pipes of only 40mm ID. An ID of 50–60mm, however, gives a better margin of error and allows for some silting in use.

A main pipe of 100mm can cope with water from a site of 1 hectare and a 150mm pipe with water from 2 hectares. Since few landscape schemes exceed 2 hectares and gradients mostly lie in the range between 1 in 50 and 1 in 200, drainage schemes commonly involve laterals of 50–75mm diameter feeding mains of 100–150mm.

Backfill Materials and Depths

Lateral pipes can be laid trenchless by machine, or laid onto the trench bottom or bedded on gravel. Where corrugated plastic pipes are laid automatically by trenchless drainage machines there may be no facility for totally encasing the pipe in gravel. However the accuracy of the machine laying system and the lack of disturbance from digging can avoid any significant movement or settlement of the pipe. Gravel fill above the pipe is provided.

Laying pipes on a gravel bed in an open trench has many advantages:

- The gravel increases the effective diameter of the pipe.
- It allows for easy truing of the trench gradient.
- Settlement movement can be minimal if the gravel is consolidated.
- The pipe is well supported all along its length.

The main disadvantage is cost.

Gravel surrounds to pipe systems are essential where the pipe is required to collect water from mole drains or sand slits, but this can be placed automatically by trenchless drainers. Where gravel backfill is used it should be continued to within 150mm of the surface, and consolidated in 150mm layers. The final 150mm should be lightly consolidated top soil unless otherwise specified. Where pipes are laid onto the trench base direct, the trench base should be cut to a 90-degree 'V' shape to the depth of half the pipe diameter and the bottom of the 'V' rounded to support the pipe. The size of gravel used depends on the pipe system and materials; in all cases it should be free of fine particles.

CLAY PIPE
This is butt jointed and the gaps between the pipe sections must not become clogged by gravel. Use 20–30mm grade clean stone (beach gravel) with no fines to a depth of 100mm over the top of the pipe. Above this is laid 5–10mm grade clean trench gravel to 150mm from the surface; if soil contamination is likely, a 50mm layer of blinding sand can replace some of the gravel.

PLASTIC PIPE
This has no open joints and stone of only 5–10mm may be used throughout, with an option of 50mm blinding sand. This also saves trenching costs (*see* below).

GEOTEXTILES
Geotextiles are useful to prevent gravel fill from becoming contaminated by soil from below. However, they readily become contaminated by soil particles and, if used to line a trench or surround a pipe, they will prevent water from reaching the pipe and impede drainage.

MAIN PIPE
Where the main pipe simply collects and carries water from laterals (restricted inlet mains), trenches can be backfilled with soil. It is important, however, that the gradient is true and soft spots well consolidated before backfilling. For this reason gravel on concrete bed is sometimes specified for unstable soils.

Trench Sizes
Trench width should be the smallest possible to accommodate the pipe plus the backfill. Clay pipes with 20–30mm stone backfill will require 50–60mm clearance each side of the pipe to accommodate the stone.

Plastic pipe with 5–10mm stone backfill needs only 25mm clearance around the pipe. Using plastic pipe can create a considerable saving in backfill materials (as much as 15 tonnes of stone in a single trench 100m long and 750mm deep). There is also a saving in time and cost of the process of trenching and backfilling.

The actual width of the trench is dependent on the tools used. Trenching machines win out over excavators on adaptability, accuracy and speed.

It is important to ensure that sufficient room is given to allow backfill materials to properly support the sides of the pipe. If this is not done, under the weight of backfill the plastic pipe will tend to squash into a figure 8 shape.

Practical Pipe Drainage

Site Assessment
Before any drainage work is undertaken the following checks should be made.

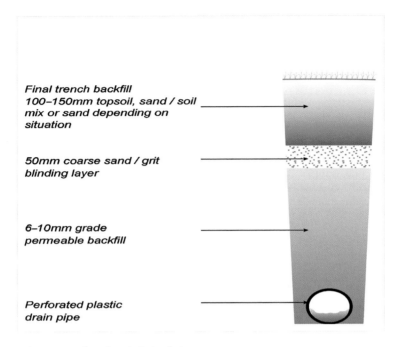

Final trench backfill
100–150mm topsoil, sand / soil mix or sand depending on situation

50mm coarse sand / grit blinding layer

6–10mm grade permeable backfill

Perforated plastic drain pipe

Figure 11   Cross section through typical pipe drain.

SOIL TYPE AND CONDITION

Drainage work involves the use of heavy equipment and a lot of soil disturbance, both of which are potentially damaging to soil structure. Damage to soil structure during installation of drainage may render the drainage scheme ineffective. Work should be confined to months when the soil is dry enough to support the excavation process.

CHECK EXISTING SLOPES

When the layout has been specified, a check should be made to ensure that the layout is feasible on site by marking the intended positions of pipes on the surface and measuring the gradient of the slopes. Determine if it is possible to follow surface gradients to achieve the intended pipe gradients without bumps and hollows rendering the pipe line:

too shallow	450–750mm
too deep	1.5m
too steep	more than 1 in 50
too flat	less than 1 in 300

UNDERGROUND HAZARDS/OBSTRUCTIONS

Researching the previous history of the site, coupled to auguring soil samples along the line of intended excavations, is essential before work commences. Old tip sites may have large stones, boulders, metal or other obstructions that require careful inspection buried near the surface. Underground cables and services pipes can be extremely hazardous in field drainage work, though they are not often found. Excessively stony ground affects the choice of machinery and cost (*see* below). Large obstructions may need to be removed before work commences, soil may be imported to bury them deeper or it might

149

entail a redesign of the system to avoid them.

Calculating Gradients

Gradients on slopes in landscape work can be measured in three ways: ratios (the most common), percentages and degrees.

RATIOS

Many people are put off by the maths involved, but in practice calculating gradients is quite simple. There are only three numbers to deal with:

- Distance from A to B (to be measured on site)
- Difference in height from A to B

Gradient Calculation Conversions		
Ratios	**Percentages**	**Degrees**
1 in 5	20.00	11.31
1 in 10	10.00	5.71
1 in 20	5.00	2.81
1 in 30	3.33	1.91
1 in 40	2.50	1.43
1 in 50	2.00	1.14
1 in 60	1.66	0.95
1 in 70	1.42	0.82
1 in 80	1.25	0.72
1 in 90	1.11	0.64
1 in 100	1.00	0.57
1 in 110	0.91	0.52
1 in 120	0.83	0.48
1 in 150	0.66	0.38
1 in 200	0.50	0.29
1 in 250	0.40	0.23
1 in 300	0.33	0.19
1 in 400	0.25	0.14

- The gradient – calculated by dividing the distance A–B by the difference in height

This may be expressed as a formula:

$$\text{Gradient} = \frac{\text{Distance}}{\text{Difference in Height}}$$

Remember that the distance and the height must be measured in the same units. It is a common error to measure the distance in metres and the difference in height in centimetres. (To convert centimetres to metres divide by 100.)

As an example, if the distance between A and B is 40m, the gradients may be calculated from the given differences in height of A and B, as shown in the table on p.151.

CALCULATING CHANGES IN LEVELS TO CREATE SPECIFIED GRADIENTS

In order to lay drainage to a specified gradient you must be able to calculate what difference in height is required between the top end and bottom end of the pipe. The formula is simple:

Difference in height required = Distance divided by the specified Gradient

$$\text{Difference in Height} = \frac{\text{Distance}}{\text{Gradient}}$$

As an example, therefore, where the distance A to B is 40m and the gradient required is 1 in 100:

Change in height from A to B	= 40 ÷ 100
	= 0.4 metres

Equipment for Measuring Gradients

The equipment traditionally used for measuring gradients comprises a spirit

Distance	Change of height	Gradient
40	0.01	1 in 40 ÷ 0.01 = 1 in 4,000
40	0.05	1 in 40 ÷ 0.05 = 1 in 800
40	0.20	1 in 40 ÷ 0.20 = 1 in 200
40	0.35	1 in 40 ÷ 0.35 = 1 in 114

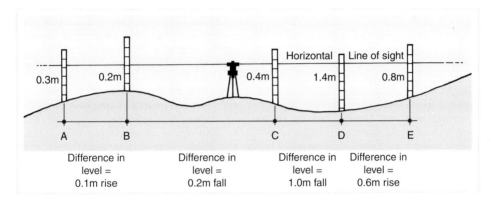

Figure 12   Levelling.

level and straight edge, boning rods and a Cowley level. These all use natural vision, which limits their scope to a maximum of about 30m. Distances involved in field drainage pipes often exceed this and systems using telescopes, such as an Auto level, or electronic methods, including lasers or an electronic distance meter (EDM), are required. Many specifications insist that lasers or an EDM should be used for measuring and creating gradients.

Principles of Measurement

The level is set up so that the telescope or laser is truly horizontal; this is set automatically in a laser level. Take a reading off a staff at A and another at B; the difference between readings is the change in level from A to B. The distance from A to B can be measured by tape, but both Auto levels and EDMs have facilities for calculating distances directly. To take many readings

simultaneously the level can be positioned at mid-point and focused on the relevant positions in turn. It is important to set up the level to a true horizontal through 360 degrees in this situation. A laser level will do this automatically.

Slope Attachments

Most levels have optional attachments that allow a gradient to be measured direct, which is a great asset for drainage, and avoids mistakes in calculation. Work stations will go one better and produce complete contour maps of a site from readings taken automatically and recorded on a portable computer. These can be recovered in the office as a plan drawn by the computer.

Equipment Used to Achieve Gradients

Much modern trenching equipment is able to install pipe automatically to the correct gradient. Where this equipment cannot be used, owing to hard digging and the need to use excavators, then two systems operate.

SIGHTING BOARDS
This is similar to the familiar system used with boning rods. Fixed boards are set up at each end of the trench and every 30–40m in between, so that when viewed from one to the other they are at the specified gradient.

$$\text{Difference in Height} = \frac{\text{Distance}}{\text{Gradient}}$$

The trench is excavated to the specified depth at the lower end of the trench and a travelling staff (or boring rod in short trenches) set up in the trench and a cross-piece fixed where sight rails indicate. This traveller is used along the line of the trench as it is excavated.

ELECTRONICALLY GUIDED TRENCHING
Pipe lasers are used to check pipe alignments and gradients, but rarely for guiding trenching operations. A more useful piece of equipment for guiding trenching operations would be an EDM, which can measure gradients directly.

Choosing and Using Trenching Machinery

Except for the shortest of drain runs and situations where machinery cannot gain access, hand-digging of trenches using sighting rails is now obsolete. Instead three types of machine are commonly used: trenchless drain layers; continuous trenchers, such as chain trenchers; and excavator diggers, including JCBs.

For reasons of cost, trenchless drainage machines will be used to lay lateral pipes and continuous trenchers for the main and outfall pipes. If accuracy is paramount, which it rarely is in landscape schemes, then continuous trenchers should be used wherever possible. Excavators should be used for sections where soil, slope or depth is difficult.

Trenchless Drainage
These machines cut a slot in the ground down to a channel. Continuous plastic drain pipe is fed into this channel as it is cut and gravel backfill is placed over the pipe as it is laid. Thus, pipe and backfill are placed in position in a single pass. Depths up to 2m and pipes up to 150mm diameter can be laid. Machines with twin hoppers can lay gravel backfill topped with blinding sand.

ADVANTAGES
* The cheapest and quickest means of laying drainage pipe.
* Automatic depth control is available.
* Causes less surface disturbance than excavating trenches.
* Little wear on the soil-cutting blade.
* Low maintenance costs.

DISADVANTAGES
* Causes considerable surface heave, which must be amended.
* Large stones deflect the depth control and cause uneven gradient.
* Smaller stones can be brought to the surface.
* With no open trench, the pipe run cannot be examined.
* In wet clay the blades smear the soil profile, inhibiting water reaching the pipe.
* Unsuitable for main pipes as there is no facility for connecting the laterals.

Continuous Trencher
These machines are also known as chain trenchers. A continuous chain like a toothed conveyor belt cuts a trench through the soil, raising the spoil either to the sides of the trench for later backfilling or onto a chute that can feed an attendant lorry if the spoil is to be taken off site. Thus topsoil is kept separate from subsoil.

Pipes up to 150mm diameter can be laid into a grove at the base of the trench as it is cut. Simultaneous backfilling is not normally carried out as the whole point is to have the pipe available for inspection and making connections.

Automatic depth control down to 2m is possible. Widths down to 50mm have become possible to facilitate sand slitting, but more commonly the minimum width is 150–200mm.

ADVANTAGES
- Less sensitive to ground conditions or obstructions.
- Pipe is available for inspection and jointing laterals, trench widths can be narrower than those possible with excavator buckets, so reducing backfill costs.
- Automatic gradient setting is possible.
- Spoil can be removed in one operation.

DISADVANTAGES
- Difficult on very stony soil.

- Causes severe wear on the cutting teeth and there are high maintenance costs.
- Loose soil tends to fall back in the trench if work is careless, causing soft and uneven pipe bedding.
- More expensive than trenchless drainage.

Excavators
These are totally uneconomic for large-scale drainage schemes and also the least accurate. There is no automatic depth control, pipe laying or backfilling. Spoil is stockpiled and has to be loaded as a separate operation if taken off site. The usual minimum trench width of 225mm is excessive for plastic pipes of 100mm diameter or less.

Excavators, however, have their uses in the following situations:

- All ditch work where a 'V' shape trench is required.
- Drains deeper than 2m.
- Work on hard or very stony soils.

Trench excavation by machine for drainage installation. (J Mallinson (Ormskirk) Ltd)

- Work on difficult, uneven or steeply sloping sites.
- Small drainage runs where an excavator is already available on site.

Since hard or stony areas are likely to be encountered in all schemes, many continuous trenchers come equipped with 'back-actors' to deal with these occasional problems. In this case the use of the excavator will be limited to ditch work, interceptor drains, deep drains and small runs.

Backfilling

In order to avoid undue settlement, it is common practice to consolidate permeable backfill in 150mm courses, particular care being taken to consolidate the fill around the pipe and up to 150mm above the pipe. Where the spoil is to be used for backfilling this is normally turned back into the trench by a plough on a blade grader mounted on a tractor. Care should be taken, however, not to disturb the pipes by crude backfilling methods. Some specifications will not allow tipping or machine backfilling until the pipe is covered by 150–300mm of fill. Again, consolidation in layers is normal practice, care being taken with the fill adjacent to the pipes not to disturb them unduly. Where topsoil forms the final layer of backfill, this should be consolidated but not compacted, and left level with the surrounding surface. Small amounts of excess soil can usually be dispersed locally over the surface.

Materials Inspection and Storage

Clay pipes: These are prone to cracks and distortion. Any such pipes should be rejected at the expense of the subcontractor or supplier. Pipes with badly cut ends, causing poor jointing, should also be rejected. Special pipe-cutting tools should be used. Tiles must be kept covered and dry to avoid frost damage.

Rigid polythene pipe (uPVC): More commonly used in domestic hard landscaping schemes, this material is flexible and may warp if exposed to strong sunlight.

Stocks should be kept protected from sunlight, and stacked no more than six high on timbers at 1.5m centres. Joint flanges should protrude from the stack to avoid bending stresses.

Corrugated plastic pipes: This is delivered in rolls that can be stacked on their sides to a convenient height. Rolls should be protected from sunlight as a matter of good practice; this is essential where storage will exceed twelve months.

Permeable fill materials: These are specified to size grades and contain no fines. Beach gravel has a rounded profile to aid drainage; angular stone should not be substituted. Visual inspection should be made to confirm grade and shape. All these materials must be stored covered and on hard standing, so that no contamination with soil occurs during storage on loading.

Specialized Systems for Sports Turf Drainage

The key aim of sports turf drainage is to transmit rainfall rapidly to the subsoil. This is achieved by one or a combination of two methods. The first method is a system of close-spaced vertical drainage channels filled with permeable material installed to transmit water to a pipe drainage system, thus bypassing the bulk soil. The second method is a rootzone, in which the particle size distribution guarantees adequate percolation overlying a permeable subsoil or permeable fill linked to a pipe drainage system.

Sand Slit (Bypass) Systems

The objective of sand slit systems is to provide a bypass system for water from the surface to the under-drainage. For satisfactory results the system must be correctly designed and maintained. Many different systems have been used, although the basic principles are the same. They range from a do-it-yourself system using a trenching machine to techniques used by contractors

Critical Processes to be Inspected: a Supervisor's Checklist

The following list provides a checklist to aid to supervision of the installation of a field drainage system.

1. Soil conditions permit operations to commence. Layout and pipe positions conform to specification.
2. Ditch conforms to specification for:
   Bottom width
   Batter
   Gradient
3. Outfall conforms to specification:
   Headwall
   Splash plate
   Pipe material
   Vermin trap
4. Silt trap conforms to specification.
5. Open trenches conform to specification for:
   Position
   Spacing
   Length
   Width
   Depth
   Gradient
6. Open trenches show good workmanship:
   Cut by appropriate machine
   Absence of loose fill in base
   Arisings piled 600mm from edge of trench
   Large stones removed from arisings
   Top soil for backfill separated from subsoil if required
7. Trenchless drains show good workmanship:
   Heaved soil free of stone and other debris on the surface
   No observed problems during laying or all problems reported and dealt with
8. Pipe materials inspected for quality:
   Correct dimensions
   Correct materials
   No distortion
   No cracks
   No damaged ends
9. Pipes inspected for workmanship:
   Correct gradient
   Even gradient along drain run
   No kinks or displacement (NB clay tiles)
10. Joints inspected for workmanship:
    Corrugated plastic uses manufactured not hand-cut joints
    Rigid pipe is correctly seated at joints
    Angle of joint from lateral to main is correct
    Water observed to flow in pipes
11. Backfill material conforms to specification:
    Correct materials – beach gravel, lytag etc.
    Correct size grade
    Uncontaminated with soil
    Correctly stored
12. Backfilling shows good workmanship:
    Well consolidated around pipe
    Replaced in layers and consolidated at every 150mm depth
    Fill not crudely tipped directly onto pipe, proper equipment used
    Permeable fill finishes at correct height above pipe; especially important where moling or sand slitting will follow
    Topsoil lightly consolidated to finish flush with surface
13. Secondary systems inspected
    Soil conditions suitable for subsoiling or moling
    Moling as a specified
    depth
    diameter
    gradient
    spacing
    Sand Slit as specified
    depth
    width
    spacing
    backfill materials
14. Surface finish acceptable
    Soil heave from trenchless installation cultivated and reduced if necessary
    Arisings from operations removed from site
    Steps taken to re-establish vegetation over disturbed ground if appropriate
    All excess materials and machinery removed from site.

either in constructing new grounds or modifying existing drainage systems. The term 'slitting' indicates that soil is removed, while 'injection' is applied to systems where no soil is removed.

The following example is a design similar to many installed at various football grounds. The system, designed to cope with rainfall of 5cm per day, can be split into three stages:

1 Coarse slits, 5m apart, 7.5cm wide and 60cm deep, running from touchline to touchline, backfilled with 25cm gravel and 35cm coarse sand.
2 Fine slits at right angles to the coarse slits, 30cm apart, 2.5cm wide, 30cm deep, filled with medium sand to the surface.
3 Topdressing of whole pitch with fine sand.

MAIN DESIGN POINTS AND INSTALLATION TECHNIQUES

The following considerations must be observed in all sand slit systems.

• Fine gravel in coarse slits must link to the backfill over the drains. In this design 2 × 90mm pipes, 15m in from each touchline, would be sufficient to remove the water.
• Fine slits must link to the coarse slits and the fill material must be graded so as not to seep away.
• Fine slits must remain open to the surface. This is achieved by top dressing with fine sand (also acts as a wick to aid water movement into the slits).
• The slit dimensions and materials must be carefully chosen so that the required design rate is achieved (this is possible using Hooghoudt's Equation).

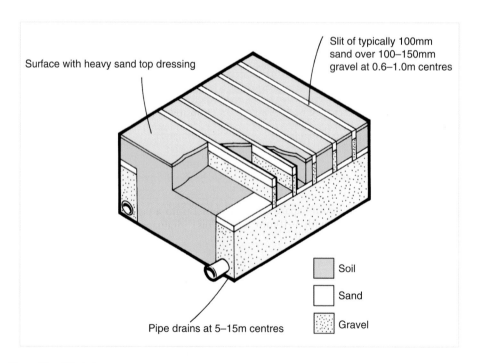

Figure 13 *Slit drainage system.*

When considering the improvement of a sports area by sand slitting, there are usually two alternative methods to be considered, depending on whether or not there is an existing drainage system.

Using an Existing Drainage System

If you are improving an existing drainage system the following points must be considered:

Are the existing drains still working? If they are, then OK; if not, can they be cleared?

Is the existing backfill adequate? Is there enough backfill to enable you to connect up the slits to it? Is it the correct size or will you have to blind it before putting in the slits?

If any of the above are doubtful, will the cost of cleaning and digging be greater than that of ignoring what is there and installing a completely new system?

With a conventional herringbone system, will the slits be connected with the drains at right angles (two runs) or will they be left to connect up at an angle?

Installing a Complete New System

There are a number of possible ways of installing a system. Exactly which you choose will depend on many factors. Depending on whether or not the top soil has been removed, two possible ways are described here.

TOPSOIL REMOVED FROM SITE
* Install main drains 30m apart in straight lines and backfill with 3–10mm gravel.
* Install subsurface, using very coarse sand (1–2mm) and slits 100mm wide and spaced 3–5m apart, making sure that they connect with the backfill of the drains.
* Replace topsoil and establish the sward.
* Once the sward has established, inject the thin surface slits, using medium/fine sand, to the surface (30cm between slits).
* Topdress the surface before use with 75 tonnes/ha of medium-fine sand and top up each following year with 25 tonnes/ha.

TOPSOIL LEFT ON SITE
* Install main drains 15m in from each touchline, backfill with 3–10mm gravel to within 150mm of surface, blind with coarse sand and fill to the surface with medium/fine sand.
* Establish the sward.
* Install 100mm wide slits (medium/fine sand over coarse/medium sand) to connect with the backfill of the drains.
* If slits are installed every 30cm, then complete the system by top dressing with 75 tonnes/ha of medium/fine sand prior to play and 25 tonnes/ha every subsequent year, or
* Install the slits every 1–2m, then install sand grooves at right angles to the sand slits.

Maintenance Problems and Techniques of Bypass Systems

Bypass, or sand slit, systems are usually installed when the top soil is unable to transmit water downwards at an adequate rate. The inadequate drainage rate is frequently caused by the soil becoming destructured during intensive use in the winter months. The sand slit system provides a means of removing the excess water from the surface through channels into a piped drainage system.

This drainage technique is often regarded as an 'engineering solution to a biological problem', the reason being that soil structure is often forgotten or ignored once a slit system has been installed. Soil aggregates are formed and stabilized both by physical and biological means. The actions of worms, growing roots and micro-organisms are intricately involved in aggregate formation and stability in addition to the natural weathering cycle and the groundsman's activities. Slit systems can remove surface water, but are they curing the basic problem of the soil not being suitable or in the right condition? Remember that the soil between the slits represents a high proportion of the playing surface and is of utmost importance in sward establishment and development. Indeed, the soil is expected to support a healthy sward tolerant to wear. Certain problems have arisen on slit areas but it is not easy to identify individual problems as a cause of an effect. The following is an attempt to rationalize the problems and suggest techniques to alleviate their effect.

SOIL COMPACTION

Compaction, already mentioned as a reason for installing slit systems, is usually alleviated by contractors prior to sward establishment. The soil between the slits, although being firm, should have a reasonable structure. It should allow root and water penetration, although excess water will be channelled down the slits.

During the playing season compaction of the soil will occur due to either, or both, of the following causes:

- Physical disintegration of the aggregates.
- Water slaking of the aggregates.

Compaction will occur easily because the structural stability of the soil will be very low. Remember, it has been destructured and lying wet for a long period, and has only recently been restructured. It will break down into a single grain state very readily, as can be illustrated by measuring its dispersion coefficient. Its stability will be more like a subsoil containing low levels of organic matter.

Even if the sand topdressing protects the aggregates from physical damage by boots, it is very unlikely they will be water stable. The resulting effect will probably be:

- Rapid wear of the sward and a slow recovery rate.
- Wet patches and much developing between the slits, with eventual 'capping' of the slits.
- Increase in the proportion of annual meadow grass in the sward, which in this situation will be shallow rooted.

CAPPING OF THE SLIT SYSTEM

'Capping' of the slit system is a common, yet very serious, problem because the water infiltration rate will be reduced to almost zero. A combination of factors is involved:

Development of wet patches and mud during play: As described above.

Worm activity: Soil brought to the surface on worm casts will nullify the effect of the sand topdressing and lead to 'capping'. Worms commonly bring 2–3mm of soil to the surface each year.

Dry summers: Soil shrinks and cracks as it dries during the summer. This tends to deepen the slits and causes the sand level to drop. When the soil is wetted it swells and closes over the top of the slits. The heavier soils are particularly prone to this phenomenon. Another side effect of cracking is the production of a 'corrugated' playing surface.

Silt: Silt appears on the surface, especially in the lower spots. Some of the silt will be from the underlying soil but a certain proportion will be brought in from surrounding areas by the wind.

TEXTURAL BREAK

This occurs due to the pore sizes in the sand and in the underlying soil being different. It has a direct effect on water relationships between the two layers and therefore an indirect effect on rooting characteristics. If a capillary break occurs between the sand topdressing and the underlying soil, a 'suspended water table' will be produced. This is the principle on which some 'all-sand' and 'sand/soil mix' constructions are based. The surface layer of sand will transmit water, but only when it has filled completely with water. This occurrence will lead to rooting problems especially if the underlying soil is 'firm'. The summer rain, or irrigation water, will moisten the sand topdressing and stimulate surface rooting. There will be a definite tendency for the roots to grow into the sand topdressing and into the slits.

The effects expected would be:

- Rapid wear
- Reduction in efficiency of slit system
- Lack of root binding in the underlying soil

The damage could be localized or widespread over the pitch. The main objective would be to prevent the development of wet patches, which are the precursor for wear and mud formation. It is therefore critical to prevent 'ponding' between the slits by allowing the water to flow adequately across the surface. Careful replacement of divots and application of sand topdressings are essential at this stage. The degree of wear is governed by many factors. For example, local climatic conditions and intensity of use are two key factors. (Play during frosty periods is often responsible for a high degree of wear.) But let us assume that as the season progresses the sward will wear and the soil will become more compact. As spring approaches the sward will begin to recover but unfortunately this will be accompanied by the invasion of annual meadow grass. In this situation the annual meadow grass produces a poor quality sward, very intolerant to wear during the following season.

End of Season Maintenance

It is likely that the groundsman will be faced with a compacted soil supporting a shallow-rooted, annual meadow grass-dominated sward. His objective should be to repair the season's damage and establish a healthy sward prior to the next playing season. The time available in many situations is limited. The main objective should

be to restructure or 'open up' the compacted soil to stimulate the development of a deep rooting sward. Root and worm action can stabilize aggregates and a sand topdressing can protect the aggregates from physical damage. The following scheme could be followed:

Repair the deep divots: Should these be filled with the sand topdressing or a suitable sand/soil mix? Remember that, to be removed, the excess water must flow across the surface into the slits.

Restructure the soil

- Surface cultivation by discs or rotovator. This technique will lead directly to surface capping and severe problems the following season unless sufficient amounts of the correct sand are mixed with the cultivated soil.
- Cultivators by specialized machinery: the Verti-Drain could be used, for example, depending on soil type and degree of compaction.
- Spiking or slitting. As the soil begins to dry, spiking should be fairly effective in aerating the soil. It will also produce weakness planes in the soil, which should lead to more cracking as moisture is lost by evaporation/transpiration. It is doubtful whether spiking alone is sufficient to restructure the soil effectively.

A combination of the above operations, in conjunction with sand topdressings, can usually produce a topsoil capable of supporting a healthy sward.

Sand topdressing: Some sand will already have been applied during the playing season. It may be necessary, and probably worthwhile, to apply more sand during the renovation work or later during the summer. The reasons for applying it would include:

- 'True' the surface.
- Counteract worm activity.

- Replace the sand mixed into the soil during play.
- 'Loss' of sand as slits shrink during drought.

Half the sand could be applied prior to contravating the seed and the rest applied later in the summer along 'crack lines'. A total depth of 10–15mm would appear to be reasonable.

Soil structure problems will still pose problems to the groundsman after installation of a slit scheme. The establishment and maintenance of a healthy sward able to withstand intensive wear and possess a quick recovery rate is the major problem. Soil biology will be a key factor in his success or failure.

Sand/Soil Systems

Suspended Water
Table Constructions

The main construction type for sports field developments constructed to the highest standard is the suspended water table construction. The objective is to provide a free draining construction that will allow play all year in various conditions. A gravel raft is used to create a capillary break, thus forming a suspended water table. Although this system usually has an 8–10 per cent silt/clay element in the rootzone, it is possible to replace this with peat, thereby having a sand/peat (rather than sand/soil) mix. A perched water table can be formed when an impenetrable layer under a sandy layer stops drainage. You can also have a perched water table with coarse sand over a layer of fine sand. The pore water is stopped from draining by surface tension set up between the fine-to-coarse layers. The coarse sand may not act as a drain. The behaviour is dependent on the ratio between the pore sizes of the two soil layers. By having the impenetrable barrier of clay at the bottom of the construction, the perched water table forms and no more water moves to the drain once gravitational pressures from surface water cease. Capillary action now takes over and, because of cohesion and

adhesion, this action brings water up into the rootzone. From this it can be seen that in drier weather the rootzone will retain a certain level of moisture for the plants and so reduce the need for irrigation.

Sand-Based Constructions

Sand-based constructions are expensive to maintain and their management, and performance, can be sporadic. In general these systems are no longer installed but one may come across them in some established pitches.

Permanently elevated water table or enclosed systems: In these constructions water is retained in the rootzone by a plastic lining that separates the construction from the surrounding soil and again creates a suspended water table. Examples of this type of construction include:

- The 'Cell System' by Chipman
- The Purr-Wick (Plastic Under Root zone Reservoir with Wick action)
- The PAT (Prescription Athletic Turf System)

They utilize the principle of a permanently elevated or adjustable water table in contrast to the suspended water table concept. As the drainage pipes are laid over the plastic lining, it is possible to sub-irrigate the construction through them. Water is readily transported upwards through the sand by capillary action. Peat may also be incorporated into the surface during seedling establishment to retain moisture and prevent localized drought at this critical stage. Construction depths of sealed systems are normally in the range of 40–50cm with a uniform rootzone material comprising mainly medium/fine sand. Purr-Wick constructions require the installation of an overhead irrigation system, whereas a Cell System incorporates a method of sub-irrigation. These systems did not survive for too long. They were very expensive to install, difficult to maintain and disease in the form of black layer

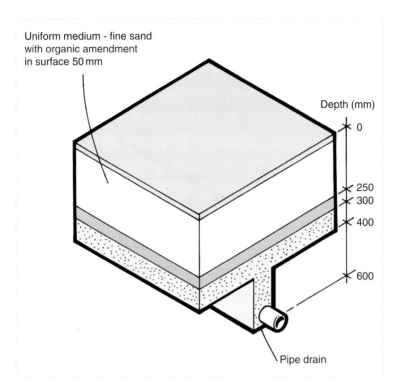

Uniform medium - fine sand
with organic amendment
in surface 50 mm

Depth (mm)

0

250
300
400

600

Pipe drain

Figure 14   Suspended water table.

was a major problem with this type of construction. As the drainage system was installed within the cell and they had a pure sand construction, blockages in the drainage system were not unknown and both irrigation and drainage became difficult to control.

Sand Carpet Construction: This type of construction is composed of a drainage system covered by a 100–150mm layer of medium/fine sand. Sand carpet constructions can be used to great effect in the construction of sports fields where the costs of suspended water table or sealed systems are prohibitive. It is possible to build up a similar construction by repeated topdressings over a number of years on existing sand and slit drainage system. The sand carpet provides a free-draining, non-compacting surface. However, the grassroots should be

encouraged to grow into the soil base, thus preventing a root break at the soil/sand interface. The big disadvantage of this system is the movement of the sand in dry conditions and it is necessary to install an irrigation system to make the system work. If the issue of saving money is of prime consideration in the construction, you will almost certainly not have the finances to install the irrigation that is needed.

NATURAL SOIL CONSTRUCTIONS

In the early days pitches were constructed of the only material that was available to the builders: soil. They realized that they needed a soil with a silt and clay content because it was possible to retain moisture and nutrients in the rootzone with those materials. Football pitches are still constructed out of soil, especially in local authority situations, because it is the

161

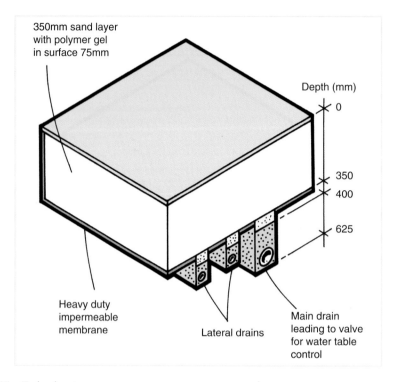

Figure 15   Enclosed system.

cheapest way to build them. The problem with this type of construction is that, if the weather is very wet, a lot of matches end up being cancelled because of the muddy conditions. To overcome this, a system of intense slit drainage can be used to improve surface water removal, as has already been explained. Soil structure for football pitches can also be improved by the addition of amendments, the most common being sand. Before attempting sand amelioration on a football pitch, a great deal of time should be given to comparisons between a rootzone mix and amelioration of an amendment.

SOIL AMELIORATION

Soil amelioration is commonly conducted in order to improve surface drainage. In winter sports pitches such amelioration is often essential in order to facilitate a suitable playing surface. It is, however, useful for any surfaces that are liable to be played upon in the winter or other situations where improved drainage is necessary.

Soil pores less than 0.4mm do not drain well, because of surface tension forces. The particles that constitute these pores are less than 0.1mm in diameter. One should aim, therefore, to have more than 75 per cent of the particles within the range of 0.1mm to 0.5mm to avoid interpacking. For amelioration purposes, this corresponds to medium/fine sand (particle size range 0.125–0.5mm). Soil amelioration will only be successful where the underlying subsoil is sufficiently permeable to allow rapid drainage from the sand/soil mix through to the drains.

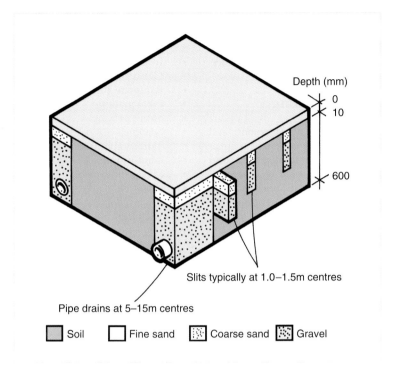

Figure 16   Sand carpet.

Amelioration is best achieved during the construction stage when all the ingredients can be mixed thoroughly to achieve a suitable rootzone material. It is advisable that all materials undergo laboratory analysis for hydraulic conductivity and particle size range before they are used for a rootzone material.

The equation used for soil amelioration is:

$$X = \frac{100\ (D\ P)}{Y\ D}$$

X   amount of sand needed to improve 1cm of soil over 1 hectare (given in tonnes/hectare).

D   desired percentage of medium/fine sand in mix (75 per cent for winter sports pitches).

P   percentage of medium/fine sand now present in the soil.

Y   percentage of medium/fine sand to be used.

NB Allow for 25 per cent settlement.

Amelioration can be carried out over a period of time by removing a limited amount of the existing topsoil and replacing it with suitable sand. This is most commonly achieved by hollow coring, followed by application of sand topdressing.

It should also be noted that soils can be ameliorated with other materials in order to improve nutrient and moisture retention. This is most commonly achieved by using the following methods:

• Organic materials, such as peat, slurry or seaweed conditioners

- Mineral-based materials, such as calcined clay, vermiculite or perlite
- Set forming polymer materials, such as polyvinyl alcohols and polyacrylamides

Construction Planning

For effective project management and resource utilization it is necessary to plan the works to be executed if a successful outcome is to be achieved and desired standards achieved. There is much work to be conducted prior to actual commencement of physical works on site by both employer or representative and also the appointed contractor. For a start the employing agent will need to collect all relevant information relating to the contract. This should include:

- Plan and detailed drawings
- Planting plans
- Material and construction specifications
- Site reports (site analysis if available)
- Bills of quantities
- Client brief and consultation
- Information from the site visit
- Environmental impact assessment

The type of information available will depend on the size and nature of the work to be undertaken, but it is essential that before works start one has a clear understanding of what is required. Component parts of a sports field construction project and a contract may include the following:

- Construction planning: architect choice, design
- Plan acceptance: design chosen, contracts drawn
- Materials sourced
- Survey and staking
- Weed control
- Site clearance/grubbing
- Selective thinning of trees
- Topsoil removal
- Main drain installation

- Grade, sub-grade and landscape features
- Earthmoving/shaping
- Install features, irrigation and drainage
- Construct playing surfaces bases
- Reinstate topsoil
- Final grading
- Stone picking
- Seeding
- Turf establishment
- Landscaping
- Final assessment
- Open for play

After determining the extent of all works it will be necessary to write Contract Documentation for tendering and ultimately contractor and works management. Specific advice on procurement and contract management is given in Chapter 2 above, but following provides notes more pertinent to constructions works.

Specifications: Include a description of the work in detail, the character and quality of materials, and special responsibilities. The specification of works is often provided by the consultant. There is no such thing as a standard specification. Each site is different and each specification will be different. A specification of works is a very detailed description of the methods of construction, the materials to be used and the standards of workmanship to be achieved; all of that, together with the drawings and the bills of quantities, will form the contract and tender documents. There should be precise details of the materials to be used, and only materials that have been approved by the architect or his consultant should be employed in the construction. This would involve testing materials as the contractor forwards samples for approval. Approved samples should be kept on site once the project starts, and they should be compared with materials actually arriving on site so that they are seen to match up properly. The standards of workmanship should be

Summary of Major Sports Turf Drainage Systems

System	Major uses	Benefits	Disadvantages
Slit Drainage	Winter sports pitches Horse racing tracks	Economical use of drainage materials More rapid return to use Useful method to improve existing pipe drainage Retained soil in system acts as nutrient/water buffer	Slits can open (backfill sinks) on heavy soils Uneven surface with wetting/drying cycle Capping of slits with adjacent soil Difficulty of establishing grass on sand (seed) Slit lines prone to erosion with loss of cover Areas between slits more prone to compaction
Sand/Soil Systems	Bowling greens High quality football pitches	Entire surface can remove water (theoretically) More stable/firmer surface Soil component affords nutrient/water retention Surface trueness is not disrupted	More expensive (than slits) Requires complete turf re-establishment Decreased water/nutrient retention (Can achieve greater retention if rootzone overlies soil and not drainage raft) Danger of material segregation
All Sand Constructions	Very high quality sports pitches Arid climates	Firm surfaces Rapid drainage Exceptional wear tolerance/playing quality	Generally cost prohibitive Water management difficult Irrigation essential Nutrient management difficult Inert rootzone (no microbial activity) Unstable with loss of cover Not suitable for sloping conditions (erosion) Dry patch

accurately described in the specification of work.

Bills of Quantities: Lists items providing quantities and brief descriptions of the work. It is used during the tender evaluation to compare tenders submitted by the contractors and also during construction to assess work completed to date. With accurate scale drawings and a detailed specification of work, it is possible to item-ize, in terms of volume, area or number, all the constructional operations for which the contractor submits prices. Accurate bills of quantity are essential to get as realistic and genuine a contract price as possible. Detailed and accurate bills of quantity will also allow proper payment for work done, and fair costing of any variation of the works during the construction (important information for the client, the architect and

View of developing rootzone profile, here showing heating cables in a football pitch. (J Mallinson (Ormskirk) Ltd)

the contractor). Every single item in terms of materials and working practices is clearly measured and listed, together with a rate given by the contractor and an ultimate cost for that operation.

Drawings: The architect will have started out by having a comprehensive site survey carried out, often recorded on a 1:2,500 scale plan, perhaps showing contours on that survey at 1m intervals. Important site features should be recorded on the plan and the architect will eventually produce his layout on the plan. This plan is an essential drawing and forms part of the contract documentation. The next set of drawings should be individual drawings (such as specific sports surfaces), often drawn on a different scale, probably 1:200, showing existing and proposed levels. These particular detailed drawings are essential. There may well be sectional drawings where appropriate, for example when there are major changes in levels or if large volumes of soil have to be moved. Plans for tree planting may be

drawn that can be put onto the original layout plan (the 1:2,500 scale plan). All of these drawings should be accurate, to scale and detailed. As they are working drawings, they should also be simple to understand.

Resource Planning

Pre-construction planning should involve an assessment of the activities and resources that must be arranged prior to initiating actual construction. Resource planning involves three primary areas:

- Manpower
- Materials
- Equipment

The contractor and employer should carefully examine the architect's plans and specifications to determine the exact activities to be performed and assess the resources required to accomplish these tasks. The main contractor must decide which activities will be accomplished within the organization and which activities are to be subcontracted. Similarly, for materials acquisition, it must be decided what materials, if any, are to be purchased by the main contractor and which must be furnished by the subcontractors involved. Any of the survey-staking, clearing, rough grading, irrigation system installation, drainage system development and final seeding phases may be accomplished under separate subcontracts. The main contractor must usually specify the materials, equipment, construction permits and inspections to be secured by a subcontractor. This process, or resource planning, aids the contractor in pre-determining activities and resources that are essential for efficient implementation of each construction operation contributing to the overall project. Contractors may draw up a resource flow plan, which is basically similar to a construction flow plan. The resource flow plan is closely interdeveloped with the construction flow plan. It should indicate what equipment and materials are to be available on specified workdays on the critical path. Due consideration must be given to the lead times required for ordering, manufacture and delivery of specific items.

Sourcing Materials

In constructing sports pitches, one of the most important aspects to achieving a very high quality product is to select the correct products. Obviously the products that are selected to complete the project are dependent on other factors, such as cost of the materials, availability of materials and budgetary restraints. The costs of materials vary considerably depending on the size of the project, where materials are sourced and where the quarries are located (transport costs).When you have to choose a gravel for construction or drainage purposes the nominal size is usually in the range 4–9mm and for sports turf use there is not normally a need to go larger. To go larger

is to invite problems of infiltration by soil or sand above the gravel, which leads to the need for blinding layers. Gravels of the size 4–9mm are used for the following purposes:

- As a drainage bed beneath a specially constructed topsoil
- As a backfill over perforated plastic drainage pipes
- As the fill in a pipeless drainage channel
- As the gravel layer in two-part sand/gravel slits

STONE TYPE

Gravel must be very carefully selected when deciding to do any drainage or construction work. There are several types of stone sold for use in drainage: crushed limestone, crushed granite and river rock or gravel (mainly quartz). Granite and quartz gravel are best as they are stronger and less likely to be crushed. Softer gravels such as limestone may break down over time due to the weight of overlying soils and to chemical reaction with acidic water. Gravel that is suspected of being soft should be tested by a laboratory.

SANDS

Sand for construction purposes depends on three factors:

- Average particle size
- Uniformity of particles
- Correct mixing of sand with amendments

All sands are not created equal. Uniform sands are better for constructing sports pitches and less uniform are better for making things like concrete. Sands that are uniform are characterized as having the most individual particles of a similar size. This is termed narrow particle-size distribution. This narrow particle-size distribution is very important because like-sized particles do not interpack and result in good stable porosity in the soil. In contrast, non-uniform sand

	Very fine sand (0.050–0.125mm)	Fine sand (0.125–0.250mm)	Medium sand (0.25–0.50mm)	Coarse sand (0.50–1.00mm)	Very coarse sand (1.0–2.0mm)
All sand constructions for winter games		�©	▓		
Amelioration for winter pitches		▓	▓		
Soil amelioration for fine turf		▓	▓	▓	
Slit drains			▓	▓	▓
Blinding layers			▓	▓	▓

particles range between very coarse to very fine in size. This range of sizes can lead to interpacking. The accompanying table illustrates a range of sands, their particle sizes and suitability for different applications.

Gravel Choices

The choice of filter material to surround a drainage pipe should be made on the basis of the type of soil or sand that will cover and surround it and the situation and construction type.

The following must not be used for drainage:

- Soft limestone
- Soft sandstone
- Shells
- Any material that will breakdown during weathering

Selecting the Correct Material

For any construction work the only way to determine the correct materials is to have them analysed by a laboratory. The accompanying gives a comparison of two analyses

for two drainage materials – good and poor! The important factor to remember is that materials should be tested and compared to the specification determined for that specific project.

Workmanship

After all the careful selection of materials it would be very foolish to go ahead with any project without having the skilled staff to do the job. In any major project these days there will be a clause in the contract about using only qualified staff. This is very important because if you use staff without the knowledge to use the materials selected you will find that the project can fail (probably not immediately but shortly into its use) and the remedial costs will be very expensive for the want of picking a skilled workforce.

Rootzone

The only other material that is going to be required for the sports turf area is the rootzone. This is the area above the gravel drainage layer and is very important as this

168

Category	Diameter (mm)	High drainage rate material (% retained)	Poor drainage material (% retained)
Stones	>8.00	0.0	0.0
Coarse gravel	8.00–4.00	0.0	0.0
Fine gravel	4.00–2.00	0.0	1.5
Very coarse sand	2.00–1.00	0.0	6.0
Coarse sand	1.00–0.50	4.2	16.5
Medium sand	0.50–0.25	66.0	31.0
Fine sand	0.25–0.125	27.5	26.0
Very fine sand	0.125–0.063	1.8	12.5
Silt/clay	<0.063	0.5	6.5

has to support the sward and retain water and nutrients to a pre-determined level. The rootzone will vary from construction to construction. Sand-based rootzones will be sand and an organic matter mixed together to give the most satisfactory growing medium. The one thing to remember if you require rootzone material is to have it mixed off-site at the suppliers. This makes for much more accurate mixing and also prevents contamination of the mixture.

Construction Management

Good construction of sports turf surfaces comes about with very careful planning and management. Attention to detail, and having a team who understand the technicalities of construction, can make or break a project. Everyone involved in a major project has a big part to play in making it work. Without communication between all the managers, a project could so easily fall apart. The key personnel and their roles are as follows:

Contract Manager
This could be either the architect or consultant, depending on the size of the project and their qualifications. The contract manager represents the client's interests and ensures the day to day running and organization of the project. They must be fully conversant with the details of the specification and able to interpret the specification in a sensible and straightforward manner. The contract manager will be named in the specification and deals with the contractor/representatives at all levels. The administration duties completed by the contract manager include:

- Regular assessment of progress
- Authorization of interim payments
- Keeping of records
- Issuing supplementary instructions
- Issuing variation orders as and when (if) required
- Involvement in communication with all interested parties
- Complaints/requests etc.

Architect/Consultant
The architect can also be the consultant, depending on his qualifications and experience. The role of the architect is to design whatever you are going to construct and make sure that the site is suitable for the project.

He will also be responsible for the following:

- Site assessment
- Environmental impact assessments
- Legal restrictions, such as public rights of way
- Anything of archaeological significance on the site
- Engineering qualities (soil moving, subsoil and so on)
- Sporting and safety implications
- Economic feasibility of the project

These responsibilities could also come under the consultant's brief (if one was employed). The architect and consultant would also be responsible for any agronomic issues that need to be taken into account. Good architects and consultants also work very closely with the appointed Head Grounds Person or Manager, as it will be the Grounds Manager that has responsibilities for maintenance after the construction period. It also gives them the knowledge about the construction system upon which to base their ongoing maintenance plan.

Site Supervisor (Clerk of Works or Supervising Officer's Representative)

The Site Supervisor/Clerk of Works/ Supervising Officer's Representative may variously be termed a Contract Inspector, Supervising Foreman or some such similar title. The supervisor's responsibilities will be to liaise between the contract manager/ supervising officer and the contractor's on-site foreman, and by his daily presence on the contract site to provide a direct front-line link between contractor and client. The supervisor will be authorized by the contract manager to act on his or her behalf with regard to the day-to-day supervision of the contract and thus be able to relieve the contract manager of a great deal of minor but nevertheless important detail. The supervisor's duties will be many and varied. To carry them out effectively he or she will need to be aware of the contrac-

tor's working programme. He or she may well liaise with the contractor's foreman from time to time in drawing up a programme of site work for the weeks ahead. At the very least, the supervisor needs to know when the contractor will be on site and the nature of the work he or she will be doing in order to utilize his or her own time to maximum advantage. The supervisor will constantly check that the contractor is keeping up with the programme so far as weather and site conditions allow. Some of the construction operations will require to be performed at particular times of the year, or at stated frequencies, and it is important that these times are adhered to.

The standard of work will be under continuous surveillance and must never be allowed to fall below that required by the Specification. The first few weeks of a new contract are vital in this respect, as it is then that the supervisor will establish the standards required and ensure that the contractor appreciates what is acceptable and what is not. If inferior work is allowed to be performed in the early stages, without demur on the part of the supervisor, it is very difficult to correct this at a later time. Any short comings in this respect should be brought to the attention of the contractor without delay. The supervisor, with his or her superior knowledge of the contract site, should ensure that no part of the site is being abused or any part of the Specification being overlooked. It sometimes happens that odd areas tend to get neglected or mistreated, particularly if the contractor is unfamiliar with the contract site.

Another important aspect of the work is the maintenance of safe working practices and compliance with the Health and Safety Regulations. The Specification will have something to say about this and the supervisor must ensure that the contractor is aware of its requirements and is complying with them. This is particularly important where machinery is involved or when pesticides are being used. The Pesticide Regulations require that Certificates of

Competence be held by persons using herbicides and other chemicals and an important part of the supervisor's job will be to check that certificate holders are present and in a position to supervise that operation is in accordance with the requirements of the Regulations. The supervisor should also ensure that appropriate records are kept by the contractor of all the pesticide operations, and that copies are regularly transmitted to the contract manager. The supervisor will no doubt be required to make regular reports to the contract manager and certainly all disputes and differences of opinion should be reported without delay so that the contract manager may be kept fully informed of the current situation. With regard to the regular checking of the progress of the works, some form of simple checklist might be found useful. This form of regular progress report will serve as an early warning system for the contract manager, enabling him or her to decide when their personal intervention is required, as well as providing a written record of the progress of the contract works. It will be clear from the foregoing that the Site Supervisor/Clerk of Works will have much with which to occupy his or her time on site. A supervisor's workload is difficult to establish and will vary according to a number of factors. Principal among these is the nature of the contract itself. Clearly some contracts will be more demanding than others in this respect.

Maintenance of Drainage Systems

Regular maintenance of ditches and land drains is essential in order to sustain suitable conditions for plant growth and, in the case of sports turf, a surface that is playable. Ditches become gradually blocked by silt and debris that collects in the ditch and impedes the water flow. Ditches are also prone to vegetation overgrowth and collection of litter and other extraneous materials. The bottom of the ditch begins to 'silt up' as material that would normally be carried away settles on the bottom and builds up, eventually raising the ditch bottom until the drain pipes emptying into the ditch are themselves underwater. They in turn will silt up and cease to work effectively.

Surface Indications of Poor Drainage or Drainage Failure

One of the most important aspects of managing a drainage system is being able to detect early indications of system failure or evaluating ground conditions that may exhibit a need for a system to be installed. As part of routine maintenance, the person responsible for an area of grassland or turf needs to inspect the areas that may require preventative or renovation works on the system in place. Many of these indicators become more apparent during times of wet weather, especially during the winter, but this should not preclude inspections at other times of the year. These surface indicators will often mean further investigations are necessary, requiring excavations and possible installation of new sections for the drainage system.

Areas displaying such indications should be marked as appropriate so that they can be later investigated more fully in drier conditions. Excavations will be easier, for instance, when any surface water has eventually disappeared.

A field inspection may provide indications of poor drainage and its effects, such as:

- Surface ponding or standing water. This is a very obvious indication of poor drainage. It may only be due to surface compaction, but this is not necessarily so and will need further investigation.
- Boggy conditions occur in the main if a problem with surface water is not rectified and water lies in place for some time.

- Water emerging at surface, a sure sign of blocked drains and also of spring water in the area.
- High water levels in ditches.
- Rutting or surface caused by machinery and vehicles.
- Damage (such as divots) readily caused by players, especially on winter sports where areas are wet or 'cut up' badly.
- Poor or surface rooting of grasses.
- Foliage colour is often yellow or pale, but certainly discoloured.
- Greater incidence and depth of thatch build-up is primarily due to less bacterial breakdown in the soil.
- Surface vegetation, with water-loving plants present within the sward.

Plants as Indicators of Drainage Condition

Wild plants can very often be useful indicators of soil moisture status and its drainage condition. In some areas they may be the first sign of a problem that, if not rectified, will surely become more severe. Some plant communities can, at a glance, indicate ground and soil conditions to an experienced investigator long before a more detailed site survey is carried out. Some plants are truly aquatic, others range through bog, marsh and fen to land of only moderate wetness. Apart from indicating wet land, some plants have other significance for drainage. Plants that thrive in acid conditions are a warning that care is needed in considering the use of concrete pipes and structures. Rushes often colonize seepage lines but other species may also be present or indeed be the main indicators: Silverweed (*Potentilla anserina*) and the Horsetails (*Equisetum spp.*), for example, occur at less vigorous seepage areas of an intermittent nature. Often, where the excessive water is of an intermittent nature, there will be no real development of wetland species, but instead a flush situation where nutrients and even the temperature of groundwater encourage a rich growth of grasses. Sometimes a stronger growth of grasses will indicate drain locations, either because of a more open soil structure over a drain, or because of the available moisture flowing in a drain. The availability of water in a drain can also encourage the development of water-loving plants such as Horsetails to such an extent that the drain can become blocked by the plant roots.

Ditch Maintenance

The first task will often be to remove any overhanging vegetation to allow inspection and/or access to the ditch. This will need to be cleared away from the immediate area. Brushing hooks and billhooks will be useful for cutting and clearing grass and other vegetation. This material should be stacked well clear of the ditch for carting away later or burning on site. An inspection of the ditch can then be conducted to ascertain any signs of water flow impediment, such as silt build-up in the ditch. Remember to inspect outfall pipes and culverts for signs of damage, silting or debris restricting the flow.

The silt and debris will need to be cleared from the ditch to obtain an adequate water flow. Dig out using a shape spade and shovel all materials impeding flow of water to expose the ditch bottom. Take care not to dig below the original ditch level and ensure you maintain an even fall or gradient. The spoil removed from the ditch must be thrown well back from the ditch bank so that it cannot fall back.

Pipe Drainage Maintenance

Drainage rods are used to clear load drains, which have become silted up or otherwise blocked. Be sure to rotate rods *clockwise* as you push those forwards. Add further sections to prevent them from becoming disconnected and remaining in the drain, especially at withdrawal. There are a number of different types of head that can be fitted to cope with a variety of situations. Support or replace badly damaged or misaligned outfall pipes. Cut back the bank to expose and encase in blocks or bricks to support the outfall pipe. If using a face plate, ensure it is cut into the bank to prevent it slipping and displacing the pipe.

Drain Jetting Equipment

There are several drain jetting machines on the market. The smallest machines can be attached to a tractor's three-point linkage and powered via the PTO shaft. Larger machines are mounted on trailers. Both of these types take their water for jetting from the ditch adjacent to the drain to be cleaned. Water tanks are available for times when the ditch is dry and water is not available. Larger machines, usually used by specialist contractors, are mounted on their own four-wheel-drive vehicle with an independent storage tank to carry a supply of water for jetting.

The procedure involves feeding a special nozzle on a flexible pipe up the land drains. Water is then pumped under pressure through the pipe and nozzle to loosen any deposits further along the pipe. Others have a positive feeding system that forces the pipe along. Placing the pipe manually on the drain outfall can be rather an unpleasant task and models with hydraulic arms have been developed that enable the whole job to be done from the tractor feet.

Specialized equipment is available to locate drains. Nozzles that emit radio signals can be used if blockages are encountered that cannot be cleared by jetting and so excavation becomes necessary. A receiver above ground detects the signals and indicates when the listener is directly over the nozzle.

Working in ditches and with drains could result in tetanus infection, so always ensure that your vaccinations are up to date. Always wear gloves, overalls and Wellington boots to protect yourself.

For the maintenance of any pipe drainage system, you will also need to pay particular attention to such as silt traps, inspection chambers and pipe junctions, which are all prone to silting up and need periodic inspection and clearance to

maintain water flow, as do culverts with ditch drainage systems.

Subsidence

This is an indication of drainage failure at the extreme. It is not unknown for pipes in drainage systems to collapse, often with dramatic results. A drainage system may have been *in situ* for years and otherwise forgotten about until collapse and subsequent ground subsidence indicates its position. The likelihood of a drain collapse depends in the main upon its age, the materials used and the use to which the surface is subjected. Naturally such subsidence will need immediate attention and repair if the area is to be usable again. One should be vigilant with ground conditions, especially where it is known or suspected that there is an old drainage system still in place. Collapse could prove to be disastrous for both vehicular and pedestrian users of the area. Severe injury may be caused to players and/or animals that may even be fatal. Where possible try to locate any old plans of the area to help in the location of such drains.

Pavilions and Clubhouses

The pavilion or clubhouse is an integral part of the sports ground complex and an essential facility if the maximum use is to be made of the playing surfaces and if tournaments, competitions or other events are ever to be considered and held at that venue. In planning applications it is usually the actual buildings that are the focus of attention by the authorities, since they have the biggest effect on the landscape and in development terms they are often the most expensive single item. It is critical that proper evaluation of user needs, scale and scope of sports, additional activities and possible future developments be considered at the outset. The advice of a qualified architect experienced in such developments should be sought and adopted. The maximization of space within the building 'footprint' and catering for all user needs is a demanding task and requires skilful planning, attention to detail and knowledge of constructional limitations and requirements. Remember too that it is far more efficient to get these aspects right in the first place and have a well-designed building (with possibilities for future extensions) than to cope with a poor building ill suited for the identified requirements. Later alterations are nearly always overly costly unless planned for initially in the design. It should also be remembered that the pavilion or clubhouse will often serve as an essential means of income resource for the club, especially where there is a bar or catering facility.

Location and Orientation

The physical features of the site and usually planning limitations will dictate the actual siting of any pavilion or clubhouse. The prime considerations will be site access from roads and the ingress points of necessary services, such as water and electricity. Provision must be made for vehicular access and parking, including access for emergency services and possible overspill parking for events. There should be room for future expansion where this is deemed necessary. It is not always possible to foresee all future provision, but all organizations should have strategic plans for their future activities. Building entrances should be orientated away from the direction of the prevailing wind. Viewing of pitches should be planned to avoid the setting sun. The orientation compass on the earlier illustration concerning the layout of pitches can be used as a guide for the siting of pavilions and clubhouses.

Accommodation

The size of the sports ground, the number of sports catered for and the standards of provision will influence the specific accommodation requirements but the following will normally be needed:

- Changing rooms
- Showers and dry-off areas
- Toilets

- Officials' accommodation
- Meeting/social rooms
- Cleaners' stores
- Entrance hall
- Disabled changing/toilets
- Heating/electrical plant room

The facility may have need also for:

- Committee rooms
- Kitchens
- Bar/lounge/dining areas
- Physio/treatment rooms
- Score box
- Offices
- Staff accommodation

Planning

When planning and designing pavilions and clubhouses:

- Always include an entrance hall within the building.
- Keep wet/dirty changing areas separate from social areas.
- Plan for flexibility in terms of male and female usage.
- Plan simple circulation routes.
- Corridors should be at least 1.5m wide (2.7m where there are lockers).
- Ensure access for disabled users (comply with the requirements of the Disability Discrimination Act).
- Plan for convenient access to pitches and courts.
- Provide satisfactory viewing of playing areas.
- Never plan grass pitch changing rooms with stair access at first-floor level.

Floodlighting

Floodlighting can help to achieve greater levels of pitch use and flexibility. It is especially valuable in maximizing the use of non-turf or artificial surfaces in the short days of winter. Such surfaces can provide for far more play during the winter months with floodlights. It is possible for such surfaces to achieve up to sixty hours of use each week with floodlights, although restrictions on working practices and social conventions often mean that this will often be nearer to forty hours in practice. This figure, though, still exceeds that normally provided by natural grass pitches, the use of which rarely surpasses seven hours without serious damage to the playing surface resulting. The design and installation of floodlighting schemes is the business of specialist qualified engineers and will depend upon a number of site-specific criteria including:

- Types of sport and standards of provision.
- Amount of usage.
- Requirements for spectators.
- The likelihood for future upgrading.
- Any need for additional amenity, security or emergency lighting.
- Effects on local residential properties.

There are many factors to consider, not least of which is planning permission. All floodlighting schemes require planning permission under the Town and Country Planning Act of 1990. Negotiation with the electricity supply company will also be needed, with early consultation to establish loading requirements and operational hours for lighting use in order to set tariffs. A key factor in the design of any scheme is the planned illumination measurement or the average light level over the area on the horizontal plane. This should never be less than 70 per cent, as measured in lumens per square metre or lux. The design needs to be such that it limits potential for light pollution and nuisance to neighbouring properties.

Appendix 1: Theoretical Field Drainage Calculations

In order to design a practical system the follow process has to be followed:

- Decide how much rain will fall on the site.

- Decide how much of this rainfall will reach the pipe.
- Determine the Design Drainage Rate.
- Decide what size, spacing length and gradient of pipes is required to remove this water as fast as it reaches the pipe.
- Ensure that the outfall ditch can cope with the flow.

Step 1: Determining the Rainfall
Tables are available for average rainfall for any district of the UK. To be on the safe side, drainage engineers prefer to take the wettest five days of the wettest year in ten and establish the average daily rainfall in mm per day from this figure. Ready reckoners are available with this information (*see* Appendix 2).

Step 2: Determining What Proportion of Rainfall will Reach the Pipes
Not all the rainfall will percolate through the soil to the pipe. There are losses from:

- Surface run-off
- Subsurface run-off
- Evaporation
- Transpiration from plants
- Water percolating below pipe level

On the other hand there may be gains from water running onto the surface from adjacent slopes, unless there are intercepting drains.

The pipes will also tend to silt up over time and calculations should allow some over-capacity in the system to cope with this. Finally some extra capacity may be required if the site is mole-drained or sand-slitted, because water reaches the pipe system very rapidly and this peak flow can overwhelm the system. For agricultural purposes on vegetated sites, it is commonly assumed that about 60 per cent of rainfall will reach the pipe; for sand-slit sports turf and hard landscape a figure near 100 per cent is assumed.

Step 3: Determining the Design Drainage Rate

It will be noticed that nearly all of the above calculations will be based on educated guesswork. Accordingly many designers of small drainage schemes ignore the two steps above and use average values based on the use of the site and whether any auxiliary drainage is employed, such as mole drains. The rate at which water is designed to be cleared from site is called the Design Drainage Rate. A number of Design Drainages Rates in common use include:

Remember this is not the actual rainfall; it is a figure that has been chosen because it works for the situations quoted.

Design	Drainage rate
Agriculture/landscape planting schemes	13mm/day
High quality landscape/ amenity grassland	26mm/day
As above in high rainfall areas	35mm/day
High quality sports turf	>50mm/day

CALCULATING THE VOLUME OF WATER TO BE REMOVED

The design drainage rate can be used to calculate the total volume of water to be removed. For a 2 hectare sports field drained to a single outfall, for example, the calculation is as follows:

Area of site is 2 Ha (20,000m²)

The design drainage rate is 50mm/day (0.05m/day), so the maximum volume of water to be removed through the outfall in one day is:

Area of site × depth of water
 = 20,000 × 0.05m³
 = 1,000m³/day (1 million litres)

This equates to 41.67m³/hour or 11.57 litres/second.

So the main drainage pipe must have a flow rate capacity of at least 11.57 litres/second.

Step 4: Determining the Pipe Characteristics Required to Achieve the Design Drainage Rate

LATERALS

The actual volume of water that a lateral pipe will have to discharge depends on the area of soil feeding that pipe (volume = area × design drainage rate). The area depends on the pipe length and spacing, in other words the layout of the system. In practice the direction of the pipes will follow site gradients to the outfall, and the spacing will be determined by soil types and site use.

PIPE SPACING

Pipe spacing can be calculated from the Hooghoudt formula:

$$\text{Spacing} = \frac{4Kh^2}{V}$$

K Hydraulic conductivity of the soil
h Depth of permeable material (rootzone)
V Design Drainage Rate

Or rearranged as follows to determine the design drainage rate (V):

$$V = \frac{4Kh^2}{S}$$

In practice these values are difficult to determine and often simply confirm common practice. Many designers prefer to use ready reckoners based on soil type or average figures, such as:

Heavy clay	4–10m
Loams	10–20m
Sandy loams	20–30m

PIPE GRADIENT

Cost-effective pipe installation requires that pipes follow site gradients where they fall in the range 1 in 50 to 1 in 300. Some adjustment is possible by aligning pipes across slopes rather than up and down. Where following site gradients gives either poor or excessive flow rates, adjustments can be made by altering spacing or pipe diameter.

PIPE LENGTH

Once pipe direction has been decided by the site gradients, and the spacing determined as above, the proposed pipe lengths are known and the area served by each pipe can be calculated. Restrictions on maximum pipe length can sometimes affect pipe sizing (*see* below).

PIPE DIAMETER

Determine the flow rate: Once the area in hectares served by a pipe is known, and a design drainage rate in mm/hour decided, the required flow rate of the pipe in litres per second is obtained from the following formula:

$$\text{Flow rate (l/sec)} = \text{Area (in hectares)} \times \text{Design rate (mm/hour)} \times 0.116$$

Example 1

Main pipe accepting water from laterals covering 1 hectare
Design Drainage Rate 26mm/hour

$$\text{Flow rate} = 1 \times 26 \times 0.116$$
$$= 3.0 \text{ litres/second}$$

Example 2

Lateral pipes 50m long at 10m spacing

$$\text{Area covered} = 50 \times 10 = 500\text{m}^2$$
$$= 0.05 \text{ hectares}$$

Design Rate 26mm/hour

$$\text{Flow rate} = 0.05 \times 26 \times 0.116$$
$$= 0.15 \text{ litres/second}$$

Determine the pipe diameter required to give the designed flow rate: Charts are available from manufacturers that show the flow rate for all available pipe materials, of different diameters and set to various gradients (*see* Appendix 2).

Example 1

The flow rate calculated for our main pipe is 3.0 litres/second.

This flow rate can be discharged by any of the following pipe/gradient combinations.

| 85mm/1 in 200 |
| 85mm/1 in 100 |
| 100mm/1 in 300 |

Knowing the layout of the system and therefore the proposed gradient for the main pipe, a suitable diameter pipe can be selected from the options above.

Example 2

The flow rate of the laterals in the system is 0.15 litres/second.

This is achievable by almost any size pipe even if laid to the shallowest gradient.

Limiting effect of drain length: The theoretical maximum lateral pipe length can be calculated from the following formula:

$$\text{Max. length} = \frac{\text{Flow rate of pipe (litres/sec)} \times 3{,}600}{\text{Design drain rate (mm/hour)} \times \text{spacing (m)}}$$

In practice, other than high quality sports turf, the calculation of the limitation of pipe size by pipe length is usually ignored and the chart referred to in Appendix 2 is followed.

Step 5: Determining the Ditch Capacity

The flow rates of ditches can be determined from charts in the same way as pipe flow rates (*see* Appendix 2). The key criteria are ditch bottom width and gradient.

It is important to remember that the site you are working on may only be a part of the total catchment area of the ditch. You must use the total catchment area when using the tables.

Summary

The first principles of drainage calculations are lengthy and complex, but essential when large and complex drainage schemes are involved.

Most land drainage designers involved in field drainage, however, will soon find that as a rule of thumb most schemes rely on a main pipe of 100–150mm with laterals of 65–75mm. These figures are not arbitrary, but based on a sound theoretical basis, as illustrated below.

Theoretical Bases for Pipe Sizing Rules of Thumb

If we assume that gradients of at least 1 in 200 are usually viable on landscape sites, and that areas served by main pipes rarely exceed 2 hectares, and laterals 0.2 hectares (100 × 20), the maximum flow rates may be taken as follows:

	Max. area	Design rate (mm/h)	Flow rate (litres/ second)
Mains	2 Ha	13	3.0
		26	6.0
		50	11.6
Laterals	0.2 Ha	13	0.3
		26	0.6
		50	1.16

Referring to the previous table on pipe diameters, we can see that a 100mm main at even 1 in 200 gradient will cope with basic drainage (13mm/day) for a 2 hectare site, and a 150mm main at 1 in 200 will suffice for the most sophisticated drainage schemes (50mm/day).

In theory all the lateral pipe discharge rates (0.3–1.16l/sec) can be accomplished by a pipe of only 65mm diameter laid to a gradient of 1 in 200; 75mm will give excess capacity to cope with rapid discharge from sand slit systems.

There is then a sound theoretical basis for the 100/150 main, 65/75 lateral rule of thumb option.

Appendix 2: Practical Field Drainage Design

Calculating drainage requirements from first principles is rarely done other than by drainage engineers – most designers use ready reckoners.

Use of Ready Reckoners

Several of these exist: one of the easiest to use is an HMSO publication, *The Design of Field Drainage Pipe Systems*, originally published for the Ministry of Agriculture, Fisheries and Food.

The first section of the booklet identifies rainfall rates for all different areas of the UK and gives simple methods of calculating design drainage rates that take account of:

• Run-off
• Gradient
• Soil permeability (hydraulic conductivity)
• Use of site
• Secondary drainage system (subsoiler, mole drain)

The design drainage rate for a given area is given directly in litres per second, rather than mm/day.

The second section consists of manufacturers' charts that show the flow rate for pipes of different materials, of different diameters set at various gradients (given as per cent).

Thirdly, there is an Appendix showing the maximum drain length possible for laterals, depending on area covered and spacing.

If desired, the drainage flow graphs in the second section can be used with the rule of thumb design drainage rates (*see* Appendix 1), after converting them from mm/hour to litres/second. This is most easily done as follows:

Flow rate = Design drainage rate
× area in hectares
× 0.116 in mm/hour

Example 1

Design rate = 26mm (amenity grassland)
Area   = 0.5 hectares

Flow rate   = 26 × 0.5 × 0.116
            = 1.5 litres/second

Example 2

Design rate = 50mm (sports turf)
Area   = 0.1 hectares

Flow rate   = 50 × 0.1 × 0.116
            = 0.6 litres/second

Determine the gradient to be used and select the graph for the relevant pipe material. Find the flow rate and gradient on the graph axes and, where the two meet, find the first line to the right of

this point. This is the pipe diameter that must be used.

Ditch Capacity
A ditch must have the capacity to accommodate:

Design rainfall (pipe discharge)
+ groundflow
+ other inflow

In most situations existing ditches already take the flow from the landscape site, and all that a pipe system will do is transfer the water more rapidly then before.

If the existing ditch is coping adequately, it is unlikely to be overwhelmed unless large areas of hard landscape are involved.

Example 3

A 2 hectare sports turf site produces a calculated discharge into the ditch of 11.6 litres/second: what the table shows is well within the capacity of a 200mm wide ditch at a gradient of only 1 in 1,000.

Ditch Gradients
To obtain self-clearing flow rates, speeds of 0.5–1.5m/second are required, while 0.75m/second will prevent weed growth. These flow rates give rise to the range of gradients shown in the box below.

All of these tables tend to confirm that most existing ditches will suffice for discharge of landscape drainage, unless the sites are very large or significant amounts of hand landscape are involved.

Bottom Width	0.5m/sec	0.75m/sec	1.5m/sec
0.2m	1 in 400	1 in 180	1 in 40
0.3m	1 in 700	1 in 330	1 in 70
0.4m	1 in 1,000	1 in 400	1 in 100
0.5m	1 in 1,500	1 in 600	1 in 150

7 Mechanization, Materials and Equipment Management

The management of physical resources such as the machinery and materials utilized in the maintenance of playing surfaces and ancillary areas is an important part of sports ground management. Effective management is necessary to exploit the full benefit of such resources and to ensure that playing areas are maintained and presented in best condition throughout the playing season. The 'heart' of the sports ground is the maintenance building from which work is planned and executed, and where physical resources are stored and maintained. This facility is the operational centre and should be planned, designed and constructed in accordance with the requirements for physical resources, staffing levels and areas to be maintained. The selection of machinery is also an important management task that requires careful consideration and planning as this will have major implications both for finance and, not insignificantly, upon the quality of playing surfaces and facilities. There are many types and manufacturers of sports turf machinery and equipment, and sourcing the best machine for the job at the most competitive price is crucial for overall resource management. After labour, machinery and equipment represent the biggest cost for turf maintenance and so it is imperative that they be managed proactively and that a planned approach is taken. The standard of the maintenance facility and the sports ground machinery and equipment is often indicative of the standard of the facility itself. This chapter provides guidance for turf maintenance buildings, storage areas and the selection, maintenance and management of sports ground machinery and equipment.

The Turf Maintenance Facility

A purpose-built and well-designed turf maintenance building will have many beneficial effects for the organization, its staff and the actual playing surfaces. These can help to:

- Increase machinery and equipment 'life expectancy'.
- Increase staff productivity.
- Improve stock and inventory control.
- Provide a safe and desirable place to work.
- Reduce insurance and other liabilities.
- Promote health, safety and good working practices.

Planning and Site Selection
The site for the maintenance building should be such that it is easily accessible but separate from pavilions and player changing rooms or other facilities. Screening from players and site security should also be considered. The building will need to be accessible for turf maintenance staff and to receive deliveries from companies arriving with large items of plant and machinery or

Make sure that your maintenance facility does not look like this; it is unprofessional and a hazard.
(Waste2Water Europe Ltd)

bulk materials without interference to players or visitors. The location should also permit easy and efficient access to all areas of the site to reduce operator-travelling distances, facilitating more efficient working or rapid response to incidents within the curtilage of the facility. Services such as electricity, water and waste disposal are essential and therefore consideration regarding connection and costs incurred for these is required. The site should be on flat ground that is not liable to flooding or the possibility of subsidence and there should be sufficient land capacity around for machinery manoeuvring, outside storage and working. The siting of service roads both within the site and especially in relation to highways needs planning and is subject to local planning authority scrutiny and constraints, as of course will be the detail of the building type, size and construction. On most sites, the location of the maintenance building will be constrained by the actual siting and requirements for the actual sports surfaces, available finance, planning restrictions and the size of the facility.

The Building

There may be a building already *in situ* that is suitable to serve as the maintenance facility. Equipping and fitting out an existing building, however, can be problematic, expensive and even be restricted by planning or building regulations. Older buildings often do not meet modern standards expected for heating, ventilation, security, space or health and safety. Often the use of an existing building leads to compromises that have an impact on overall efficiencies for working practices, building maintenance and servicing. The opportunity to build anew and start with a 'blank canvas' is usually the most desirable situation, since all necessary work, storage and support infrastructures and services can be planned for greatest efficiency and most competitive costing. This will ensure that the resulting building is fit for purpose and most suited to the specific requirements of that sports ground. An important consideration at the planning stage and when choosing a building type is to allow for possible future expansion.

The building will normally fulfil several functions, as it most often will have rooms or spaces for:

- Staff offices
- Staff rest/changing areas
- Machine workshop/service area
- Parts storage
- Materials storage (grass seed, fertilizers and so on)
- Tools and small plant storage
- Machinery storage
- Fuel/pesticide stores

The space allocated for each particular requirement will obviously vary according to the size of the facility, number of staff and range of machinery, among other factors. There are many sports grounds that manage with less space but also many that are struggling with cramped and outdated facilities. It should not be forgotten that effective management of the facility is essential if the most efficient operation is to be maintained. Space should be apportioned in large open plan buildings for each type of use and all need to be kept in a clean and tidy state at all times. The accompanying table is for general guidance and will be most useful where a purpose-designed building can be procured.

The most basic facility will be a large shed that is subdivided with internal partition walls for the different rooms and working or storage areas. Most constructions today tend to be prefabricated steel or concrete beam shells with concrete block walls, plastic-coated steel-clad agricultural type buildings. Sliding doors, large enough to cater for the biggest machines at either end can be useful where through traffic is required; obviously there must be separate entrance and exit doors for personnel. Concrete block walls up to 1.2m in height are useful for storing loose materials against, but any higher and they may need to be buttressed. These walls also serve to enhance building durability and integrity, while helping to protect the metal cladding above from damage. Eaves and lintel heights should be tall enough to allow in the highest vehicle comfortably; any higher results in large roof voids, which lose heat and are unnecessary space. In some areas, notably staff room and working areas, it is advisable to add insulation. In storage areas plywood, hardboard or MDF materials can be used to accommodate shelving and other storage requirements.

Suggested Space Allocation for a Large Sports Ground Maintenance Facility

Facility and type of use	Suggested space allocation (m²)
Staff office	30
Staff restroom/lockers	40
Workshop and parts store	100
Tools and small equipment store	40
Machinery storage area	200
Dry goods storage	40
Total floor space	450m² (This equates to a building 18 × 25m)

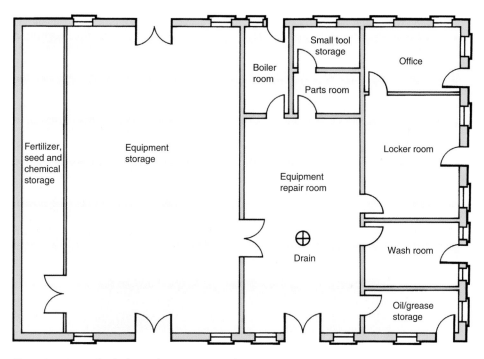

Figure 17   Example of a layout for a maintenance facility.

Foundation depth and construction will be specified by the architect and flooring should incorporate drains as required. Floors should be sloped towards these drains as required. The load-bearing needs of the roof must be considered, as buildings with large floor areas may need internal supports for the roof. These will obviously affect the layout and use of the space available inside the building; you need to know such requirements before planning internal divisions and work areas. Guttering is often neglected on prefabricated buildings but is an important consideration. Care taken during the design and planning stages will minimize future problems with the building structure and its use. Several techniques used in the actual design process that are summarized in the accompanying table.

Design Methods for Buildings	
Method	**Comment**
Models	They give a three-dimensional view and show special relationships
Line plan drawings	Used for simplicity
Cardboard scaling	Scale drawing with cut-outs in scale
Interaction net (matrix)	Allows relationships with other areas to be considered

Security and Health and Safety

It is a fact that many turf maintenance buildings are prone to vandalism. Often they are sited in locations away from public view on the urban fringe or in localities that are more rural. Special measures should be taken to preserve security that need to be planned from the outset. Management systems, such as careful monitoring of resources with accurate inventory control, may also be needed in order to discourage internal losses. In planning the facility, the following measures can be considered to enhance security:

- Minimize windows to decrease break-ins and reduce energy losses. A view of the sports ground from the office, however, is invaluable for monitoring sports ground security. Windows fitted with wire screens or bars, where necessary, will still allow light into the building.

- Install outside lighting, including motion-sensitive security lighting in sensitive areas.

- Use locks that can easily be changed. Limit the number of keys issued and keep track of them. Change security codes regularly on doors where fitted. Issue pass codes only to those that really need them.

- Install electronic security and alarm systems.

A purpose-built workshop is a real benefit for the large sports ground or contractor. (TORO)

- Security fencing around the maintenance building should be installed especially where any items of plant or equipment are stored outside.
- Consider the use of protective materials such as anti-climb paint, barbed wire or other similar products.

In respect to Health and Safety, plan with safety in mind. Use protective screening, barriers and bollards where necessary. Consider non-slip surfacing, handrails, steps and ramps. Make sure that adequate provision is made for first aid, fire extinguishers and hydrants, and that there is adequate signage for these items as well as emergency exit points.

Machinery Workshops

When designing the actual machinery workshop area (or building where this is separate) consider:

- The type of work that needs to be undertaken
- The space required (or available)
- What services are needed?
- What tools will be needed?
- Access to other areas
- Health and safety requirements
- Environmental issues and waste disposal
- Available finance

The type of work undertaken will depend upon your machinery management policy and whether there is a full-time mechanic or technician employed at the sports ground. Many sports grounds will conduct only basic maintenance and utilize the services of contractors or machinery dealers for more complex repairs or maintenance works. The ownership of the machinery will also affect what can be done 'in-house' and what cannot. Machinery servicing ranges from daily checks maintenance and routine servicing through to major overhauls, repairs and fabrication. In terms of space requirements, the figures in the box below can be used as basic guidelines when planning.

Where major repairs and servicing is conducted there will need to be areas where laid-up machines can be stored while work is taking place on other machines. Machines not in use can often be out of commission for weeks. The availability of parts and dealer service are significant factors here. Services are essential, particularly electricity where both 110V and three-phase supplies may be needed. The accompanying table gives a brief overview of small plant items and tools that may be needed in the workshop.

Provision must be made for the storage of oils, lubricants, solvents and cleaning chemicals. Particular attention must be paid to the disposal of such materials. Specialist contractors can be employed to remove such products and you will be required to register with the local authority.

GRINDING AREA

It is desirable to have a designated grinding area or room where in-house cylinder grinding and bottom blade and rotary mower blade sharpening is practised; this will minimize dust and grit exposure to other staff and working areas. The area should be well lit, soundproof and power ventilated with extractor fans fitted. Dust

Operation	1st Mechanic	2nd Mechanic
Mechanic at work bench	8m²	5m²
Mechanic assembly or repair	15m²	12m²
Welding and fabrication	12m²	8m²

Equipping the Workshop	
Hand tools	Complete set including spanners, screwdrivers, hammers etc.
Jacks and axle stands	Use industrial ones
Lifting ramps	New types now available for turf machinery and tractors
Compressor	Can get silent ones housed indoors
Bench drill, grinders	Inexpensive tools
Cylinder grinders	Specialist mower equipment
Battery chargers	Need ventilated areas
Welding equipment	Arc and Mig
Benches	Need to be strong and stable
Cupboards/shelving	For security and greater 'life expectancy'
Manuals	Complete set in an organized 'library' of all machine operator and service manuals
Accessories	Oil cans, grease guns, brushes, funnels, trays etc.
Test and diagnostic equipment	Specialist equipment as required

A cylinder grinder is an invaluable machine in contemporary sports turf management. (Bernhard and Company Ltd)

All topdressings and sands should be kept under dry cover, such as this purpose constructed storage bay. (Stewart Brown)

and grit removal will be further enhanced by vacuum exhaust system attachments to the grinding equipment.

ANCILLARY AREAS

Within the vicinity of the maintenance building, there will be a need to accommodate several other material and allied resource management requirements for overall sports ground management. These also require detailed planning if they are not to negate efficient operational management in the sports ground environs.

SOIL, TOPDRESSING AND SAND STORAGE

Bulky materials such as topdressings are required for turf maintenance. To preserve their appearance and quality, clean storage facilities should be provided. For loose materials, constructed bays with concrete bases and solid walls with some form of open roofing should be built. These are open to one side and of sufficient size to facilitate material handling with tractor fore-end loaders and deposit using tipping trailers or trucks when deliveries are made. If appropriate, an area of hard-standing can be included where in-house mixing of topdressing is practised.

FUEL TANKS

Large sports grounds may have their own petrol and/or diesel tanks and pumps. Specific legislation and health and safety requirements apply to such facilities. Specialist advice should always be sought and the appropriate authorities such as the local council and fire service consulted. These facilities should be sited away from the main building with provision made for possible leakage and security. There are many manufacturers of smaller fuel tanks suitable for sports ground installations.

PESTICIDE STORES

The requirements for pesticide storage are again covered by legislation, which must be adhered to. Specialist small storage bins, lockers and containers can be purchased that suffice for most sports grounds. The

187

A 'model' outside work area for a large sports ground complex. In the picture can be seen fuel tanks, pesticide stores and machine washdown area. (Waste2Water Europe Ltd)

basic requirement is that they be fireproof, able to contain leaks and secure.

PARKING

There should be adequate vehicle parking for staff and occasional visitors who may call upon the maintenance building. This should be clear of the main working areas and not obstruct access for turf maintenance machinery or equipment.

OUTSIDE WORK AREA

An area of hard-standing, preferably concrete or macadam, should be present in order to provide temporary parking for machinery. This will be used most often for machine adjustment. It may also serve to receive deliveries of machinery, equipment or materials.

MACHINE WASHDOWN AREA

An area should be constructed specifically for washing down machinery after use. Washing turf machinery leads to a significant

amount of grass clippings, greases, oils and fuel deposits, which need to be contained. New regulations require that washing operations must be carried out in a designated kerbed area that drains into a foul sewer or a closed loop recycling system.

LANDSCAPING

Providing landscaping to provide both screening for the turf maintenance building and associated work areas is beneficial from both aesthetic and safety considerations. Sometimes there may be topsoil left over from that excavated for the building works. This can be used to great effect, possibly in mounding to provide partial screening or at least in use with borders for ornamental planting. The use of groundcover, hedging and tree planting can provide sufficient screening and an attractive landscape feature. The use of low maintenance plants and native species is ideal for most sport grounds situations.

188

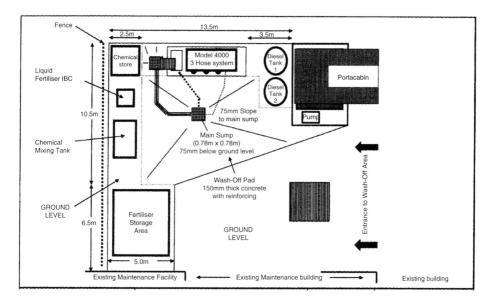

Figure 18   Example of maintenance facility yard layout.

Machinery for Sports Ground Maintenance

Turf surfaces today are largely maintained using machinery that has been developed over many years to high levels of engineering, safety and operator comfort. Most tasks associated with turf maintenance, renovation and presentation are now wholly or partly mechanized. This increasing use of machinery during the latter half of the twentieth century and up to the present day has brought several benefits to the sports turf industry. Mechanization has led to better working conditions for staff, greater productivity and quality of surfaces. It has also reduced the need for manual work, which of course has reduced staffing requirements. The selection of machinery for turf maintenance works is a very important part of management in the industry today and requires careful evaluation, assessment and decision-making. Choosing the right machine for the job can sometimes be a daunting task when the choices appear to be endless.

Machinery Selection Criteria

The following factors should be used to evaluate machines for sports turf machinery for use on the sports ground.

MACHINE COST AND BUDGET

This is probably the most obvious factor but should never be used as the sole determinant in choosing new machinery. The initial purchase price is not the only consideration in costing machinery. One must also consider likely service and maintenance costs, predicted operational life and any warranty benefits.

SURFACES TO BE MAINTAINED AND STANDARDS

The particular surfaces to be maintained and the level of provision, whether for professional sport or amateur and recreational use, will have a large influence on the machines required. The number of

189

games or events will also need to be considered. Often ground staff have a short period between fixtures and machinery needs to be fast in operation while not reducing the quality of the playing surface.

GROUND AND
ENVIRONMENTAL CONDITIONS

Different surfaces have different maintenance requirements and will vary in condition depending upon prevailing weather conditions. One also needs to consider the actual ground and soil or substrates conditions, particularly drainage, topography and terrain. Can the machine operate in a range of climatic conditions? The size of the facility in terms of hectare and number of pitches, courts or greens will also be a factor here.

MACHINE EFFICIENCY

The major consideration here is just how quickly a particular machine can complete a task at a given cost. Will the machine actually do what is claimed or specified? What are the costs in fuel and operation? Onsite demonstrations can be invaluable here, especially where you can see similar machines working against each other.

OPERATOR COMFORT AND ERGONOMICS

Many tasks, such as mowing, involve many person-hours sat on a machine and therefore operator comfort and safety are essential criteria to assess. Good ergonomics and ease of operation are not luxuries; a comfortable operator will be more productive and there is less chance of operator stress. The seating position, where relevant, and positioning of controls are important, as are factors such as anti-vibration devices.

LABOUR AVAILABILITY AND COMPETENCE

Are there staff available that can operate the machinery, safely and efficiently? Are there sufficient staff and do they have the necessary levels of skills or competence? It may be necessary to undertake training needs analysis and training programmes

implemented either in-house or using external training courses. Some machines and items of plant, such as sprayers and excavators, require competence certificates. This factor can also have cost implications.

MACHINE RELIABILITY AND QUALITY

Durability is important for professional turf machinery, as it will have to perform many hours or work in sometimes testing conditions. Machinery developed for the amateur market is not sufficiently robust for commercial use and should never be considered for such work. The machine should be of a sturdy construction while being easy to maintain and adjust, and have a proven record of accomplishment of service. Commendations from other grounds

---

Fuel Types

For most turf machinery, the main choice remains that of either petrol or diesel, with conventional internal combustion engines being the norm. There are machines, including mowers and utility trucks, powered by electricity and Liquefied Petroleum Gas (LPG) available on the market for use on the sports ground. The major problem with electric vehicles is the capacity of batteries to retain charge and the often-limited operating hours between charging. Electricity is, however, a cleaner power source. Currently LPG is more costly than the red diesel used with many tractors but it has become more common with now even small engine conversions being available and more dependable. A more recent development has been the growing interest in bio-diesel, which may in time prove to be a long-term replacement for conventional diesel. It is worth investigating alternative fuel and power sources, but the commercial range of machines is limited. Professional advice should be taken, especially with respect to implications for fuel storage and machine efficiency and running costs.

persons can be very valuable here when investigating new machines.

The availability of parts and back-up service from the machinery dealer is critical. Machine downtime can have an adverse effect upon productivity and even income for the business. This is not acceptable. Suppliers should be questioned upon their back-up service, particularly in respect of response time to call-outs and parts delivery. It is often worth spending more money initially when purchasing a machine if service back-up can be assured.

Machinery Needed for a Sports Ground

All sports grounds need machinery and equipment for maintenance. Some operations are so intrinsic for routine maintenance that it is imperative that machines are owned for these tasks. These include mowing, aeration and scarification. Many other items are more sports specific and will need to be procured for those facilities, for example, a heavy roller for cricket squares. The listings below provide a basic framework for four sports turf surfaces: a winter games pitch, a bowling green, a cricket ground and a tennis court. These recommendations would apply to a single pitch or green and multiples of machines listed will often be needed for sports grounds containing more than one such surface. This is not to say that it will always be necessary to have two mowers instead of one. One may be able to use larger capacity machines on many sites. Some machines can obviously be used on more than one surface type where these are on the same site.

WINTER GAMES PITCH

30–40 hp tractor
Set of 3–5 trailed gang mowers *or* large pedestrian cylinder mower with trailed seat (76–90cm)
Tractor-mounted scarifier/rake/harrow
Light roller (250kg)
Tractor-mounted heavy duty aerator

Tractor-mounted topdresser
Pedestrian powered aerator
Tractor-mounted sprayer (optional)
Powered overseeder
Range of hand tools

BOWLING GREEN

Pedestrian cylinder mower (9–12 bladed and 46–61cm width of cut)
Pedestrian powered scarifier (with a range of reels/brushes)
Pedestrian powered aerator (with slit, solid and hollow tines)
Rotary mower (possibly hover type for ditch banking)
Fertilizer/topdressing spreader
Pedestrian 'walkover type' sprayer
Light roller (250kg)
Lute (3–5m width)
Dragmat
Drag brush
Range of hand tools

CRICKET GROUND (SQUARE)

Pedestrian cylinder mower (9–12 bladed and 46–61cm width of cut)
Pedestrian cylinder mower (61–71cm width of cut)
Pedestrian powered scarifier (with a range of reels/brushes)
Pedestrian powered aerator (with slit, solid and hollow tines)
Heavy roller (0.5–2 tonnes)
Light roller (250kg)
Pedestrian 'walkover type' sprayer
Line marker
Range of hand tools

CRICKET GROUND (OUTFIELD)

Large pedestrian cylinder mower with trailed seat (76–90cm) *or* set of 3–5 trailed gang mowers
30–40 hp tractor
Heavy duty aerator (slitter)
Tractor scarifier (or chain harrow)
Tractor mounted sprayer (optional)

GRASS TENNIS COURT

Pedestrian cylinder mower (9–12 bladed and 46–61cm width of cut)

Pedestrian powered scarifier (with a range of reels/brushes)
Pedestrian powered aerator (with slit, solid and hollow tines)
Fertilizer/topdressing spreader
Pedestrian 'walkover type' sprayer
Light roller (250kg)
Line marker
Dragmat and drag brush
Range of hand tools

Without sufficient machinery and equipment in good working order, it is not possible to maintain satisfactory playing surfaces. The quality of the playing surface is directly related to the availability and proper use of these resources. All too often, many sports grounds are expected to maintain surfaces with second rate or even inappropriate machinery. The results are entirely predictable and should come as no surprise to management or players. Naturally, it is critical that such expensive machinery and equipment be housed and maintained in good working condition at all times. Neglect is wasteful and often even damaging.

Machinery Management

Machinery is a significant resource that needs to be managed if one is to gain the greatest efficiencies in both economic and operational terms. It is not unusual for some sports facilities to have up to £500,000 worth of machinery in their premises and to be over 75 per cent mechanized in operational activity. This scale of resource demands proactive management; it is a major budgetary expense and impacts directly upon the quality of the surfaces and ultimately the profitability of the business. In order to maintain a professional machinery management approach, an organization should have a written policy. Sports facilities are judged by the quality of their playing surfaces and this is directly related to the provision and management of machinery. Machinery purchase, maintenance and operation should all be part of a managed process. A management strategy must be adopted and should be renewed on at least a five-year cycle. Review the strategy on an annual basis so that current trends and developments can be taken on board.

It is worth remembering that investment in machinery will bring several benefits to the organization including:

Improved working conditions: Many tasks on the sports ground are now mechanized and this has directly improved working conditions for staff as it has reduced much physically demanding and repetitive work.

Productivity: Machinery allows faster and more efficient completion of works. Output per operative will be significantly greater where the task is mechanized as opposed to manually executed.

Quality: The quality of work and playing surfaces has improved almost immeasurably since the Second World War as machinery usage has increased. This is apparent with many machines. The increasing use of cylinder mowers in particular has greatly improved the quality and presentation of turf playing surfaces since their invention.

Cost reduction: Mechanization has reduced the need for large staffs where much manual work was once commonplace. Modern machinery is available for many maintenance tasks and can have a large capacity for work and greater work efficiency rates. This has led to significant reductions in operational costs.

THE NEED FOR PLANNING

Planning is an important part of the management process. Better control of resources will be achieved where these are planned, organized and managed. The planning of sports turf mechanization is necessary as it has several key impacts on the organization:

Profitability and cash flow planning: After labour machinery, this is the most significant cost to the sports ground business. Mechanization management will allow decisions to be made based on facts and true costs, thereby real profit margins can be determined and greater control of cash flow facilitated.

Staffing organization and labour costs: Improving or increasing the level of mechanization can reduce labour requirement and therefore costs. It may be pertinent to consider alternatives to staff when they leave or retire.

Capital costs: The costs of machines generally continue to rise as costs in manufacturing and distribution are passed on to the customer or end-user. New advances in technology and machinery and research and development must be paid for!

Fixed and variable costs: The costs of power and machinery can be as high as 90 per cent when labour is included at some facilities. Matching machinery to resources can avoid over-mechanization. Variable costs such as fuel use can be decreased with careful management.

Timing of works and soil or surface damage: The timing of many turf maintenance works is important to surface quality and playability. Having machinery on site and ready to go is often vital when working with the vagaries of the weather. Some operations such as aeration are reliant upon soil or rootzone condition for their success. Much damage is often done to playing surfaces using machinery in inappropriate conditions.

Machinery efficiency and fuel efficiency: Machinery should be working to capacity if the greatest returns on investment are to be had. Labour and machinery need to be working as a unit. Understanding the machines' capabilities and matching requirements will reduce fuel usage.

Machinery ownership: Knowing the true costs of owning and operating machines will allow alternatives to be investigated and comparisons made. All aspects of machinery use need to be evaluated and reviewed.

Effects on other activities: Improving the output of machinery can affect other areas of the business or work, for example it may free up staff for other work.

Future expansion and developments: Management may have plans for future expansion of facilities in order to cater for demand or attract more business. This may require additional machinery resource but it is imperative that the utilization of existing machinery is considered first before rushing out and buying more.

Monitoring machinery usage: Keeping records is important regarding machine repairs, fuel consumption and servicing. This will allow trends to be highlighted and costly machines identified. The future of such machines can then be reviewed.

Depreciation and taxation: Depreciation is a significant cost in owning machinery. Machinery replacement needs to be planned. Operators can do much to reduce depreciation costs by careful use and diligent maintenance of machinery. Advice on taxation should be sought when procuring new machinery.

Health and Safety: Legislation often requires changes in working practices or modifications to machinery. The manager needs to review existing machinery and its suitability for purpose and compliance with legislation on a regular basis.

MANAGING AN EFFICIENT 'FIELD' OPERATION
The management of machinery should include that of managing their use in the 'field', that is when in actual operation as well as their procurement and maintenance. A number of factors can be identified that have a direct influence on field efficiency that management (staff) can address.

Operator competence: This will have an impact upon work output per hour or day and the number of breakages or downtime. Training may be necessary for new equipment and some machines require a certificated operator. Safe and efficient machine operations are prerequisites for effective machinery use. Consider the level of experience and training required to do each job.

Operator instruction and motivation: Clarity of instruction is important. The operator needs to know what to do! The level of involvement for that operative is also crucial if the best results are to be achieved. Does that person consider they are just an employee with no incentive? If so it may mean they 'just do the job' without attending to peripheral issues. Staff holding a level of responsibility are better motivated to address these issues and give a better performance.

Field procedures and facility size/ shape: The size, shape and topography of the site may be fixed but one can still plan some operations such as mowing to provide more efficient working. Regular shapes, including square, round and triangular, are time consuming – rectangular shapes are the most efficient. Straight boundary fences are an asset. Obstacles such as electricity pylons, trees and ponds are time consuming and there is a need to follow a procedure when working around these and to plan your route/working pattern.

Speed of operation and machine adjustment: The actual speed of operation possible and therefore the output will largely depend upon the capacity of the machine including its power rating and effective working width. Machinery should be carefully matched to site requirements. Where using machines attached to a power unit, such as a tractor, these need to be carefully matched too. It is important that all machines are adjusted correctly to site conditions; incorrectly adjusted machinery can increase the power requirement by 25–30 per cent.

Ground conditions: Virtually all operations are determined by the weather and ground conditions. Too dry or too wet will be most often problematic for proper machine use and surface maintenance works. Drainage or irrigation practice will often have to be considered and acted upon to redress any extremes of soil moisture status affecting turf cultivation practice. Often previous work will have a direct influence upon following treatments or operations. There can be a real danger of 'forcing' work through when conditions are unsuitable, for example seedbed preparation in wet conditions. The power commonly available in machinery today enables this to

be done. The experienced operator should know when to start or stop, but novices will need close management if damage is not to result to the surface.

Machinery Costs

The annual costs of operating a machine can be divided into two categories.

Fixed Costs

These are generally constant per annum; the cost per hectare or hour, however, will decrease as the annual use of the machine increases. Fixed costs consist of:

Depreciation: This is an estimate of the amount that a machine (or other asset) falls in value during the period of ownership. All machines will decline in value as they get older and will be worth less than the initial amount paid, even after only a few months of ownership. Ultimately older machines may be 'written off' as having no monetary worth to the business even though they may still be working.

Insurance: Comprehensive cover should be procured for all items of plant and equipment in the fleet.

Buildings/workshops: These are essential to provide cover for machinery from weather and for security. Machinery stored outside will decline as frost, rain and sunlight will corrode and degrade machinery parts. The costs of machine housing can be significant and should be added to the machinery budget. Such housing, however, will ensure that machines remain in good condition with greater resale value and less money spent on repairs.

Road Fund Licence: This is a legal requirement for some land-based machinery using the public highways, most commonly tractors but also ride-on mowers. This should not be forgotten by those maintaining sports surfaces on different sites.

Finance charges: These are levied by banks and other finance houses on capital borrowed from them.

CALCULATING DEPRECIATION COSTS
There are three main methods of calculating depreciation for machinery:

Straight line method: This figure represents the average annual loss in value or depreciation.

Example

A ride-on mower costs £15,000 and its estimated resale value in 5 years time is £3,000:

$$£15,000 - £3,000 = \frac{£12,000}{5 \text{ (years)}} = £2,400$$

The annual rate of depreciation is £2,400. Calculating replacement of this machine can be assumed to set aside the annual depreciation figure plus inflation.

Diminishing or decreasing balances: Depreciation is calculated as a constant percentage of written-down value:

Example

Depreciation rate = 25%
Machine cost £15,000

Year 1 £15,000 − £3,750 (25%) = £11,250
Year 2 £11,250 − £2,812.50 (25%) = £8,437.50

This method reflects depreciation more accurately, showing that the machine loses value rapidly at first, but that this slows down as the machine gets older.

Sum of the digits: This method is rarely used and assumes a value of the machine after its useful life.

Example

Cost of machine   £15,000
Value after 5 years   £3,000

Add up the years 5 + 4 + 3 + 2 + 1 = 15

$$£15,000 - £3,000 = £12,000$$

$$\frac{£12,000}{15}$$

$$= £800$$

Depreciation in Year 1 = £800 × 5
= £4,000
Depreciation in Year 2 = £800 × 4
= £3,200
Depreciation in Year 3 = £800 × 3
= £2,400
Depreciation in Year 4 = £800 × 2
= £1,600
Depreciation in Year 5 = £800 × 1
= £800

RUNNING COSTS
These are constant per hectare or hour but they increase in proportion to annual use. Running costs include:

- Service costs and maintenance
- Labour
- Fuel and oil

Operating costs: Machinery can be costed on a per hour basis depending on circumstances or how the information is required. It can be difficult to start calculating costs when machinery is purchased new. One can be more accurate once you have a number of years' figures for reference. Keeping accurate records is an essential activity that should be an integral part of machinery management. All costs associated with machinery, including depreciation, can be better determined when previous records are available and the experience of individuals within the business with personal experience is used as a basis for more accurate costs estimation.

Total mechanization costings should include the cost of all machines and equipment. This enables managers to produce an accurate estimate for the operation. The table on p. 197 illustrates clearly the significance of labour in sports turf operations.

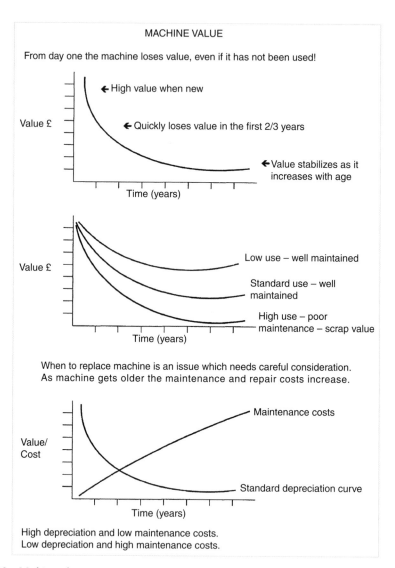

Figure 19 Machine value.

Managing Machinery Costs

The aim of any good business is to make a profit to provide reward and cover future investment. Cost control is vital and attention to detail is important: good managers control their machinery costs. Careful planning and analysis will help with future investment decisions. Identifying, monitoring and reducing machinery costs will help the organization plan effectively and with confidence.

A systematic approach is required to evaluate and monitor machinery costs, as is shown in the accompanying figure.

Calculating Operating Costs

To calculate the operating costs of an item of machinery it is necessary to take various factors into account. The example here details the costs over a twelve-month period of a 25kW ride-on mower:

New mower cost £15,000
Value at the end of 5-year period
Average annual use

Depreciation (over 5 years)
20% of purchase price (£3,000)
420 hours

Cost item	Annual cost	Cost per hour	Comment
Depreciation	£2,400.00	£5.04	Straight line method
Tax/insurance	£300.00	£0.71	(2% of £15,000)
Repairs/maintenance	£900.00	£1.42	(4% of £15,000 ÷ 420 hours)
Fuel consumption (4.47 litres per hour)	£657.09	£1.56	'Red diesel' costed at £0.35 per litre
Labour	£10,500.00	£25.00	
Storage	£750.00	£0.08	(5% of £15,000)
Totals	£15,507.09	£33.81	

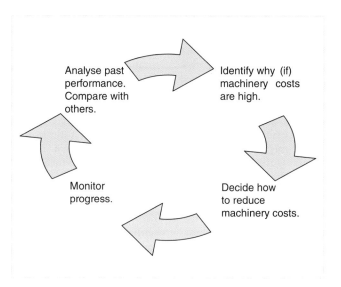

Figure 20   A systematic approach to evaluating and monitoring machinery.

Reducing Costs		
Depreciation	**Maintenance**	**Fuel**
Obtain a better trade	Select machinery for its simplicity and ease of maintenance	Encourage good maintenance
Maximize resale value	Record and pinpoint where money is spent	Test the main machines with a dynamometer each year
Obtain the correct machinery in the first place	Provide facilities for better on-site maintenance	Eliminate unnecessary journeys and works
Extend planned replacement periods	Choose the best source of skilled labour for repairs	Match the correct tractor to the implement
Consider alternative methods of machinery acquisition	Choose the best source for spare parts	Select energy-efficient machines
Provide good operator skills	Ensure adequate operator training	Adequate operator skills training in order to ensure fine tuning/adjustment of machinery
Buy quality second-hand machines	Develop a bonus system to reward operators who look after equipment	

Reasons for High Mechanization Costs

There are many reasons why expenditure on machinery may be higher than that desired by management. These factors need careful scrutiny and investigation if 'true' costs are to be determined and then options for action formulated and implemented. Some facilities may actually have too much machinery; this over-mechanization is not cost-effective as many machines will lie idle for long periods. In turf maintenance many tasks are often conducted by machinery simply because it is at hand, when in fact manual methods can be more effective and beneficial to the turf sward. Machines may be too large for purpose and have excessive capacity not required for the scale of that facility. The opposite can also be true sometimes, which is why careful matching of machine to site and operating conditions is important in procuring new machines. Replacements must be planned and advice sought over the 'best' finance arrangement for that business. Remember that new machinery may not always be the best deal; there is much good machinery available on the second-hand that may be more cost-effective. Operators will only give of their best if they are trained, skilled and motivated and machines are maintained properly. Finally the use of contractors is not a panacea for turf maintenance works, although they have a role to play. This again needs management if costs are not to escalate. The more significant costs with machinery include depreciation, repairs and maintenance and fuel.

Machinery Records

Keeping machinery records provides management with information on:

- The true cost of owning/operating a machine.
- Utilization and performance of the machinery stock.
- Trends in repairs and maintenance costs (allows early identification of problems).
- Planning maintenance schedules to reduce downtime.
- Easy access to physical data on each machine as an aid to ordering spare parts.
- The need for workshop facilities and equipment.

Machine Maintenance

Maintenance for machinery is essential in order to ensure that it is available in a satisfactory working condition for operation when required by grounds staff. Maintenance will assist in meeting the following criteria:

- Health and Safety
- Machine functionality and operation

- Prevent breakdowns and lengthen machine life
- To save on unnecessary expenditure
- To extend machine working life
- To comply with warranty requirements

Machine breakdowns are not only frustrating but can also be very costly. Such incidents often have adverse effects on business income, such as the cancellation of matches or fixtures. Additional machines may have to be hired to cover and obviously there will be costs associated with parts and labour in repair works. It is not unusual for machine breakdowns to cost hundreds of pounds or more. Planned maintenance can reduce breakdown incidents and costs as it will detect faults early when remedial works will prevent further more expensive problems arising later. Preventative maintenance should include daily checks to the machine and necessary adjustments, including scheduled tasks such as oil changes. When machines break down it is important to

Machine Record Card				
Machine Type		**Machine Ref No.**		**Department**
Registration no.		*Unit*	*Type*	*Quantity*
Make		Engine oil		
Model		Gearbox oil		
Serial no.		Transmission oil		
Chassis no.		Hydraulic oil		
Purchase date		Power steer oil		
Purchase price		Fuel		
New/second-hand		Water		
Sale date		Antifreeze		
Sale price		Battery		
Date sold				
		Tyres	Size	Pressures

Machine Job Card							
Machine details	**Department**			**Start date**			
				Finished date			
Work carried out/instructions	*Hour meter*	*In workshop*	*In the field*				
	Technician's name	Date	Time	Total hours	Rate	Cost	
TOTAL							

remedy the cause of the problem and not just its effect – prevention though is always better than cure. Today there are computer management programmes available that can offer several advantages for the manager and can provide:

- Planned preventative maintenance schedules
- Minor works recording
- Full asset history
- Fault analysis
- Full machinery reports

There are times or situations when machine maintenance cannot be conducted 'in-house', for instance when the item is under warranty, on a service contract, on hire or demonstration period. This needs to be made clear to operators as it affects individual machines on the premises. The basis for machinery maintenance should be a 'maintenance plan'. Resources and facilities will need to be made available including finance, technical expertise and an equipped workshop. The maintenance plan will need to include an inventory of all machines in the fleet together with manufacturers' maintenance instructions and operator manuals. There is a need for an administration system that will record works executed to individual machines and also identify when such is required. Machinery and maintenance records can be kept on paper or electronic form using purpose-made record cards. A couple of examples are given here.

Mower Maintenance
Mowers are probably the most important and heavily used items of plant on the sports ground. Proper maintenance, servicing and sharpening of cutting parts and units is critical to the quality of the playing surfaces. More and more sports grounds are investing in their own cylinder grinding and rotary blade sharpening equipment as they recognize the importance of maintenance and the cost-effectiveness of investment in such equipment, when there may

Testing a cylinder mower for cutting sharpness after grinding. (Bernhard and Company Ltd)

be many machines and many sharpening occurrences required in the season.

CYLINDER MOWERS

Modern sports complexes using up-to-date, state-of-the-art mowing equipment need equally modern equipment to keep the machines sharp. If the blade cutting surfaces are rounded over, nicked or damaged then the cylinder will need to be sharpened on a grinder. Spin grinding has been accepted as the norm. Using this technique the whole surface of the blade is sharpened flat leaving a large surface area. The more modern approach is to relief grind, leaving only the leading edge on the blade. This is a secondary grinding process after spin or single-blade grinding. A portion of the cylinder blade surface is removed to reduce the area of contact. Reducing the blade thickness by three-quarters reduces the torque required to turn the cylinder and the subsequent load on the engine. Back-lapping is a method of maintaining the

keenness of the cylinder cutting edge by reversing the direction of the cylinder, applying lapping compound to the blades and adjusting it until metal contact is made. Most modern machines are now made with a backlapping mode available. This allows for backlapping and resharpening of the cylinders while they are still attached to the machine. Each time you grind the cylinder you should grind the bed knife to suit: if not, the cylinder to bed knife clearance may vary along the length of the cylinder. This then will affect the quality of cut. Bed knives can be reground, or replaced and reground as required. Replace the bed knife when it is worn to the point where it can no longer be ground with a correct top face angle.

ROTARY MOWERS

Rotary blade sharpening is probably the one thing that many grounds staff neglect and pay insufficient attention to. A rotary blade cuts by high-speed impact and so, regardless of the condition of the blade, it will smash the grass in the same way that a flail mower does. Rough cut 'smashed' grass will always result in die-back, leaving the grass with a tatty, ragged appearance that does not look good even for rough and amenity grass areas. Therefore keeping a relatively sharp edge on a rotary blade will add to overall appearance, and moreover will result in less strain on the power unit and so will ultimately extend the life of the machine. Rotary blades are sharpened on two opposite faces. A properly sharpened blade has a cutting edge that is swept back rather like an aeroplane wing. The blade maintains its original width at the inner end of the cutting edge, while the outer end gradually recedes with each sharpening. The first step is to inspect the blade for damage and see if there are any nicks or cracks in the cutting edge. Check the blade wing tips for excessive wear at the point where the wings turn up. Sharpening should be done lightly using a bench grinder or small angle grinder. A bench grinder is probably better as you will have more control over the cutting edge. To check for sharpness, do not use your fingers; hold the blade up to the light and look down the cutting edge, with light reflected off it: it should look like a thin black line. After sharpening, the final procedure is to balance the blade. This is vital as unbalanced blades will case vibration and greater strain on engines and drive mechanisms.

Machinery Procurement

It is a fact that machines will come to the end of their useful working life and will need to be replaced periodically if playing surfaces and facilities are not to be compromised. The number of years that a machine should be retained before replacement is that which minimizes its average annual cost. The main factors will include:

- The annual rate of depreciation.
- The annual costs of maintenance and repairs.

- Any interest charges on borrowed money.
- Tax relief obtained on depreciation, interest charges and repair and maintenance costs.

The manager should consider whether the existing machinery is reliable and if indeed the new machine is essential or not. One should refer to repair and maintenance records when reviewing machinery requirements and also consider workloads and machine capacities for both existing and possible new purchases to determine any real benefits that may accrue from a new purchase. Investigate finance options and seek advice, not least from the bank manager. There may be trade-in options and discount deals that can be exploited to good effect. Do not forget to establish machine reliability and reputation by seeking endorsements and recommendations from users at similar premises. The proximity of dealers for sales and back-up service will often be a significant feature. The effect upon staff morale should also be considered, together with their competence and any training needs that may result from new machinery acquisition. Finally, always bear in mind the company's policy and plan for renewal and whether all alternatives have been considered.

THE BENEFITS OF SOLE OWNERSHIP

There are many benefits to owning machinery as opposed to the many other options available today, and it is worth remembering these when reviewing management procurement options. Machinery that is owned adds value to the business in the form of an asset and is not subject to external management charges or finance costs. It is always available, subject to maintenance, when you want it and therefore operations need not be delayed and can be conducted in the most appropriate conditions. Machinery should be carefully matched to your requirements and thus should attain the most effective operation. Owning machines also ensures that the maintenance history and machine performance is fully known and therefore full costs. Ownership also allows contracting out of machines to be conducted if required.

SOURCES OF FUNDING

Investigating funding sources and arrangements needs careful investigation and it is always best to seek genuine independent

Main Finance Options and their Merits

Finance Option	Advantages	Disadvantages
Capital purchase	May get a discount No interest payments No debt Immediately added to asset register Capital at end of a period to put towards another purchase	Capital tied up in machine (could be invested) Large expenditure can seriously affect cash flow Value of capital reduced over time If it is paid for, will it be maintained?
Bank loan	Company owns the machine Repayments can be arranged to match cash flow Spreads the cost of machinery purchase Easily accessible if you have credit or assets to cover loan Can pay off loan early	May need an initial deposit There may be arrangement fees Interest rates may change Planning cash flow more complex
Bank overdraft	Company owns the machine Lower interest rates than a loan Variable rate of interest Take advantage of cash 'deals'	Not a term agreement – must be repaid on demand Uses up credit at the bank Heavy penalties if overdrawn without permission
Hire purchase	Offered by the dealers through a finance house – convenient 'one-stop shop' Payments are fixed and regular	No ownership until final payment Expensive method of purchase due to high interest rates Usually a deposit is required Potentially dangerous to extend credit without bank manager's knowledge
Leasing	Rentals are shown on liability sheet Tax relief Secondary period at nominal cost Regular change/upgrade (3–5 years) Servicing often included No initial capital outlay Use your own capital for other items No security needed as lease company owns the asset	Never own the machinery Not included on asset register Payments must not exceed the life of the machine Potentially dangerous to extend credit without bank manager's knowledge Nothing to trade in or sell later towards a new machine Fixed interest rate

advice before committing yourself or your organization to any one 'deal' or arrangement. Do not be 'sold' by any single dealer or supplier before you know the full implications to the business, both in financial and operational terms. The bank manager must be consulted and kept informed of any machinery arrangements or purchases. The main options available for the sports ground manager are briefly described below:

Company capital reserves: This is in effect cash buying, using the company's financial reserves to buy machinery outright. Forward planning is necessary with a purchasing policy. A percentage of the profits made each year can be set aside, invested and utilized for such purchases.

Banks: Banks are a useful source of finance by making use of overdraft facilities or loans. Interest rates can be fixed or variable but base rates may be higher than those of other finance companies.

Finance companies: Many finance companies will loan money for the purchase of equipment. They may be more flexible than banks in the way the money is repaid, and may also offer services such as lease purchase or lease hire.

Manufacturer/dealership arrangements: Finance can be arranged through manufacturers and their dealership network. This is usually handled by a large finance company aligned to the manufacturer and may offer better terms and conditions than approaching the finance company direct.

Sponsorship: Sponsorship deals can take many forms, but in the main sponsors are looking for high-profile advertising. If you are staging a major event that will attract the news media, and in particular the television companies, equipment could be procured for the duration of the event and may be retained afterwards.

ALTERNATIVE METHODS FOR MACHINERY PROCUREMENT

The present economic climate and operational costs are encouraging sports ground managers to reconsider their mechanization policy. Machinery is expensive, increasingly sophisticated and often rapidly changing. It does not make economic sense to purchase some highly specialized machines, particularly some associated with renovation and construction works. A number of 'other' alternatives are available to the resourceful manager.

Machinery rings: Here a group of users form a consortium. Each user or business contributes to a central fund by means of a membership fee or levy (based on a sliding scale linked to the size of the enterprise). This levy is used to cover administration costs and members of the consortium contribute to the ring by the offer of specialized machinery. Equipment is used by individual users as required, either as a direct exchange or hired. In some cases the machinery is owned by the ring (it is possible to gain large discounts by having a large buying power) and the user hires the machine from the ring.

Using contractors: Here the business employs an outside company that specializes in the specific nature of work required. Such is the development of the contracting business that for a small sports ground all the work may be undertaken by a 'contractor', and sometimes even the management of the operation itself. Using this method has distinct advantages:

- Modern equipment is used to complete the job.
- There are no (minimal) machinery costs incurred by the business.
- Trained operators do a professional job and are familiar with equipment.
- Contractor comes in and does the work, then goes onto the next customer.
- Quality clauses can be included in the job contract.

Care must be taken when using a contractor: the cost of doing the job must be weighed against your quality requirements.

Machinery hire: In some areas there are companies that specialize in the hire of equipment and machinery to sports grounds and facilities. This concept is very popular in the construction industry, where virtually all equipment is hired. The hire company purchases the machine and rents it to the hirer. Usually all repairs and maintenance are the responsibility of the hire company, but damage is the responsibility of the hirer. Machinery hire is a growing trend in the sports turf industry to hire such as tractors and mowing machines.

PART III

Sports Pitches and Surfaces

8   Winter Games Pitches

Winter games pitches in the UK are those that are mainly used for field sports such as football, rugby (Union and League codes) and to a lesser extent hockey. Other sports such as American football, Gaelic football, lacrosse and hurling are played on similar surfaces. Thus we have sports where the primary objective is to kick, throw or carry a ball into the opponent's goal or territory and those that have the same objective, but where a stick and ball are used. In recent years 'higher level' hockey has moved to synthetic pitches with now very little being played on 'natural' turfgrass surfaces. There is some hockey played on grass at schools level and in local authority recreational grounds. Football and rugby are mostly played on 'natural' grass surfaces and in terms of their construction, and indeed their maintenance, there is actually very little difference between these two sports. Differences are minor and may often be no more than the grass height of cut and the actual pitch markings for play. The common factor with most of these sports is that they are played primarily in the winter

months when ground conditions are often wetter and grass growth reduced. Some sports, for example Rugby League, are playing more fixtures in the summer months at a professional level but still it is the case that for the majority of players and surfaces games are played over the autumn to spring period. This has significant impacts for management and many surfaces today at club and local authority provision level often end up as bare muddy fields when grass has been eroded and drainage impeded, and where resources cannot sustain the desired level of quality grass pitches. The grounds personnel in charge of the maintenance of winter games pitches often have one of the most demanding jobs in the sports turf industry.

Playing Quality Characteristics for Winter Sports

Most of our current knowledge regarding playing quality and surface standards is based on research done on football pitches

Surface Standards and Performance Criteria

There are obviously great differences in the games of football, rugby and hockey in terms of the surface requirements for play. An overview for each is given here.

FOOTBALL

The main objective is to provide a smooth surface of a regular gradient or slightly crowned that has no potholes or undulations. The ball should run true and evenly without deviation and should not be retarded as a result of the condition of the surface or the foliage. In wet conditions water should not remain on the surface. The surface should be firm (not hard) and there should be sufficient 'give' to allow players to stop and turn without undue strain on their anatomy. It should not be unduly abrasive. Markings should be clear.

RUGBY

The main objective for a rugby pitch is to provide a surface that is firm but also with sufficient resilience to allow players to stop and turn without due strain. The surface should be level and free from holes and undulations, and the grass should be kept at such a height

as to encourage tillering of the sward and reduce the tear factor. The grass should form an additional protective carpet to afford a falling player protection. The grass should be maintained at a height that, depending on its density, will achieve this objective. Markings should be clear and discernible even when travelling at speed.

HOCKEY

The surface should be smooth and the ball should run true, travelling without deviation or bobbling. There should be no humps, potholes or undulations that are likely to make the pitch dangerous to the players. The density and length of grass should permit the ball to travel in a straight line at the appropriate pace as required by the player: therefore the grass should be short. The pitch should be firm and have sufficient resilience to allow the player to stop, turn and change direction without strain on his or her anatomy. Marking should be clear and easily distinguishable by the player running at speed, and should be on the same level as the rest of the surface. The turf should form a closely knitted, well-tillered sward, grown in a well-structured soil through which water is able to filter rapidly.

by organizations such as the Sports Turf Research Institute and individuals such as Peter Dury. Research has indicated that for such winter games pitches the following criteria, divided into two categories, are significant:

Ball/Surface Characteristics

- Ball rebound resilience (how much it bounces)
- Ball roll, or rolling resistance

Player/Surface Characteristics

- Player traction (the amount of grip that a player can get when he is turning on the surface)

- Surface hardness

Further properties of the sward that are not strictly measures of playing quality, but are directly related to it, are:

Surface trueness: A very bumpy surface will detract from the playing quality of the pitch.

Grass ground cover and species composition: A bare mud surface is going to have a completely different set of characters from one with a full grass cover, and weed grasses such as annual meadow grass have inferior playing quality to the desirable grasses such as perennial ryegrass.

Water infiltration rate: Standing water on the surface grossly detracts from the quality of the surface for play.

Apparatus and Test Methods
Used for Football Pitches

REBOUND RESILIENCE

A 3m high pole with a means (a cup) of dropping a ball freely without any spin or downwards impulse is used to test rebound resilience. The pole has a graduated scale on its front and ball bounce against this scale is recorded. This is usually done by eye or, for more accurate recording, by the use of video equipment. The degree of ball bounce is recorded as a percentage figure.

ROLLING RESISTANCE

A ball is released from a height of 1m down a ramp of 45 degrees. The ramp has a curvature at the bottom to ensure that the ball does not bounce when it hits the turf. The distance that the ball travels from the end of the ramp is measured and recorded in metres.

PLAYER TRACTION

A mechanical device consisting of a sole plate about 150mm in diameter (roughly the same size as a size eight boot), into which are screwed six football boot studs and on top is placed 40kg of weights, is used to assess player traction characteristics. The sole plate sits on the sward and an industrial torque wrench is used to measure the force or torque needed to tear turf as the sole plate is turned. The basic idea is to measure how much force a player can exert on a surface before he or she starts to slip. The torque (or force) required is measured in Newton metres (Nm).

SURFACE HARDNESS

This is assessed using a Clegg impact soil tester. This device consists of a 0.5kg hammer that has an accelerometer fitted inside. The hammer is connected by a wire to a readout. The hammer is dropped down a guide tube from a set height of 300mm. The harder the surface the greater will be the deceleration experienced by the accelerometer. This deceleration is shown in Gravities on a liquid crystal display.

SURFACE EVENNESS

This can be tested using a profile gauge. This is a frame that has ten pins within it that are free to move vertically. The pins are placed onto the surface and then locked into position – the tops of the pins represent a profile of the surface. Each pin has a scale in mm, which is used to take readings. The 'roughness' of the surface is recorded as the Standard Deviation (the average deviation measurements).

Construction of
Winter Games Pitches

Soccer, rugby and hockey are played when grass growth is minimal and soil very wet. Frequently grass cover is worn at the beginning of winter and quagmire conditions can develop in high wear areas of the pitch such as goalmouths and centre circles. As a result players are unable to experience a satisfactory quality of game. The pressure to get matches played means they often take place at inappropriate times, for example during heavy rain. Frequently maintenance routines during and after the season are unable to restore the pitch to an adequate state for quality play. A vicious circle of deterioration sets in, directly related to poor drainage and compaction of the playing surface. The majority of playing surfaces require a designed drainage system to provide satisfactory playing conditions throughout the playing season. Upgrading a poorly drained pitch or constructing a new one does not necessarily solve the drainage and usage problem. Poor construction, lack of effective maintenance and overuse of the pitch will, eventually, lead to poor drainage and unacceptable playing conditions. It is essential that pitches are designed taking account of the estimated intensity of use.

Standards for Football Pitches

The tables here show standards proposed for use with football pitches as developed by Mike Canaway and others at the Sports Turf Research Institute about 1990.

Rebound resilience	Minimum (%)	Maximum (%)
Preferred limits	20	50
Acceptable limits	15	55

Distance rolled	Minimum (m)	Maximum (m)
Preferred limits	3	12
Acceptable limits	2	14

Traction	Preferred minimum (Nm)	25
	Acceptable minimum (Nm)	20

Surface hardness	Minimum (Gravities)	Maximum (Gravities)
Preferred limits	20	80
Acceptable limits	10	100

Surface evenness	Preferred maximum Standard deviation (mm)	8
	Acceptable maximum Standard deviation (mm)	10

The above figures thus give an indication of the specific surface requirements for football pitches. They, as yet, are merely guidelines and are not, in any way, mandatory requirements for play. Clearly there are different levels of sport from professional to lower league and schools provision, and not all surfaces will be able, nor will they be needed, to reach the highest performance criteria. Such performance indicators enable the grounds staff and management to assess the quality of their surfaces and therefore make more effective decisions in deploying resources for maintenance or in deciding whether surfaces are suitable for play. For more detailed information regarding playing surface standards and performance testing there is a wealth of information available from organizations such as the Institute of Groundsmanship and Fields in Trust (formerly the National Playing Fields Association).

Players under the age of 15 are judged to inflict about half as much damage to a pitch as their more senior counterparts. Therefore, a pitch used predominantly by juniors can accommodate approximately twice the capacity of one used solely by more senior players. The pattern of use must be taken into account when designing a pitch. Where use primarily takes the form of a large number of games played during weekends with little play during the rest of the week, demand cannot be staggered to make best use of a single high-specification pitch. In these circumstances general upgrading of

An exceptional standard of presentation – maybe not always achievable at lower league and club level but at least a goal to aim for! (J Mallinson (Ormskirk) Ltd)

pitches using slit-drainage and sand amelio-ration would be more appropriate than the creation of a single 'premier' pitch.

Main Options for Construction and Drainage

The need for good drainage on winter pitches cannot be disputed. Facilities on naturally free-draining soils may only require grading and routine cultivation to provide the basis for a good pitch. Such conditions are exceptional, however, and considerable work and expenditure is required to provide satisfactory drainage on heavier soils during the winter months, not only for play but also effective maintenance. The need for drainage increases with the intensity of play and the quality of surface required. Commercial facilities, such as League football grounds, require the most rapid drainage because of the quality of playing surface needed and the cash penalties involved in cancelling matches as a result of waterlogging. On new sites generally, the fewer earthworks and less

regrading required to produce satisfactory levels the better. Where soils have to be stripped and graded, the work must be done in dry weather to avoid damage to the soil structure. Soils worked in wet conditions will show drastic deterioration in drainage properties. An important consideration when deciding upon a construction system is the 'carrying' capacity of the surface, that is how many hours of use or number of games a surface can sustain. The accompanying table illustrates some of the main options available and their 'carrying' capacity.

The descriptions below cover the most frequently encountered systems in the UK (for further notes *see* Chapter 6). There are few situations when pitches of this type will provide a sustainable, quality playing surface. They are likely to be of use only on naturally well-drained soils such as sand, shallow soils over gravel, limestone or chalk.

PIPE DRAINAGE

Where natural drainage of the site is inade-quate, the basic requirement is for a pipe

Type	Construction detail	Time from construction to use	Life span	Games per season	Match cancellation rate	Matches per week
Undrained	No installed drainage system	n/a	<5 years	50–75	10–50%	1.4–2
Pipe drained	Basic lateral pipe drains at 5m spacing	4 months	<5 years	Up to 50	10–50%	>1.4
Slit drained	Sand/gravel slit drains at 1m spacing intercepting lateral pipe drains at wide spacing	4 months to 1 year	<5 years	50–75	5–15%	1.4–2
Sand carpet	100mm medium fine rootzone sand overlying an intensively slit drained area	1 to 1.5 years	>15 years	75–100	>5%	2–2.8
Suspended water table	250mm of medium/fine rootzone overlying a gravel drainage raft	1 to 1.5 years	>15 years	>100	>1%	>2.8

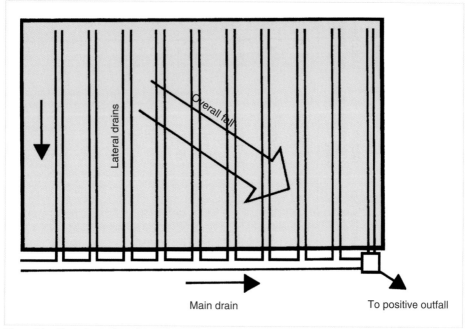

Figure 21   Typical pipe-drain layout for soccer/ruby/hockey pitches and training areas.

drainage system. This will consist of a comprehensive system of lateral drains usually at a spacing of 5–10m. A simple layout with the minimum number of junctions is the best approach. Where possible, it is better to avoid installing mains drains within the pitch. Drain trenches should be backfilled with a clean, hard stone to within about 150mm of the surface, blinded with medium/coarse sand and topped up with sand or sandy soil. There is no doubt that pipe drains alone can improve conditions dramatically on very wet sites or where there is a high water table in more permeable soils. However, good surface drainage is usually the most important criteria and pipe drainage may not be adequate, particularly on heavier soils or where a better, more reliable standard of playing surface is required.

SLIT DRAINAGE

Slit drainage provides a secondary 'bypass' system, intercepting surface water and conveying it to the pipe drains. The slits are excavated across the pipe drains, preferably along the line of play and at a spacing of 0.6–1.0m. It is essential that the pitch is topdressed with sand before using the pitch to ensure the sites are not smeared over and capped with soil. Topdressing with sand should form part of the ongoing maintenance programme to ensure the continuing effectiveness of the slits.

SAND CARPET

A further option is to install a basic pipe and slit drain system and, instead of dressing heavily with sand over a period of years, spread a full 100mm of sand during construction. The sward is established in the sand but is also capable of rooting through and drawing both nutrients and moisture from the underlying soil. To aid establishment, amendments such as soil, organic matter, peat and/or seaweed products can be incorporated into the surface of the sand. Some form of irrigation will be required to facilitate renovation and in the drier parts of the country a fully automatic sprinkler system may be needed.

DRAINAGE CARPET/SUSPENDED WATER TABLE CONSTRUCTION

Where even higher standards of construction are required, such as at many League football clubs, multiple-use stadiums or sports complexes, the option may well include complete stone drainage carpets with a rootzone of either a pure sand or sand/soil mix. Most systems of this type involve a pipe drainage system under a base of 100–150mm of clean, hard stone over which is spread a 50mm blinding layer of coarse sand/grit and then 250–300mm of the appropriate rootzone. Moisture is retained within the rooting medium by capillary forces to create a water table suspended over a drainage layer. Because of the exceptionally free draining nature of these constructions, a fully automatic irrigation system is essential for grass growth.

This summarizes the main options, but clearly there are variations that could be incorporated depending on individual circumstances. The choice of the correct system depends on a thorough knowledge of the site and the requirements in terms of the standard of construction and anticipated usage, as well as the budget available. In order to provide good playing surfaces for football and other winter games it is essential that water is rapidly drained away from the surface. This means the correct specification of a construction and drainage system appropriate to the client's needs. On a Football League ground one might need a full sand or sand-ameliorated construction overlying a gravel drainage carpet; on the other hand, for a local authority ground a slit-drained construction plus sand top would be perfectly adequate. Materials need to be chosen after laboratory tests and correctly placed in the construction and drainage works. Finally, in order to get the best out of the previous stages, there needs to be good aftercare and maintenance.

Surface Preparation and Grass Establishment

General cultivation is an essential part of seedbed preparation. Cultivation at a deeper level may be necessary on sites levelled by major grading. It is important that the works are correctly timed and that soils are only worked in appropriate conditions. To achieve the desired tilth it is essential that the appropriate equipment is used. With stony topsoil allowance must be made for the removal of stones or other debris using appropriate stone-picking/rotary equipment. The final seedbed must produce a smooth surface that is uniformly firm but not over-compacted. An appropriate fertilizer dressing should be applied prior to the establishment of the grass. The drainage characteristics of existing topsoil can be improved by adding suitable sand. The quantity of sand required should be determined by laboratory analysis. In some cases the sand will be mixed with the topsoil off-site, with the final rootzone spread over the prepared base.

GRASS COVER

The cheapest means of establishing grass cover is by seeding. It is essential that seeding is uniform over the working area. For rugby and soccer pitches the seed mixture must be composed predominantly, if not entirely, of hard-wearing and fine-leafed cultivars of perennial ryegrass. On hockey pitches slightly finer textured seed mixtures can be employed, particularly if the pitch doubles as cricket outfields in the summer. Pitches can be established using purpose-grown imported turf, although this is a more expensive option. The turf must contain hard-wearing grass cultivars suitable for winter games and be predominantly weed-free. The turf must be grown on light sandy topsoil and should not be excessively fibrous. On specialist constructions a washed turf may be considered. This is where the entire topsoil base has been washed away before laying.

213

Turfed pitches often require intensive hollow tine aeration in order to assist surface drainage in the early years of establishment.

Winter Games Pitch Maintenance

There are many maintenance tasks that are common to all grass winter games pitches. Typically, post-match work will involve divoting and this may require the application of topdressing material to the most badly damaged areas of turf. Sand topdressing is absolutely essential in winter games pitch maintenance, particularly for lower grade constructions, but it also has benefits for sand carpet and pure sand constructions. The sand topdressing helps to ameliorate the surface and prevent slit drains from becoming capped. While the capping is much reduced by the presence of a sand layer at the constructional stage, as in the slit drain plus sand top, the addition of further sand is still beneficial. Ensure provision of a reasonable quantity of topdressing and that adequate storage facilities are available to keep it dry. To restore the pitch for the following season a number of operations may need to be performed at the end of the playing year. Provision should be made for mowing,

fertilizer application, irrigation, aeration and renovation.

Pitch Size and Wear

A factor not often considered is the available space and its effects on wear, which impacts directly upon the nature and extent of maintenance and renovation works required. Most sports pitches have a range of possible sizes and it is useful to remember that in smaller pitches wear will be far more concentrated and severe. The table below illustrates how different sports compare in terms of size and, more significantly, the actual area per player. More players equates to increased wear and tear and, while one cannot change this factor, the grounds staff often have the option of increasing the pitch size within permitted parameters.

Intensity of Use

The management of fixtures and timing of games also has a large influence on pitch quality and the nature and extent of maintenance works and renovations needed. As already stated, it is a fact that these sports are played primarily in the winter months when ground and environmental conditions are often particularly challenging for the maintenance of surfaces fit for play and indeed for any sustained level of grass growth. In larger stadiums this has also

Sport	Number of players per game	Typical area of full-size pitch (m²)	Area of turf per player (m²)
Rugby Union	30	9,936	230
Rugby League	26	8,296	262
American Football	22	5,348	203
Football	22	7,700	350
Gaelic Football	30	11,234	374
Hockey	22	5,027	229
Lacrosse (men's)	20	6,400	320
Hurling	30	11,234	374

Effect of Intensity of Use of High Quality Natural Turf Winter Games Pitches on Percentage Ground Cover in High Wear Areas at the End of the Season

Number of games per week	Number of hours play per season	Mean % ground cover	% of pitches with no ground cover
2 or less	100 or less	40	0
2 or 3	100–150	32	0
3 or 4	150–200	21	43
Over 4	Over 200	0	100

Many professional football clubs are using smaller cylinder mowers to achieve quality of cutting comparable to fine turf surfaces. (Ransomes Jacobsen)

been exacerbated by shade from roofs. In recent years advances in science, technology, education and training have led generally to better-quality pitches at all levels of sport and the 'mud baths' of yesteryear, although still found, are no longer the common sight they were. Pitches often exhibit a 'diamond wear' pattern, especially on football pitches where the goalmouths and centre of the pitch receive the greatest wear. The table above shows the relationship between the amounts of play pitches can have and the effect on the amount of grass cover existing on the pitch at the end of the playing season. Clearly the greater the number of games played the less grass cover may be present at the end of the season. This is certainly true for pitches based on local soils. Excessive play or, more frequently, play occurring on inappropriate ground conditions leads to soil compaction, impeded drainage and loss of grass cover.

215

Generic Management Operations and Methods for Winter Sports Pitches		
Operations	**Objectives**	**Suggested methods**
Control height	To maintain a playing surface	Mowing options: pedestrian controlled cylinder, ride-on or gang units.
Correct compaction	To improve aeration and drainage and hence sward growth and playability	Aerate regularly
Control thatch	To improve surface drainage and grass growth and limit disease	Harrow, scarify; maintain pH and nutrients at adequate levels
Feed	To maintain sturdy growth under mowing regimes and hard wear	Apply fertilizer
Level	To create firm, level playing surface after disturbance by frost heave, repair work etc	Harrow/roll when necessary and when soil is not wet
Repair work	To maintain an intact playing surface; speed up natural regeneration, prevent weed ingress	Cultivate worn areas and reseed or turf badly damaged parts. Top-dress and overseed minor damage
Improve drainage	To facilitate all year round play and surface integrity	Spike; tine; topdress work sand; cultivate sand into top horizon; sand slit; improve under drainage. Remake pitch.
Control unwanted species/pests/ diseases	To remove harmful species that may weaken the sward and reduce cover	Spray with suitable approved pesticide

This is the perennial battle for those managing winter games surfaces.

Maintenance and Presentation

The table above lists the basic maintenance tasks for winter games pitches. Such pitches have many common requirements, with the different works required often only varying in details such as mowing height or level of renovation works required due to the amount of play encountered with a particular pitch. There will also be differences because of levels of game played: professional standard pitches need to be maintained at a higher standard and most often they have better resources (materials and equipment especially) to achieve this. Thus all maintenance works need to be tailored according to the sport played, level or standard of game and resources available. Prevailing environmental conditions, especially rainfall, have a large effect on works too. Of great importance is presentational maintenance. The visual appearance of pitches can be enhanced by mowing, brushing and rolling operations. Mowing and/or brushing the pitch in different directions can be used to create pattern effects on the sward that are visually appealing. Clippings should always be removed when mowing for presentational effect. Of even greater significance is for pitches to be correctly marked out with well-defined clean white lines. Line marking is covered in greater detail at the end of this chapter.

MOWING

Mowing should be carried out on a regular basis to encourage a good sward density to be produced. The height of cut for professional football pitches will be in the region of 25–37mm, depending upon how near it is to the first match being played. Local authority and school football pitches will typically be maintained at between 37 and 50mm. This higher cut height will also help to retain more ground cover at the start of the season and may be especially important for the limited budgets available to the majority of sports clubs and local authorities. Pitches with little or no artificial drainage will also benefit from this height of cut, helping them to wear better.

The disadvantage of this is that ball bounce and ball roll will be less than at a shorter height of cut. This should not be too great a concern as the early part of the season is fairly dry and the benefits will be appreciated later on in the season. During the growing season mow rugby pitches at 25–50mm and cut at 50–75mm in the playing season. As with many operations, the type of machinery used will depend upon available budgets and the standard of the pitch to be achieved. Professional pitches may be cut with a pedestrian cylinder mower, while local authority pitches will most likely be cut with tractor-operated gang mowers.

Sport	Suggested height of cut
Hockey	12–25mm
Football	25–50mm
Rugby	25–75mm

SCARIFICATION

As part and parcel of sward growth, a build-up of dead or decaying organic

Large cylinder mowers with trailed seats are ideal for most winter games pitches. (Ransomes Jacobsen)

Tractor-powered scarifier unit suitable for most winter games pitches. (SISIS Equipment (Macclesfield) Ltd)

material (fibre thatch) develops that lends itself to a soft surface. Therefore it is important to ensure that scarification is implemented to help counteract such developments. A tractor-mounted unit can be conveniently utilized. This basically consists of a series of revolving blades flicking through the turf surface, removing debris and reducing prostrate growth. If the unit does not possess a collecting box it is important to ensure that all resulting arisings are removed from the pitch, for example by using a leaf sweeper. Scarification can be appropriately timed for late summer during a period of good growth to allow sward recovery.

AERATION

A vital aspect of pitch management is having a routine programme of aeration work. This relieves compaction and improves water, air and nutrient circulation through the soil. In the playing season slit tine spiking should occur regularly, on a weekly basis if possible, ground conditions permitting. Slitting when the ground is very wet will cause more harm than good. When slitting aim for penetration of at least 125mm. A tractor-mounted slitter is usually adopted. Hand-forking of localized wet areas and subsequent topdressing with suitable sand also has the added effect of drying the immediate surface. At the close of the playing season, if the soil profile has become compacted to depth, deep aeration by verti-draining to maximum penetrable depth is essential. However, if the compaction is concentrated at the surface then thorough slitting will suffice. With all treatments the ground must be receptive, that is just moist enough for full benefit. During the summer months aeration work should not be neglected, but continued with regular spiking when ground conditions are receptive. Slitting in dry weather can be problematic, in that the ground is not very receptive and any slits present will open and crack, weakening the turf surface.

When conducting deep aeration work, penetrating to 300mm or so, be wary of any underground heating or irrigation pipes (these generally occur at a depth of 250mm or so) and ensure that the depth of penetration is adjusted to ensure the pipes are not punctured. Sand topdressing is

Irrigation should never be overlooked, especially in periods of grass establishment post-renovation. (TORO)

sometimes applied before Verti-draining so that some of the sand is 'punched' into the rootzone. Applying sand before verti-draining may be more useful on surfaces that are bare and muddy, as the sand will help to dry the surface providing an improved grip for the tyres. Additional topdressing may be needed following the verti-drain operation, although this will depend upon how much material is required to produce the desired standard of surface evenness. Hollow-coring of the surface layer of the rootzone, to 100mm depth, using 10–20mm diameter tines can also be carried out as a way of further reducing compaction in the surface layer. The extracted cores can either be removed from the pitch, especially if the aim is for soil exchange to improve the underlying rootzone, or can be re-cultivated and broken down where they are ejected, allowed to dry and then worked back into the rootzone. This second procedure is suitable if the cores are of an appropriate textural composition and the aim was just to relieve surface compaction. Solid or slit tining to 150mm depth

may only be required if the pitch does not need much in the way of renovation.

IRRIGATION

Watering facilities are required for winter games pitches, not only for initial grass establishment but to assist with renovation of the playing surface. Due to high percolation rates, well-drained pitches will require intensive irrigation to combat problems caused by drying out during periods of low rainfall. The minimum requirement for all pitches is conveniently located hydrant points where a hose or mobile sprinkler can be connected. For free-draining rooting mediums over drainage carpets an automatic pop-up irrigation system is essential.

FERTILIZER APPLICATION AND NUTRIENT REQUIREMENTS

Fertilizer application is necessary to provide the growing grass plant with nutrients and sustain and promote growth. The accompanying table suggests annual nutrient requirements for different pitch types. The significant variables when arriving at

Annual Fertilizer Requirements for Winter Games Pitches			
Type of pitch	**Fertilizer requirement kg/hectare/year**		
	N	*P₂O₅*	*K₂O*
Local authority pitches or school or club pitches (clippings not removed, earthworms present, loamy soils)	35–45	5–15 P₂O₅ and K₂O can be applied every third year	10–20
As above, but on loamy sand or sandy loam soil or having been slit drained	45–65	15–25	20–40
Major sports stadia (free draining, intensively used, clippings removed, irrigated)	160–240	60–90	140–200
Soil rootzone (clippings returned)	180–100	20–50	20–50
Soil rootzone (clippings removed)	160–200	80–100	80–100
Sand rootzone (clippings removed)	250	80–100	80–100

specific fertilizer programmes for winter games pitches are soil type/rootzone and whether clippings are removed from the sward. Many sports clubs and schools have pitches on unmodified soils and are mown with gang mowers where clippings are not collected. These pitches need less fertilizer than more sophisticated constructions with sand dominant rootzone and where clippings are frequently collected.

ROLLING
Some rolling work is required on pitches, especially hockey, to assist in producing a surface that is fast, firm and true. Repeated heavy rolling should be avoided as this will smear the surface and cause considerable compaction within the profile, leading to associated problems with impeded drainage and waterlogging. In addition severe compaction at the surface will encourage the spread of shallow-rooted annual meadow grass. The majority of pitches can be rolled perfectly satisfactorily using a cylinder mower, cutting blades raised, perhaps with some added weight in the front box. However, any form of rolling should always be avoided when the ground is very wet as

the risk of compression of soil structure will then be at its greatest.

TOPDRESSING
Topdressing will generally be with medium/fine sand and applied at a rate of up to 10 tonnes per 1,000m². A full-sized football pitch will therefore require between 60–80 tonnes. It is often more practical to apply the topdressing in two parts: 30–40 tonnes first and then work it in; followed by overseeding and then the remainder of the topdressing. It is also possible to use a general topdressing such as a '70/30' (70 parts sand and 30 parts soil, by weight), '80/20' or even '90/10'. Always have an analysis conducted for all topdressing materials to ensure a proper particle size analysis, otherwise it can be quite feasible to end up topdressing a pitch with a material that contains an excessively high amount of poor quality soil or worse. Work the topdressing in by drag-brush to ensure a fairly even spread. Where a deep spiker has been used, and especially if the weather is dry afterwards, the pitch may require additional topdressing applications. Pitches that have a slit system will require a regular

A tractor-drawn sweeper is invaluable for collecting arisings in renovation work or leaves in autumn. (SISIS Equipment (Macclesfield) Ltd)

topdressing maintenance programme. If this is not undertaken then the slits will deteriorate. The type of material used for topdressing a sand slit pitch will need to be compatible with the sand in the slit to ensure continuity is maintained between the pitch surface and the slit. Failure to maintain a sand slit system properly will result in the design failing, and result in a poorly drained surface again.

RENOVATION

Renovation work must be planned well in advance. All materials required, such as grass seed and fertilizer, should be ordered so as to be available when required, thus enabling work to proceed as early as possible. Depending on the prevailing ground and weather conditions, renovation should commence immediately after the season's final fixtures have been completed. This is important because a good recovery of the turf is essential so that the pitch will be in a presentable and playable condition when play resumes at the start of the following season. One of the first major operations of renovation is aeration work, to try and alleviate the compaction that has built up in the topsoil during the season. If the compaction is limited to the surface then the use of a deep slitter, making several passes over the pitch, will suffice. If deep-seated compaction is present, however, then deep aeration by verti-draining would be needed to maximum penetrable depth. At this point localized, badly worn areas such as goalmouths and centre circle areas may need to be cultivated thoroughly using a hand fork digging down to 100mm depth and relevelling. The prepared areas can then either be seeded or turfed, with deep turves being particularly suitable for these high wear areas.

Following aeration work a dressing of a medium/fine sand is desirable and must be worked well into any aeration holes with a drag mat; 40–60 tonnes/ hectare of lime-free sand should be sufficient. Extra light dressings can be given to localized low spots in an attempt to build them up. Where a number of pitches need renovation, specialist minimal cultivation equipment is sometimes used – this introduces the seed into the slit prepared by the machine. Several passes are usually necessary (in different directions), but used properly on reasonably level surfaces with no compaction present the result can be more than satisfactory.

During the renovation programme a spring fertilizer may be applied to assist pitch recovery from the season's play. This may involve using a high nitrogen-only application or a complete fertilizer product. Again this is best determined by reference to recent soil analysis as well as appraisal of turf condition.

OVERSEEDING

On completion of topdressing the pitch should be overseeded with a suitable grass species. Large-scale overseeding is most conveniently carried out by the employment of a machine that introduces the seed into the bed. For football and rugby the grass seed mixture will either be 100 per cent perennial ryegrass (with blends of different cultivars) or one that is predominantly perennial ryegrass, for example 60–70 per cent, with the balance being made up of smooth-stalked meadow grass, strong creeping red fescue, browntop bent or tufted hairgrass. A typical application rate will vary from $17–50g/m^2$, which works out as between two-thirds and two bags (of 25kg per bag) per 1,000m²; a 6000m² pitch would therefore require some four to twelve bags. The seed can be applied using a seed-drilling machine, especially if only a small amount of topdressing is being planned. If a further topdressing is being applied following the application of the seed, then broadcasting with a spreader might be quite acceptable, although scarification should ideally have been carried out beforehand to aid subsequent seed establishment. Sowing grass seed at too high a density can result in narrow, relatively weak plants that struggle to develop due to increased competition,

producing a turf that is not as wear tolerant as it should be. Hockey pitches are mown at a lower height of cut than other winter games, while also subject to wear, and in such situations the finer grass species of fescue and bent need to be considered. However, due to the wear factor involved, it is also advantageous to introduce perennial ryegrass into the seeds mixture, selecting 'dwarf type' cultivars that tolerate low mowing, including fineness of leaf, in the calculations. The ryegrass strengthens the sward and it is advantageous to sow high rates of perennial ryegrass in high-wear areas such as goalmouths.

Germination sheets can be used to protect a seeded area, although these should only be used for a short period of time (no more than five days) to allow germination to take place. The sheets should not be left down for too long otherwise disease attack will occur. There will be a higher risk of disease due to the germination sheets effectively nullifying any wind aeration and increasing humidity and temperature beneath the sheets. Raising the sheets for part of the day and making sure they are left in place overnight might help to reduce the problems associated with leaving the germination sheets down permanently for the few days they are down.

PLAYING SEASON REPAIR WORK

To assist in maintaining surface quality, repair work should be undertaken routinely after matches, replacing divots and forking up deep scars as required. Wherever possible, the divots should be trodden back down and replaced by hand immediately the game has finished. Wet and worn areas can also be in filled with an appropriate grade of sand topdressing (medium/fine), imparting a drying effect. Depending upon the level and intensity of play, this can take up to a day or two to complete in its entirety. Realistically, such levels of detail can only be achieved on the more professional pitches. Lower standard pitches will usually have to make do with a short spell of divoting by the groundstaff, with a chain harrow (smooth side down) being used to finish off and tidy up the surface, with excess divots being removed from among the links of the chain harrow.

PESTS, DISEASES AND WEEDS

Be vigilant against disease attack. To help prevent this, make sure that the grass is kept relatively dry and free from dew, and that adequate air circulation and light levels are maintained. Fusarium patch disease can be a problem on heavily maintained areas that are enclosed within stadiums. In such circumstances, light levels and airflow are reduced, increasing the likelihood of a disease attack. Fungicide application will most likely be the only realistic control method. Black layer can be a problem on some high sand content pitches. Deep spiking, hollow-coring and sanding is sometimes used to help alleviate the problem, although this may not provide a solution. Power harrowing can cultivate the surface layer, exposing and breaking down the black layer, which results in a significant increase in aerobic exchange. Ultimately, however, the pitch may need to have the rootzone removed to the depth of the problem. The most likely pest damage will be from earthworm casting and this will start to smother the sward unless remedial action is taken. Dispersion of the casts, when dry, through brushing or chain harrowing will be necessary. The chemicals that are currently available only appear to give limited control for a short period of time. A slight acidification of the surface may be considered, however; both perennial ryegrass and smooth-stalked meadow grass thin out with acidification. The low pH levels that can be sustained by fine turf swards are not suitable for football pitches, as the suitable grasses would not grow to any extent. Leatherjackets can be a serious pest, feeding on the grass roots over the autumn and winter period. If they are present they will probably need to be controlled with the use of approved pesticides,

typically in October or November when the grub is large enough to absorb the dose and yet not so large that the thick cuticle of the grub effectively resists the chemical. If a selective herbicide is to be applied to a pitch, then the grass should be in a strong, growing condition and any areas that have been renovated should not be sprayed too soon after seed germination. A realistic time for herbicide application is some six to eight weeks after the renovation work has been completed.

FROST PROTECTION

During the winter a very common occurrence is the cancellation of matches due to hard ground caused by severe frost. This is frustrating for player and spectator alike. Numerous methods have been developed to protect winter pitches from the effect of frost. Unfortunately the most effective methods requiring the least labour to operate, for example the introduction of underground heating cables or pipes that conduct warm water, are also the most expensive. They can also hinder deep aeration work, which is vital in sustaining good drainage. Pitches can also be prevented from freezing by the use of insulating blanket covers, but these too have inherent drawbacks, such as labour and storage. Straw is the traditional material in this category, but various types of insulating blankets have been tried with varying degrees of success. The major disadvantages of this approach are the labour requirements of dragging the cover on and off the pitch and the damage to turf and playing surface that accompanies this procedure. It should also not be forgotten that the insulating properties of a long grass cover of 50–75mm, with air trapped between leaf blades, can be effective against the less severe late autumn frosts.

PITCH ROTATION

By the middle of winter the pitches may be looking worn, possibly because of overuse. Perhaps the surface is being subjected to regular training or far too many second team games and it is showing significant wear despite good drainage and maintenance. If a spare ground is available then this should certainly be used for training. If more than one pitch is available, then rotation of games between the pitches is also sensible. If one pitch is notoriously wet then the drier pitch is better employed during wet periods. Management of pitch use is important:

- Where possible rotate pitches to spread play over all available turf areas.
- Use separate pitches for early and late season (keeping the drier pitches for the wet part of the season).
- Use any spare ground for training (consider a synthetic pitch for training purposes).
- Prior to matches pitch condition should be assessed and if necessary matches cancelled.

Line Marking for Winter Games Pitches

In sports turf management the final presentation of the playing surface is of great importance and can be improved, or alternatively marred, by the standard of marking out operations. Uniform and positive line marking is not only pleasing in appearance but it is essential to all participants and spectators in order that the rules of the game can be correctly interpreted. There are a variety of marking materials available for machine application and that can be used on many different surfaces. Clearly the persistency of materials varies and some are better suited to hard surfaces than to turf. In general, an ideal marking material should be waterproof, quick-drying, not easily rubbed off or liable to flake or powder. It should also meet health and safety requirements. Various practices have been used in the past for the application of white lines to football pitches. The objectives of such practices have been to both reduce

labour and materials costs, while endeavouring to keep the lines visible for a greater length of time. Some of these practices have led to injury and subsequent court action being taken against managers and clubs.

Types of Line-Marking Materials
WET LINE MARKING

Here the marking material is in a liquid formulation. Such materials are frequently used on both grass and non-turf surfaces. Lime mixed with water was the common material traditionally used, but this has now been replaced by commercial line marking solutions. Lime can be dangerous to players, especially if it gets into the eye, which is why in the main the newer non-toxic marking compounds are used today. It is necessary to overmark the lines after the initial marking. Overmarking frequency will depend largely upon pitch/court usage, material longevity and the prevailing weather conditions.

DRY LINE MARKING

Various non-toxic whiting powders are available, based on ground natural calcium carbonate, that can be used wet or dry. They are safe to use provided Control of Substances Hazardous to Health (COSHH) principles are applied. Under COSHH the user would be required to wear gloves and eye protection, and to wash off any in contact with the skin as a precautionary measure. Most powders are supplied in a fine form. Hydrated lime (calcium hydroxide) should never be used for line marking. It is toxic and can give rise to chemical skin burns and irritations. It can cause serious damage to the eyes and skin on contact in both its dry and wet form. Its use is not recommended under any circumstances.

PAINT MARKING AND MARKERS

There are two types of paint marker, those that use paint and those that use aerosols. The first type is used on macadam and similar surfaces, while the aerosol can be used on similar surfaces but also on grass. If paint is used then it should be a special type that gives a good line without the application being thick. If the application is thick then it can affect the bounce of a ball if it hits it. Because the paint is special, they often use special thinners and these will be required to clean out the paint tank and rollers after use. Permanent paints are based on pigmented viscous liquids that can be applied either in a diluted form or neat.

Line-Marking Machines

Line marking needs to be accurate. Officials, players and spectators all need to observe that the game is played within the playing area and within the rules of the sport. Part of the accuracy and precision of line marking comes from the skill of the groundsman, while part is dependent on the machine used, the type of white line-marking compound or paint and, importantly, the conditions at the time. Ideally the machine and the paint should be chosen to give the best results depending on the weather and ground conditions, and also the requirements of the match. Having the right machine really can make a difference. Although there appear to be many different types of machine, there are in fact only two main techniques employed in linemarking. There are wet marking systems, where a liquid compound or paint is rolled or sprayed onto the ground, and dry markers that use a powder. In adverse or muddy conditions it is best to avoid equipment that transfers paint or compound onto the ground through mechanical contact. Such equipment, using transfer wheels or belts, can easily pick up mud and loose debris, which then clogs the wheels or falls off as a thick messy dollop at the end of the line. Non-contact markers, such as dry powder or spray markers, are preferred in wet conditions, though dry markers will require a relatively wind-free day for application if crisp lines are to be created. Spray-on or pressurized markers have the advantage that they work well in both wet and dry conditions. On these machines a

trigger is used to release the paint solution from a nozzle. They do tend to be more expensive to buy, and the paint can be too, but the line may last longer. This is because the paint is usually more rain-fast and when it is applied it marks both the grass blade and the ground below, so mowing will not remove it all. Changing conditions may mean it is desirable to have more than one type of marking machine. Budgets, however, usually mean only one machine can be bought and that machine has to cope with all sites and all conditions.

One should also consider the type of surface to be marked. Spray-marking systems and aerosols are often chosen for the marking of synthetic or hard, porous facilities. Another factor to consider is the number of facilities to be marked. Where there are many pitches on one site, a good option is a ride-on marking machine. Ride-on units speed up the rate of marking in terms of metres per minute and, because of their large tanks, they also reduce downtime in terms of mixing and refilling with marking paint. Other factors to consider include the required density, brightness and longevity of the white lines. It is worth remembering that these properties may be influenced by expected grass growth, mowing frequencies and height of cut, as well as by the paint and the machine applying it.

The wheel-to-wheel transfer marker remains a popular option because of its relatively low purchase price and, since these machines take most wet marking compounds, their low running costs. Transfer markers are also simple to use, making them ideal for those situations where trainee groundsmen or volunteers do the over-marking. The skill of the groundsman can do much to produce a straight line but there is now a machine available that incorporates laser technology. This machine uses a laser and digital recognition software to produce perfectly straight lines time after time, irrespective of the operator's experience. The system also produces perfect right-angled corners. A sprayer tank fitted with a tracking arm follows the laser beam and turns on and off the paint spray as required. Any deviation from the laser beam is immediately compensated for by an adjustment of the tracking arm to deliver paint in a true straight line.

The variety of marking machines available can be generally categorized according to working principles and type of surface that they can mark. These categories include:

Dry line markers: As the name implies, these are applying dry powder compounds.
Pressure pump markers: A wheel-driven pump forces marking fluid through a jet or spout directly onto the turf surface.
Electric pump markers: These are battery driven to constantly maintain the required pressure and direct the liquid onto the turf surface.
Belt feed markers: These have a moving belt system that conveys a

continual supply of liquid onto the turf surface by contact.
Wheel transfer markers: These convey the liquid via a rotating wheel onto a tray and then via a sponge wheel directly onto the turf surface.

All of the above markers are obtainable from most sports ground suppliers. Before purchasing any marker, have a demonstration first and ensure you get the right marker for your requirements.

To summarize, when deciding upon a specific type of line-marking machine it is worth considering a few key points:

- The machine should ideally have a splash-free container when it is moved around.
- Machines on larger wheels are easier to push than those on small wheels.
- Grass and soil should not pass back to the tank when marking. It reduces the

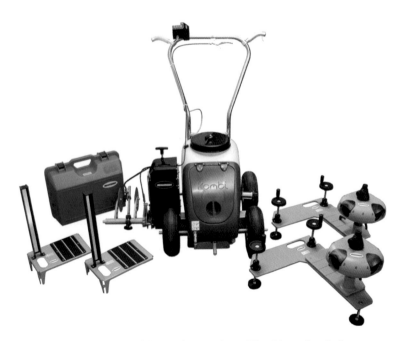

The future of line marking? Laser-guided line marking machine. (Fleet Linemarkers Ltd)

capacity of the tank and also discolours the marking material.

- It should be possible to switch off the machine for transport purposes.
- It is desirable that the machine is capable of producing differing line widths to cater for different sports.
- Those machines that have the actual applicator out in front are easier to use on bends than those at the rear.
- The machine should be easy to clean out after use.
- It is desirable that the machine should be able to handle as wide a range of different marking materials as possible.

Immediately after use, marking machines must be cleaned thoroughly to avoid marking material hardening in the tank and interfering with future operations. There are combination line marker/sprayers available. Even greater care is required with these to ensure that chemical residue is thoroughly washed out to avoid a carry over to the next operation.

Some Aspects of Legislation Relevant to Line Marking

The main governing factors for marking out white lines are the same as those for other routine tasks in the workplace. Under the Health and Safety at Work Act 1974 every employer has a duty of care to ensure the workplace is safe for their employees, contractors, visitors, players and spectators. The Control of Substances Hazardous to Health Regulations is in place to prevent ill health from exposure to any hazardous substances present in the workplace.

Risk Assessments are required for all tasks carried out in the workplace: in relation to the nature of the hazard, worst outcome, person(s) at risk, current precautions, estimated risk and further precautions. If all three of the above are addressed satisfactorily, this will automatically govern what to use for white line marking, ensure best practice and, above all, safety. It is the duty of all managers to ensure that all the regulations are adhered to, as they are ultimately responsible in the eyes of the law. If line marking is carried out by contractors, then a specification should be drawn up to include all the safeguards outlined in these guidance notes. This could also extend to include specifying a particular product.

USE OF HERBICIDES TO
REINFORCE LINE MARKINGS

Until the Food and Environment Protection Act 1985 (FEPA) was introduced, many grounds staff and club members used various herbicides mixed in with whitening compounds to keep the lines in longer and more visible during the winter playing season. It is, however, only permissible to use a herbicide approved for use on sports turf and this is likely to be a total herbicide. COSHH and Risk Assessment must be carried out prior to any application. A further governing factor is that the user must have obtained his/her Certificate of Competence in Use of Pesticides (PA1, PA2A and PA6A).

Any herbicide product for line marking must be used within the conditions of approval granted under the Control of Pesticide Regulations 1986 (COPR) and as outlined on the product label. There should be no risk to players by contact or transfer of the active herbicide to any part of the body. The addition of herbicides to whitening materials is not a recommended practice, unless carried out by a competent, certificated person. Creosote is another compound used in the past to mark and reinforce line markings but it is not approved for use on sports turf under COPR. Its use is therefore not recommended under any circumstances. The use of hydrated lime, herbicide additives and creosote can result in serious injury to players, which can ultimately lead to actions against both clubs and individuals. Play safe – use only safe and approved compounds that are currently available on the market. Do not use old compounds.

Surface Preparation for Line Marking

Surface preparation prior to marking out is all important in improving the efficiency and persistency of the marking material, particularly on grass areas. When marking out on turf, the grass should not be too long; where mowing is necessary, the clippings should be removed, at least in the vicinity of the line marking. When marking out playing areas with a slightly longer grass cover, such as rugby pitches, it can be useful to mow the grass shorter just along the lines that are to be marked out with a pedestrian mower. Generally, wet marking produces best results on a dry surface, but the dry line materials work better on wet grass. Dry weather conditions are desirable for either method. Prepare the marking solution carefully to ensure it is not lumpy. Lumps could cause application problems, particularly where pressure jet machines are to be used. Regular stirring may also be necessary to keep the material in suspension. To obtain good results from marking out, the following points should be observed:

- Dry materials such as marking compounds should be carefully and thoroughly sieved.
- Agitate the mixture thoroughly to ensure good mixing of materials.
- The grass on the area to be marked should not be too long nor should it harbour any grass clippings or other debris. It is often a good idea to mow out the lines prior to marking and to 'box off' the clippings.
- Ideally dry conditions should prevail when marking out, although the surface may be slightly moist. This will aid retention of the marking material, especially so with dry line materials.

It is advisable to determine the exact location of pitches on a scale plan before attempting actual marking out. The first task is to fix all four corners of the pitch. Right angles can be obtained using the 3:4:5 triangle method. Often pegs or holes are sunk into the ground to act as a guide of the pitch for future seasons (obviously only where the pitch is not moved). Centre spots can be determined by intersection of diagonals from the corner points. The remaining lines must be located by using a tape measure, long lines, pins and, in the case of the 9.15m centre circle and penalty areas, a cord revolving around a pin. When re-marking lines, especially broken ones, it is strongly recommended that a string line is used to ensure that these lines are in fact straight and true.

Sports Pitch Markings

Football Pitches

Colour of lines	Not specified, traditionally white.
Width of lines	120mm maximum. The goal line shall be marked the same width at the depth of the goal posts.

External dimensions include width of lines. The centre of the penalty kick mark is measured 11m from the outside of the goal line. The dimensions for the centre circle and penalty area arcs are measured from the centre of the field and penalty kick mark respectively to the outside of the lines. The inside faces of the goal posts are 7.32m apart and the measurement between the ground and the underside of the crossbar is 2.44m. Goalposts and crossbar may be of square, rectangular, round, half round or elliptical cross-section. They must be of wood or metal (steel or aluminium) or other material approved by the International FA board. They should have a white finish. Nets should be attached to the two posts, the crossbar and the ground behind the goal, and should be supported. Four flags and flag posts should be placed at the corners. Posts should not be less than 1.5m high. If desired, optional flags may also be placed to mark the centre line and should be at least 1m outside the touchlines.

PITCH SIZES

International matches	110 × 75m (maximum) 100 × 64m (minimum)
Other matches	120 × 90m (maximum) 90 × 45m (minimum)
NB The length in all cases exceeds the breadth.	

Rugby Union Pitches

Colour of lines	Not specified, typically white
Width of lines	75mm preferred

External dimensions exclude width of lines; other dimensions indicated are measurements between lines. Touchlines are therefore in touch; goal lines are in the 'in goal' area. Dead ball lines are not in the 'in goal' area. The distance from the goal line to dead ball line should be not less than 10m where practicable and 22m maximum. The six short lines 5m in front of and parallel to the goal lines at the 5m and 15m lines, and in front of each goalpost, are each 1m long. The goalposts are on the goal lines and should be 5.6m apart (internal measurement) with 3m from ground level to the top of the crossbar. Posts should be at least 3.4m high. Flags marking halfway and 25 yard lines should be at least 1m outside the field of play. These and the flags at the junctions between touchlines

and goal lines should be a minimum of 1.2m high.

Rugby League Pitches

Colour of lines	Not specified, typically white
Width of lines	Typically 75mm

External pitch dimensions exclude width of lines; other dimensions indicated are measurements between lines. The broken lines shown consist of marks or dots on the ground not more than 2m apart. It is of advantage for transverse broken lines to be marked across the full width of the pitch but if restricted then each shall not cover a length less than 15m long. Goalposts are on the goal line and are 5.5m apart, this being the internal measurement. The bottom 2m of each post may be padded. Height above ground to the lower side of the crossbar is 3m and the height of the goalposts should be a minimum of 4m. Flags may be placed as indicated: corner posts are in touch and in goal. Posts should be of non-rigid material and not less than 1.25m high. Flags should be at least 1m outside the field of play.

HOCKEY PITCHES

Colour of lines	Not specified, traditionally white; white or yellow on synthetic grass pitches
Width of lines	75mm

The field shall be rectangular, 91.4m long and 55m wide. Its boundaries shall be clearly marked out according to the plan illustrated. The longer lines are known as side lines and the shorter ones as back lines, the length of back line between the goalposts being the goal line. A centre line and two 25 yard lines shall be marked throughout their length on the field: the middle of these lines to be 50 yards and 25 yards respectively from the outer edge of the back lines. To assist in the control of the hit-in, across the centre line and each 25 yards line, parallel to and 4.5m from the outer edge of the side lines, a mark of 1.83m in length shall be made. A mark 0.3m in length should be marked inside the field of play on each side line and parallel to the back line and 14.63m from its inner edge. For penalty corner hits, the field shall be marked inside the field of play on the back lines on both sides of the goal at 4.55m and 9.10m from the outer edge of the nearer goalpost, such distance being to the further edge of those lines. For corner hits the field shall be marked inside the field of play on the back lines 4.55m from the outer edge of the side lines. All the marks to be 0.3m in length. A penalty spot 150mm in diameter shall be marked in front of the centre of each goal; the centre of the spot shall be 6.40m from the inner edge of the goal line. The two striking circles are made up of two quarter circle arcs of 14.63m radius, measured from each goalpost and joined by a straight section 3.66m long, the latter being the width of the goals.

Marking Out an Association Football Pitch with One Person

Equipment: Line marker, marking fluid, tape, lines, pins, paint brush, wheelbarrow if necessary.

1. The method described is for one man and assumes that goalpost holes are already in place.
2. Place pins A and B adjacent to the goalpost holes at one end of the pitch, and measure and place a further pin C halfway between the goalpost holes. Attach tape to pin C. Tie a line on to pin B and pull this through pin A, extending it (with the tape) to the corner of the pitch D. The width of the pitch can vary between 45–90m, depending on space available and the requirements, so the distance from pin

C to the corner, being half the width of the pitch, will depend upon local circumstances.

3. Repeat the operation from pin A pulling the line and tape (from pin C) out to the other corner point E. The goal line has now been fixed.
4. Measure 9.16m from pin C towards pin D and insert pin F and 20.16m from pin C towards pin D. Insert pin I. These mark the extents of the goal and penalty areas respectively.
5. Repeat the operation on the other side on pin C and insert pins G and H. Remove tape from pin C.
6. Walk to the opposite end of the pitch, taking with you a line attached to pin D. Refer to the diagram, repeat the operation carried out at the opposite end and insert pins J, K, L and M. Attach the string you brought with you from D to M, giving one touchline. Measure for O and N. Attach line from K through L, J to P and insert pins P, Q and R.
7. Remove tape from pin L, attach line to pin P and walk back from P towards E, measuring 5.5m from E towards P. Insert pin S. Measure 16.5m from E towards B and insert pin T. S and T give extents of the goal and penalty areas respectively.
8. Continue from E towards P and insert pin U halfway between E and P. This gives the position of the halfway line. Repeat the operation from P towards E to give the goal and penalty areas at that end, and insert pins V and W.
9. Repeat this operation between M and D. Inserting pins X, Y and Z, 1 and 2.
10. String between 2 and S, T and 1, Z and U (inserting pin 3 to give centre spot), V and Y, and X and W.
11. String between Q and M, G and R, N and C, F and O, N and I.
12. Obtain marker and mark in all lines, including corner quadrants (1m radius) and centre circle, radius 9.15m.

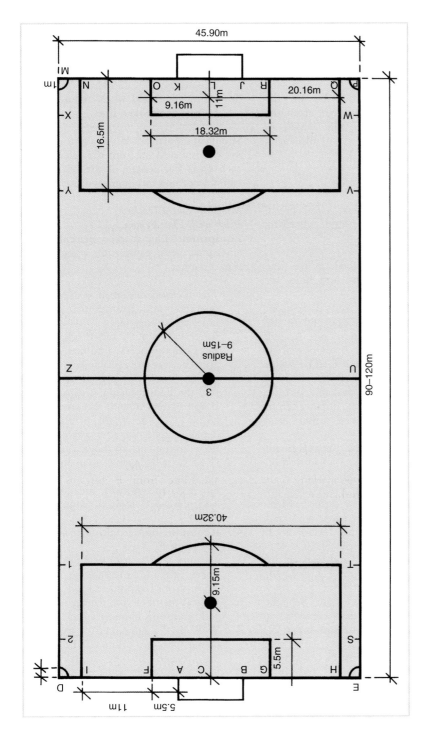

Figure 22   Marking Out a Football Pitch.

231

13. Measure up 11m from C towards L and mark the penalty spot and semi-circle radius 9.15m. Repeat this at the other end.

Should the goalposts not be in, the touchlines must be squared off from the goal lines at one end. The length of the pitch, according to circumstances, varies from 90–120m.

Marking Out a Rugby Union Pitch with One Person

Equipment: Line marker, paint brush, pins, tape, lines, marking fluid, wheelbarrow if necessary.

1. The method described is for one man and assumes the post holes are already in.
2. Insert two pins A and B adjacent to the post holes at one end of the pitch. Tie a line on to pin A, pull this through pin B, extending it to the corner of the pitch C. The width of the pitch can vary between 60–70m, depending on space available and the requirements, so the distance from B to C will depend upon local circumstances.
   Measure in 5m from C towards B and insert pin D. Measure 15m in from C towards B and insert pin E.
3. Repeat the operation, pulling the line out to the other corner, point F. Measure in 5m from F towards A and insert pin G. Measure 15m from F towards A and insert pin H.
4. Fix a line onto pin F and walk to the other end and insert pins I, J, K, L, M, N, O and P.
5. Pick up the line you brought from corner F and extend it (for schools use) 10m past point N, inserting pin Q.
6. Walk back down from N towards F. Insert pin R 22m from N and pin S halfway between F and N. Pins T and U fall 10m either side of S. Insert pin V 22m from F towards S. Extend the

line 10m beyond F and insert W, the position of the dead-ball line.
7. Repeat the whole operation on the opposite side of the pitch inserting pins X, Y, Z, 1, 2, 3 and 4.
8. String all around, mark in, taking care to note the broken lines.

Should the posts not be in, the touchlines must be squared off from the goal lines at each end. The length of the pitch again varies according to circumstances.

Marking Out a Hockey Pitch with One Person

Equipment: Line marker, marking fluid, tape, pins, lines, paintbrush, wheelbarrow if necessary.

1. The method described is a one-man operation and assumes the goalpost holes are already in.
2. Insert two pins A and B adjacent to the goalpost holes, find the halfway point between the goalposts and insert pin G. Hook the tape on to pin C. Pull the line from pin A through pin B and extend it with the tape to the corner C. The width of the pitch depends upon the area available and the requirements, so the distance from G to C will depend upon local circumstances.
3. For women's hockey measure back 4.55m from C towards B and insert pin D.
4. Repeat the operation to give corner E and point F.
5. Measure 4.57m from goal post A and insert pin I, measure a further 4.57m from I and insert pin K.
6. Repeat the operation from goalpost B and insert pins H and J.
7. Walk to the other end of the pitch, taking with you a line fixed to pin C (for women's hockey also take a line from pin D at the same time).
8. Repeat the operations above to give points L, M, N, O, P, Q, H, S, T, U, and V.

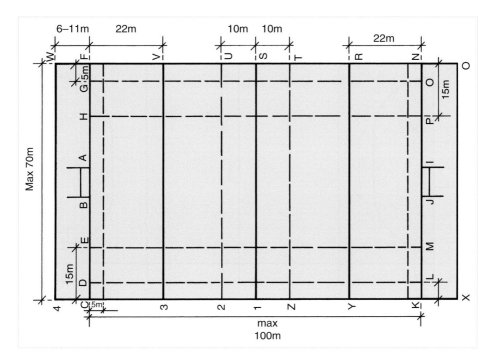

Figure 23   Rugby Union.

9. Walk back from O towards C, after fixing the lines from C and O to pins O and P, measure 23m from O towards C and insert pin W. Insert pin X halfway between O and C. Measure 23m from C towards O and insert pin Y.

10. Repeat the operation on the other side of the pitch and insert pins Z, 1 and 2 and lines E to Q and F to R.

11. Pull lines between pegs A, G, B and L, N, M at opposite ends of the pitch (these lines will cut the striking circle at points 3, 4, 5 and 6 and the positions can be dotted with a paint brush).

12. Obtain marker and, starting at peg O, mark in the outside of the pitch and the 4.55m marks at the corners.

13. Fix the tape at pins M and L and mark in the striking circle (radius 14.63m) to points 5 and 6. Mark in the straight line between these two points. Repeat at the other end of the pitch.

14. Mark in the 4.55m dotted lines F to R and P to D, if pitch is required for women's hockey.

15. Mark in centre line, 23m lines and centre spot.

16. The lines form part of the pitch so the marker should run inside the lines.

Should the goalposts not be in then it will be necessary to square off from the goal lines at one end. The length of the pitch will vary according to local circumstances.

Important note: These notes are intended solely to provide helpful guidance for club managers and grounds

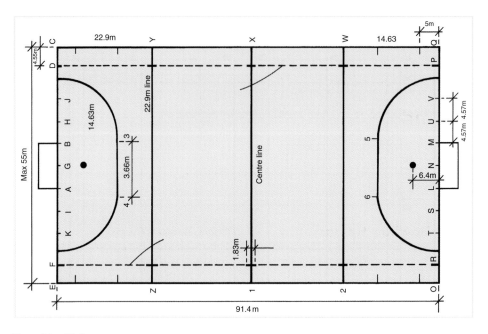

Figure 24   Hockey.

staff. The information may vary or change from time to time, as a result of directives issued by governing bodies or government departments. Always check details with sport governing bodies for the latest requirements regarding measurements and pitch markings. One must also follow the latest Health and Safety and Materials Handling Legislation and seek guidance from product materials suppliers.

9 Bowling Greens, Croquet and Pétanque

Lawn Bowling Greens

There are two distinct types of green and forms of the game in the UK: Flat and Crown.

Flat Bowling Greens
This is the dominant game in both the UK and abroad, including Canada, Australia, New Zealand, South Africa and the USA. There are more than 5,000 flat greens in the UK.

GREEN SIZE
The green is surrounded by a ditch between 50mm and 200mm deep and 200–380mm wide. The green is often enclosed by a bank (35 degrees from the vertical). The bank should be not less than 230mm above the playing surface. For play the green is divided into parallel rinks of between 5.5m and 5.8m (18–19ft). These rinks may be reduced to 4.8m (14ft) for domestic play. It is usually possible to have six playing rinks on a standard green.

Crown Bowling Greens
This is the dominant game in Northern England (Lancashire, Cheshire), the Midlands, North Wales and the Isle of Man. There are around 3,500 crown greens in the UK.

GREEN SIZE
Crown greens are usually similar in size to flat greens, but can be up to 55 × 55m. Unlike flat, crown greens occur in most shapes and sizes (including circular ones). The crown (centre) is between 200mm and 450mm higher than the corners of the green; the recommended height of crown for a 36 × 36m green is 380mm. The game is played in *all* directions across the green with *no rinks*. Ditch requirements/measurements are less stringent than for flat bowling greens.

Bowling Green Surface Standards

The playing surface standards for flat bowling greens have been studied in detail in the UK, while those for crown bowling

Flat Lawn Bowls Dimensions	
International competition size	34m (direction of play) minimum
	40m (side) maximum
National games	31m (direction of play) minimum
	40m (side) maximum

greens have not. This is primarily due to the dominance of the flat green game, which has spread nationwide while crown greens are almost exclusively confined to the north-west of England, predominantly in the counties of Lancashire and Cheshire.

Flat Bowling Greens

Four criteria are recognized to be impor-tant components of natural turf bowling surfaces for flat greens:

- A fast green speed
- An even draw on both backhand and forehand
- A level surface
- A good cover of fine turf grass

These have been developed most exten-sively by the STRI and the English Bowling Association. A bowling green must also be able to drain sufficiently quickly to permit play after rain, but be relatively unaffected by drought.

Green Speed

In the past, the performance of a bowling green was described using qualitative crite-ria such as 'slow', 'heavy' or 'fast', but now the quantitative criterion of green speed is used extensively. This is defined as the time in seconds for a biased bowl to travel from a bowler's hand and stop within 0.15m of a jack located 27.4m (30 yards) from the front edge of a bowler's mat (English Bowling Association). The more seconds a bowl take to travel, the faster the green. Thus, a 9 sec-ond green is 'slow', but a 14 second green is relatively 'fast' by British Standards.

Green Speed: A Method for both Crown and Flat Greens: Record the time taken for a bowl (wood) to reach the opposite side of the green when bowled from another side.

The rate of travel for a slow green is faster due to the fact that a wood must be bowled much harder and faster to reach the opposite ditch. Although a bowl

18 seconds	a very fast green by average club standards
14 seconds	generally considered satisfactory
12 seconds	too slow for most players

decelerates more rapidly on a slow green, it leaves the bowler's hand at a much greater speed and hence crosses the green more rapidly. The above figures are for a stan-dard 42 × 42 yards green; add one or two seconds for a 60yd × 60yd green.

12–13 seconds	acceptable speed
10 seconds or less	unacceptably slow

EBA Approved Method: Bowl a wood from a mat to the jack 30 yards away. This method caters for all sizes of green:

Draw

The amount of 'draw', that is, the width of the curve taken by the wood as it travels towards the jack, is related to the speed of the green. The more the green allows the wood to trickle slowly before stopping at the end of its run, the more it will curve. The bias on the wood is a fixed and con-stant imbalance but the extent to which it causes the wood to curve will increase in relation to the time it takes the wood to cover a particular distance. Thus, the slower the wood travels (but continues to travel) the more it will draw. On very fast greens (18 seconds or more) it is possible for the extent of the curve to cause problems during games because the woods are increasingly likely to cross rink boundaries, causing possible interference or collision with bowls in adjacent rinks. The unique feature of the draw and the green speed are the two most important playing quality characteristics of flat greens.

Green speed increases with increasing hardness of the surface, closeness of cut and dryness of soil and turf. The average speed of flat bowling greens in Britain is about 11 seconds, with a typical variation of between 9 and 14 seconds around the country. In cooler and wetter conditions soil organic matter contents are usually greater and soil and turf are more frequently moist; thus green speed generally declines the further north and west one travels.

SURFACE LEVELS

Flat greens: Survey levels can be taken at 2m grid pattern and, ideally, recorded heights should be within 6mm for a flat green. Variations of plus or minus 18mm can usually be corrected by maintenance work, for example by topdressing.

Crown greens: For crown greens it is difficult to put exact figures for surface levels. Very few crown greens conform to the theoretical requirement of a uniform 'mushroom-top' contour – many show quite considerable humps and hollows. Crown green bowlers seem happy with the situation. Carrying out a survey, though, will identify surface extremes of level for correction.

With the widespread availability of laser technology for surveying equipment, it has been possible to make detailed studies of the levelness or evenness of flat bowling greens and to make recommendations based on survey results. Results from such surveys have shown that the levels on bowling greens in the UK vary greatly. It has been recommended that levels of newly constructed greens should be within 6mm of the average height of the green.

Caution needs to be used when judging the levelness of a green solely on the basis of the difference between the highest and lowest spot height (the height range). It is possible to have a perfectly good playing surface with a 50mm difference between the highest and lowest areas, provided there is a gradual fall from one end of the green to the other. Such a fall represents a gradient of less that 0.15 per cent, which is negligible. Variation around the average height (the standard deviation) and the minimum allowable difference between adjacent spot heights are more relevant criteria for the levelness of the surface.

Bowling Green Construction

The effort and organization involved in constructing a new bowling green or

Playing Quality Standards for Flat Bowling Greens			
Standard	Surface evenness for individual rinks		Green speed for individual rinks (seconds)
	Difference between adjacent spot heights (mm)	Standard deviation of spot heights (mm)	
Preferred maximum	6	10	
Acceptable minimum	10	15	
Preferred minimum			12
Acceptable minimum			10

reconstructing an existing one is considerable. It is too big a job for most people to do themselves and it certainly should not be attempted before evaluating fully all aspects of the work. Where full construction is intended, an early start to the planning is essential since 'timeliness' for many operations has a great bearing on the final result. Advice should be obtained at an early stage on the particular problems of the site, drainage layout, suitability of existing topsoil and general construction procedure appropriate to the type of green (crown or flat) required.

Site Considerations

Consider the following points when selecting the location for a new bowling green:

- There must be sufficient land available to accommodate the required

dimensions of the green and its immediate surrounds.

- Allowance should be made for a surround path, usually 1.5–2.0m wide, and outer planting borders/grass verges as required.

- A detailed survey drawing of the site will be required to establish finished levels relating to the surrounds and to establish the relationship of the pipe-drainage system to finished levels.

- Ideally, to avoid subsequent settlement problems, bowling greens should not be built on 'filled' areas.

- The green must be located away from tall buildings and trees that may cast shadows over the bowling surface, thereby affecting turf performance.

- Avoid tall plantings around the bowling green.

- There must be good access to the site to facilitate construction work and

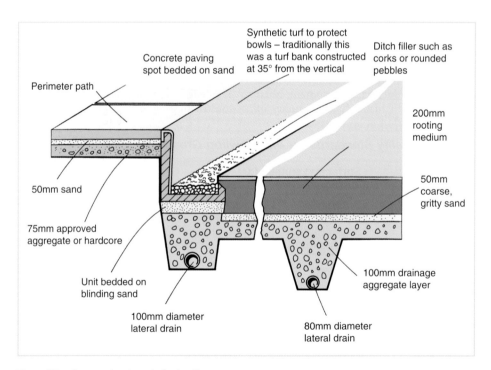

Figure 25   Cross-section through flat bowling green.

subsequent maintenance operations. Narrow gateways may prove inconvenient for delivery of machines, materials and so on.

- The basic construction of flat and crown greens is similar: both require the formation of a smooth and uniform bowling surface.

The following sections cover the main stages of construction and the requirements for both types of green.

Grading

Flat greens: A completely level and smooth subsoil formation surface must be prepared with a tolerance of ±15mm. Allowance must be made for the various layers of materials used in construction and for making the surface of the green a minimum of 230mm lower than the surrounds.

Crown greens: Adjustment to subsoil levels must allow for a crown formation between 254mm and 380mm above the corner levels. A 380mm crown is the Crown Green Bowling Association's recommended height for a 37 × 37m green (pro rata for other sizes). Figure 26 illustrates a possible construction profile for construction of a crown green.

Drainage

Greens constructed over porous subsoils, such as gravel or sand, may not need any special drainage measures but this is

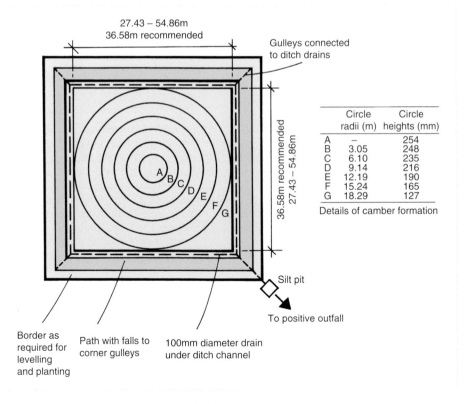

	Circle radii (m)	Circle heights (mm)
A	–	254
B	3.05	248
C	6.10	235
D	9.14	216
E	12.19	190
F	15.24	165
G	18.29	127

Details of camber formation

Figure 26   Crown green showing contours and ditch drain.

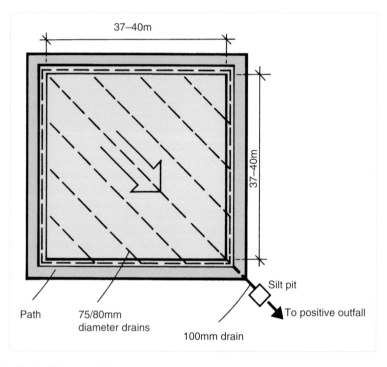

Figure 27 Flat bowling green drainage system.

exceptional. Most sites will require a drainage carpet and an underlying system of pipe-drains. Flat and crown greens require a perimeter drain laid beneath the outer ditch channel.

Flat greens: 'Emptying drains' should be installed through the graded subsoil formation surface, usually at 5–8m centres.

Crown greens: 'Emptying drains' are normally omitted from the body of the green as the contouring of the formation allows speedy surface and subsurface water run-off. All drains must be laid to an appropriate fall with pipe work conforming to the relevant British Standard. All junctions, end stops and so on must be provided as required. All drain trenches must be backfilled to the formation surface with a 6–10mm layer of

hard gravel. A suitable silt chamber should be provided at the lowest point of the drainage system on the green surround. A sealed outlet pipe will be required from the silt pit to a positive outfall such as a watercourse or surface water drain. Once the pipe-drains have been installed, a 100–150mm deep drainage layer of 6–10mm hard gravel is spread over the graded formation surface. The layer is then blinded with coarse, gritty sand to a firmed depth of 50mm.

Ditch channels
Flat greens: The dimensions of an outer ditch channel must conform to the statutory criteria laid down by the English Bowling Association (EBA). The height of the outer path surround above the bowling surface is critical. Traditionally, treated

timber boards and/or precast concrete kerb edgings haunched on concrete were used to form the ditch channels. More up-to-date forms of ditch channel are now available in the form of precast concrete, glass-reinforced cement and moulded polyethylene plastic. These are manufactured to conform to EBA criteria. In most cases some form of protection is required to protect the bowls when striking the outer ditch face. This can be in the form of treated wooden battens, artificial turf or rubber 'bumper' bars. Some form of ditch filler will also be required, such as corks, rounded pebbles or other suitable inert, durable material that will not harm the bowls.

Crown greens: For crown greens, where ditch requirements are rather less rigid, traditional timber edging or precast concrete kerbs are usually used. Additionally, crown greens require treated timber striking boards along the outer ditch kerb. Alternatively, synthetic turf may be used.

Rootzone

A free-draining rootzone is required for both crown and flat greens, particularly where local rainfall levels are high. Sufficient rootzone material should be prepared to provide a minimum of 200mm firmed depth over the blinded drainage layer on completion. Depending on the location of the green, it may be possible to utilize indigenous topsoil if it is light sandy loam in nature. Some preliminary screening of the topsoil to remove larger stones and other debris may be required prior to spreading. In some situations the drainage qualities of the topsoil might be improved by adding approved sand. Quantities are determined by laboratory analysis and mixing should be done off-site in dry conditions, using appropriate shredders/screeners to ensure the production of uniformly blended topsoil. If local topsoil is unsuitable, provision must be made to import suitable commercially prepared sand/soil rootzone material. The approved rootzone must be spread using appropriate equipment, taking care not to disturb the underlying blinded drainage layer. Seed/turf bed preparation will comprise alternative hand-raking and heeling in order to produce a fine, smooth and evenly consolidated tilth. Note that for all greens it is imperative that a level survey be carried out to ensure that accurate levels aid the setting out.

Flat greens: Levelling pegs must be set up on a 3m grid or alternatively 'screeding battens' can be used to accurately set out the levels. Final levels must be to a tolerance of $\pm$ 6mm.

Crown greens: It is important to maintain correct contours and levels by setting up level pegs at 3m centres on each contour line.

Surface Preparation and Grass Cover

In the final stages of seed/turf bed preparation a suitable fertilizer dressing should be well raked into the surface. Grass cover can be established by seeding or turfing, the choice of which depends upon budget and the time available before the facility is required for use. Seeding is the cheaper option but a longer establishment period is required, usually eighteen to twenty-four months. The seed mixture should contain approved cultivars of fescue and bents. Most often, mixtures comprising Chewings Fescue and Browntop Bent are used. A sowing rate of $35g/m_2$ is normally used. Turfing is more expensive, but requires a shorter period to become established (usually between six and nine months). Turf must be purpose-grown on a light sandy topsoil containing fescue and bent grasses and free of broad-leaved weeds and weed grasses. Traditionally turf is supplied in narrow rolls (approximately 300mm wide) and laid by hand working from boards. Wider rolls, up to 1m across, are now available. These can be laid directly from tracked machines or compact tractors.

Irrigation

During construction works a suitable irrigation system must be installed. This is necessary to assist establishment of the grass sward and to aid future maintenance of the green. A basic system would comprise one or two water hydrants located around the outer edge of the green. These can be used for supplying portable sprinklers, spray lines or self-travelling sprinklers, given adequate pressure. A more expensive option would be to install an automatic pop-up irrigation system. This would comprise between four and eight sprinkler heads located outside the bowling green perimeter. This system would also include a storage tank, pumps and control. All will require safe and secure housing near the bowling green.

Green Surrounds

Some form of path will be required on the outside of the green for pedestrian access and/or spectator viewing. The following must be considered:

- The perimeter path must be formed from a durable level material such as brick/slab paving or, when the budget is a consideration, from tarmacadam.
- Provide safe, easy access to the green for wheelchair users.
- Outer borders may be required for the planting of ornamentals, shrubs and/or perimeter hedging.
- Tree planting demands a cautious approach owing to the potential for harmful shading of the green, as well as penetrating root systems.
- A perimeter boarded fence can be provided for shelter and security.
- Make allowance for sufficiently wide access gates through the fence for maintenance machinery and so on. Access should be wide enough to allow entrance for compact tractor-sized vehicles and equipment.
- Facilities such as seat recesses, litter bins, path drainage gulleys and access

ramps to the green must also be provided.

Initial Maintenance

Whatever method of establishment is adopted, good initial maintenance is essential. Top-dressing in particular is needed to help perfect surface levels, and adequate quantities of sandy compost (similar to the topsoil mix) should be prepared and stored. The need for extra fertilizer dressings, especially for sown areas, should be borne in mind.

- Mow when grass reaches 40mm with a hover rotary mower and remove the clippings.
- Roll with a 250kg hand-roller or pedestrian cylinder mower on a non-cutting setting.
- Gradually reduce cutting to 12mm before growth ceases for the year.
- Topdress the following year with the special soil mix – several applications may be needed to perfect the bowling green surface.

Surrounding Bank

This should be created using turves held down with pegs onto 75mm firmed topsoil. Brush topdressing into the joints.

Bowling Green Maintenance

Maintenance requirements will depend upon site conditions and prevailing growth. Proper management will be vital to the achievement of the best possible playing surface and topdressing the green will be crucial in achieving this. The following equipment is fundamental to successful maintenance:

Mower: a high quality professional cylinder mower, the most expensive and important piece of maintenance machinery.
Aeration machine: ideally a powered, pedestrian version.
Scarifier: the most efficient are powered, pedestrian models.

Cylinder mower suitable for bowling green maintenance. (Dennis)

Sprayer: for pest and disease control.

Spinner-type pedestrian distributor: to achieve even application of granular materials, especially fertilizers.

Water square or spray line: to water the green in the absence of an automatic pop-up system.

Hand tools: including a switch, drag mat or drag brush, edging shears, fork, spade and springbok rake. A large lute will be required for flat greens.

Expensive equipment that will rarely be used, such as a punch-action hollow tine machine or top dresser, can be hired as and when required.

Mowing

Heavy mowers should not be used on a bowling green. A good quality mower having a thin bottom blade, ten or twelve knives to the cutting cylinder, and that provides a minimum of 110 cuts per metre is very suitable. In the early spring, before the green is put into use, mowing should be carried out as grass growth demands and at this time the sward should be 'topped' about once a week, the mower being set to cut at a height of about 8mm (the thickness of five fivepence pieces).

As more frequent mowing is needed due to increased growth, the height of cut should be reduced in stages to 5mm. Height of cut is determined by placing a straight edge from the front to the back roller then measuring the distance between the straight edge and the upper lip of the bottom blade. During the playing season mowing should be frequent, say three times a week or more when the grass is growing vigorously. The mower should not be set to cut more closely than 3mm, even on flat greens, and this should be increased to 5mm during dry spells when growth is slow. In the autumn as the rate of grass growth decreases, the height of cut should be increased in stages to 8mm. Mowing may have to be continued into the early winter, when the work should be done during suitable ground and weather conditions. The cover should never be allowed to exceed 13mm before any winter 'topping' is done. Cuttings (except in very special circumstances) should be boxed off the green each time it is mown.

243

Verticut unit fitted to a cylinder mowing machine. Part of the innovative cassette system developed by Dennis.
(Dennis)

Verti-cutting and Thatch Control

Grass does not only grow vertically; use verticut reels to remove lateral growth of grasses on a regular basis through the playing season, say every seven to twenty-one days. Blades should be sharp and set to cut into the base of the turf. The tramlines produced should grow out within four days of each operation: much sooner and the blades are not set deep enough, much longer and you are scarifying! The use of a grooming reel or rake attachment on the mower will also reduce lateral growth. An excessive amount of spongy thatch to the turf produces a soft and slow surface. Deep scarification in conjunction with top dressing practices can reduce thatch and help produce a firmer, faster surface.

During the early spring preparation of the green, thorough but gentle scarification is often needed to remove fibre and straggly growth. This treatment should only be done when grass growth has become quite steady and it should be avoided at all times during dry weather. During the bowling season, light

scarification at intervals of two to three weeks proves beneficial as long as it is done when growth is occurring. This light scarification assists in the production and maintenance of fine, dense, healthy turf and in checking the growth of undesirable grass, such as Yorkshire fog, and weeds that have a straggly habit of growth, such as mouse-ear chickweed and clover. Early autumn is particularly suitable for more thorough scarification, which should be done prior to the autumn and compost top dressing. Local scarification of undesirable grass and weed patches can be done with Springbok rakes but for general treatment, scarification machines may be employed. Grass combs (for fitting to mowers) are useful for frequent, light scarification. Scarifying machines take the form of hand-operated wheeled rakes or engine-driven machines in which a series of rotating blades or wire tines do the work. When using any machine, particularly the engine-driven types, care must be taken to ensure that scarifying is not done too severely as damage to the grass and the bowling surface would result. For regular, routine scarification, rotary scarifiers should be adjusted so that their blades or wire tines only just affect the turf surface, but these may be set a little more deeply for more thorough work in the early autumn.

Fertilizer

A well-fed lush turf increases resistance on the bowl, which reduces pace. Follow a lean feeding regime to attain better pace. This may not produce the colour that impresses but it will give you a better playing surface. Colour can be improved for major events with one of the chelated iron or seaweed soil conditioning products without producing more grass. Overfeeding is also a waste of money as you simply take off more grass when mowing.

Recommended annual nutrient application		
Nitrogen	N	8–20 g/m²
Phosphorus	P₂O₅	2 g/m²*
Potassium	K₂O	6–15 g/m²*
* depending on soil analysis		

On sand rootzone constructions the nitrogen application rate should be $25\,g/m^2$ and the potassium application at the high end of the range given above. The annual application would be split into three or four dressings starting mid–April, with the last application being before the end of August. Nitrogen content in the final dressing should be low and of ammonium sulphate alone in order to prevent the encouragement of disease from organic nitrogen sources. Autumn application of nitrogen fertilizer is generally not required as mineralization of soil organic matter releases adequate nitrogen to the turf. In regions that experience relatively mild winters and warm springs, extra spring dressings of ammonium sulphate may be necessary. A dressing to provide $2\,g/m^2$ of nitrogen during mid- to late March

would be appropriate. If phosphate and/or potassium are to be applied, then the phosphate should be applied within the first main spring dressing as super-phosphate. Potassium should be given in two applications, one in the main spring treatment and the other in mid- or late summer. It is usually applied as potassium sulphate.

Irrigation

Many bowling greens, especially those with less than 150mm depth of soil, are particularly vulnerable to drought. Suitable water supplies and methods of watering should, therefore, be arranged and the green adequately irrigated during dry periods. The aim should be to commence watering in good time and not to wait until the dry period is well advanced before starting. Watering should be continued right up to the end of the dry period and the soil never allowed to dry out completely. Spiking before watering will aid penetration. Keep a dry, firm surface and you will get more pace. Irrigate early morning to allow optimum penetration and minimum evaporation. Only irrigate when necessary and hand water any local area that seems to be suffering rather than the entire green. Use aeration and wetting agent to assist rapid penetration. If you cause some damage through under-watering this can always be made good at the end of the playing season. Giant water squares are appropriate for irrigation but installed pop-up sprinklers are more efficient in labour requirements.

Aeration

Regular aeration is helpful for improving surface drainage, soil air supply, root growth and for relieving compaction. Hollow tining is the best method of dealing with the latter but it is usually restricted to once every three years, except in special circumstances. This work is normally confined to the autumn period prior to topdressing. Solid or slit type tines that create minimal surface disturbance can be used when appropriate: the former throughout

Drag brushing can be conducted to disperse surface dew or incorporate topdressings. (SISIS Equipment (Macclesfield) Ltd)

the year as necessary, whereas the latter are best confined to the spring and close season. Some form of mechanical aeration will be required to relieve 'compaction' and to improve water and air infiltration into the top 100mm of the rootzone. Spiking at least once a month to 100mm depth with an appropriate machine is desirable. Shallow spiking (pricking) with a Sarrel roller on a weekly basis will also be beneficial. Intensive splitting/hollow coring is done in the autumn as part of the renovation works. Remedial treatment for deep compaction may be required from time to time.

Topdressing

This is normally applied as part of autumn renovation with spiking and scarification. This is necessary to:

- Restore surface levels.
- Maintain particle size distribution in soil surface.

- To control/reduce organic matter content of soil/rootzone surface.

Ideally the topdressing should closely match the soil or rootzone mix used in construction of the green. Topdressing should be spread, avoiding smothering, in a screened and dry condition onto a dry surface and thoroughly worked into the turf. A drag mat or drag brush can be used for this purpose on a crown green, but on a flat green a screeder with a straight edge should preferably be used.

Quantity
After solid spiking   approx 4 tonnes
After hollow coring   5–6 tonnes

Materials
70/30 or 80/20 sand/soil mixture

Autumn Renovation: A Quick Guide

Fifteen days before work commences apply selective weed killer if weeds are a problem.

Ten days before work commences apply systemic fungicide to whole green and order all grass feed and topdressing to ensure delivery can take place on the date you require.

PROGRAMME OF WORK
- Brush off surface with drag brush.
- Mow to a height of 3–4mm.
- Scarify to a depth of 5–6mm in two directions (not at right angles). Remove all debris from the surface.
- Solid spike or hollow core as required. Remove cores.
- Oversow with appropriate seed mix, such as 80:20 fescue/bent at 20–30 g/m².
- Apply topdressing at approximately 5 kg/m². Work well into surfaces with lutes, dragmats and brushes.
- Apply autumn feed if required.
- Keep a regular look out for fungal diseases (Fusarium) and treat when necessary.
- Drag brush heavy dew from green surface throughout the winter.

Rolling

Rolling should be kept to the minimum conducive to satisfactory playing conditions. Excessive rolling compacts the soil and leads to a gradual deterioration of the turf. In the spring it is usually necessary to roll before the commencement of the season to firm the surface after it has been puffed up by winter frosts. A hand roller weighing about 250kg and with a width and diameter of 750–900mm is generally used in the spring. During the bowling season lightweight wide rollers may be used to help maintain the trueness of the bowling surface (Trulevel type rollers are particularly useful). All rolling should be avoided when the green is in a

Overseeding is necessary at the end of the season if grass cover is to be maintained. (SISIS Equipment (Macclesfield) Ltd)

247

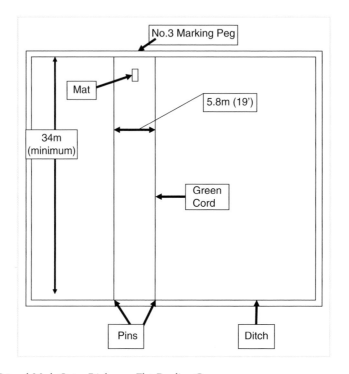

Figure 28   Set and Mark Out a Rink on a Flat Bowling Green.

wet condition. There is clear evidence that rolling fine turf with a lightweight roller, for example of the turf-iron type, can produce greater pace without causing problems of soil compaction. The frequency of such rolling will vary according to other maintenance practices, such as aeration and mowing.

Rink Management

Preservation of the bowling green surface is greatly assisted by sensible rink spacing. Direction of play may be varied to the degree of wear imposed by the players on the green and any one point. A common practice is to change the direction of play every fourth day, or reduce the width of the rinks and move slightly left or right. Rink management depends on several factors: the greenkeeper's experience, amount and type of play on the green and weather conditions.

Set and Mark Out a Rink on a Flat Bowling Green

The accompanying diagram shows the marking out of the No. 3 rink on a flat bowling green for international standard of play.

REQUIREMENTS
- 4 pegs, white, 50mm square, 60cm long
- cord, green, minimum length 80m
- tape measure, minimum length 40m
- numbered metal markers
- rubber mat, 60 × 35cm
- hammer
- plan (*see* below)

Procedure

1. Install first peg 11.4m from corner of green.
2. Install second peg 14.1m from corner of green. Mark rink 5.7m wide. Repeat operation on opposite side.
3. Fix all pegs flush to the face of the bank.
4. Attach thread to first peg, draw line tightly along surface of green and then attach to corresponding peg on opposite side of green.
5. Establish centre of rink.
6. Place mat lengthwise on centre line of rink, the back edge to be 1.2m from the rear ditch.
7. Place metal marker number 3 on the bank in line with the middle of the rink.
8. Leave the site clean and tidy.

Care of Ditches, Banks and Surrounds

Maintenance of these in a clean and tidy state should be an integral part of the management programme.

Ditches on Flat Greens
• No less than 50mm or more than 200mm below green.
• Most common ditch infilling material is smooth rounded pebbles, usually between 12mm and 18mm in diameter.
• An alternative material is Lytag 10–12mm grade.
• Sand is also common; it can scratch woods, however, and stick to the woods when wet.
• For flat greens many clubs have used plastic duckboarding as a final ditch surface.

Ditches on Crown Greens
• Where a wood is dead when it enters the ditch requirements are less rigid; infill is commonly pebbles or sand.

• Where pea gravel, rounded pebbles or Lytag is employed, the material should be taken out of the ditches and washed at intervals, usually an annual operation.

Weed growth in ditches is sometimes a problem, particularly in sand-filled ditches. Use non-residual total weedkiller, taking great care not to damage the edge of the green.

Banks
The major task in the maintenance of banking is to keep it mown and weed free. 12mm is the norm for cutting height, which can be achieved by ether pedestrian rotary or cylinder machine. Keeping banks weed free through the use of approved selective herbicides or hand weeding will ensure that such cannot contaminate the green. Repairs to the banking may be needed from time to time and this is best done through the use of turves. Striking boards may need periodic repair or painting and these should be checked annually.

Green Surrounds
The surrounds to bowling greens including landscape features, hedges and trees should be maintained in sound horticultural practice. It is important that trees and hedges do not cast shade on the green, a consideration that must be born in mind when planning new greens, as this restricts grass growth and leads to worn damp areas as well as incidents of disease. Similarly the roots of hedges and trees must not be allowed to enter the green substrate as they will disrupt levels and take moisture form the grass roots. Path surrounds should be kept in good condition. Moss and weed growth can be a source of infection for the playing surface and suitable herbicides should be used if necessary.

Croquet

The origins of croquet are obscure; however, it is known that the sport was

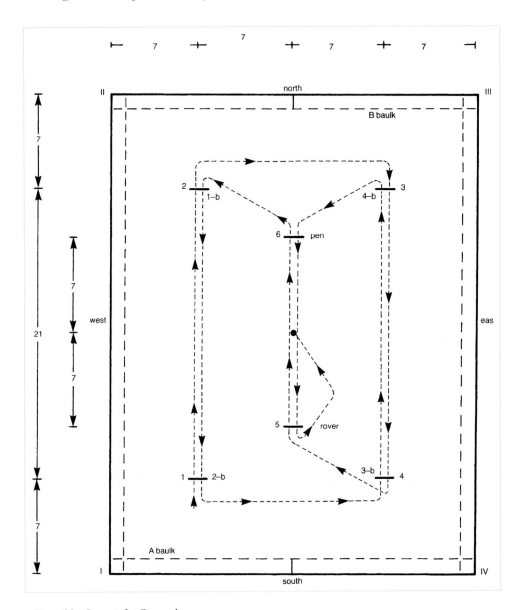

Figure 29   Layout of a Croquet lawn.

introduced to England from Ireland in the 1830s. In the latter part of the nineteenth century and early twentieth it grew very rapidly in popularity, being an agreeable pastime for the upper classes, while being played on equal terms by men and women, the old and the young. When lawn tennis took off croquet declined in popularity and a large proportion of courts were turned over to the new game. Indeed, the dimension of a tennis court owes itself to two fitting snugly within the area of one croquet court. At the height of its popularity croquet spread throughout the British Empire and this laid the foundations of the game's strongest supporters being within the present Commonwealth.

The Game
Croquet is played on a lawn or 'court' of dimensions 32 × 25.6m (35 × 28 yards). Almost all croquet is played on completely flat, closely mown fine grass (similar to bowls). There are three main variants of the game: Golf Croquet, Association Croquet (International Rules) and American Croquet. In Golf Croquet the objective of each player is to get his ball(s) though each hoop first. When the first hoop is scored all players move on to the second hoop, and so on. Each turn comprises only one stroke. The merit of Golf Croquet is simplicity and an analogy between it and Association Croquet is like that between draughts and chess. It is Association Croquet that is mainly played at the highest levels. There are regular World Championships and also an international team event played irregularly between the top nations. The third variation belongs exclusively to North America, where a significant variation to International Rules evolved. It differs from Association Croquet in the same way that Rugby League differs from Rugby Union.

Lawn Speed
For croquet the speed of a lawn is defined as the time in seconds taken for a croquet ball to travel the full length of a standard court when it just comes to rest on the far boundary. On a fast lawn a relatively gentle shot will be adequate for the full traverse, so a fast lawn corresponds to a longer time of transit. Since it is not easy to hit a ball so that it travels exactly one court length, the recommended procedure is to time and measure the length of several shots of approximately court length (32m/35 yards) and to interpolate or extrapolate to the time for the exact distance. Measurements in opposite directions are averaged. Alternatively, speeds may be determined in accordance with the method defined by the World Bowls Board by measuring the distance travelled by a standard, unbiased bowl launched from a defined ramp.

Pétanque

Pétanque or boules, as it is sometimes known, is a game that is played all over France and its former colonies and has also been growing in popularity in the UK since the formation of the British Pétanque

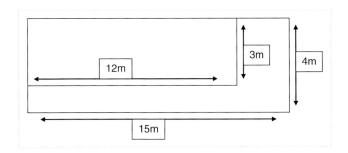

Figure 30   The Piste.

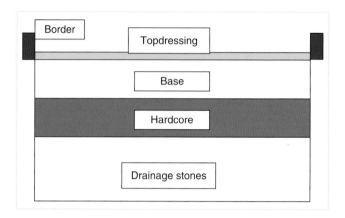

Figure 31   Piste construction.

Association in 1974. There is much evidence that the game did in fact originate in England. The metal boules used today are not unlike the round shot used in the naval and military cannon of the sixteenth century and it is likely that the game that Sir Francis Drake played on Plymouth Hoe while watching the progress of the Armada was an early form of boule.

Playing Surface Requirements

The game can be played on almost any surface, such as a beach or a car park, but for competition play a surface with a well-drained base with a thin layer of loose material is required. The playing surface should not be so smooth as to enable the boule to be rolled in a straight line. Nor should it be so soft as to restrict the forward movement of the boule once it has landed. For this reason lawns are not considered as suitable playing areas. The area on which the game is played is known as a piste or terrain. The piste should be at least 3m wide by 12m long. Ideally it should be 4m by 15m, as this is the size required by the international governing

body, the Fédération Internationale de Pétanque et Jeu Provençal.

Piste Construction

Where the land is poorly drained or low lying it will be necessary to construct a piste over a drainage carpet or aggregate base. The topsoil should first be removed and then the area excavated to a depth of 400mm. Over the drainage stones and hard-core layers a good base can be made from 3.5cm crushed quarry reject gypsum or the kind of crushed limestone often used as a base for roads. This is often referred to by builders' merchants as No.3 limestone and it is better than some materials in that it contains less clay and therefore drains better. Whatever material is used for the base, it must be well tamped down and rolled before the final topdressing of sand/gravel (cheapest) or '4mm to dust' pea-beach or granite chippings is put on. The ideal topdressing depth is about 6–15mm, which will allow the boule some grip on landing without sinking too deep and making the game difficult to play properly. The terrain will need a protective surround of some sort. This is usually made of wood and railway sleepers are ideal for this purpose as they can well withstand the impact of the boules. The terrain border should be about 230mm to 300mm in height.

Size of Terrain

A piste can cater for up to six people as the most common form of the game is 'triples' (two teams of three). Most clubs are run on either six or eight pistes and can therefore cater for up to thirty-six or forty-eight people at one time.

3 × 12m × 6 pistes	216m^2
3 × 12m × 8 pistes	288m^2
4 × 15m × 6 pistes	360m^2
4 × 15m × 8 pistes	480m^2

10 Cricket Pitches

Cricket is fundamentally different from most other sports in terms of the requirements for play and the severity of some turf maintenance practices. The main criteria are for ball bounce and pace. In this respect it is most like tennis, but the game demands far harder and faster surfaces than tennis. These requirements for pace and bounce mean that surface preparation and maintenance practices are often against the principles of normal turfgrass growth. Pace and bounce are achieved by the use of heavy clay soils, which are compacted by rolling with heavy rollers. These are difficult conditions to grow grass in and thus demanding for the grounds staff to sustain. The grass is primarily required on pitches for its roots, which help to bind the surface and prevent surface degradation. When prepared for play, individual pitches are virtually shaved of any top growth, leaving only the crown of the plant to recover later when top growth is allowed after pitch use and during renovation. Such treatment again is harsh on the individual grass plant, and although grass is remarkably resilient, it requires careful monitoring and nurturing to recover. The cricket square where pitches are prepared is the most important part of the cricket ground and the focus of most work and attention. The other part, the outfield, can be more easily sustained by conventional turf maintenance practices, principally mowing. It should be level and reasonably smooth, with good grass composition. The situation is more complex on some sports grounds where the cricket outfield is used for winter games. Here more intensive maintenance and management will obviously be needed. The ECB, through their publications and county pitch advisors, are an invaluable source of information on the management of cricket pitches at all levels of provision.

Playing Surface Standards

It is important to consider the level of provision being catered for when preparing, maintaining or constructing cricket pitches. It is no use having hard, fast, bouncy pitches if the players cannot cope with them. Indeed, such surface reactions may even cause them to give up playing. The higher the quality of game, however, the more bounce and pace is required. In fact, the faster and more bouncy the better, as this encourages good players to become even better. At club level, and indeed at parks/recreational level, a lower bounce and more easy paced pitch are desired by the majority of players. A cricket pitch should ideally be:

- Even throughout with no undulations or depressions.
- Well consolidated giving good and appropriate ball bounce.
- Covered with a dense sward of desirable grasses that have good root density and depth.

An essential part of managing and maintaining cricket facilities is to monitor the condition of the square, pitches and the outfield throughout the year, particularly during the playing season. In order to determine whether pitches are to a satisfactory standard, there are a number of simple tests that can be carried out by the club grounds staff. Five basic items of equipment can be used to make measured assessments on a square or prepared pitch. Once trained, any competent turf manager can purchase or make their own and use them to monitor their own facilities. There are other forms of equipment that can be used for more serious problems, but these are costly and perhaps preferably hired in or a qualified consultant employed. The key tests and equipment recommended by the ECB are:

- Soil profile sampler and measure to assess the profile make-up and depth of rootzone.
- 3m straight edge, spirit level, graduated wedge or measure for determining the evenness of the surface and localized gradients.
- Square quadrant frames, divided into 100 equal squares for identifying percentage values of ground cover composition, pests and diseases.
- Ball drop device, measuring post and good quality cricket ball for testing vertical ball bounce on a pitch. The bounce test results have been used for more than thirty years to determine the binding qualities (that is, the clay content) of a pitch and its potential pace, which is here expressed in percentage terms as a guideline:

Less than 8%	very slow pitches
8% to 11%	slow
12% to 16%	easy paced
17% to 21%	fast
22% to 24%	very fast

The last major testing procedure for cricket soils is the Adams Stewart Soil Binding Test (ASSB), more often known as the Motty test. Motties were clay balls once used as marbles and thus the term is used since balls of clay are used in the ASSB method. It is used to determine soil binding strength, which is of great importance with soils for cricket. It is well worth the cricket ground staff learning this simple test. (For a description of the method, *see* Appendix 1.)

Cricket Square Construction

The amount of effort and organization involved in preparing a new cricket square table on an existing playing field or new site depends on the site, standard required and the finance available. At its simplest, where soil and drainage are suitable, and where surface levels and turf are reasonable, an intensive maintenance programme can achieve all that is required. At the other extreme, where full construction is necessary, an early start to the planning side is essential since 'timeliness' for many operations has a great bearing on the final result. There is no doubt that the best surfaces are to be found on those squares that have been constructed correctly. This work may be carried out by contractors or by the clubs themselves; in either case it is necessary to have a plan and details of construction.

The first requirement is to identify the level of cricket to be played and thereby the standard of pitch required. It is feasible to plan for the square to have a lifespan of twenty-five years. The boundary should be a minimum of 45.72m from the centre of the pitch in current use. Pitches must run approximately north–south to minimize the risk of batsmen or bowlers facing a low sun. The pitch axis must point in a direction between 325 degrees and 55 degrees on the compass. One pitch area is 22.86m long by 3.05m wide. The size of the cricket square is determined by the number of pitch areas required in a season. To calculate this, quantify the total number of matches to be played during the season and then estimate the number of times each strip can be used during the playing season.

This is variable but could be between two and five times, dependent on the type of cricket, the standard of maintenance and the time available to the ground staff to maintain and prepare the pitches. Calculate the number of pitches required and hence the total width of the square: the number of matches to be played divided by the assessed number of games per pitch gives the total number of pitches required.

Loams for Cricket Squares

Cricket requires a heavy topsoil with good binding qualities to produce the desired type of playing surface (a firm, level surface that provides consistent bounce and pace). The soil has at the same time to be fairly free-draining. For county standard tables, however, much heavier soil is used (invariably quite slow-draining material), but this is often offset by protecting the surface with covers at critical times. Most loamy clay soils will give reasonable results provided they are not mishandled so that soil structure is destroyed during construction. Soils that contain much grit, sand or small stones are not satisfactory and it could be necessary to replace, say, 75mm firmed depth of the top surface with imported clay loam topsoil. If this is necessary, early location and quotations for suitable soil are essential. The choice of soil used is very important and a laboratory analysis is essential. The selected soil will have a major influence on the physical characteristics of the playing surface and will also affect the selection of grass cover. The nature of the existing topsoil will determine the extent of the construction works required to develop the square. For different standards of pitch the minimum clay content should be:

first class and county	28–35%
club	25–30%
school	23–28%

Where existing topsoil is unsuitable, make allowance for importing appropriate cricket topsoil from a specialist supplier. To accommodate the imported topsoil an equivalent depth of existing material must be removed. The imported topsoil must be compatible with the indigenous topsoil. Selection of the wrong sort of loam (or taking the cheaper option) could be the cause of future problems. All loams should be obtained from recommended suppliers. The accompanying table below gives an indication of how much soil may be needed per pitch (wicket).

Irrigation

Provide at least one hydrant point at a location convenient to the square. A hose or sprinkler can be attached for general

Quantity Guide for Soil Requirement
(per pitch area of 22.87 x 3.05m (75 × 10ft) and inclusive of allowances for consolidation and element of wastage)

Depth (mm/in)	Exact quantity (m³)	Suggested delivered quantity (m³)
25 (1)	2.2	2.5
50 (2)	4.4	4.5
75 (3)	6.6	7.0
100 (4)	8.8	9.0
125 (5)	11.0	11.0
150 (6)	13.3	14.0

watering of the square and/or preparation of pitches.

Construction Methodology

It is not appropriate to standardize on a type of construction for a cricket square as a number of factors are involved and the cost of such provision may be unnecessary, bearing in mind the condition of the site and what materials are available. Existing material on site may be suitable and all that is needed is to grade out an area to the required gradients followed by cultivations and seeding. On the other hand a total excavation may be required.

As a general rule squares are made up of:

- A clay-loam surfacing zone laid on an
- Intermediary zone, which supports the clay loam,
- Supported by a free drainage zone, which may or may not require a blinding layer to prevent particles migrating into the free-draining layer.
- Around the perimeter an interception drain may be desirable.

The depth of each zone shall be consistent but will vary depending on the ground conditions, the topsoil and subsoil profile in the location where the square is to be laid, prevailing climatic conditions, and the grade of cricket to be catered for. At club level the clay loam shall have an ASSB soil binding strength of no less than 45kg, whereas at higher levels a binding strength of no less than 60kg is more desirable. Typical consistent depth of each zone shall be within the range indicated in the accompanying diagram.

SITE EXCAVATION AND GRADING

The specialist equipment necessary for substantial level adjustment is usually hired and the work should be carried out under dry ground conditions in summer. Depending on the degree of levelling necessary, the topsoil should be scraped off and preserved in a spoil heap away from the immediate working area. The exposed subsoil should be carefully graded to the levels required, the work being extended over adjacent outfield areas as necessary to marry levels through neatly. Where a drainage carpet is required, allow for the necessary depth of excavation. Any filling should be done in layers that must be adequately consolidated. Pegs should be set at the correct levels and the subsoil graded to conform to these, using boning rods to ensure a true, even surface is produced. Allow for disposal of surplus subsoil to a tip.

DRAINAGE

The drainage system will comprise a single perimeter drain around the outer edge of the square. Except when designed

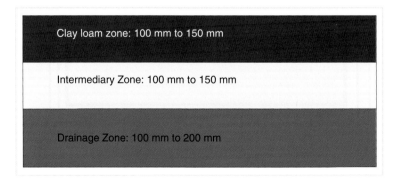

Figure 32   Profile of a Cricket Square.

with a drainage raft, never install a pipe-drainage system under the square as this will result in differential drying out at the surface. Drains should not be laid with falls less than 1 in 200. 'Drainage rafts' are required only in exceptional circumstances, such as on very wet sites or where the highest standards of construction are required, for example at county level. Drainage pipes, where used, are normally 100mm plastic perforated corrugated pipes laid to a minimum depth of 600mm with a minimum gradient of 1 in 100. The level should be checked before backfilling. Backfill all drains with 3–10mm of angular stone to the top of the formation. A drainage layer of a similar filling to the trenches can be laid to a consolidated thickness of 100mm over the entire construction area and then covered with a 50mm layer of coarse sand laid to form a blinding layer, ensuring that the correct level is formed ready for the clay loam. Rake the blinding layer to form a key for the loam.

SUB-BASE AND CONSOLIDATION

If the depth excavated exceeds 100mm then a loam can be used as a sub-base. This should be as compatible as possible with the shrinkage values of the topsoil and thoroughly keyed in during construction. Consolidation is the most important element of construction: uniform consolidation should be undertaken approximately every 50mm by using an appropriate method. The best and time-honoured process is by 'heeling', but it is very time-consuming and too labour-intensive to be cost-effective for most contractors, who

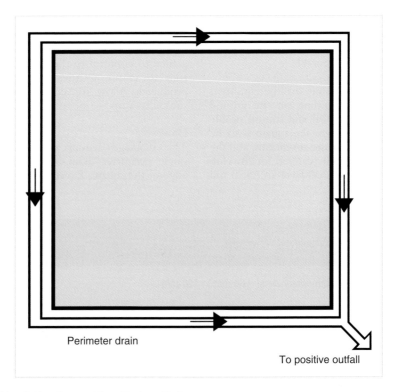

Perimeter drain

To positive outfall

Figure 33   Cricket Square without Drainage Raft.

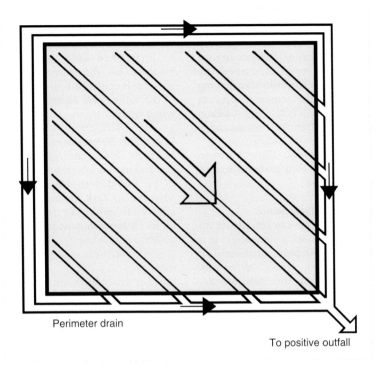

Perimeter drain

To positive outfall

Figure 34   Cricket Square with Drainage Raft.

prefer to use appropriate machinery, such as caterpillar tracks, tractor tyres or 'sheep's foot' rollers. Whatever method is used, care must be taken to ensure uniformity with no air pockets remaining and each layer to be keyed in. The projected optimum playing performance rating will only be achieved if this process is completed correctly. The final surface levelling should not be done by a heavy roller as it may leave isolated and uneven pockets.

ROOTZONE
Spread and grade the clay loam in to a depth of 50mm and consolidate as required. Rake the surface to create a key for the next layer. Add further 50mm layers until the total depth of 100–150mm is achieved. The final surface should be level along the direction of play, although a fall of 1 in 100 is acceptable with a cross fall of 1 in 60 to

1 in 80. In all cases the square should blend smoothly into the outfield and be finished proud of the surrounds by 25mm to allow for water run-off and prevent standing winter rainfall to the detriment of grass health. In the direction of play, the ideal gradient is 1 in 80 to 1 in 100, but not more than 1 in 60, though it can, if required, be flat.

SEEDBED PREPARATION
AND GRASS ESTABLISHMENT
Turfing a pitch or square is strongly discouraged; rarely will there be turf available that has the appropriate soil type. Most commercial turf is produced on sandy loams totally unsuited for cricket squares. Grass cover will normally be established by seeding using appropriate cultivars of suitable grass species sown, usually blends of perennial ryegrass cultivars at a rate

259

of 35g/m². Irrigate when necessary to encourage germination and establishment. Germination sheets can be considered to facilitate and prevent the occurrence of damage from wash-off caused by severe rain storms. Erect protective fencing around the area of the square to prevent unwanted encroachments and follow the appropriate aftercare maintenance measures.

It is essential that you allow between eighteen months and two years before the square is ready for use.

Post-Construction Maintenance

In order to allow the cricket square to settle and mature, it is essential that proper post-construction maintenance works are deployed. This will ensure good performance of the new cricket square.

MOWING

The first cut can be with the usage of a hover-type rotary mower ensuring sharpened blades to avoid tearing or pulling at the delicate new grasses. This should occur about four weeks after germination depending on climatic conditions and growth rate or at least when the sward is around 50–75mm. Gradually reduce the cutting height after this using a cylinder mower until a maintenance height of cut is achieved of approximately 20–25mm in winter and 15–20mm in summer.

WEEDS AND WORMS

Broad-leaved weed species will normally succumb to close mowing regimes; once the sward is strong enough, an application of selective weed control will account for the remaining weed content. Cricket loam companies will not normally supply sterilized loam unless specifically requested and this is usually at a higher cost. There are no chemical worm eradication products available but there remain for an uncertain period of time products classified as worm control. These should be applied by a competent and certified operator whenever worm activity is present. No chemical control measures should be undertaken until the grass plant has matured to the three-leafed stage of growth. Regular brushing or drag-matting of the square will assist in dispersing casts when friable.

FERTILIZER APPLICATION

Nutrient levels are generally in more demand in new constructions so these need to be attended to when necessary. It is advisable to seek a nutritional analysis at intervals to ensure the correct nutrient and Ph levels are maintained for optimum grass health.

ROLLING

Rolling procedures are one of the most important yet least understood operations that are essential towards achieving the deep-seated consolidation required of cricket squares. This is an essential operation towards the requirements of the game of cricket: good pace, carry and consistency of even bounce. The timing is not an exact science but the condition of the soil profile and optimum moisture content is the key. A 36in motor mower weighs around 254kg (5cwt) and is ideal for initial settlement, especially during winter months when the soil is in a 'plasticine' condition. The cutters can be engaged during mild spells to tidy up the sward.

The decision will have to be made to when introduce the heavy roller and this will depend on the moisture content of the new square, neither too wet nor too dry. It is advisable, though, to err on the side of caution for the initial rolling so as not to cause pushing the surface in a 'bow-wave' fashion and capping the surface or induce 'rippling', which can lead to very unsafe playing conditions. The operation should not be overdone in the first year and priority should be given to cross and diagonal passes with speeds progressively slower as even consolidation is achieved.

SURFACE LEVELS

A feature of newly laid squares or pitches is that a certain amount of settlement can occur, the severity of which usually depends on how well the construction methods were applied, specifically the condition and quality of rootzone materials and consolidation. This may appear as overall (slight or deeper) sinkage or excessive cracking. Wide cracks should be methodically filled with finely screened loam and firmed using an implement such as a builder's wide cold chisel and seeding in order to knit the cracks together. By use of a 3m straight edge or similar device, routine checks on surface levels should be made especially if 'rippling' has occurred, so that, where considered necessary, carefully applied topdressing can be administered to correct levels. It is important though to thoroughly incorporate the dressing and not trap organic matter in low spots as it would lead towards a root-break discontinuity in the profile years later after many seasons of applied clay loam topdressings.

Cricket Outfield

The outfield must comprise a field with smooth and even levels that permit balls to roll freely across the surface. If the outfield is to be cut from existing grassland the site must be checked for:

- Uneven surfaces
- Inadequate drainage
- Inappropriate grass species

Where the quality of turf is satisfactory and site undulations are isolated it should be sufficient to strip away portions of turf and, where necessary, adjust the underlying ground level. The turf is then replaced to form a level and firm surface. Where site undulations are more severe but there is a

There are many machines suitable for mowing cricket outfields. For the best finish, choose one that can remove the clippings. (Ransomes Jacobsen)

good depth of topsoil, it may be enough simply to regrade the site to a uniform surface. Where existing gradients are too steep, more drastic level adjustment may be necessary involving the removal of topsoil and grading of exposed subsoil, followed by topsoil replacement. The outfield need not be completely level and a slight gradient of up to 1 in 50 may assist shedding of surface water.

Construction Methodology

The playing quality of any newly constructed outfield facility and the associated financial income and expenditure is substantially governed by the ability to ensure maximum playability and maintenance conditions within as short a time as possible after the cessation of rainfall and to restrict the effects of localized flooding and high water tables, especially where situated on a flood plain. This is especially important where winter sports are to be played on the outfield area. In recent years many first class cricket grounds have had their outfields reconstructed to ensure matches can be played after heavy rainfall. Thus, fewer matches need to be cancelled and less income is lost.

DRAINAGE

Where rainfall levels are low and topsoil is naturally free-draining there should be no need for artificial drainage, particularly if the outfield is to be used for summer cricket only. If the ground is relatively impervious some form of pipe-drain system may be required. Where the outfield will be used as a playing surface for soccer, rugby or hockey, construction should follow recommendations for those sports. While supplementary slit-drains may be used on cricket outfields, caution is advised owing to the possibility of settlement of backfilling material within the slits during dry weather. This will result in an uneven playing surface that is potentially dangerous for fielders. Make allowance for topping up the slits with suitable sand when settlement occurs.

Drainage systems are normally laid with lateral drains of 80mm at specified intervals and at an angle of flow to the main 110mm carrier in a grid or herringbone design across the outfield area. Drainage trenches are backfilled using 6–10mm gravel to within 150mm of the finished surface level, followed by a 50mm layer of blinding sand and then a sandy, free-draining topsoil or imported rootzone to the surface.

IRRIGATION

Increasingly, where they can be afforded, pop-up sprinkling systems are being considered at the construction stage to ensure optimum and effective irrigation of outfield areas.

GRADIENTS AND TOPSOIL PLACEMENT

Final gradient levels can facilitate drainage but may be determined by the local topography of the site. It is an advantage to have a slight slope, ideally running away from the centre of the square where appropriate, but in all cases not exceeding 1 in 50. Topsoil should be replaced to the original depth subject to an absolute minimum of 100mm consolidated.

SURFACE CULTIVATION

A satisfactory seedbed can be produced using approved harrows and roller or purpose-made seeding implement, as necessary, to form a fine tilth for grass seeding. The seedbed should be fine, smooth and evenly firm but not compacted. Shortly before seeding, apply evenly to the outfield a suitable pre-seeding fertilizer and lightly harrow fertilizer into the immediate surface. During the above operations all surplus vegetation, debris and all stones having one dimension in excess of 38mm should be removed from the outfield area.

SEEDING

For the finest quality outfields, mixtures containing appropriate species of fescue and bent are most appropriate. Where winter games are to be played on the outfield the inclusion of a proportion of perennial ryegrass is essential to maintain the hard-wearing quality of the surface in anticipated wet winter playing conditions. The cultivars chosen should have a high tolerance of close mowing. A seed mixture containing between 40 and 60 per cent by weight perennial ryegrass would be suitable for most winter games situations. Seeding should be carried out during suitable weather conditions. The total quantity of seed required should be divided into half and each half sown in transverse directions and then lightly chain harrowed into the immediate surface.

Post-Construction Maintenance

Standard turf culture maintenance practices will apply to outfield areas during the post-construction stages and involve removing any stones remaining on the surface and picking if necessary, initial topping of the grasses when the grass reaches a height of 50mm to encourage tilling and subsequent mowing operations, light rolling, fertilizer applications when required, control of worm and weed activity and regular brushing/drag matting. Frequently a feature of newly constructed outfields in the first year of usage is that they can become very firm, prohibiting player safety and preventing water percolation in the event of prolonged periods of rainfall. Some form of de-compaction may be required by deep aeration methodology.

Cricket Square Maintenance

The maintenance of specialized areas of turf can only be carried out provided a suitable work programme for the year is drawn up and adhered to. Cricket requires a good firm flat surface upon which the ball will bounce and not deviate from its true path. Both batsmen and bowlers should be able to execute their true skills without fear of the ball 'flying off a length' or keeping 'low'. Above all else, the surface should be 'true' and 'fair' to both batsmen and bowlers alike. The outfield must be firm and flat to enable the maximum of runs and should be free from undulations. To achieve this end, it must be borne in mind that a work programme will go a long way to achieve the required result. However, the programme is only a guide and does not take into consideration climatic conditions from area to area, and most important of all, the different types of soil structure. From a practical point of view, it is most important that anyone engaged in looking after the square must be trained and competent.

MOWING

In spring gradually reduce the height of cut on the square to a height of 12mm from the winter height of cut of 12–25mm. This height should be maintained all season over the square, with it being cut at least once a week, if not twice during growing conditions. Always ensure blades are kept sharp and set correctly to ensure a good clean cut with no 'ribbing' or tearing. Mowing should be done with a pedestrian cylinder mower with all clippings removed.

IRRIGATION

Irrigation will be required throughout the season to maintain not only a good surface but to allow the soil particles to be compacted together during the process of rolling. The use of rotary type sprinklers can result in uneven coverage, which in turn can produce an uneven ball bounce. It is important to irrigate to a suitable depth, to at least 75mm, and not just to penetrate the immediate surface of the soil. Most grounds utilize portable overhead spray irrigation lines for this purpose.

ROLLING

The most significant and difficult part of pre-season cricket maintenance is rolling. This is usually a blend of art, science and local knowledge. Pre-season rolling is absolutely crucial to the production of fast pitches, as the cricket square requires a firm, even surface and rolling should commence as soon as conditions permit. The groundsman onsite is the only person who can decide when conditions are suitable. The use of rollers to firm the surface over a period of several weeks will slowly consolidate the square. Use a light roller at the earliest opportunity in the spring, possibly at the end of February or the beginning of March, gradually increasing the weight, if possible, up to a 2,028kg (2 ton) heavy roller.

Rolling Weights	
Light roller	up to 254kg (5cwt)
Medium roller	up to 508kg (10cwt)
Heavy roller	1,014kg (1 ton) or more

The pitch should be rolled in all directions, with the emphasis on cross rolling in the early stages, but finish on the line of the pitches. The aim is to consolidate the square to a depth of 100mm before the commencement of the season.

TOPDRESSING

It is important to ensure that not only is an appropriate material used with the required soil strength for the standard

A heavy roller for rolling cricket squares. Rolling is fundamental to producing pitches fit for play. (Autoguide Equipment Ltd)

of pitch, but the material must also be compatible with the existing soil profile. Problems of using incompatible material and resulting layering are well documented and this results in low and uneven bounce. The use of the right soil is most important for the production of pitches of optimum playing performance. The soil must have strong binding qualities and this is dependent on the percentage of clay content in conjunction with the other constituents of the soil structure. A sandy soil must never be used as a top dressing. The soil selection is dictated by the standard of pitch required:

First Class and Premier Leagues	Minimum of 28–35% of clay
Club standard	Minimum of 25–30% of clay
School	Minimum of 25–28% of clay

The binding strength of soil, measured using the ASSB method, can be suitably determined by a groundsman. The results of the soil strength tests indicate the ability of the soil to bind together when prepared as a pitch by rolling. Soils that have a breaking strength of less than 35kg will not hold together when dry under the impact of the ball and therefore such soils should never be allowed to dry out. Soils that break between 45kg and 55kg can be allowed to dry out but preparation must be very good. Soils with a breaking strength of 56–75kg are ideal for club cricket and, provided they are prepared well, can be allowed to dry out.

Under 45kg (100lb)	poor soil
55–65kg (120–145lb)	good for club cricket
65–90kg (145–200lb)	good for county cricket
Above 91kg (200lb)	difficult to manage

The aim of topdressing is to restore the levels of the pitch to produce a consistent surface while also maintaining the quality of the playing surface. The use of topdressings on a cricket square must follow two fundamental principles:

- It must be compatible with the existing soil in terms of particle size distribution.
- It must be compatible with the existing soil in relation to swell/shrinkage characteristics.

Topdressing involves the application of sieved/screened clay loam to the surface of the square to improve the surface and ameliorate the underlying soil. The topdressing should be a heavy clay loam with a binding strength of between 55–90kg (120–200lb) and approximately 25–35 per cent clay, with sand and silt fraction ranging between 25 and 50 per cent. The organic matter content should be between 2 and 8 per cent with the pH above 5.5 and the soil screened through 4mm mesh. As a working estimate the depth of clay loam applied as a top dressing should be 2–3kg/m^2 (4–6lb/yd^2).

AERATION
Aeration has always been considered as one of the most essential requirements of managing a healthy soil profile, in particular relieving the dense consolidation, a natural feature of all cricket squares, which impedes the pore size and air spaces between soil aggregates and severely limits the depth and health of the root system. Traditionally, this operation was done before topdressing but rarely sufficient depth of penetration was achieved due to the density of the subsurface in late autumn. It is now recognized that the roller drum type of spiker with a consistent depth of tine can be detrimental to any square with underlying layering and root-breaks due to its pulling action.

It is now recommended that cam or vertical punch type of aerators, fitted with a solid 'pencil' tine, be used on cricket squares at a minimum depth of 100mm at 50–100mm centres. The timing of the operation is now later in mid-November when the soil profile is more likely to be moist and in a more receptive condition after early re-establishment of the grasses, while the soil temperatures are favourable and topdressing has been weathered in.

For many grounds, consideration for hiring aeration equipment may prove more favourable rather than having a capital item sitting in the workshop for the best part of the working year. Soil exchange or hollow core aeration tines have traditionally been used before topdressing to remove plugs of layered and buried fibre and replace with fresh loam or as a means to introduce a different loam into the profile. There is some debate on the effectiveness as the operation is seldom achieved efficiently, since it is quite impossible to fill the void of the tine hole with a sufficient volume of loam. It would now be considered more practical to undertake some form of removal of the offending profile by use of modern innovative procedures such as fraise topping restoration, which to date has been monitored to great success at affordable costs, where they met the right criteria.

SCARIFICATION

Thatch and fibre can be a major problem in cricket squares and these can have a significant effect on the surface, absorbing energy from the cricket ball and consequently reducing ball bounce and slowing the speed of the ball during delivery. Unpredictable deliveries can also result from thatch and fibre, making for a potentially dangerous pitch. Light scarification may be necessary in the early spring, but this should only be done in moderation with great care being taken not to destroy grasses sown in the previous autumn. Heavy mechanized scarification/verti-cutting that would cut into the surface may well lead to cracking of pitches later in the season; a scarifying unit with brush attachment, however, is recommended. The pitch should be given a thorough scarification to remove any surface thatch as part of the end of season renovation.

NUTRIENTS AND FERTILIZER

Nutritional analysis of the soil is a must and will assist decision making. A light application of a fertilizer during the middle of March may be considered, possibly including iron. Adequate nutrients will need to be applied during the growing season to ensure a hard-wearing sward is maintained. Typically $8–12g/m^2$ of nitrogen may be applied over the growing season with phosphate and potassium needs being determined by soil analysis. An end of season fertilizer might typically be given towards the end of August. It should be low in nitrogen and an appropriate amount of phosphate should be included to aid seed establishment.

WEEDS, PESTS AND DISEASES

The need for any control measures will depend on weather conditions and the condition of the pitch. Fusarium might be a problem following any early fertilizer application that might take place in March, while earthworm activity can be a problem as the winter frosts recede and the spring approaches. May is usually a good time to carry out any herbicide application for weed control. Growth is usually good at this time of year and this allows for an effective elimination of most weeds.

DRAG BRUSHING

Use a drag brush regularly to keep the grass upright, which will help to keep adequate airflow around the grass blades. Earthworm casts, if present, will be dispersed on a regular basis and this will help to prevent the grass from becoming smothered. A consequence of leaving undisturbed earthworm casts on the pitch is that the underlying grass will die out and weeds will be able to invade the weakened areas.

Pitch Preparation and Repair

When the fixture list is available the grounds manager plans a programme for pitch allocation for the whole season. The aim should be to produce equal usage of each pitch. It will be necessary to place the more important fixtures towards the centre of the square and then work out accordingly. Consecutive matches should not follow on adjacent pitches as this could mean using a strip that may be damaged from the bowler's run-off from a previous match. The two outside pitches are often reserved for junior games or practice/artificial pitches. To facilitate this, the table should be 'squared off' prior to the playing season, using the '3–4–5 triangle' method to establish the corners, stump lines and individual pitches set out with white 'T' markings.

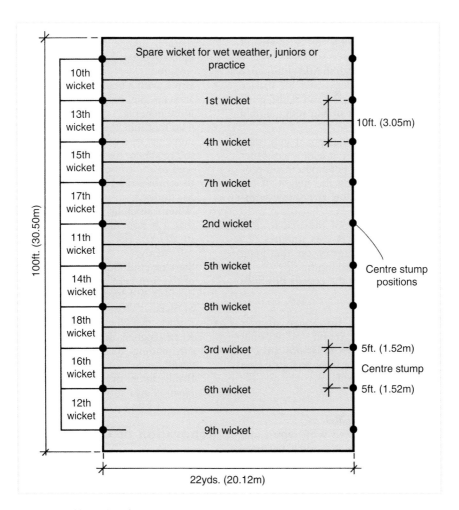

Figure 35   Possible Wicket Plan.

Pitch Preparation Prior to a Match

- Commence works at least 14–10 days prior to the match for first Class cricket or at least five days in the case of clubs, schools etc.
- Select the pitch to be used and mow to a height to 6mm. Remove as much grass as possible using one or more passes.
- Scarify the pitch using pedestrian or mechanical brush/rake machinery to reduce the density of grass and taking care not to disturb the soil surface.
- If the surface is dry, water copiously to soak the profile to a depth of 75–100mm.
- Rolling of the pitch should commence with a light roller when all surface water has disappeared and as the pitch dries, the weight of the roller should increase.
- For the remaining pre-match days mow every day or at least every other day between the popping creases progressively lowering the height of cut to 3–5mm or as low as possible without scalping.
- On the morning of the match close mow and roll for twenty minutes.
- Mark out the creases on the pitch clearly using a marking frame.
- Set the stumps in the correct positions on the crease.

A pitch prepared in the above manner should, given good ground and weather conditions, be expected to last for three to five days of first class or three to four games of average club standard.

After Match Pitch Repairs

It is essential to proceed with repairs and renovations as soon as the pitch becomes available after play. Un-repaired ends on used/worn pitches can be dangerous and are not conducive to a good game of cricket. The selection and rotation of fresh pitches, of a good standard, will become increasingly difficult if the ends are not repaired promptly and correctly.

Maintenance and Repairs to Foot Holes

In matches of two days or more, as soon as is possible after the conclusion of each day's play, bowlers' foot holes will be repaired If the pitch is to be used the following day they will need to be filled in using the following method: recommended by the ECB:

- Screen clay loam soil into a wheelbarrow and sprinkle with water until there is sufficient moisture to have a light covering. Keep under cover until required.
- Brush with a besom within the creases and up the pitch cleaning out any loose material.
- The footholds need to be thoroughly drenched to create a bond for the new soil to adhere to. By adding some grass seed to the soil there will be no need to remove the repair once the match has finished.
- When infilling depressions ensure that it is done in one mass, if applied in layers, the soil will not bind sufficiently.
- Start to consolidate from the outside of the foot hole and tread down with the foot or with a heavy panner made of metal.
- Ensure that the finished filled area is no higher than the rest of the surrounding surface with a suitable straight edge.
- Brush some dry soil/dust over the repaired area and mark out afresh.

Renovation of Used Pitches

As soon as possible after the game is over, reinstatement of the whole pitch must commence. First vigorously brush the pitch with a besom or yard broom to remove any loose soil and debris. Check that no foreign objects such as studs have been left on the playing surface; if they are not picked up they could seriously damage the mower. Worn bowler's footholds need particular care and attention. Flood the pitch three or four times, until the surface is soft enough to take a sarel spiked roller or studded type overseeding device, which will produce a good seedbed of many small holes. It is a waste of time and money to merely scatter seed on an unprepared surface. In order to give the seed a better chance of germinating it is important that it is well embedded in the surface. The making of a seedbed is essential and the seed worked/brushed well into the holes produced by the overseeder. Do this by raking lightly to form grooves, or use a border fork, or dibber to loosen the base. Evenly sprinkle the grass seed into the repaired footholds by hand and cover with a light coating of loam. Always use a straight edge to level off with the surrounding area to prevent raised bowling ends and a saucer-shaped square. Any deep ball or heel marks should be attended to by raising with a knife and plugging with moulded loam, level to the surface, and consolidated. Finally, overseed the rest of the pitch, brushing the seed into the holes made by the overseeding equipment. Apply an autumn fertilizer at a rate recommended by the manufacturer. If needed give a light dressing of loam, work in and lightly water with a sprinkler. In normal British summer conditions, grass seed will germinate with the pitch ready for use in four to five weeks. Use of germination sheets will speed up the recovery of the surface.

End of Season Renovation

Post-season cricket square renovation forms the foundation for quality pitches throughout the forthcoming season. For many clubs this work can often be difficult due to lack of resources, either in funding or lack of machinery/materials or plain absence of knowledgeable trained manpower. All materials required should be ordered and delivered to site well in advance to ensure that all workings are commenced and completed at the earliest opportunity as soon as the playing season is over, while climatic conditions promote grass seed germination and early growth. There is never a guarantee that completion of recommended operations will result in improvements in quality playing standards. This is especially so if the correct aftercare and resources are insufficient to maintain facilities.

RENOVATION PROCEDURE
At the end of the playing season any remaining worn bowling ends should be filled and consolidated level to the surface and seeded. The entire square is brought to a condition for the renovation programme down to 3mm (match height), or as low as possible without scalping the surface. Use a well-set cylinder mower with a low height of cut to provide a clean surface; this may take two or three cuts. Soften the surface sufficiently prior to further operations by irrigating the square. It is imperative that weather conditions are taken into consideration before commencing. The entire square is then heavily scarified in preferably two or three directions (diagonally and in line with play), according to density of surface vegetation, by a machine capable of penetrating the surface. All resultant arisings must be removed from the surface. The linear grooves created by the scarifier create a receptive surface for overseeding and keying in loam topdressings, although an overseeding implement such as a sarel type spike roller or studded vari-seeder would maximize application of recommended grass seed at a maximum of $50g/m^2$ for the square and brushed into the surface. An application of a suitable pre-seeding fertilizer should be applied to encourage an aggressive primary root growth. Some grounds managers prefer to apply fertilizer a week or so prior to commencement of renovations and follow up with another

application later on when the grasses are fully established. A nutritional analysis beforehand is always advisable to determine the specific requirements of the square.

Apply topdressing of a suitable loam ideally in continuity of that already established in use or as close a match to the properties of the indigenous loam. This should be spread by hand or machine and thoroughly incorporated into the surface by use of a wide tru-lute or straight edge at a rate of approximately eight 25kg bags per pitch (2.85kg/m² or 5.5lb/yd²). Where pronounced saddled ends are evident, dressings should be applied only to where levels meet the rise. Any small deviation in the levels should be corrected at this stage. It is important to maintain the same consistency of top dressing and it is often advisable to order a small surplus to store for seasonal repairs. Irrigate the square if necessary during prolonged dry spells and lightly top off the grass sward when the seed has germinated.

Overseeding and Grass Species
Pace and evenness of bounce can be influenced by the growth habit and performance of the turfgrass cultivar(s) and/or specie(s) used. Today all first class county squares use a 100 per cent perennial ryegrass blend, although some squares in lower standard and club cricket still include a few traditional species such as Chewing's fescue (*Festuca rubra communtata*) and brown top bent (*Agrostis capillaris*). Advice on particular cultivars can always be sourced by consulting the STRI or individual feed companies. Some cultivars perform better than others according to location, topography and prevailing climatic conditions. To ensure evenness of application, spread the seed in several directions. In addition, it can sometimes be beneficial to 'drill' seed into the surface by using a seed-drill machine. The turfing of pitches or square is not advised.

Winter Work
Further operations may include supplementary aeration during the winter months.

It is generally recognized that all aeration operations should cease by mid-January. Maintain ongoing regular inspection and brushing/drag matting to minimize the opportunity of any disease developing and ensure the dispersal of worm casts, if present. Occasional surveillance of the square will provide the opportunity for investigating any outbreak of fungal disease, treating with fungicide when the first signs appear (following any legal requirements) and also enable the detection of any excessive grass growth. In any mild spells it may be necessary to top the grass to ensure that the sward growth is not too retarded in the spring by removing too much growth in a short period of time. Any growth over 25mm should be lowered to 18–20mm. It may be necessary apply additional nutrients, especially during mild winters, but it is recommended that you are guided by professional analysis. If the presence of moss algae is detected, they should be treated with a suitable proprietary product at the first opportunity and the possible cause investigated. When the surface conditions allow, regularly walk the square to remove any debris that may have accumulated to ensure that no damage will be caused to equipment and to keep a watchful eye for damage caused by animal activity. During prolonged wet spells, heavy frost or under a blanket of snow it is advisable to stay off the area completely. It is often advisable to 'rope off', the square when not in use over the winter.

Surface Stabilization Agents (SSA)
In 2006 of the England and Wales Cricket Board (ECB) sanctioned the application of a surface stabilizing agent, in particular PVA (polyvinyl acetate) adhesive, solely for county one day matches. PVA works by binding the surface to prevent excessive deterioration. It can also be useful for club level cricket in retaining safe playing surfaces in times of drought and subsequent watering restrictions. It should never be applied with the notion of turning a pitch

with poor playing characteristics into a good one, nor a substitute for a correct maintenance regime.

The optimum time to apply is the evening before match day, when all pitch preparation is complete. Allow approximately forty-five to sixty minutes to cure and dry before putting the covers on for the night. On the morning of the match, a quick cut, if necessary, and light roll will suffice. This procedure can prolong the lifespan of grass practice facilities, especially where confined or restricted by available space. When no longer in use, the pitches are easily reinstated and renovated simply by vigorous brushing of the surface, thorough watering and overseeding under normal procedures. The use of such products is still under evaluation and presently mainly confined to 'professional' standard facilities. There are other products on the market based on 'molasses', which claim to be effective for cricket. At club/local authority level it would be better to stick to more conventional methods at present.

Fraise Topping and Fraise Mowing

Many town and village cricket grounds have been established for well over a century, as they have on the playing fields at some of the oldest public schools. Such pitches are often reported as playing notoriously low and slow. This can be observed by examination of the soil profile. Years of applications of topdressings can be seen forming layers, often with differing loams that became incompatible or separated by bands of buried fibrous organic matter. A common problem encountered on cricket squares, with the continuous application of topdressing material onto the pitch, is the formation of a 'saddle' where the ends of the square become raised and higher than the centre. Many cricket squares also have significant depths of surface thatch acting as a cushion and preventing water and air from promoting a healthy sward and vital root establishment. Strictly

speaking they are the results of incorrect management procedures over many years. Finding a remedy in the past to such issues necessitated excavating the offending profile and replacing with a new approved cricket loam. This is of course an expensive exercise implemented over a number of years to complete the whole square. Few sports grounds could contemplate such a cost. A previously used remedial measure was to aerate using hollow tines to remove plugs of at most 75–100mm of the top profile and work fresh loam into the holes. If done proficiently this operation did improve some poorly rated squares but it was more the exception to the rule, with no real estimation of a realistic time span to enhance and improve the playing characteristics.

The range of Field Top Makers Machines now available in the UK have been used for restoring cricket squares very cost-effectively and swiftly (in most cases one or two days given favourable weather conditions), generally without compromising the club's fixtures the following season yet drastically changing the levels, quality of grass content and overall playing performance characteristics, but only where the correct conditions of the profile have been identified by qualified advisers as being suitable. The machinery is basically a tractor-mounted surface planing device, similar to a flail mower, that can remove the top surface down to a maximum depth adjustment of 40mm in one pass with all arisings deposited on a conveyor belt straight into an accompanying trailer. An average ten pitch square (100 × 75ft or 30.48 × 22.86m) can be stripped of years of history in a couple of hours. Experience has guided experts and contractors who understand the unique dynamics demanded of cricket squares into three types of restoration operations, according to soil profile make-ups and adviser's recommendations.

Fraise topping: This is the most popular method of swift restoration, whereby

The field top maker machine has been used successfully to renovate many cricket squares. (J Mallinson (Ormskirk) Ltd)

the device removes the grass surface and underlying soil.

Fraise topping and cultivation: Here the top surface is removed with the planing device almost acting as a turf cutter. A suitable implement is used to cultivate the layers and indigenous soil into a fine tilth.

Fraise mowing: This operation is simply the machine being set at an adjustment height to remove only the herbage, whereby the surface is cleaned out of shallow rooting *Poa annua* and any thatch accumulations. Deeper rooting ryegrass is also removed, including old 'woody' stems and crowns, but the body of the plant remains intact allowing for regeneration to take place.

The Outfield

The outfield should provide a fast and true surface for the ball to run without deviation and should be firm enough to provide a good and safe foothold for the fielder. Some outfields perform a dual role and will be utilized for football or other winter sports after the cricket season. In these circumstances there is a greater opportunity for the provision of a wider range of machinery and equipment for the outfield. Mowing is the main operation carried out on the cricket field; the standard and quality of the facility will determine the height of cut. A good outfield should play true if maintained on a regular basis at 10–12mm. Any unevenness in the surface would prevent close mowing and a cutting height of up to 25mm will be required. Every opportunity should be taken to enhance the presentation of the ground, for both spectators and players. This can be achieved easily by the sensible use of the mower (or trailed equipment, such as the brush or harrow). For best results the outfield should be cut with a 36in (90cm) box cylinder mower. The use of a roller-mounted trailed seat with the mower will

It is well worth devoting some time and effort to maintaining the cricket outfield. (Harrod UK Ltd)

assist the smoothness of the surface. A Triplex type ride-on mowing unit will also produce a similar quality boxed finish, without affecting surface consolidation, while allowing increased time efficiency. Where the grass clippings are removed regularly, there will unfortunately be a greater demand on the nutrients and additional fertilizer applications may be required. Many small clubs have the outfield cut by gang mowers towed behind a tractor or other vehicle. These will reduce the cutting time and return the clippings to the surface. The lack of rolling from the gang mowers will reduce the need to aerate the outfield with spiking equipment.

A light rolling prior to the start of the playing season will resolve soil disturbance and firm the sward. A larger mower, with the cutting cylinder disengaged, will prove ideal for the purpose and may also be used during the playing season to firm the outfield, should the need arise. This latter difficulty often arises when gang units are used as the sole means of cutting the outfield. Although fertilizer on the outfield is not as important as on the square, one dressing a year, usually in spring, is sufficient for most grounds. However a supplement at the end of the season to enhance growth for winter sports may be useful. Other maintenance operations could include the control of weeds, pests and diseases, as required. Where provision is allowed for the irrigation of the outfield areas, either by self-travelling or pop-up systems, these should be used at the discretion of the groundsman. The whole of the outfield will benefit from aeration, subsequently improving the sward and also the drainage. The most common method of aeration is by tractor-drawn slitter. Aeration is even more necessary when winter games are played on the outfield. Drainage is another major problem on the outfield and the installation of a pipe drainage system may be required. The outfield should ideally be made up of a good free-draining loam with suitable grasses and weed free. It must be cleared of any objects that could cause injury to players or damage to machinery.

There are many grounds in the UK historically sited or newly constructed within residential areas with adjacent housing, or with railway lines or public highways in close proximity to the boundary extremities. Over the years there have been reported incidences of damage to property and persons. Insurance company indemnity policies have become costlier and increasingly reluctant to cover without the consideration, on safety grounds, of installing protective ball stop netting situated reasonably high enough to prevent the trajectory of a hit cricket ball encroaching outside the ground perimeters. Where installation is contemplated, local planning permission should be sought, although there is on the market a temporary system that can be erected and dismantled as required, without the need for planning approval.

Cricket Field Marking Out and Dimensions
CRICKET AND WINTER GAMES

Cricket outfields are often used for hockey or football during the winter after the cricket season has finished. This does cause some problems, particularly during the change-over period from one sport to another, but it does mean that a limited size of field can be successfully used for more than one sport.

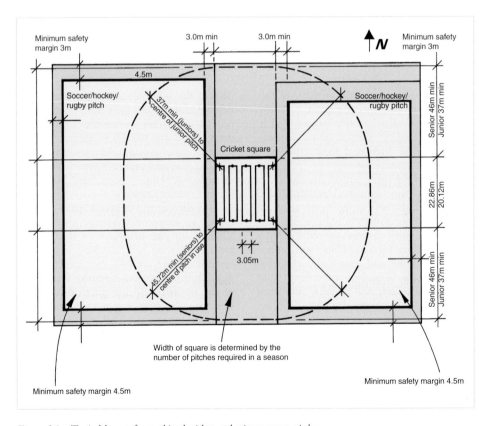

Figure 36 Typical layout for combined cricket and winter games pitches.

CRICKET TABLES

To ensure that all wickets are accurate in length and that they are set squarely on the table, mark out a rectangle with its corners just off the table edges and having a dimension of exactly 20.12m in the direction of play. The corners may be permanently sited by driving metal tubes into the ground. These can then act as sockets with their tops flush with or just below ground level. When marking individual wickets, pegs can be placed in the sockets and string run along the line of the wicket ends. It is important to ensure that the centre stumps are always equidistant from the corresponding sockets at each end of the table. In this way all wickets are parallel and wicket ends in line. Creases can then be marked by placing a template over the centre stump position.

Colour of lines	White
Width of lines	25mm recommended for creases

The pitch is the area between the bowling creases (the bowling, popping and return creases). It measures 1.52m in width on either side of a line joining the centre of the middle stumps of the wickets. Two sets of wickets, each 228.6mm wide and consisting of three wooden stumps with two wooden bails upon the top, are pitched opposite and parallel to each other at a distance of 20.12m between the centres of the two middle stumps.

The bowling crease is marked in line with the stumps at each end and is 2.64m in length, with the stumps in the centre. The popping crease, which is the back edge of the crease marking, is in front of and parallel with the bowling crease. Its back edge of the crease marking is 1.22m from the centre of the stumps and extends to a minimum of 1.83m on either side of the line of the wicket. The popping crease is considered to be unlimited in length.

The return crease marking, of which the inside edge is the crease, is at each end of the bowling crease and at right angles to it. The return crease is marked to a minimum of 1.22m behind the wicket and is also considered to be unlimited in length. A forward extension is marked to the popping crease.

Although only one pitch is indicated in the diagram, in practice a square suitable for the preparation of a number of wickets is the centrepiece of the cricket field. Typically squares are either 18.29m or 27.44m wide.

The boundary in the field is marked by a white line, a rope laid on the ground, or a fence. If flags or posts only are used to mark a boundary, the imaginary line joining such points is regarded as the boundary. For senior cricket matches, the boundary is set out with a minimum dimension of 45.72m, measured from the centre of the two middle stumps, and continued parallel to the length of the pitch.

MARKING OUT A CRICKET
SQUARE AND WICKET

Equipment: Template, brush, marking fluid, tapes, pegs, lines

Squares: Four permanent pegs should be placed *in situ* at the corners of the square at the beginning of the season as indicated in the accompanying diagram. When putting in the permanent pegs, the distance between the pegs in the direction of play must be 20.12m. Right angles must be taken to ensure that all wickets are square at a given distance.

Wickets: Wickets are marked out using the following procedure:

1. String a line between points A and B.
2. String a line between points C and D.
3. Place marking frame at the desired place on the line.
4. Place a line down the side of the frame as indicated E–F.

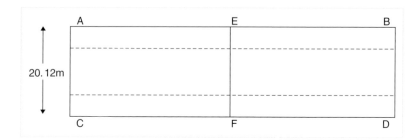

Figure 37 Marking Out Wicket.

5. Mark out end 1.
6. Move frame to the other end.
7. Place frame on the lines.
8. Mark out.
9. Remove frame from the square and clean.
10. Remove links.

If the ground is very dry it may be necessary to damp the area to be marked with a small amount of water.

Appendix 1: Adams and Stewart Soil-Binding Test (ASSB)

The procedure for making and testing a motty has a number of stages.

Place on a saucer a golf ball-size sample of soil, roughly 50g (2oz) for a mineral soil. Then add 15–20ml of water, using a lesser quantity for sands.

Rub down by firm thumb pressure, smearing on the surface of the saucer to break down all aggregation.

Make into a ball and thump down on to absorbent paper to test for, and eliminate, excess moisture. Samples that are too wet will smear and stick to the paper; too dry samples will shatter and crack. If it is too wet to thump drier, leave to stand for a while in contact with absorbent paper. If it is too dry, add 1ml water, knead to incorporate and try this stage again, adding further 1ml increments of water if necessary.

Place clod on dish in one drop of water, and cover with a small glass or cup. Leave to stand for several hours or overnight. This will allow time for the water to become uniformly dispersed.

Check on the moisture state of the clod after equilibration, then:

*   If too dry the surface will be dull and it may be necessary to add a further drop of water;
*   If too wet there may be a pool of water in the dish and the clod will glisten. Pour off any free water and leave the wet clod to dry for a while on absorbent paper;
*   If ideal, the soil ball will be glistening wet but there will be no free water in the dish.

When the clod is satisfactorily wet, rework in the hand and then roll into a cylinder 25mm in diameter. Avoid incorporating folds and cut off any involuted ends. Cut the cylinder into three or four 20mm lengths, discarding any residue. Ensure that all sections used are of equal size.

Mould cylinder sections into round balls, avoiding folds. Add one drop of water and thoroughly rework if there is a tendency to crack. Round off by progressively rolling more firmly between the palms of both hands for at least forty-five seconds.

With strongly coherent soils, such as loams and clays, maximize consolidation by repeatedly throwing the ball down on to a smooth, solid surface covered with clean absorbent paper. Roll to restore shape after each throw. Continue until the reduced earthy staining of the paper on impact indicates that all excess water has been squeezed out, and then round off for the last time, aiming to form a perfect sphere with a smooth, polished surface.

With silts and sands there may well be insufficient cohesion to enable a moist ball to hold together on impact. Therefore, consolidation and removal of excess water will have to be achieved at the ball-forming stage by very careful squeezing and then blotting during the rounding-off process. This can help if the ball is left to stand periodically on absorbent paper, but great care will be required when handling during the rounding-off process as any motty with little or no clay will become brittle as it dries out. In every case, aim to form a perfectly smooth, well-consolidated sphere, with no cracks.

Leave the moulded soil balls uncovered overnight to begin drying. If they have been rolled too wet they will be moist and flattened at the base next morning and may stick to the dish. They should be left to dry out completely over a period of five days at normal room temperature.

On the sixth day, crack the dry motty between two smooth, hard surfaces laid one over the other on the platform of a bathroom scales. Apply foot pressure from above and record weight required to shatter the dry motty. Zero the scales, plus any baseplate used, before applying pressure from above. If the motty is well made the shatter point will be well defined and sudden.

Because of the risk of errors in preparation affecting individual motties, eliminate the lowest breaking value in every three determinations before averaging the remaining values to give the rating for the sample. The accompanying table can be used to interpret the results.

Classification of Clay Content and Breaking Strength (ASSB) Values

ASSB value	Equivalent clay content	Strength
113kg	Over 55%	Exceptionally strong
91–113kg	44–55%	Very strong
68–91kg	33–44%	Strong
45–68kg	22–33%	Moderately strong
23–45kg	11–22%	Weak
9–23kg	4–11%	Very weak
Less than 9kg	Less than 4%	Non-binding

11 Tennis Courts

Selecting the right court surface to satisfy club requirements, the aspirations of coaching staff, junior players, competitions, social and senior club play is a tough challenge and one of the most important decisions for anyone involved in a project to build tennis court facilities. Selection of the right surfaces will attract and retain players and contribute to the success and viability of the facility. Inevitably, however, some level of compromise will be necessary, so it will be important to prioritize any conflicting requirements. There are many factors to take into consideration before making a final decision, not least the playing characteristics of the different surfaces. Not only is there a generic range of surfaces but each of these has a number of sub-classifications as well as different proprietary names. Cost is clearly an issue and can be a deciding factor from the outset of a construction project.

The question of whether courts should be pervious or impervious is often dictated by the weather, the size of the facility and available resources, including staff expertise, for court maintenance and management. No one has yet invented an inexpensive, free-draining, non-maintenance and long-lasting surface that suits everyone from beginner to top player. In recent years some manufacturers have focused on providing all-year round surfaces that are relatively low in maintenance and have similar performance characteristics to traditional tournament surfaces such as clay and acrylic. Examples of these surfaces are often well established abroad and manufacturers have classified them under 'porous acrylic' and 'artificial clay'. The subject of sports surfaces and their construction is also becoming increasingly scientific with test methods being developed and refined that can describe and quantify, on an objective basis, the different playing characteristics of alternative surfaces and products. While this information can be helpful, it remains essential that any existing surface type or product under consideration should be inspected and played on in order to make a full assessment of its relative playing qualities. A cross-section of players should test the surface in both dry and damp/wet conditions and it should be borne in mind that the performance of the surface can vary according to its age and condition, as well as the prevailing weather conditions at the time of the play test. Try to establish the surface history, maintenance involved and likely replacement cost. The addition of floodlighting to all-weather courts can extend playing time by up to 35 per cent or approximately 800 hours per year per court. Courts built with a solid foundation and well maintained will play well longer. The building of new courts or conversion of existing courts to seasonal surfaces should be done to Lawn Tennis Association (LTA) recommended specifications and dimensions.

Tennis Court Surfaces and their Playing Performance (Lawn Tennis Association – LTA)

Surfaces		Playing characteristics						Player surface	
		Ball surface			Spin				
		Speed of court	Height of bounce	Trueness of bounce	Topspin	Slice	Sliding /firm footing	Traction (slip or non-slip)	Shock absorption (hardness)
All Year Round	Porous macadam	Slow	High	Almost consistent	Yes	Little	Firm footing	Non-slip	Hard
	Artificial grass	Medium to fast	Medium to low	Variable	Little	Yes	Firm footing	Mainly non-slip	Medium to soft
	Impervious acrylic	Medium	Medium	Consistent	Yes	Yes	Firm footing	Non-slip	Hard to medium
Seasonal Surfaces	Clay	Slow	Medium	Almost consistent	Yes	Yes	Sliding	Non-slip	Medium to soft
	Grass	Fast	Low	Variable	Little	Yes	Firm footing with partial slide	Slip	Soft

Court Surface Types

Porous Macadam

Porous macadam courts are constructed with two layers of open grade modified bitumen macadam laid on a granite aggregate foundation and are fully permeable, hard-wearing and frost resistant. These courts have been a very popular surface, representing approximately 80 per cent of courts in the UK. The surface can be painted, which assists surface wearing properties and visual appearance.

Artificial Grass

Artificial courts consist of a tufted synthetic carpet laid on a base usually constructed from porous macadam. They are a popular club and recreational tennis surface used for club and county competitions, but are not considered as a higher level tournament or competitive surface. They are not as consistent as a hard court such as acrylic because the playing characteristics can vary from one carpet to another. There are many variations on the market but the short and medium pile (10–15mm) carpets are considered better for tennis than long pile carpets (18–23mm). These have less sand and more pile density, producing a higher and more consistent bounce and slower pace.

Impervious Acrylic

Impervious acrylic courts consist of multiple applications of coloured acrylic materials installed on a sub-base, usually of dense macadam. They are a recognized Grand Slam surface and 50 per cent of ATP and WTA Tours are played on indoor and outdoor acrylic surfaces. The cushioned layers or shock pad provide some shock absorbency, making them ideally suited for all levels of coaching and training with playing characteristics to suit all standards of play up to the highest levels of competition.

Clay

Clay courts consist of a loose surface, usually sourced from local materials (brick, volcanic rock or clay), which is crushed, lightly bound by water and laid on a hard base. The base usually doubles as a reservoir for water, which reaches the loose top surface by capillary action. Additional water is sourced from above by hose, sprinklers or rain. These elements give the surface its distinctive playing characteristics: slow pace and sliding. Two types are often encountered: red and American (or fast-dry).

Red clay is another recognized Grand Slam surface but such courts are limited to play for approximately six months of the year. Their viability is seriously affected by maintenance, cost and climate in all but the drier frost-free areas of the south coast. As such they should be considered only in special circumstances and where there are resources to deal with downtime in winter and the necessary ongoing maintenance.

American or 'fast-dry' clay is sourced from the USA and is derived from basaltic volcanic igneous rock. This is a WTA tournament surface and there are more than 200 courts in the UK. They can be played on for at least ten months of the year or throughout the year in some southern parts of England. They require less maintenance and drain more quickly than European clay, making them less susceptible to frost heave. These courts should only be considered where there are skilled ground staff and the resources to maintain them to a good standard.

Grass

Grass tennis courts have three distinct components that must function effectively together to produce a good quality playing surface: the court foundations, the soil or rootzone layer, and the grass plant. They produce fast courts and require the highest levels of technical skill to maintain in good condition. Grass is a recognized Grand Slam surface but the number of grass courts has been declining in the UK in recent years, largely due to the requirement for skilled ground staff and the level of resources to maintain them to a good standard.

Grass Tennis Courts

A well-maintained, good-quality grass court is thought by many to be the best type of tennis surface. While grass remains a very popular surface, representing approximately 20 per cent of all club courts across the country, the number of natural turf surfaces is declining, as many clubs choose to convert courts to more practical surfaces in order to maximize the amount of play possible throughout the year. Many clubs are keen to retain their grass courts and, with them, a part of their tradition. But for many others, particularly smaller clubs, the relatively short playing season is too small a return for the necessary investment of the time and cost of year-round maintenance. The large number of grass courts in Britain also represents a wide range in the quality of surfaces, as a great deal of skilled groundsmanship is required to maintain natural turf in good condition. While there are many experienced and knowledgeable grounds staff, they tend to be based at larger clubs and venues, and a large number of clubs have to get by with the work being done by club members on a voluntary basis, or with the help of part-time grounds staff who have not specialized in natural turf sports surfaces. Many smaller clubs also have insufficient budgets for maintenance equipment and materials.

Playing Surface Standards

To ensure that a grass tennis court is maintained correctly, not only during the playing season but throughout the whole of the year, a number of individual performance standards are likely to be set. The combination of these standards determines the overall quality of the court. The setting of these performance standards provides a means of objectively assessing the quality of the tennis court. Most users wish to have a top-class tennis court, but the true cost in materials, machinery and, especially, the skills of qualified and experienced grounds staff do not come cheap. Realistically the aim is for a tennis court that plays well, is safe and is managed in a cost-effective manner. Uniformity and consistency are the key requirements. There must be no variation in ball bounce or speed of the playing surface. To achieve these standards a number of criteria need to be satisfied, including sound basic construction, correct maintenance of the turf and regulation of court usage. The surface should be smooth and free from any significant high spots or depressions. If the aforementioned criteria cannot be achieved, there is little chance of producing an evenly paced, consistent and predictable playing surface. It is also perhaps prudent at this stage to mention the importance of sound construction – without sound constructional standards and adequate drainage, for example, it is unlikely (indeed, almost impossible) to create a playing surface of the very highest standard.

Construction

ORIENTATION AND LEVELS

Courts must be orientated with play along an approximate north–south axis with gradients:

- Not exceeding 1 in 120 on championship standard courts.
- For general club use 1 in 100 is acceptable.

Where possible the gradient must be across the line of play and in all cases gradients must be uniform throughout.

DRAINAGE

The precise construction methods used and maintenance routines followed will vary significantly from venue to venue. The construction process for a grass court begins with the excavation of the ground to 450mm, plus an additional depth for the drainage pipework. A grid system of drains is laid, consisting of a 100mm main drain running along the length of the court to one side, plus a series of 75mm lateral drains. The lateral pipes join the main drain at less than 12m, otherwise turbulence can be caused, which may impede the flow of

Many consider grass to be the finest surface for tennis. (TORO)

water. A silt trap is also used, just outside the court, to prevent silt accumulating in the main drain. The drainage system provides significant capacity so that the court can deal easily with the heaviest rainfall. The drainage layer is made up of graded 9–12mm slightly angular gravel spread to a thickness of 150mm. On top of this is a 50mm depth of blinding layer of coarse sand or fine grit (6mm) is spread to prevent the topsoil working its way through the court and eventually reducing the drainage. This blinding layer should also be lime-free, otherwise the pH of the topsoil could be affected.

Topsoil Profile

In the majority of cases indigenous topsoil may well be acceptable for 'domestic'

courts. For this standard of surface the requirements are less exacting and the level and intensity of usage would not necessitate or justify the importation of selected loams. The soil used to construct quality championship courts should be a loamy soil with a clay content of 20 per cent. The soil is laid to a depth of 250mm. The topsoil needs to be compacted evenly all over the court if a consistent playing surface is to be produced. To achieve this the soil is laid in 50mm depths at a time, with each layer being heeled-in, raked, levelled, then heeled and raked again. Such a process is clearly very slow and labour intensive, but careful attention to detail is important to ensure a firm surface and to avoid any future unevenness through sinkage.

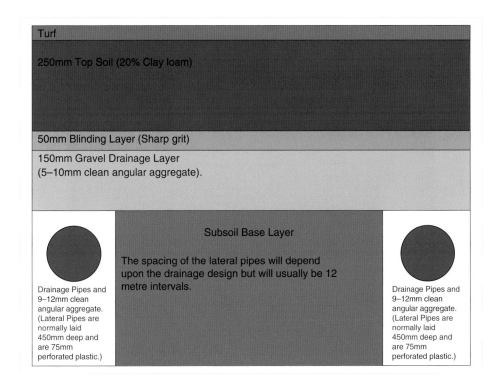

Turf

250mm Top Soil (20% Clay loam)

50mm Blinding Layer (Sharp grit)

150mm Gravel Drainage Layer
(5–10mm clean angular aggregate).

Subsoil Base Layer

The spacing of the lateral pipes will depend
upon the drainage design but will usually be 12
metre intervals.

Drainage Pipes and
9–12mm clean
angular aggregate.
(Lateral Pipes are
normally laid
450mm deep and
are 75mm
perforated plastic.)

Drainage Pipes and
9–12mm clean
angular aggregate.
(Lateral Pipes are
normally laid
450mm deep and
are 75mm
perforated plastic.)

Figure 38   Construction profile of a grass tennis court.

CULTIVATION AND GRASS ESTABLISHMENT

Initially cultivation equipment may be required to break down the soil and create a rough working tilth. The final seedbed should be produced to form a fine, smooth and evenly consolidated but not over-compacted surface. The seedbed should be graded using laser-guided equipment or by working to levelling pegs at 3m centres. During seedbed preparation all small stones and debris should be removed and a pre-seeding or pre-turfing fertilizer applied. When the soil surface has been prepared the grass surface is produced, either by turfing or seeding. Turfing has the advantage of being quicker, but can produce problems if the soil used to grow the grass is not totally compatible with that used in the construction of the court. Incompatible soils will not bind together properly, even though the grass roots will grow through – different soils will inevitably dry out at different rates, and the surface will therefore be prone to movement and break-up. The seeding method ensures complete control of the mixture of grass species used, although it usually takes one year to produce a playing surface. Seed would typically be sown in the spring, and be prepared for play twelve months later. On courts that will attract only occasional use the grass cover could contain a mixture of fine-leafed fescue and bent grasses. However, regularly used courts where a high standard of performance is required will need grass

Irrigation installed at the construction stage will be invaluable later in court preparation and maintenance. (TORO)

cover comprising predominantly perennial ryegrass. The cultivars chosen should be highly rated for shoot density and tolerance of close mowing.

Irrigation

A suitable water supply must be planned when developing a grass tennis court. This is required to help sustain normal grass growth in dry spells, as well as to assist the renovation of worn sections. A single hydrant point to which appropriate sprinklers can be attached is a basic requirement. For higher standard facilities an automatic pop-up irrigation system could be installed.

Maintenance

Good-quality grass tennis courts can only be maintained by skilled grounds staff using the right materials and equipment. Equally important is the timing of the various operations and this is when a sensible and cooperative ground committee and club administration can be of prime importance. There is no doubt that successful tennis court management is usually very much a team effort.

Court Renovation

Although the lawn tennis playing season is normally only during the summer months, maintenance continues throughout the year; as one season is completed, so preparations for the next are started. Effective autumn renovation is vital to ensure a good playing surface for the following year. Failure to do so will certainly result in a deterioration of the courts. As the playing season comes to an end the tennis courts should be closed down at the end of August/early September. Not only must the renovation programme be fully scheduled but also the necessary materials and equipment must be available so there is no delay in commencing the work. It is essential that courts are re-established as quickly as possible. A typical renovation programme includes the following operations.

Irrigation: If the court, when taken out of play, is dry, thoroughly irrigate to allow water to penetrate to a depth of approximately 100mm. This will not only assist the grass plant but will also help with the subsequent mechanical operations. The water needs to be applied at frequent intervals, thereby encouraging a steady downward movement into the soil without causing the surface to become flooded and susceptible to damage.

Scarification: Following the closure of the courts at the end of August/early September, the first task is to scarify the courts thoroughly. Intensity of treatment will depend mainly on the depth of thatch accumulation and it may be necessary to make more than five or six passes in different directions providing growth is still good. The blades of the scarifier should be adjusted to penetrate up to 6mm. This will remove any unwanted growth that may have formed and prevent the build-up of thatch. Start by working over the court, in the line of play, and then make a second pass across the line of play. All debris should be removed after each operation. Providing this has been carried out correctly in the past, ensuring a good root development, and the surface is kept moist, there

should be no risk of cubes of turf lifting out. A moist surface also reduces the amount of friction, and thus wears on the knife of the scarifier. The amount of scarification required is, as with all mechanical procedures, a matter of judgement for each grounds person. However, it is essential that it is carried out thoroughly to ensure that the best results are achieved. Late, severe scarification must be avoided as it is vital for the turf to fully recover before the onset of winter.

Aeration: The turf will require intensive aeration to improve air and water movement through the compacted topsoil. Solid or slit tines fitted on to a mechanical spiker can be used, but hollow tines should not be discounted, especially where excessive thatch or compaction is evident. The type of aeration should be decided in advance – hollow tining, solid tining or verti-draining – as it may be necessary to hire some of the equipment. If deep aeration is necessary, then a verti-drain may be the answer. This machine is very effective at relieving severe compaction but, to avoid the risk of surface damage, it is essential to have a good root system and for the soil to be in the correct moisture condition. Like every machine, it must be used correctly. When the verti-drain is not used, then the programme will, in the main, probably be one of solid tining to a depth of 100mm. However, if you have a severe thatch problem, or wish to carry out a soil exchange, then a programme of hollow coring should be carried out. There are many advantages to this treatment being carried out once every five years or so. When adopting this method, care must be taken to work topdressing down into the holes. Failure to do so can affect ball bounce. Whichever method is chosen, always first use the machine on turf away from the courts to 'shine' the tines. This will help to avoid damage from rusty tines.

Seeding: Seeding should be completed by the end of the first week in September at the latest. Seeding after this time does not produce a dense sward capable of withstanding heavy play the following spring. To ensure evenness of application, spread the seed in several directions. In addition, it can sometimes be beneficial to 'drill' seed into the surface by using a seed-drill machine. Alternatively, the use of a sarel-spiked roller can be used prior to sowing seed. These additional seeding tasks will enhance seed establishment. Use an appropriate grass seed mixture. The application rate can vary quite widely depending upon the condition of the court and grass species used. The seed might be a mixture of several perennial ryegrass cultivars or a mixture containing perennial ryegrass along with one or more of the following species:

- Slender creeping red fescue
- Chewing's fescue
- Brown top bent.

If the seeding is not completed early, then worn parts should be repaired by introducing some decent quality, mature turf. It is essential that the nature of the soil with the turf is compatible with that already on the court. Where turfing is carried out, it is important to ensure that the turves are not laid proud in anticipation of settlement. The turf should be laid on to a firm turf bed, flush with the surrounding ground, not proud. If the odd turf does sink a little, levels could be made good with some topdressing.

Topdressing: The final major operation would be to give the courts a good topdressing to provide a level surface for the following season. However, before considering the method of topdressing, it is important first to consider the material to be used. It is vital that the soil applied is compatible with the existing soil. If not, there is a risk of creating a layered effect that can cause many problems, including root fracture and the possible break-up of the court. It is well worth the relatively low cost of having an analysis carried out, and then to discuss the most suitable material with your supplier. The percentage of clay within a topdressing for a club level court will typically be within the range of 18 to 20 per cent and will provide soil strength of some 40kg.

Topdressings can be applied by hand and the procedure is very simple. Firstly, apply approximately one tonne of soil over the entire court and its surrounds. Then, with two people, a 3m lute is pulled diagonally across the court. This will help work the soil into the turf. Any low spots will be shown up and further soil can be worked into the individual area to bring it up to the required level. Once this operation is completed, a drag mat is pulled over the entire area. The court should not then be walked on until the topdressing has weathered-in properly. This material is normally applied at 1.5–2.0kg/m^2 following end of season solid/slit tine aeration and up to 3kg/m^2 after hollow tining.

Post-Renovation Work: Following renovation, the court will need to be nurtured from the end of September to December to assist in the development of a compact sward. Typical work will include:

- Mowing at around 12–15mm.
- Regular drag-brushing and switching to remove dew.
- Moss and disease control.
- Regular aeration (solid and slit/chisel tines).

MAINTENANCE OPERATIONS

Mowing is necessary to maintain the playing surface and its frequency is governed by both prevailing environmental conditions and the standard of court required. Most contemporary courts are dominated by perennial ryegrass which needs to be mown at a height of 8mm, courts consisting of more bent/fescue grasses can be mown

A cylinder mower with brush and comb attachment ideal for grass tennis court maintenance. (Ransomes Jacobsen)

lower at 6mm. Mowing will typically be required two or three times per week in the growing season whilst less frequent but regular topping of the grass should be carried out at around 12mm. For tournaments it is often desirable to mow at 5mm to achieve the necessary court speed. Most mowers used on grass tennis courts are fitted with combs or brush attachments which assist in lifting the grass for a cleaner cut. As with all fine turf surfaces clippings should always be removed.

Scarification and Verti-cutting: regular light scarification and verti-cutting is necessary to prevent a build up of thatch or fibre which would deaden the ball and result in courts with low bounce and slow pace. Scarification can be deployed monthly taking care not to damage the surface by scarifying too low or not scarifying in hot dry weather which would stress the grass plant. Similarly verti-cutting lightly on a monthly basis should help avoid the development of excessive fibre in the sward. Comb attachments fitted to mowers assist

in promoting upright grass growth and allows better cutting.

Irrigation may be necessary in periods of dry weather and there should be provision for this in maintenance programmes. Water management should ensure that grass plants are not subjected to unnecessary stress but that only sufficient water is applied to maintain plant turgor and growth. Amounts of water required will vary but it is good practice to irrigate only in the evening to avoid excessive water loss which can occur in hot weather through evapotransporation. Such practice will also ensure that courts are dry for play in the day time. Tennis courts have quite high clay content and therefore it is advisable to spike the court prior to irrigation to help water infiltration into the surface.

Fertilizer Application: fertilizer applications commencing in spring with light nitrogen feeds and continuing throughout the growing season should be based on assessment of grass growth, weather conditions and also soil analysis. This is particularly so for the inclusion of potassium and phosphates. Courts with ryegrass swards will be more nutrient demanding and require more fertilizer applications or higher dose rates whilst the opposite is the case for fescue/bent swards. Over application of phosphate in particular can lead to courts dominates by Annual Meadow Grass (*Poa annua*) which is undesirable. Therefore the exact composition of fertilizers needs careful consideration. Regular applications of nitrogen can continue until August time when its rate should be low in order to avoid flushes of grass growth and possible disease ingress at this time of year.

Aeration: regular aeration in the winter moths post renovation will help to promote vigorous grass root growth and surface drainage during periods of wet weather. Generally solid or slit tines fitted to a mechanical aerator are used to varying depth and spacing. Such practice is not advocated after early March when preparations for the playing season commence. There is a danger that to do so would lead to surface cracking when courts are in play in the summer months.

Rolling with a 250–500kg roller after winter will help settle any upheaval of the surface caused by frost and help to firm the surface for the playing season. Over rolling must always be avoided as its effects can be detrimental to grass growth and particularly soil structure and drainage. Rolling before tournaments is sometimes desirable to firm courts and promote bounce and pace. Often the use of a large cylinder mower set off cut is sufficient for this purpose.

Pests, Diseases and Weeds: ground staff should be ever vigilant for troublesome diseases, particularly Fusarium, and where necessary deploy the appropriate control measures which may require the use of an approved fungicide. Keeping surfaces clean and free from dew is always good management practice and helps to prevent such incidences. The same is true for casting earthworms which may be prevalent in wet conditions. Broadleaved weeds are best treated in May with an approved broad spectrum selective weed killer. At this time of year they are often growing vigorously and succumb readily to translocated herbicides. Repeat applications may be needed for heavy infestations. Moss may need similar treatment although often herbicides are only palliative as underlying causes such as shade or damp conditions need to be corrected for effective control of moss.

Drag-Brushing: the use of a drag brush on a daily basis will keep grass free from dew and promote upright growth which are both better for reducing disease incidence and clean cutting with the mower. Brushing will also disperse any worm casts present too. Such daily works also provide the opportunity to closely monitor the courts surface and check for any damage or scars occurring. The use of a switch will also be beneficial and is quicker than brushing but not as efficient in standing the grass up. Brushing is always advisable before mowing if the mower is not fitted with a brush/comb attachment.

Court Rotation: where there are a number of courts available, it is good policy to introduce a system of rotating the temporary closure of one or two courts to allow several days rest. This encourages the recovery of worn areas and allows time for remedial and restorative work to be carried out. With only a limited number of courts available, this system may not be possible.

Post-Match Renovation: renovation works to restore the courts surface will be necessary post match the extent of which will depend upon the level and intensity of play. Damage in the form of minor holes, depressions or areas of scuffed and worn grass will often be apparent and need repair. First it will be necessary to 'clean' the court of loose soil and arising with a brush and followed by mowing. Shallow spiking and over sowing with pre-germinated seed can then be carried out on the most damaged areas. Some areas will require lifting with a hand fork and filling with moist topdressing loam. The repaired areas need to be kept irrigated at least until grass cover is restored.

Porous Macadam Courts

Porous macadam courts are a very popular surface for tennis throughout Britain's clubs, local authorities and schools, representing approximately 80 per cent of courts in the UK. As well as being well suited to the UK's climate, porous macadam has been popular owing to:

- Its initial low level of construction costs.
- It has proved to be a hard-wearing and durable playing surface.
- Maintenance requirements are considered to be minimal.
- The surface provides a high level of court utilization during the year.
- Courts may be painted to improve aesthetics and playing environment.

Construction
Porous macadam tennis courts consist of a frost-resistant, permeable foundation of broken graded stone or aggregate on which is laid a two-layer system (65mm recommended depth) of open grade modified bitumen macadam. This forms the surface course or playing surface and binder course that improves the strength of the court. The surface course is coated with coloured polyurethane or acrylic based paint. Playing lines are painted onto the coloured surface using paint with the same specifications as that used for the entire playing area. The resulting tennis surface is fully permeable, hard-wearing, frost resistant and requires relatively little maintenance, but however modest this maintenance requirement, it is nevertheless of vital importance if the surface is to remain free-draining, aesthetically pleasing, good to play on and long-lasting. Surface coatings are usually acrylic but can be polyurethane based, and are spray applied when the bitumen has hardened.

This will take approximately three weeks during the summer months and could take up to three months in winter. It is usual for the surface coating to be allowed to harden for approximately one week before play commences with four days as an absolute minimum unless otherwise specified by the installer. Coating the surface enhances the appearance of the court and helps to prolong the life of the surface by preventing harmful UVs from penetrating and degrading the bitumen. A colour-coated macadam court can take between seven and ten weeks to total completion. This is allowing four to six weeks for construction; three weeks for the macadam to cure, one day to colour coat and a further week for the paint to fully cure.

Maintenance
Maintenance requirements are minimal, although failure to keep the upper surface free of moss, algae and debris by moss/weedkilling and power washing will cause surface water drainage problems and reduce the total service life of the court.

SURFACE CLEANING
Leaves, tree flowers, pine needles, fluff from tennis balls and other detritus should not be allowed to remain on the surface for any length of time. If this happens they rapidly rot down and settle into the pores of the surface, impairing drainage and providing a growing medium for algae and moss. A wide soft broom can be used to sweep the surface but this has a tendency to push smaller material into the surface. A rubber-tined rake is usually better, although slow and arduous. A mechanical garden vacuum cleaner will greatly speed up the operation and do it more efficiently. Mechanical leaf sweepers can also be used to good effect. The equipment should be well maintained and carefully operated to avoid contamination of or physical damage to the surface.

At least once a year the court surface will benefit from a vigorous wash. This not

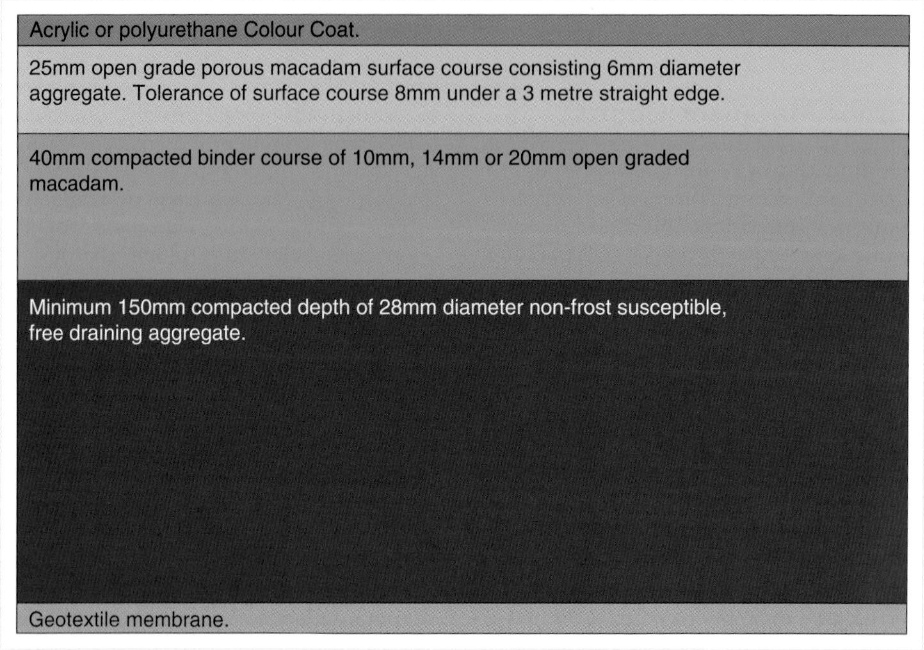

Acrylic or polyurethane Colour Coat.
25mm open grade porous macadam surface course consisting 6mm diameter aggregate. Tolerance of surface course 8mm under a 3 metre straight edge.
40mm compacted binder course of 10mm, 14mm or 20mm open graded macadam.
Minimum 150mm compacted depth of 28mm diameter non-frost susceptible, free draining aggregate.
Geotextile membrane.

Figure 39   Construction profile of porous macadam court.

only has the effect of keeping the surface pores clean and free-draining but is also essential to maintaining good foothold. Courts near busy roads are particularly susceptible to becoming coated with 'traffic film', while those near trees may become coated with sap. The resulting black film from either cause can make the courts very slippery after rain. Cold water pressure washers are recommended and are available from most equipment hire outlets. During cleaning great attention must be paid to ensuring that the process does not damage the surface by removing the coloured coating or dislodging stone chippings. A mild, non-foaming detergent increases the efficiency of the operation. Steam cleaners should not be used.

Play in Hot Weather

Caution should be taken before allowing play in hot weather as the courts may be susceptible to softening, especially in the first season after construction. Thereafter the tendency to soften should rapidly diminish. If the surface softens, stop play immediately because serious damage can result from continuing play. The first sign of the problem is usually when black marks begin to appear as a result of the paint being rubbed or scuffed off. It is sometimes possible to cool a hot surface by hosing it down with cold water to allow evening play to take place.

Court Renovation

RE-COLOUR COATING

As a guideline a new colour coating should be carried out every five years using either polyurethane or the more traditional water-based acrylic paint. Poly-urethane paints are slightly more expensive than acrylic but less prone to softening in moist conditions as they retain the texturing agents incorporated in the paint for longer. This helps to retain acceptable slip resistance. There are two types of polyurethane paint. Moist curing is solvent-based and does not soften in wet conditions. Water-based polyurethane paint is slightly cheaper (and more environmentally friendly) but offers slightly less protection against wear.

When repainting the following procedure should be observed:

- Apply a proprietary moss killer (allow approximately two weeks for the treatment to take effect).
- Remove any surface debris.
- Power wash the whole macadam area.
- Apply textured tennis court colour paint.

The paint covers only the upper face of the aggregate forming the top of the surface. While it can improve the slip resistance of the court it will do little if anything to improve the bond strength and extend the life of the surface. Once a court starts to fret the economics of repainting are often questionable, since the court is likely to require resurfacing before the full life of the new paint coating has expired.

RESURFACING

As macadam courts age the bitumen binder incorporated in the macadam will become weaker and at some point, typically after eight or more years, will no longer provide adequate adhesion resulting in the aggregate in the macadam starting to break away, a characteristic known as fretting. This will eventually lead to a potentially hazardous surface with unacceptable playing characteristics. The rate of deterioration will be dependent on a number of factors, including amount of use, maintenance and severity of winters.

In the majority of cases resurfacing merely involves undertaking preparatory works before laying a new macadam layer (normally 25mm thick) and painting. Some courts, however, will have suffered damage to their foundations, which will have resulted in an undulating playing surface. Common causes are inadequate foundation, depths and materials, settlement and root damage. In such cases the cause of the damage should be identified, normally requiring trial holes to be opened, and appropriate remedial works under-taken – in the worst case this may involve reconstruction.

If the existing court surface does not have excessive undulations the resurfacing process normally includes:

- Treatment of moss, algae and other weeds.
- Piercing at 450mm centres to help surface drainage.
- Power washing.
- Application of bitumen tack coat (to allow the new and old layers of macadam to key together).
- Laying of the new macadam layer.
- Colour coating.

The installation and painting of macadam surfaces should be undertaken at times of the year when the ambient temperature is not too cold and the weather will ensure the court surface is dry during the painting process. This is normally considered to be April through mid-October. New macadam surfaces need to be laid against a hard edge to provide protection so the material does not break away at the edges. If the existing posts and sockets are in good condition, spacing plates can normally be inserted into the sockets to raise the heights of the posts.

POLYURETHANE BINDERS

Polyurethane binders are a relatively new development in the tennis court industry and have become popular in recent years. They are clear coatings that are applied to new or old macadam surfaces to provide enhanced strength to the playing surface. They also aid the adhesion of the paint coating to the macadam surface, acting as a form of tack coat. Binders are available in either water- or solvent-based acrylic or polyurethane formulations and are spray applied. On older macadam surfaces, where the original bitumen binder incorporated in the macadam mix has aged and started to noticeably weaken, the application of a binder coat may prolong the life of the macadam surface in the short term. On very weak macadam, however, the quantity of binder required to hold the surface together may be such that it seals or partly seals the surface, resulting in a significant loss in porosity. As a general rule, if an old court starts to break up during power washing the level of deterioration is likely to be so great that an application of binder will not be effective and resurfacing is required. As binders do not have any form of texturing agent in their formulation, the resulting film coating will be slippery when wet or damp. If a binder coat is applied a court must also be colour coated. Applying a binder will not improve the texture of the macadam surface. Heavily pitted macadam will still be heavily pitted after a binder coat is applied. The cost can vary greatly and normally relates to the type of binder being applied (water- or solvent-based) and the application rate.

Sand–Filled Artificial Grass Carpet Courts

The demand for better facilities that can be used throughout the year has led to the development of a range of synthetic sports surfaces, of which synthetic grass has become one of the most widely used and well accepted. Synthetic grass tennis surfaces have their limitations for use in tennis coaching and for high-level play, but nevertheless the dramatic rise in the number of courts installed during the 1990s is evidence of the surface's popularity with many players. Short pile carpets are now the preferred surface for tennis courts as they allow the pile to be stiffer, offering more resistance to a ball as it strikes the surface, resulting in a slower surface pace. Synthetic grass carpets generally are now of a higher standard than they were during the early 1990s. Better polymers have been developed to produce harder-wearing and longer-lasting fibres, and more attention has been paid to the choice of sand used, following the early problems of compaction and drainage. Being a permeable surface, synthetic grass can be played on in most weather conditions, and can be used for twelve months of the year. Short pile carpets should only be installed above 6mm diameter open grade surface crushed stone.

Construction

A synthetic grass court is basically a tufted synthetic carpet laid on a base usually constructed from porous macadam. Installation of the base is critical if the court is to perform satisfactorily for the duration of its life, and the specification used should be tailored to the individual site. The carpet is loose laid in pieces, and seamed, either by sticking or gluing to a backing tape. Carpets are produced in a range of widths, usually between 4.0m and 5.0m: the greater the carpet width the fewer seams are required in the court, reducing the risk of premature failure of the surface. The playing lines are nearly always permanently inlaid, and can either be incorporated into the carpet during manufacture or cut and glued into the surface once it has been laid.

Sand Infill

Once the carpet has been installed, dry weather conditions are required to fill the surface with sand. The choice of sand itself

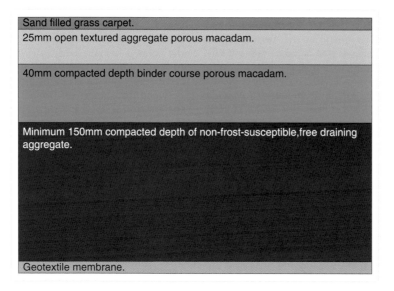

Sand filled grass carpet.

25mm open textured aggregate porous macadam.

40mm compacted depth binder course porous macadam.

Minimum 150mm compacted depth of non-frost-susceptible,free draining aggregate.

Geotextile membrane.

Figure 40   Construction profile of sand-filled synthetic grass carpet.

is vital if the court is to perform well. Many of the earlier surfaces experienced over-compaction and pollution of the sand, which led to drainage problems, and so these days larger rounded sand particles are usually preferred. Typically, manufacturers will recommend filling the carpet with sand to within 2 or 3mm of the top of the pile, but in practice this can be seen to vary considerably. During the first few months of a court's life, the sand will compact to some degree and should be topped up as necessary. It is important that not too much of the pile should be exposed, as otherwise it will flatten and can then be very difficult, if not impossible, to raise. This can cause excessive wear and tear of the fibre, and reduce the life of the carpet. Correct ongoing maintenance is also vital to keep the surface in optimum condition.

Immediately after construction there is an initial working-in period during which the final playing surface is created. Initially the court surface will be left rather sandy but full penetration of the sand infill into the pile and its subsequent compaction into a uniform playing surface occurs naturally with normal processes, especially rainfall and initial play. This usually takes one or two months.

During construction every effort should be made to ensure even distribution of sand over the whole court. Increasing the frequency of brushing in the early weeks of use is beneficial in creating the final playing surface. If areas are found that are short of sand it should be possible to brush surplus sand into them from adjacent areas, provided this is done within the first few weeks.

Maintenance

In maintaining sand-filled carpet tennis courts it is important that:

• The playing surface is kept scrupulously clean.
• The pile remains supported.
• That free drainage of surface water is maintained.
• The tennis court looks attractive and well kept.

Surface cleaning: Leaves, tree flowers, pine needles and other detritus should not be allowed to remain on the surface for any length of time. If this happens they rapidly decay forming a drainage-inhibiting skin within the surface, and providing a growing medium for algae and moss. A wide soft broom or a rubber-tined rake is ideal for removing vegetable matter and other rubbish. Mechanical leaf sweepers will greatly speed up this work. Such equipment must be well maintained and carefully operated to avoid contamination or physical damage to the surface. Both sweepers and vacuum cleaners may tend to remove rather too much sand during the first few months of the life of the surface, but thereafter should cease to be a problem. Some disturbance of the surface of the sand may be a positive benefit.

Brushing: Brushing the surface is a crucial operation if premature loss of pile and deterioration in drainage is to be prevented. The purpose of regular and fairly vigorous brushing is to prevent the formation of a compacted and impervious skin on top of the sand layer, which will inhibit drainage and encourage moss and algae. Brushing by hand is basically ineffective and hard work. A selection of mechanical brushing machines is now available that will speed up and lighten the operation and these are recommended at tennis venues where there are several courts. The machines vary in the vigour with which they treat the surface: some methods, namely rotary brushing, are rather fierce and only recommended for use by experienced operatives and where heavy remedial brushing is indicated. Combined brush and vacuum machines must be used with even greater care because sand brushed and sucked from the surface may be very difficult to replace, especially when the court is wet. The use of a small tractor with weighted drag brush is strongly recommended for the best long-term performance. The recommended frequency of brushing will depend on the amount of use the court receives and whether its location is open and clean. Once a week is a recommended norm but it may be advisable to brush more often if the court is heavily used, shaded or subject to contaminants. Similarly a little used court will come to no harm if the intervals between brushings are longer, provided the location is open and clean. It cannot be overemphasized that to neglect the brushing of this kind of court may have serious long-term consequences even if, in the shorter term, the court does not appear to suffer. Brushing need be neither time-consuming nor onerous but its benefits are profound. To omit the process may result in a court ceasing to drain at half-life or sooner. An unbrushed court will look scruffy and be susceptible to moss infestation.

Moss and algae: In certain situations and in some seasons algae or moss can become established on the court surface. Since prevention is very much more effective than cure, it is important to treat the court with a good proprietary moss killer and algaecide at least once a year. Moss is not usually found on that part of the surface that is heavily used and it may not be essential to treat these areas, although it is still a wise precaution to do so. Particular attention should be paid, however, to those perimeter and other areas that are not heavily used, especially if they are shaded by walls or buildings or overhung by trees. Any approved proprietary product is satisfactory provided it is not oil-based. The manufacturer's instructions should be closely followed. Where moss has become established, repeated applications of moss killer may be needed until the moss can be brushed and cleared away. Moss is only a serious problem if it is allowed to become established: an annual prophylactic application of moss killer is an easy way of preventing this. Regular brushing and use of the court renders moss an even less likely problem.

Play lines: The court will normally be supplied with permanently in-laid playing lines. However, if additional lines are required for special events, these can be painted onto the surface using water-based paints. Chalk lines can also be applied, but these tend to leave a lasting powder spread in the area of the line. Permanent lines require no special attention.

Stain removal: Most stains can easily be removed with a solution of hot (not boiling) water and a household detergent, such as washing-up liquid. The removal of chewing gum can be simplified by using ice cubes to harden the gum.

Surface replacement

The synthetic grass carpet is removed in its entirety and replaced with a new surface and new sand infill. In order to ensure adequate drainage for the life of the new synthetic grass carpet, the macadam base of the court may need to be pierced and backfilled before resurfacing. With medium and particularly short pile carpets there is a possibility of the pierced holes causing small depressions in the playing surface. This can distort the bounce of the ball after it has made contact and is therefore unacceptable. To ensure the holes do not become a problem it is strongly recommended that the pierced macadam surface is overlaid with a new macadam layer. Overlaying also has the advantage of ensuring the surface regularity of the macadam base for the carpet is to the highest possible standards and giving the best possible ball consistency.

Impervious Acrylic Tennis Courts

Impervious acrylic, sometimes referred to as 'American Cement' or, in the US, simply as 'hard courts', is widely used throughout the tennis-playing world. It is the surface on which many major championships are played, including the Australian and US Open Grand Slams, and around half of the ATP and WTA Tours are played

on indoor and outdoor acrylic surfaces. The number of impervious acrylic courts built in Britain has been growing steadily since 1989 with significant growth occurring during the 1990s following the recognition of impervious acrylic as a preferred performance surface by the LTA. The overall combination of the surface's playing characteristics makes it suitable for all standards of play, up to the highest levels of competition. The surface can be played on for twelve months of the year, depending on the weather conditions. The impervious nature of the surface does mean that surface water or puddles will form on outdoor courts during periods of rainfall, which will normally prevent play from continuing. This must be cleared before play can recommence; this can be achieved with the use of specific drying aids such as squeegees.

Construction

The construction of an impervious acrylic court is quite straightforward. The playing surface consists of multiple applications of coloured impervious acrylic materials installed on a sub-base, usually of dense macadam, which is laid on a suitable depth of well-compacted aggregate foundation. Most proprietary systems offer optional 'cushioned' layers of varying depth, intended to provide a degree of player comfort. Being non-porous, an outdoor impervious acrylic court is constructed with a slight slope to help water to run off. The optimum run-off of surface water will depend on the construction of an adequate gradient on the court; the LTA recommends a cross-fall of 1 in 120, up to a maximum of 1 in 100. The essential difference in the construction of an impervious acrylic court is that a dense foundation is required, compared to one through which water must pass for surfaces such as macadam and synthetic grass. The provision of adequate drainage to collect water is equally important, particularly as significant quantities of rain may need to be dealt with. It is usual

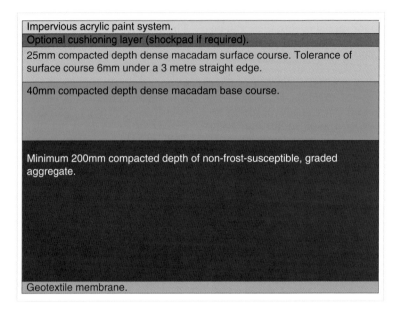

Impervious acrylic paint system.

Optional cushioning layer (shockpad if required).

25mm compacted depth dense macadam surface course. Tolerance of surface course 6mm under a 3 metre straight edge.

40mm compacted depth dense macadam base course.

Minimum 200mm compacted depth of non-frost-susceptible, graded aggregate.

Geotextile membrane.

Figure 41   Construction profile of impervious acrylic tennis court.

practice to install drainage channels within the edging along the low sides of courts, but the system must be carefully designed, particularly when blocks of two or more courts are to be built.

Maintenance

In maintaining impervious acrylic tennis courts it is important that the playing surface is kept scrupulously clean and that the court looks attractive and well cared for at all times.

Surface cleaning: Leaves, pine needles, dust, dirt, rubbish and all detritus should be removed from the surface regularly using a wide broom (medium to soft bristles, not too stiff or hard) or a garden vacuum cleaner. If the latter is used, it should be well maintained and carefully operated to avoid contamination or physical damage to the surface. At least once a year, more often if the courts are heavily used or are in a

location subject to pollution by traffic fumes, aphid secretions and other contaminants, the surface should be thoroughly washed using a cold water pressure washer taking care not to damage the surface. Stains can be removed with a mild detergent.

Surface monitoring: Keeping the surface clean is the only routine maintenance that the court surface should require. In the unlikely event of other apparent defects occurring, for instance cracks or crazing, the manufacturer should be consulted. The surface should also be maintained to enable surface recoating to be scheduled when required. A newly laid surface should give firm foothold and a good medium-paced game. As the surface is used over the years, however, it will become smoother and more polished. This may result in a somewhat faster game and, eventually, some impairment of the foothold when the surface is damp. When this happens it will be time for the surface to be recoated. The recoating requirement should be discussed with the manufacturer when the new court is handed over.

Surface Replacement

If impervious acrylic courts are well specified and well built in the first place, the top playing surface can be 'resurfaced' at a relatively low cost and have a very long life before major work is carried out. Resurfacing falls into two main categories depending on the structural condition:

- If the court is in good structural condition but has become worn and is losing colour and texture, it can be restored to 'as new' condition by suitable preparation (cleaning, power washing) and the application (by squeegee) of one or two coats of colour-finish material. Depressions or surface imperfections must be treated prior to this recolouring.
- If the structural condition of the court has deteriorated significantly, it may become necessary to superimpose a new layer of dense bitumen macadam, or to remove the top 25mm or so of the existing macadam sub-base and replace it. A completely new impervious acrylic surface is then built up.

Hard, Porous Waterbound: Red Championship Shale Tennis Courts

The vast majority of shale-type courts in this country are in a very poor condition and the reason is not hard to define: owing to the pressure on playing facilities, for the past few years the practice of taking shale courts out of use from November to April for renovation purposes has largely been discontinued. If the courts have not been brought to a satisfactory standard by the start of a new season's play, nothing that can be done during the season will remedy that situation. The result of the lack of autumn and winter renovation work is that, over the years, no new coarser

material has been worked into the surface and the old material has simply broken down into an impermeable mass that prevents water passing through into the foundations to provide satisfactory drainage. This is evident in the pools of water that lie on the surface after rain, greatly delaying the start of play and reducing the available playing hours. The real problem is that the required remedial work for courts in this condition is substantial and costly and has to take account of many years of neglect. In fact, in a large number of cases, there is likely to be little of the original surface left at all and the courts ought properly to be professionally resurfaced.

Court Renovation

The court should be taken out of use in late autumn and works commenced by removing all ash and lumps of clinker in evidence on the surface. Do not attempt to roll them back in; the baselines are usually the worst areas for compaction and loss of level. Apply sufficient medium grade dressing to that area to correct any depression in the surface. Forget fine grade dressings for this purpose. Using a lute, level out the applied dressing by eye across the area being worked on, feathering it away to nothing at the edges of the area. Use a light, thin-tined fork to lightly fork the surface until contact is made with the foundation (usually ash) and then gently raise the fork until the existing surface is lifted but not turned. Break up the lifted surface with the back of the fork (or rake) and the new material will drop into the gaps made by the fork. Complete that mixing process and then lightly roll the area in a dry condition until the surface has reached its new corrected level.

Roll in both directions but take care not to spin or twist the roller on the newly prepared area. When ground conditions are suitable, further roll the area thoroughly to consolidate the surface, watering as required. Continue such rolling over the ensuing weeks, working only when ground conditions are fit for this treatment, until consolidation to play standard is achieved. In the rolling process, in order to prevent the surface material adhering to the roller, an efficient scraper should be devised. The winter frosts will do some of the work. If a layer of medium dressing is added across the whole court area from the moment play ceases in the autumn, the upheaval of the surface caused by frost will open it up and absorb the dressing. It can then be lightly rolled back when the ground condition is right. As each amount is absorbed, further quantities may be added. The object of this renovation treatment is to get new material into the existing surface and not onto it, simply to lie loose on top.

Maintenance

There is no short cut to a well-maintained shale court when the playing surface is in a properly consolidated condition and fit for play. The following maintenance should be carried out during the playing season:

- Courts must be kept damp. A thorough watering of the surface is essential. Try to avoid play taking place on a dry surface, which will tend to break it up. If possible, provide each shale court with its own watering point, fitted with a hose and fan-shaped spraying head, so that players can quickly and conveniently spray the surface before commencing play. This will anyway produce a better playing surface for their game.

- Roll only as and when the surface consolidation requires it. Excessive rolling will do nothing but harm, panning down the surface and the foundations. A roller of 250kg is sufficient for this work.

- Any minor surface damage should be properly repaired and consolidated afterwards. Any loose material on the surface after play can be redistributed with the use of a semi-stiff broom, which should be dragged and not pushed.

- Intensive renovation work in autumn and winter, whenever ground conditions permit, is the key to success, plus the indicated regular maintenance throughout the playing season.

General Care of Tennis Courts

Footwear: Good-quality tennis shoes should be insisted on for all surfaces. Training shoes or other types of footwear with bars, studs or sharp serrations on the soles should not be used. It is useful to have a notice at the entrance to the court recommending, among other things, the correct type of footwear. A player wearing incorrect shoes with aggressive soles can do a great deal of damage in a very short time and can lead to player injuries.

Furniture and equipment: Most surfaces will be indented and therefore damaged by heavy or sharp objects standing on the court. Do not put umpire's chairs or garden seats directly on to the surface; boards or pads can be placed under the legs to spread the load. It is also essential to outlaw roller skates, skateboards, bicycles, wheelbarrows full of sand and anything else that children may bring on the court and that could do damage to the surface. Family pets should be excluded too for obvious reasons. Perhaps the simplest thing to do is to lock the gate! Machinery being used on the court surface, such as compressors and water-pumps, should stand at all times on a piece of plywood or similar.

Court perimeter: A strip of ground at least two feet wide outside the surround fence should be kept clear of vegetation at all times to form a barrier against plant and weed encroachment onto the playing surface. This may be done quite simply with an appropriate weedkiller. Climbing plants should be avoided as their roots and leaves may disturb and pollute the court surface respectively. Shading caused by the windbreaks or screens can lead to increased algae and moss development on the court surface, which may affect surface grip. Shrubs, trees and hedges should be planted as far back from the court as possible, certainly allowing sufficient room between surround fence and plants for maintenance to be carried out between them.

Tree roots: Trees, hedges and shrubs to be planted close to the court should be chosen carefully to avoid any aggressive root systems, such as poplars and sycamores. These can cause major disturbance of the surface. If their use is essential, the insertion of a root barrier between the trees and the court is strongly recommended. Planning or conservation consent should be sought where required.

Overhanging branches: Branches of trees that overhang the court invariably cause problems. Water dripping from the branches may cause slippery or discoloured patches, encourage the growth of algae or moss and sometimes even erode the surface. The secretions of aphids coat the court surface with a sticky blackish substance that may impair foothold and encourage such as algae and, in severe cases, damage the surface paint. The droppings of larger birds, including pigeons and collared doves, can cause damage especially to painted macadam surfaced during the summer months. For all these reasons overhanging branches should be pruned well back, subject to planning control requirements. Planning or conservation consent should be sought when required.

Nets and Net Posts

Do not over-tighten the tennis net. This will cause damage or even breakage of the steel cable, and in severe cases may pull the net posts inwards, occasioning a very costly repair. A common cause of the net being over-tightened is that the centre band is too short, preventing the correct height from being achieved. The centre band will be provided with a screw adjuster and this should be slackened to allow the net to be adjusted correctly and then carefully retightened. The correct height for the centre of the net is 914mm (3ft). If during the winter the court is not to be used, both

> **Substances to Keep Away from Tennis Courts**
>
> **Cigarettes:** make the court a No Smoking Area. Cigarettes are unlikely to constitute a fire hazard, but cigarette ends will leave unsightly burn marks on most surfaces.
>
> **Chewing gum and drinks:** should all be banned too. Chewing gum is invariably difficult to remove, although some advise the use of ice cubes, which harden the gum and allow it to be broken away more freely. Carbonated soft drinks leave an unsightly black stain when spilled on the court surface that is difficult to remove.
>
> **Petrol, oil and solvent:** spillages will seriously damage most surfaces, especially those that are bitumen bound or are superimposed upon bitumen bound sub-base. Great care should be taken to ensure that any machinery used within the court area is clean and in good repair and does not drip petrol or oil. It is strongly recommended that machines are removed from the court surface before refilling with petrol, diesel or oil. In the event of a spillage, immediate copious irrigation with tepid water and detergent may minimize the damage.
>
> **Salt and de-icing agents:** should never be used to remove snow or ice from tennis courts; their effect is unpredictable and they may cause serious damage.

net and net posts should be removed and stored, ensuring that they are first carefully dried. The winding mechanism should be greased occasionally to ensure smooth and quiet operation and the posts checked for rust. It can also be helpful to lightly grease the post sockets and that part of the posts that fits into the sockets. This can greatly facilitate the removal of the posts, especially if they are left in position for long periods.

Weeds

Before constructing the court, a total weedkiller should have been applied to the site. This is usually effective but sometimes weed growth may occur, either involving highly resistant species or windblown seed. Such weed growth that does occur usually represents a temporary inconvenience and only very rarely constitutes a significant threat to the court. If they appear, the solution is to deal with them promptly and not to allow them to become established. Courts sited in fields, paddocks or other weedy areas, or adjacent to suckering trees, may be at increased risk beyond the immediate post-construction period. This is because of tree roots giving rise to suckers and certain weeds such as Creeping Thistle can spread rapidly underground and may reinfest the tennis court site nearby. In these circumstances, it is advisable to maintain a weed-free cordon around the perimeter of the court(s) by applying an approved translocated herbicide regularly to a strip of a minimum width of 1m immediately outside the court surround fencing. This will check underground growth before it reaches the court.

Tennis Court Dimensions

Singles Court

The court shall be a rectangle 23.77m (78ft) long and 8.23m (27ft) wide. It shall be divided across the middle by a net suspended from a cord or metal cable of a maximum diameter of one-third of an inch (8mm), the ends of which shall be attached to, or pass over, the tops of the two posts, which shall be not more than 150mm (6in) square or 150mm (6in) in diameter. These posts shall not be higher than 25mm (1in) above the top of the net cord. The centres of the posts shall be 914mm (3ft) outside the court on each side and the height of the posts shall be such that the top of the cord or metal cable shall be 1.07m (3ft 6in) above the ground.

When a combined doubles (*see* below) and singles court with a doubles net is used for singles, the net must be supported to a height of 1.07m (3ft 6in) by means of two posts, called 'singles sticks', which shall be

not more than 75mm (3in) square or 75mm (3in) in diameter. The centres of the singles sticks shall be 914mm (3ft) outside the singles court on each side. The net shall be extended fully so that it fills completely the space between the two posts and shall be of sufficiently small mesh to prevent the ball passing through. The height of the net shall be 914mm (3ft) at the centre, where it shall be held down taut by a strap not more than 50mm (2in) wide and completely white in colour. There shall be a band covering the cord or metal cable and the top of the net of not less than 50mm (2in) nor more than 63.5mm (2.5in) in depth on each side and completely white in colour. There shall be no advertisement on the net, strap band or singles sticks. The lines bounding the ends and sides of the court shall respectively be called the baselines and the sidelines. On each side of the net, at a distance of 6.4m (21ft) from it and parallel with it, shall be drawn the service lines. The space on each side of the net between the service line and the sidelines shall be divided into two equal parts called the service-courts by the centre service line, which must be 50mm (2in) in width, drawn halfway between, and parallel with, the sideline. Each baseline shall be bisected by an imaginary continuation of the centre service line to a line 100mm (4in) in length and 50mm (2in) in width, called the 'centre mark', drawn inside the court, at right angles to and in contact with such baselines. All other lines shall be not less than 25mm (1in) nor more than 50mm (2in) in width, except the baseline, which may be not more than 100mm (4in) in width, and all measurements shall be made to the outside of the lines. All lines shall be of uniform colour.

Doubles Court

For the doubles game, the court shall be 10.97m (36ft) in width, that is 1.37m (4.5ft) wider on each side than the court for the singles game, and those portions of the singles sidelines that lie between the two service lines shall be called the service sidelines. In other respects, the court shall

Tennis Court: Court Sizes and Dimensions

Marked Out Playing Area	LTA Recommended	LTA Minimum
Length	23.77m (78ft)	23.77m (78ft)
Width (doubles)	10.97m (36ft)	10.97m (36ft)
Width (singles)	8.23m (27ft)	8.23m (27ft)
Length of net (doubles)	12.80m (42ft)	12.80m (42ft)
Width of white lines (included within court size)	50mm (2in)	50mm (2in)
Width of baseline	100mm (4in)	100mm (4in)
Runback (depth clear behind baseline at each end)	6.40m (21ft)	5.49m (18ft)
Side run (width clear beside sideline each side)	3.66m (12ft)	3.05m (10ft)
Side run between courts not separately enclosed	4.27m (14ft)	3.66m (12ft)
3 court block (width)	48.77m (160ft)	46.33m (152ft)

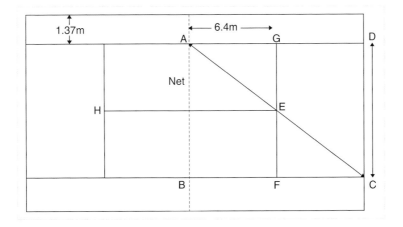

Figure 42   Marking out a tennis court with one person.

be similar to that described above, but the portions of the singles sidelines between the baseline and service line on each side of the net may be omitted if desired.

Marking Out a Tennis Court with One Person

When marking out the court, first determine the position of the net and fix, in the line chosen, two pegs 8.23m apart. Then take two tape measures and fasten one end of each to the pegs A and B respectively.

On the first A–C, measure a length of 14.46m. On the second, BC, measure 11.89m. Pull both measures taut so that at these distances they meet at C. Repeat this method to mark A–D. At a point marked F, 6.40m from B, put in a peg to mark the end of the service line. Similarly, mark G on the line A–D. The same measurements on the other side of the net will complete the boundaries of the court. By prolonging the baselines 1.37m on each side and joining the four points, the sidelines of a doubles court are made. Complete the marking by joining E–H.

12 Horse Racing Tracks and Polo Fields

Producing and maintaining turf for horse sports requires a rather different approach than the maintenance of turf for other types of sport. Whereas for most types of sports turf there is a constant war against the development of thatch or fibre in the sole of the turf, this kind of sponge development is a distinct advantage as far as surfaces for horse sports is concerned since it provides a valuable cushioning effect for the horse's hooves. This desirable cushioning effect can be produced in one of two ways: one can either cultivate a firm turf largely composed of the finer grasses, where the effect is obtained by fibre or thatch development as referred to above, or alternatively one can encourage a vigorous sward composed basically of perennial ryegrass and in such circumstances produce the cushioning effect by encouraging strong growth and by cutting at a relatively high level. The choice of approach should depend on the natural characteristics of the area where an individual racecourse or field is located. A turf made of fine grasses like brown top bent with a moderate development of fibre in the sole of the turf would be appropriate for moorland and heathland situations. In more parkland situations the aim should be to produce vigorous, strongly growing turf based on perennial ryegrass.

In general, it is easier for the turf manager to maintain a suitable surface in heathland or moorland situations than it is in parkland type areas. In such circumstances, if the soil can be kept to somewhere between 5 and 6 pH, a good resilient fibrous turf will be preserved with the predominance of natural grasses such as fescues and bents. In situations such as this the manager simply needs to preserve the natural status quo. Nature has provided ideal ecological conditions for good turf and the least interference by man the better.

Horse Racing Tracks

There are sixty racecourses spread throughout Britain and meetings are held throughout the year, including many Sundays and evenings. There are two types of racing: Flat racing, prominent in the summer, and Jump racing, which is popular in the winter. Flat racing takes place on a flat track on either turf (March to November) or an all-weather surface. Jump racing is run on turf over obstacles known either as steeplechase fences or hurdles. The governing and regulatory body for the sport is the British Horseracing Authority, whose responsibilities are wide-ranging. They include:

- Compilation of the fixture list.
- Setting and enforcing the rules and orders of racing.

- Race planning, including the supervision of race programmes and the employment of handicappers.
- Licensing and registering racing participants: jockeys, trainers, horses, owners and stable staff.
- Strategic planning and policy for racing.
- Setting and enforcing standards of veterinary and medical care.
- Protecting the integrity of the sport on and off the racecourse.
- Setting and enforcing common standards for British racecourses.
- The conduct of a day's racing.
- Central promotion of racing.
- Encouraging and fostering the breeding of bloodstock.
- Developing and maintaining programmes of training and education.
- Representing racing in dealings with Government.
- Liaison with the betting industry
- Representing British racing abroad, which includes membership of the Executive Council of the International Federation of Horseracing Authorities.

Requirements for a Race Track Surface

The 'going' (the condition of the ground) is a crucial factor in any horse race. Usually the Clerk of the Course announces the probable state of the going for a meeting some time in advance to advise trainers about the likely conditions, and will announce alterations at intervals thereafter until on the day of the meeting he (or she) declares the official state (which can alter during the course of an afternoon's racing, say in the case of torrential rain). The seven official states of the going in Britain for turf races are: -

- Hard
- Firm
- Good to firm
- Good
- Good to soft
- Soft
- Heavy

The official states of the going for all-weather races are:

- Fast
- Standard
- Slow

The ideal going is 'Good' and turf managers will always aspire to produce such ground. In the summer they may add water to the track to take away the firmness. After heavy downpours they have to rely on good drainage to stop the course turning really muddy. Unfortunately, in this country there is no accurate official measurement. The official going is often determined by placing an 'old codger's' stick or wellington boot into the ground.

The going-stick developed by TurfTrax determines going based on an average of three measurements of soil penetrative resistance and of soil shear strength. The average value is then converted to a 15 point index (see table below), which has been correlated with values of going that have been expressed by many clerks of racecourses.

13+	Hard
12	Firm
10	Good to Firm
8	Good
6	Good to Soft
4	Soft
2	Heavy

Race Track Construction

For natural turf racetracks, there is no prescription for soil type or rootzone, grass cover or any other agronomic factor. The emphasis has been on the safety of the surface for the conduct of race meetings: the ability to race a number of horses, at substantial speed, in close proximity to each other with minimal danger to either the riders or the horses. For centuries, racecourses were developed on 'agricultural' sites and laid out to fit the natural lie of the land, often on the outskirts of urban areas, with a wide variety of soil types from sands to heavy clays. The exceptional racecourse arose on deep, self-mulching, sandy loam soils. Many racetracks have been improved subsequent to their initial development. This has included refinements to the 'local' soil with the addition of sandy materials in an effort to improve both the porosity of the soil and the total soil depth. Major surface construction improvements came with the replacement of the entire rootzone with a loamy sand soil. Here a totally new soil profile is constructed in place of the 'local' soil with a loamy sand topsoil growing medium placed above a drained base layer. The inclusion of a blinding layer in this construction pattern is not common and has, in some cases, caused problems with infiltration through to the drainage system. These tracks are characterized by being uniform, having drainage capacities of around 25mm per hour, and providing fast and true racing. The agronomic factors often dictate that several species are used in order to provide satisfactory conditions for year-round racing. The sward composition of a racecourse usually becomes a blend of several grass types.

CONSTRUCTION PROFILE
The construction profile shown in the accompanying illustration is recommended for a grass racing track. The use of a natural loamy sand material overlying a gravel drainage raft will facilitate drainage but with sufficient water retention for grass growth for most of the year, while generally providing firm surface conditions for 'good' going. The use of an intermediate layer (or blinding layer) is not prescribed as such layers can often provide breaks within the water infiltration and natural drainage capacity of the rootzone medium. The use of such intermediary layers will most often restrict root growth and

drainage, especially where the material used is not sufficiently matched to the properties of the upper rootzone material and is therefore an unnecessary complication in the construction. The pipe system identified here is given as a typical example, sufficient for most applications. A full design would require a site survey and precise details regarding outfalls and land topography, together with testing of the material eventually purchased for the rootzone. It must also be noted that the surface racing conditions will be dependent largely upon rainfall and applied irrigation. The installation of an irrigation system should be considered during the construction phases since irrigation will be required in most racing seasons.

ROOTZONE SPECIFICATION
Recent constructions have normally involved the use of sandy materials variously described as sand or loamy sand. The pure sand constructions have required the use of structural materials of the like of Netlon or Turfgrids to provide sufficient structure to support galloping horses. Installations of this type have proven to be very expensive and there is little research or data published reviewing their performance. Loamy-sand soils have sufficient structure on their own to be able to conduct racing successfully and do not require the use of artificial structural materials. Loamy-sand materials produce highly satisfactory racing surfaces and, with the correct construction and subsoil drainage, are capable of tolerating heavy racing within a medium rainfall zone. The soil used should be a natural topsoil material that is free of propagules of weeds, fragments of glass, bricks, concrete, wire or other potentially hazardous foreign matter and bulk vegetative growth, in order to ensure negligible risk of subsequent weed problems (introduced in the soil) or traumatic injury. If finance allows, it is strongly recommended that the soil be screened to remove all stones greater than 20mm in any one dimension. This is

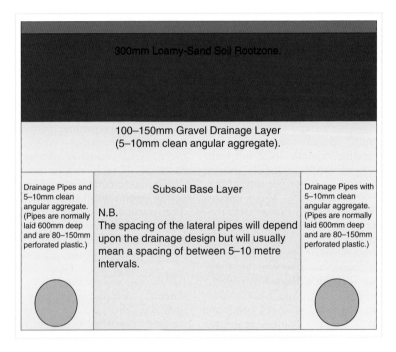

Figure 43   Construction profile of a grass racing track.

especially important for the material that will form the top 150mm of the constructed surface. The soil should have a pH value between 5.5 and 7.8 and nutrient index levels of 2 for phosphorus (P) and potassium (K).

TURF GRASS SELECTION CRITERIA
AND SEED MIXTURES
There are no edicts from racing bodies on the particular choice of grasses for racing and each course is allowed to make its own choice of preferred grass or grasses. The ideal turf grass for racing would have the following characteristics: remains green and vigorous throughout the racing season; produces medium density coverage of leaves at a 75–100mm mowing height; produces strong rhizomes that are capable of both rapidly filling into divots and holding a sandy soil profile together; and

produces little thatch. Within any environment, very few, if any, grasses meet all these criteria. The solution is one of compromise with a blend of grass types including combinations of perennial ryegrass (*Lolium perenne*), smooth-stalked meadow grass (*Poa pratensis*) and, more recently, tall fescue (*Festuca arundinacea*). The Mixtures 1 and 2 are (*see* p. 308) suitable for the establishment of the grass racing surface.

Mixture 2 is the preferred choice but needs at least twelve to eighteen months for full establishment prior to racing. Mixture 1 can be used where a faster establishment for racing earlier than this is required.

With both mixtures, the inclusion of tall fescue will ensure a surface that is resilient, capable of withstanding both drought and wet conditions. The deep roots of this

Mixture 1

45%	Rhizomatous tall fescue	(*Festuca arundinacea*)
45%	Tufted tall fescue	(*Festuca arundinacea*)
10%	Perennial ryegrass	(*Lolium perenne*)

Mixture 2

45%	Rhizomatous tall fescue	(*Festuca arundinacea*)
40%	Tufted tall fescue	(*Festuca arundinacea*)
15%	Smooth-stalked meadow grass	(*Poa pratensis*)

species and the rhizomes of the Rhizomatous tall fescue and the smooth-stalked meadow grass will provide a hardwearing surface capable of withstanding the pressures of racing and facilitating rapid surface repair.

PLACEMENT OF TOPSOIL, CULTIVATION AND FINAL GRADING

Topsoil must be handled carefully during spreading to avoid damage to the structure by machine-induced compaction. Placement of topsoil should not be carried out in wet conditions. Final grading of the top 150mm is to be carried out to ensure a true specified level and slope to avoid any dishing or other depression where water may collect. The level of the topsoil at the time of spreading is to be at least 50mm above adjacent paved areas, kerbs and other features to allow for shrinkage and/or settlement. Slopes and banks shall, where space allows, be slightly concave in section and with well-rounded shoulders and even transitions into adjacent levels and existing soiled or grass areas. Where possible, slopes are to even out into a flat area adjacent to kerbs and paved areas in order to prevent soil washing onto areas of hard-standing.

If the surface is too high it should be retrimmed and recompacted. If the surface is too low, the deficiency should be corrected by the addition of suitable material of the same classification and moisture content of other material laid and compacted to the approval of the employer. Any arisings from this operation must be removed from site. Finished levels of topsoil, after settlement, need be level with any adjacent kerb, hard surface or other level on site.

SOIL CULTIVATION AND SEEDING OPERATIONS

Where soil has been procured that has not been screened for stones, a mechanical stone burier or rake should be used to remove all stones exceeding 20mm from the top 150mm of surface soil. Bring the top 150mm of soil to a fine tilth using tractor implements and a final tilth using a harrow. Light harrow in two directions to produce a fine, smooth formed seedbed. Apply an appropriate pre-seeding fertilizer (subject to soil analysis) at a rate of 500kg/hectare. Lightly rake fertilizer into the surface with a tractor-mounted rake or harrow. Sow grass seed at a rate of 500kg/hectare using a tractor-mounted broadcaster or seed drill. Seed should be applied in two directions using one half of the total seed for each pass. Lightly rake grass seed into the surface with a tractor-mounted rake or harrow. In dry weather the seed should be watered in after seeding and surface moisture maintained subsequently to ensure germination and no checks to grass growth.

Racecourse Maintenance

As stated earlier, the maintenance of a horse-racing track is very different to the management of other sports turf surfaces, as the requirements are very different compared to the fine turf of bowling greens or even to the coarser turf of soccer and rugby pitches. The wear and tear caused by galloping horses is particularly severe, and there is a requirement for the sward to provide a significant cushioning effect if equine injuries are to be minimized. Through good management practices the aim should be to produce a level, consistent, resilient surface on which a sound horse can act to give its best performance. With experience, training and the help of specialist advisers a turf management and maintenance regime must be geared towards producing the ideal surface (meeting the description 'good to firm' for Flat racing, 'good' for jumping) through manipulating and combining the following factors:

• Soil structure
• Moisture content of soil (controlled partially by drainage and irrigation)
• Types of grasses and their structure
• Management practices:
  Mowing
  Scarifying
  Application of materials
  Aeration of soil
  Alleviating compaction
  Levelling of surface, rolling and harrowing
• Timing of fixtures
• Use of fertilizers and herbicides

Comprehensive records over the years show that the risk of injury to horses is minimized when the extremes of going are avoided. The biggest contributory factor to the state of the racing surface is the weather, which is outside the control of the racecourse grounds staff. However, by careful and planned practices, including the scheduling of fixtures, racecourses should be able to minimize the chances of producing ground that falls too far outside the ideal. Horses impart large forces to the turf and so have the potential to cause extreme damage and wear. Wear from horses has two major components arising from shear and compression forces. On firm or hard tracks, turf plants can suffer bruising with little disturbance of the growing medium. As soil water increases and tracks become softer, turf suffers shear damage during hoof deceleration and divots can be cupped out during the propulsion phase. Long-term damage to the soil is seen as a breakdown of soil structure resulting from smearing and compression of moist soil beneath the hoof. Typically, the soil from 70–150mm below the surface forms a compacted layer on racetracks. On very wet tracks more immediate damage comes from horses' hooves that may sink up to 200mm into the growing medium.

SOIL MANAGEMENT

There are a variety of soil types across the country, and an individual racecourse can feature more than one type. Although racecourses cannot do much about their soil type, the soil structure can be managed to provide optimum conditions for grass and root growth and moisture retention. Soil structure is determined by the amount of organic matter and airspace within the soil. In a natural state the activities of earthworms create fissures, enabling aeration of the soil, which in turn promotes root and grass growth. In a racing environment the course is subjected to high compactive forces from horses and maintenance equipment, which cause the air to be forced out and the soil compacted. This causes poor drainage, poor root development, less vigorous grass growth and in dry conditions an unyielding surface. A good soil structure can be maintained through management practices and scheduling of race meetings to avoid use when the structure is prone to damage, for example heavy use of clay soil when very wet. There are a number of subsurface treatments for compacted soils, including slit tine aeration and verti-draining. The choice depends on the depth of the problem. The timing of the operation is critical to the success of the treatment.

Since the most significant factor affecting the going is the moisture content, the ability to exert a degree of control over it is very important. The British climate generally produces one time of the year (winter) when there is an excess of moisture in the soil and another (summer) when there is a shortfall. To assist management to produce the ideal racing surface at times of year when fixtures are scheduled, the moisture content of the soil has to be controlled by drainage and irrigation. Determining the ideal moisture content of any given soil comes with experience, and it may be above or below the field capacity of the soil. Field capacity is an agricultural term describing the amount of water that the soil comfortably holds against gravity, after the initial excess from a soaking has drained away. Think of it as a sponge that has been immersed in water and left to drain. After a time the water stops draining from the sponge, but a certain amount is retained that could be squeezed out. Clay soils hold more water than sandy soils and also retain it for longer, making it increasingly hard for the plants to obtain it. However, the available water in a clay soil at field capacity is much greater than in a sandy soil. A loam is a good mix of clay and sand and creates an excellent soil for plant growth and for providing available water. The field capacity of a soil can be changed by drainage techniques, so in soils where the going is not ideal when the soil is at field capacity or above, the installation of a drainage system will enable a more suitable racing surface to be produced. Similarly, irrigation will improve a soil that has a moisture deficiency and is too hard for racing.

Drainage

Good drainage is also of paramount importance for satisfactory results. Slow surface drainage gives rise to going that is too soft or that causes meetings to be abandoned altogether. Wet tracks suffer under wet weather conditions and, in the winter, are more prone to freezing over. Improving natural drainage can involve the introduction of conventional pipe drainage systems, perhaps supplemented by slit drainage techniques. Vertical drainage channels filled with sand here connect with the underlying pipe drains and make for rapid conveyance of water away from the actual surface. Routine maintenance work can also be important in maintaining good drainage: this usually involves frequent slit tine spiking to maintain free-water percolation through the top few inches, which otherwise become compacted by the horses' hooves. Quite commonly there is also a requirement for deeper sub-aeration work involving the use of equipment such as the Verti-Drain, which achieves its effect by means of a long and heavy tine that levers the turf after deeply penetrating, or one of a variety of implements that force highly compressed air into the soil through a hollow probe. Implements depending for their action on a vibrating subsoil share can also be useful in some circumstances.

Irrigation

The second element in the control of moisture levels in the soil is irrigation. Drought is a soil water deficit of greater than 150mm during the period between April and September. When, by experience, racecourse managers know the soil moisture levels at which the ground provides the optimum racing surface, they can aim to reproduce it by irrigation. Actual rainfall, maximum and minimum air temperatures, surface and subsurface ground temperatures and irrigation applied must be recorded on the racecourse. Typically the grass may need 20–30mm of rain per week in the summer. Knowledge of soil types can reveal how much water may be available, which affects the frequency of irrigation – more often on sandy soils and less often on clay soil. However, clay soil has the extra hazard of cracking if it gets too dry. All irrigation must be recorded, so the balance of rain and irrigation against losses is monitored. It makes good sense to irrigate when it is raining or at night, as evaporation losses are reduced. When irrigating, allowance should be left for the possibility of a heavy deluge in the hours or days when racing. However, irrigating little and often will draw the grass roots to the surface, whereas the ideal is to produce deep-rooting plants, so irrigation should give the ground a good soaking and draw the roots down, with a reasonable gap between treatments: 25mm of water once a week may be needed in a dry summer. Typically a racecourse is about 32m (35 yards) wide and 2.2km (11 furlongs) round, covering about 6.9–7.3 hectares (17–18 acres). Applying the equivalent of 75mm of rain requires about a million gallons of water.

The management of irrigation systems is often a difficult point in racecourse management. Many courses now have automatic watering systems and water is of course commonly used not only for ensuring satisfactory grass growth in dry weather but also in order to influence the going. Agonizing decisions need to be made sometimes to water or not to water. If the weather remains dry and no watering is done then the grass may suffer and going may be too firm for the next meeting; on the other hand, if the turf is watered and it rains shortly afterwards the going may become too soft. As in other forms of turf culture, calculated risks must be taken from time to time and all modern weather forecasting resources must be drawn upon. Long experience of the local weather conditions at a particular course is a marked advantage for judging how and when to water. The use of water on racecourses, particularly if it is hard water containing some lime, tends to influence the botanical composition of the sward generally, encouraging perennial ryegrass, for example, at the expense of other species like the bents, which like more acidic conditions and do not have such a high water requirement. In situations where there are two race tracks on a single racecourse – flat and steeplechase – the latter is rarely watered in summer because it is used for racing mainly in winter, and often has the finer turf because lack of summer watering encourages the finer grasses.

MOWING

As far as mowing is concerned, for horse-racing purposes it is usual to cut the grass at a higher level than is normal for other sports, usually within the range 75–100mm (3–4in). The higher cutting levels are usually more appropriate for the ryegrass type of turf. Grass should never be allowed to grow too long in the autumn as this can leave an excessively heavy cover of grass for the winter. Under severe weather conditions longer grass is liable to suffer not only direct winter kill by low temperatures, but also by attacks of Typhula Blight (snow mould disease), which produces large areas of bleached and dead grass.

Gang mowers, often powered rather than wheel-driven, are usually favoured for racecourse mowing, although rotary cutters are sometimes used. Powered gangs give a cleaner finish, particularly under difficult ground and weather conditions. It should be remembered that gang mowers tend to leave the grass lying at an angle and that horses running along turf in the same direction that the gang mower has travelled can average about 3 miles per hour faster than if they are galloping against the line of cut.

NUTRITION AND SOIL pH

For racecourses where there is no natural advantage as far as the type of land is concerned, a more precise programme of maintenance is required to preserve a good racing surface. Here, more alkaline conditions would be advisable in order to encourage the vigorous growth of perennial ryegrass. At least one and possibly two fertilizer dressings per year would also be required for ryegrass turf in order to maintain growth and vigour. If the pH starts to drop too low, then consideration would have to be given to a light application of lime in order to correct this trend. Regular soil testing is therefore a useful indication as to the direction in which future maintenance should take and tests should be carried out at least once every three years.

Front-mounted rotary mowers are ideal for cutting the relatively long grass of racetracks as the tractor wheels do not flatten the grass before the mower. (John Deere)

Soil testing not only indicates whether over-acidity is developing but will also give an indication as to nutrient levels and allow the correct proportions of plant nutrient to be maintained, so ensuring good grass growth. Sometimes it is appropriate to give the entire course a spring fertilizer dressing, with perhaps a summer booster dressing for the area in front of the main grandstand and finishing straight. The finishing straight is often subject to particularly heavy wear and the additional fertilizer dressing here is also useful from the point of view of encouraging an attractively coloured sward for an area that is very much in the public eye. The application of spring fertilizer during late March or early April, depending on the weather conditions, also aids in thickening the sward. A granular fertilizer with an analysis of 9 per cent nitrogen, 7 per cent phosphorus and 7 per cent potassium should be applied at 350kg/hectare. During the summer months a further application of fertilizer may be necessary depending on the condition of the turf, but the application of too much nitrogen

should be avoided or soft lush growth will occur.

TRACK REPAIRS

Immediately following a race meeting the track should be thoroughly spiked to help relieve surface compaction and the localized use of hand forking is advised in obviously compacted spots. Divots should be repaired throughout the usage period, generally using a sand/soil/seed mix. Sand should be predominant but should not be too fine. A 'turf nursery', where a piece of infield is treated in a similar manner to the track, is a useful precaution. Turves can be taken from this area to effect repairs. Following returfing, the area must be well watered regularly as it re-establishes: thick turves fare better in drier conditions. Timing is very important for repair work, as usage and seasonality may conflict since repairs are best done in spring and autumn. As turves establish, any gaps between them must be filled with topsoil.

The amount of wear on well-used racecourses can be extremely heavy but tends to be much localized – the areas near the inside rails on the bends and, of course, on either side of jumps and hurdles are particularly prone to wear damage. On the other hand it is probably true to say that large parts of each race track area are in fact hardly used at all. Renovation of a Flat racecourse is a continuous process, hoof marks being filled in after each meeting with a mixture of soil, sand and soil. A National Hunt course, on the other hand, where horses race over jumps through the winter, comes in for main renovation in spring when the course enters the resting phase until the autumn. Rough areas, particularly on the inside of bends, need to be smoothed out by harrowing and ring rolling and must be oversown where necessary with a seeds mixture suitable for the particular course. Hand work, including forking and raking, may be necessary for take-off and landing areas on either side of jumps and sometimes some scraping back of soil is needed on the take-off side, since horses tend to push it up to the base of the jump as they gather themselves for the leap: if this is allowed to go too far the jumps may become not high enough due to the build-up of soil.

Overseeding

Most race tracks will eventually exhibit signs of severe wear when the grass becomes thin and coarse tufted grasses begin to invade. Under such conditions thought should be given to a general overseeding programme of the offending areas using a 'sod' seeder. Grass seed can be sown in late August to early October, and in April. A slot or slit seeder works well, as it gets the seed below the surface where there is more moisture. Grass seed added to a 60:40 mix of sand and soil mix can be used for small hollows, as well as after deeper aeration treatment. Perennial ryegrass can be used at $35g/m^2$. In recent years plant breeders have developed new and much improved varieties of turf type perennial ryegrasses, which give a far superior performance over the old varieties. These hard-wearing

grasses can be relied upon for rapid establishment and will produce a compact and dense sward. They also require less cutting because of their natural shorter leaf length. These varieties are all well proven for wear tolerance, resistance to wear and disease resistance. They are modern turf-type amenity ryegrasses that are compact and have a high tillering capacity. In cases where rapid establishment is required, ryegrass alone may be used. If, however, a wiry resilient turf is required in the longer term the following mixture should be used:

Topdressing

The overall topdressing of race tracks with soil materials is not usual, but can be carried out on occasions either to improve the depth of soil, where this is inadequate, or specifically to improve the characteristics of the going. For example, a sandy material might be used to produce a firmer and drier turf and hence a faster going, while an excessively hard surface might be softened by dressing with peat or other organic material, such as spent mushroom compost. All topdressing needs to be applied evenly in order to avoid smothering the existing sward. With this in mind materials are best applied while there is vigorous grass growth so that new foliage may quickly grow through the top dressing. Topdressings are most effective when applied in dry conditions and keyed into the surface, which can be achieved by spiking and forking before and after application or, on larger areas, a light harrowing or drag matting.

Running Rail Movement and Crossings

The worn area on the inside of bends should be given the best chance of re-establishment by moving the rail a little to provide the best possible ground, while mindful of race distances. Pedestrian and vehicle crossing points produce particular problems of wear and compaction. Artificial surfaces should be level with the racing surface and, if possible, be of a similar colour, particularly for Flat racing.

Jump Areas, Fences and Hurdles
The chief problem for the turf manager is to keep the take-off and landing zones in good order. Repair work carried out between circuits and between races greatly helps both turf and horses. Divots should be replaced and well trodden back into place. Work carried out when the turf is moist and there is some cut in the ground, particularly round the bends and in the home straight, will provide better turf for the future. On a hot or windy day a turned-over divot can dry out quickly. Turf damaged immediately in front of a fence must be filled in with free-draining material. At an open ditch the material should be packed tightly against the board. Though shallow, the ditch makes it difficult to keep the soil sufficiently moist to grow well enough to take the wear. It is important that a horse cannot drive a forefoot under the guard-rail or take-off board. Where a flight of hurdles has been moved on to fresh ground, the old sitings must be meticulously backfilled and made good.

Steeplechase fences (except water jumps) must be lower than 1.37m (4ft 6in) in height. Plain fences are usually constructed of birch packed together and held in place by a wooden frame on the ground; on the take-off side an apron of gorse is sloped to the fence to encourage horses to jump, and painted rails along the ground provide a 'ground line' by which the horse may judge when to take off. An open ditch incorporates a ditch protected by a low rail on the take-off side, forcing the horse to make a bigger jump than it would at a plain fence. In the first two miles of a race there must be at least twelve fences and in each succeeding mile at least six. For each mile there must be at least one open ditch. (The fences on the Grand National course at Aintree are of an unorthodox build: thorn dressed with gorse, fir and spruce.)

Hurdles are constructed like sheep hurdles, with gorse and birch woven into a wooden frame, which is driven into the ground: they give if clouted. They must not measure less than 1.07m (3ft 6in) from the top bar to the bottom bar. In the first two miles of a hurdle race there must be at least eight flights of hurdles, with an additional flight for every completed quarter mile beyond that. Experiments have been undertaken using an alternative form of hurdle, constructed from plastic birch like a small steeplechase fence. These have generally been well received by jockeys and trainers, but for the majority of hurdle races the traditional sheep-hurdle construction is likely to remain.

All-Weather Tracks
The five courses in the UK that currently stage all-weather flat racing are Lingfield Park, Wolverhampton, Southwell, and the more recent tracks built at Kempton Park and at Great Leighs in Essex. As the traditional flat racing turf season comes to a close in the autumn, so the all-weather championship kicks into gear. Two types of sand are used. All-weather races held at both Wolverhampton and Lingfield are now run on a substance called Polytrack, which is a kind of rubberized sand minimizing the impact of 'kickback', the effect the horses produce as they thunder over a loose-topped sandy surface. Polytrack's consistent nature means that most races can be run at a good pace.

A different racing material known as Fibresand is used at Southwell. Generally speaking, this produces a more demanding surface compared with Polytrack. If all-weather racing at Wolverhampton and Lingfield is the equivalent of fast going on turf, then Southwell's Fibresand is closer to a turf equivalent of racing on soft or even heavy ground. All-weather track maintenance consists of cultivating the surface with a power harrow to a depth of 100mm in order to relieve surface compaction and then restoring a level

Some all-weather racing tracks offer evening meetings with floodlighting. (Stewart Brown)

Close-up of Polytrack racing surface, clearly showing sand and rubber fill material. (Stewart Brown)

surface for racing with a gallop master (spiral rollers).

Polo

Polo is played in eighty countries worldwide. It was an Olympic sport from 1900 to 1939 and has now been recognized again by the International Olympic Committee. The Hurlingham Polo Association (HPA) is the governing body of polo in the UK, Ireland and many other countries throughout the world. As such, it is responsible for the regulations and rules under which the game is played. This includes the handicapping of anyone playing in the UK or Ireland. The object of the HPA is to further the interests of polo generally and support by all possible means the common interests of its affiliated clubs and associations. The HPA is currently made up of the following clubs and associations:

55 outdoor clubs in the UK
11 outdoor clubs in Ireland
28 arena clubs in the UK and Ireland
6 associations in the UK and Ireland
25 overseas clubs and associations

Polo Turf Maintenance
The principal aim should be to produce a smooth, level, well-drained, consistent surface on which polo can be safely played to a high standard from April to September. In the production of a management programme the following aspects are considered essential if the desired standard is to be attained. Correct timing, frequency and intensity of treatment are vital in achieving the best results. It is appreciated that there will be different site conditions and each operation may have to be subtly amended to take into account, for instance, soil conditions, state of growth, prevailing weather and usage. It is vital to bear in mind that

any extension of the playing season and an increase in the number of matches per year can significantly affect the success of treatments given. It should be appreciated that even with good management the end result relates to sound initial construction, including drainage.

Mowing
The aim is to produce a well-presented, level playing surface and a uniform, dense sward. The recommended choice is hydraulic gang mowers. In comparison with rotary, flail and trailed gang mowers, hydraulic gangs develop a more uniform surface, enhance presentation, give an improved dispersal of clippings and cause less damage to the grass plant. Ride-on triple and quintuple units can be employed, especially for prestigious events and for boxing off clippings. The recommended winter height of cut is 37mm, which gives a good balance by protecting the sward against winter weather, yet avoids the development of a lush, straggly turf that would increase the chances of disease and a weakened sward for the following season. The recommended summer height of cut is 19–25mm, which provides a good balance between maximizing playing quality and avoiding a deterioration of the turf in the short and long term, that is by weakening and thinning of the turf cover. For winter, top as growth dictates to maintain the 37mm height of cut. Never allow the grass to grow above 50mm, which will tend to encourage disease and the formation of a thin, straggly sward. Gradually reduce the height of cut in the spring in increments of about 6–8mm. Reverse the procedure when returning to the winter length. The summer mowing frequency in good growing conditions would be on average twice a week. Clippings are normally returned for cushioning and recycling nutrient, but if in excess sweeping would be appropriate to avoid smothering, promotion of worm, weed and disease activity as well as loss of presentation.

ROLLING

Rolling negates the positive effects of aeration, particularly in wet weather. However, rolling may be employed in drier conditions to enhance the playing surface and appearance. Use a light roller only and avoid rolling when the surface is wet.

SCARIFYING

To achieve a better end result with fewer disturbances to the surface, use a flail, trailed or hydraulic scarifier with sweeper in preference to chain harrows. Debris must be removed. Scarify twice a year, starting with a light spring treatment before play commences, with a deeper treatment in the autumn after the end of the season. Light scarifying treatments may be desirable in the playing season but care should be exercised not to disturb the playing surface and reduce the cushioning effect, so making it hard and uneven. A well broken-down organic layer is desirable for cushioning, yet excess would lead to surface moisture retention, a deterioration in turf vigour and rooting, followed by a rapid decline in playing quality.

AERATION

Aeration is carried out to relieve compaction, improve overall drainage and aerate the soil profile. This in turn encourages root growth and natural organic matter breakdown through bacterial action, thereby producing a healthy, dense turf. Due to the wide range of subsurface problems that can occur, specific recommendations are difficult to make. However, a range of equipment is available to tackle surface and deep compaction caused by the effects of play, the quality of drainage and the nature of the soil profile. As a general guide, aeration should be minimal through April to September to preserve the playing surface. More intensive, deeper treatments, such as Verti-Draining, hollow tining and vibro mole ploughing, are normally confined to the period from September to November, so allowing the maximum time for recovery and to tie in with autumn renovation. Other treatments such as slitting and solid tine spiking are acceptable up to February. The best results for good tine penetration and fracturing of the soil are gained when the soil profile is no more than moist. Caution should be exercised, especially with deeper, more intensive treatments where severe compaction and significant stone content would cause serious surface disturbance. A trial run off the main playing surface with the equipment being used will give a strong indication as to any problems.

DRAINAGE

Improvements can be made through management, particularly aeration and topdressing. However, if soil conditions significantly restrict drainage rates to below the desired standard, then the next step would be to introduce an integrated pipe drainage system to a positive outlet. If lateral water movement to the drain lines is still slow after one or two winter periods, consideration should be given to slit drainage systems and so increasing the water flow to the drains. To avoid soil capping the slits and so reducing surface drainage, annual topdressing with sand is considered essential. If drainage is undertaken, great care must be paid to ensuring a safe surface for play is produced.

TOPDRESSING AND SURFACE RENOVATION

Topdressing is applied to provide a level surface, secure footing for the horse and to improve surface drainage and air circulation. There are a number of options from a trailer/shovel through to purpose-made bulk dressers with a 5 tonne capacity. To restore the playing surface and encourage rapid recovery following wear and tear through play, end of season renovation will be required. For oversowing there is a range of machinery including contravators and direct-drill units. Immediate restoration of the surface through treading back divots and forking up will increase the chances of recovery by aiding turf knitting together and developing root formations.

Timing is the key: the recommendation would be to start renovation immediately after play. For deeper scars infill with a screened mix (no stones) comprising soil, sand and seed. The soil/sand ratio will vary according to site conditions and prevailing weather but as a guide, increase the soil content for drier conditions (for example from a 70 per cent sand and 30 per cent soil mix to 50 per cent sand and 50 per cent soil). It is recommended that sand alone be avoided due to the low recovery rate and the tendency to blow away when the weather is dry and windy, as well as avoiding 100 per cent soil because of drainage implications. For general oversowing at the end of the playing season, the recommended overseeding rate is $20g/m^2$ (200kg/hectare or eight 25kg bags per

hectare). For totally bare ground increase the rate to $30g/m^2$ (300kg/hectare or twelve 25kg bags per hectare). In both cases this would be the optimum rate.

FERTILIZER APPLICATION

In order to provide the desired amount of nitrogen per annum, three or four applications are required during the main growing season. In terms of area to be treated with fertilizer, this is normally 10 acres or 4.047 hectares ($40,470m^2$).

Applying 20:10:10 at 187kg/ha ($10,000m^2$).

For the area in question we require
$$\frac{40,470}{10,000} \times 187kg \text{ per pitch}$$

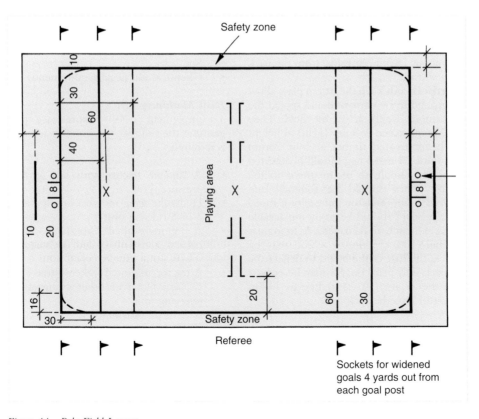

Figure 44 Polo Field Layout.

In terms of 1cwt or 50kg bags this approximates to 15 bags per pitch per application.

Layout of the Field of Play
Length: 275m (300 yards) maximum, 230m (250 yards) minimum.
Width: 183m (200 yards) maximum unboarded, 145m (160 yards) maximum boarded.
Safety zone: At sides about 9.1m (10 yards), at ends about 27.4m (30 yards).
Markings: Broken lines or full marking may be used across the grounds. Marks on the boards or flags (clear of the safety zone) are useful as a guide to the umpires.

A line of tees approximately 600mm (2ft) apart, clear of the centre spot, should be marked on the centre line. A double tee as shown will help keep teams apart at the throw in. These should be 910mm (3ft) apart. A line of about 46m (50 yards) in length should be drawn on the end safety zone about 18.3m (20 yards) from the back line a shown.
Boards: Boards keep the ball in play, allow the ground to be narrowed and spread the game more evenly across the field. They should not exceed 280mm (11in) in height and be of treated timber at least 25mm (1in) think. A metal peg should be inserted down the middle to secure them to the ground. They should be tongued and grooved at the ends or joined by a metal plate. A board should be easily replaceable during a match if damaged. A triangular arris rail (100 × 50mm/4 × 2in) may be fitted at the base of the board to deflect the ball back into play. Boards may be curved from the 27.4m (30 yards) line to 13.7m (15 yards) into the back line.

Basic Management Requirements for Horse Racing and Polo Surfaces

From the above, it can be seen that specialized techniques of turf management are required for good racecourse surfaces, and hence the work of the racecourse grounds staff involves interesting differences of approach as compared to a sports ground groundsman or a golf course greenkeeper.

Records and Measurements
Record information in a diary form that can be used for forward planning, reference and budgeting. The main points are:

- Background information on site conditions, including grass composition, soil type, existing drainage system and so on
- Usage
- Movement of playing area in relation to spreading wear
- Record daily maintenance treatments
- Daily rainfall
- Water volume applied through irrigation system
- Drainage problems
- Soil tests
- Chemical use (legal requirements)

Basic Machinery List
To implement a full maintenance programme the following essential machinery is required:

- A suitable tractor with low ground pressure tyres
- Hydraulic gang mowers or alternative 3 or 5 ride-on unit
- A short-toothed grassland chain harrow and flail, trailed or hydraulic scarifier unit plus sweeper
- A tractor-mounted spiker/slitter
- A Verti-Drain or other compaction-relieving unit
- A fertilizer distributor
- Tractor-mounted spraying equipment
- A topdresser for sand application
- An overseeder
- A light roller
- Irrigation equipment
- Hand tools, including strimmers and hand forks
- Line marker

13 Synthetic Turf Pitches and Athletics Tracks

Synthetic Turf Pitches

The first synthetic turf pitch was installed at the Houston Astrodome, Texas, in the early 1960s and since that time they have been developed for a range of sports. The early products were very expensive and mainly installed in the United States for American football and baseball. The surfaces were harsh, causing considerable skin friction. However, the huge benefits were that matches were not cancelled due to weather conditions and the quality of surface underfoot was predictable and clean. Several pitches that followed this original specification were installed in the UK, including those at Islington and later at Hackney during the early 1970s. These facilities were used for non-league soccer and hockey. The sport of field hockey adopted this new technology with enthusiasm and was quickly transformed in pace and skills. The competitive hockey leagues throughout the UK have gradually made the use of artificial grass mandatory for matches under their jurisdiction.

For many years now all international matches and tournaments under the auspices of the International Hockey Federation (FIH) have been played on artificial grass surfaces. The story with football on artificial grass is altogether different: the early pitches were hard and very fast, bearing little resemblance to natural grass and threatening serious injury to the over-enthusiastic tackler or acrobatic goalkeeper. Not until the advent of the sand-filled grass systems in the early 1980s did the soccer authorities look closely at developing a set of performance criteria to help classify these pitches. There were two main types of artificial grass pitches: sand-filled and non-filled. In the UK, the most common synthetic surface is the sand-filled grass pitch. These sand-filled surfaces are found throughout a wide range of sports including hockey, soccer, five-a-side soccer and tennis, as well as in multi-sports areas. The reason for their popularity probably stems from the fact that this type of construction is the best value for money of all modern synthetic surfaces and, in theory at least, requires the least attention throughout its life. The non-sand-filled pitch is sometimes referred to as a 'wet-field', due to the fact that these surfaces require to be regularly watered to cut down the player surface friction, reduce surface temperature in hot climates and regulate the ball speed over the carpet surface. The FIH recommends that an irrigation system be installed with the capacity to deliver 3mm over the entire playing surface at each application. The pitch would normally be watered prior to a match and, if necessary, again at half time. The provision of such a watering system has obvious implications on costs, both in the initial investment and ongoing annual charges for running the facility.

The development of artificial grass surfaces continues and new products appear on the market every year. Currently a series of products is being marketed, primarily for soccer (Third generation or 3G pitches), that utilizes longer fibres in a reduced density and filled with a mixture of sand and rubber granules. It is claimed that this type of surface allows the use of a normal football boot and replicates a good natural grass surface. With the arrival now of 3G pitches, the governing bodies of football are once again looking at synthetic turf pitches as a viable surface, particularly in climates not wholly suitable for sustaining natural grass pitches. The FIH is working towards specifying a water-free synthetic turf for top level hockey and a multi-sport turf for other levels. Developing a water-free turf is an important project because of the environmental concerns about water usage. Manufacturers are now attempting to reduce the volume of water required to keep a wetfield wet during play by introducing a thick geotextile into the carpet construction, so slowing the rate of percolation through to the base. Much work is also being done on the techniques of combining natural and synthetic grass. The synthetic fibres are being promoted as reinforcing elements in a natural grass sward. They improve the wearing properties of the turf and also promote healthy root growth by taking surface water down into the rootzone. This system is particularly useful in areas of heavy wear, such as goalmouths. Specialist advice for all types of synthetic sports surface can be obtained from the Sports and Play Construction Association.

Construction

GROUNDWORK

The extent of earthworks depends on ground conditions and site topography. Pitches are laid to very flat gradients, so sloping sites will require more extensive earthworks compared with relatively flat ones. The cheapest option will be the one that produces the least amount of spoil or

---

Playing Characteristics

Different sports require different playing characteristics and their respective governing bodies stipulate precise requirements. Once the priority sport for a planned synthetic turf pitch has been decided, and the governing body consulted, a large number of the design parameters will have been determined. Choosing a priority sport may mean that certain playing characteristics are not ideal for or even not compatible with other sports. Frequently there will be performance requirements for the artificial grass surface for the individual sports such as:

Ball – surface properties

- Ball roll
- Ball rebound
- Ball-to-surface friction
- Surface pace (angled ball behaviour)

Player – surface properties

- Traction coefficient
- Slip resistance
- Sliding distance
- Force reduction
- Vertical deformation
- Abrasiveness

Construction tests

- Porosity (or permeability)
- Slope
- Evenness

Durability tests

- Joint strength
- Tests on simulated use
- Tests including artificial weathering

---

minimizes the amount of imported stone. The most expensive tasks are transporting earthworks materials to and from site and the disposal of surplus materials.

Pitches need to be founded on solid and stable ground. Topsoil, turf and vegetation are not suitable and therefore must be stripped from the site. Topsoil can be reused for landscaping or spectator mounds if space allows. The 'formation' is the level ground on which the pitch construction is built. It is preferable that the formation is natural ground because soil is usually stronger when it is undisturbed. The formation should be treated as part of the finished pitch. It is vulnerable to softening in wet weather and therefore has to be covered as soon as possible. Any soft spots in the formation must be dug out and replaced with imported crushed rock, such as that used for the sub-base. The finished formation should be trimmed to a tolerance of ±25mm. Following excavation and levelling, the site should be treated with an appropriate approved residual herbicide.

DRAINAGE

A suitable drainage scheme should be installed to:

• Ensure that all surface water is removed from the site at a rate that will safeguard against surface flooding occurring.
• Prevent excess water remaining present in the construction, which might result in a reduction of the load-bearing capacity of the formation.
• Protect the installation from the effects of ground or surface water from the surrounding areas.

Lateral drains may be incorporated beneath the pitch, the centres of which shall be determined by the composition of the subsoil and the designed infiltration rate. Centres usually range from 5–15m. The ends of lateral drains should be capped to prevent contamination, and connectors should be used when joining lateral drains to collector drains. Collector drains should be located on the outside of the perimeter edging. Perimeter drains, which may act as collector drains, should be installed at the toe of any embankments to prevent run-off

from surrounding areas. Silt/inspection chambers should be constructed where perimeter/collection drains change direction, and the provision of rodding eyes should be included at the head of collector drain runs for ease of access for maintenance. Drains usually consist of perforated plastic pipes, bedded on, and backfilled with, clean stone. No drains should have less than 150mm cover over the top of the pipe, and no drain should be laid to a fall of less than 1 in 200 unless advised by manufacturers' instructions. In certain subsoils where silting up may be a problem, a geotextile membrane may be used to line the trench prior to backfilling. Wherever possible drains should discharge into an existing outlet or natural watercourse or, if necessary, ground conditions may permit for a soakaway construction.

THE SUB-BASE

The sub-base to any synthetic pitch should be designed to meet the following criteria:

• It should be capable of supporting and transmitting to the existing ground the loads of all vehicles, plant, machines and materials to be used in the construction, without causing deformation of the site.
• After the pitch is built, the sub-base should be capable of supporting and transmitting all loads on the playing surface without permanent or long-term deformation of the playing surface. Such loads arise mainly from players and maintenance equipment.
• It should ensure that water, whether rainwater or natural groundwater, will drain away freely through the sub-base material, either into the natural subsoil or into the drainage system.

Foundations should be constructed using hard, clean, crushed frost-resistant aggregates. The grading of the sub-base material must be such as to provide stability while at the same time remaining porous. The material should be laid in layers not exceeding 150mm, each layer being compacted before the next is laid. The minimum compacted thickness of sub-base stone should be 200mm. Upon completion there should be no detectable movement under the roller. The sub-base material should be compacted and the surface level tolerance be within ±10mm of the design level when checked with a 3m straight edge. In order to prevent contamination from the subgrade it may be necessary to install a geotextile membrane on the formation prior to installation of the sub-base.

Base Construction

Three alternative constructions may be used:

ENGINEERED BASE OF BITUMINOUS MACADAM

Engineered bases are the traditional form of road construction, consisting of a single course or two courses of open-textured bituminous macadam.

Two-course construction: An open-textured base course consisting of 40mm nominal compacted thickness (minimum compacted thickness not less than 30mm at any point) of 14mm or 20mm nominal-sized aggregate, plus an open-textured binder course consisting of 25mm nominal compacted thickness (minimum compacted thickness not

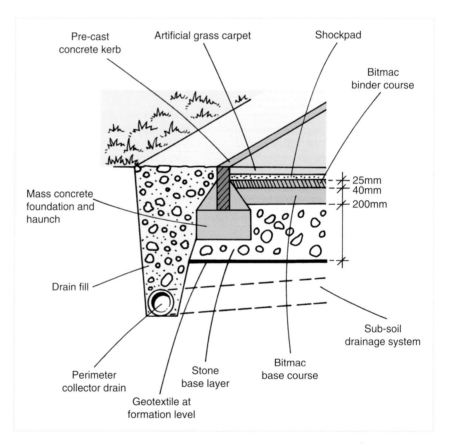

Figure 45   Cross section of a synthetic turf pitch.

less than 15mm at any point) of 10mm nominal sized aggregate.

Single-course construction: An open-textured blinder course consisting of 40mm nominal compacted thickness (minimum compacted thickness not less than 30mm at any point) of 10mm nominal sized aggregate.

The choice of single-course or two-course construction will largely depend on the available budget and the design criteria of the installation.

DYNAMIC (UNBOUND) BASE

The most common type of dynamic (unbound) base consists of crushed stone or sand. This base may have a geotextile membrane above and/or below it. The choice of the grade of stone, the thickness it is laid and its degree of compaction will have a profound effect on the ultimate playing characteristics of the pitch. Some unbound or dynamic bases may consist of 25–50mm, compacted thickness, of graded hard stone (size 6mm down to dust). In certain cases 50–75mm thickness of unbound material may be used: for example sand (50mm) or two layers (50–75mm) of compacted stone (6–10mm and 3–6mm clean stone) are used as part of the 'performance control' layers. In these instances, when also combined with suitable separation geotextiles, it is possible to select more single-sized clean aggregates and so improve drainage qualities and minimize the risk of any movement.

DYNAMIC LAVA/RUBBER BASE

An alternative type of dynamic system uses a mixture of lava rock and rubber crumb instead of stone or sand. This is sometimes called a 'soft compo' base and is one of a number of systems used on the continent. The lava/rubber ratio will depend on the priority sport. When laid to a suitable depth with laser-controlled machinery, the need for a further resilient shock-pad layer is eliminated.

Shock Pads

The introduction of a resilient layer between the base and the artificial grass carpet is used to provide a degree of comfort to players and to create defined playing characteristics for specific sports. There are a number of ways of achieving this resilient layer, with assorted laid *in situ* shock-pad systems, prefabricated or combinations of both. Typical components of *in situ* systems are rubber crumb/shred mixed with a resin binder. In the case of pre-formed systems, the shock pad is delivered to site as rolls of prefabricated material. In the case of *in situ* systems the components are mixed on site and laid to form a continuous layer of material.

Artificial Grass

There are a large number of artificial grass systems on the market, most of which look quite similar but may be made of different materials, manufactured by different techniques and designed for use in different ways. There are many fibre producers and even more carpet manufacturers and installers. It is therefore essential to establish or specify the precise materials and carpet types required for the particular pitch to be constructed. The preferred playing characteristics should be specified at tender stage, and each tender submission should be accompanied by independently certified proof of the proposed system's performance together with a reference sample.

The most basic distinction is between 'filled' and 'non-filled' artificial grass systems. In filled systems, the pile of the artificial grass carpet is generally filled to within about 3mm of the fibre tips with a fine granular material such as silica sand, which may represent more than 90 per cent of the total weight of material. Play takes place on the composite bed of fibre and sand. Non-filled systems consist of carpet alone, and play takes place entirely on the fibre. The pile of the carpet necessarily has to

323

be much denser per unit area to support the players and withstand the stresses of play, and it is usually also considerably shorter.

Other variables distinguishing different artificial grass carpets include:

- The polymer used for the fibre yarn: The two main groups used are polyolefins (which include poly-propylene and polyethylene) and polyamides (nylons).
- The cross-sectional area of the indi-vidual ribbons of fibre: This varies considerably from product to product. The unit of measurement for the weight of the fibre is Dtex – the higher the Dtex, the greater the weight of fibre per unit length.
- The method of carpet manufacture: The main methods are tufting, knitting, weaving and needle punching.
- Pile height and pile density: Pile density has two components, the density of tufts per unit area and the composition of each tuft in terms of number and thickness of fibres.

Sand-Filled Systems: Filled systems are significantly less expensive than non-filled. The tufting method is the most widely available. Both polyolefin and polyamide yarns may be used. The silica sand infill should consist of non-abrasive, non-staining, well-rounded, dust-free particles of uniform grading and density, free from extraneous contaminants. The sand infill is normally taken to within 3mm of the fibre tips. The sand and fibre combine to form the charac-teristics of the playing surface and it is essential that the level of sand fill is main-tained throughout the life of the facility. Sand-filled systems do not normally require to be irrigated in the UK climate.

Non-Filled Systems: Non-filled systems differ distinctively in design and appear-ance from filled pitches. They are often referred to as 'wetfields' or 'water-based pitches', due to the fact that water needs to be applied (on the majority of surfaces for hockey) to the surface immediately before play. The presence of water reduces the player/surface friction, modifies the speed of the hockey ball and cools the surface in hot climates. When designing a non-filled installation, due consideration must therefore be given to the means of applying sufficient water over a short period of time.

Sand-Dressed: Recently designs of so-called 'sand-dressed' carpets have started to become more available in the market. These are intermediate in properties between traditional filled and non-filled carpets. They have a shorter, denser pile than the standard filled grass systems with a reduced quantity of sand fill, normally approximately 75 per cent of the pile height. Sand-dressed systems are commonly specified as alternatives to the non-filled, irrigated fields for hockey.

Third Generation (3G): The so called 'third generation' system has found favour with the football and rugby governing bodies and has been approved for football at the highest level. Surfaces falling into this category differ from standard sand-filled systems in the height of pile, com-monly up to 65mm long, and the infill used, normally two-thirds of the pile height. The infill to the 3G system is normally designed to provide some of the shock absorption by using rubber granules. The rubber granules are sometimes mixed with sand or incorporated with sand in layers. Among the benefits this system brings to sports such as football is that a full stud can be used on the surface and the football/surface performance properties are similar to natural grass.

JOINTING AND PLAY LINES

The carpets are manufactured on looms, which normally have a maximum produc-tion width of around 4m. The strips of carpet produced by this method need to be joined on site to form the continuous surface of the pitch. This is normally achieved by using a backing tape under the butted joint of two adjacent carpet strips.

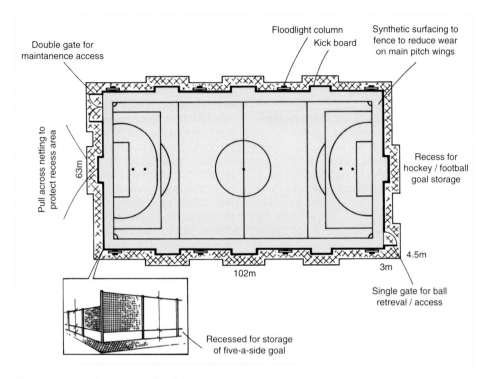

Figure 46   Typical synthetic turf pitch layout.

Both edges are bonded to the backing tape to form a continuous seam. These seams are normally laid across the width of the pitch. Play lines within the playing surface can be incorporated during manufacture, using a different-coloured fibre, or can be inlaid (cut in) on site. Play lines may also be painted but these can only be regarded as temporary. Depending upon climatic conditions, dryness of carpet and depth of sand, such lines may last only a couple of weeks.

FITTINGS
Freestanding equipment is preferred for fittings such as goals, because sockets, in time, may present a health and safety risk from trip edges. The investment in good-quality fixtures and fittings will pay dividends throughout the life of the facility. All freestanding equipment should be

substantial and robust in design whilst remaining easily manoeuvrable. When in use, freestanding equipment must be anchored by methods approved by the equipment supplier to prevent overturning. The load from the equipment should be equally distributed to the surface with no sharp edges protruding. Separate storage areas must be provided for equipment. which should never be stored on the pitch surface or within the overruns for health and safety reasons.

IRRIGATION
Non-filled carpets installed for hockey require to be watered to comply with the requirements of the governing body. The system will normally comprise six variable angled rain guns fitted with intermittent dynamic jet breakers to influence uniformity. Additional pop-ups will normally be

325

specified to further water goal areas on days of high evaporation or for short/long corner practice without having to utilize all rain guns.

Maintenance of Synthetic Turf Sports Surfaces

Non-filled surfaces (First Generation): Most non-filled artificial grass sports pitches consist of a permeable base, usually of macadam, upon which are laid a resilient shock pad and then a tufted or woven carpet of polypropylene or nylon fibre. The fibres vary in length and density. The carpet may be loose laid or stuck to the shock pad and is normally stretched and anchored at the periphery. Play lines are either tufted into the carpet during manufacture or are subsequently cut in using similar carpet materials of the appropriate white or yellow colour. Occasionally play lines are painted onto the surface, but these are decidedly temporary and need frequent repainting. The resulting sports surface is fully permeable, hard-wearing and requires only a modest amount of maintenance. This basic maintenance is, nevertheless, of vital importance if the surface is to remain good to look at, consistent in play, permeable and long lasting. Indeed, the installer's guarantee will usually be conditional on the recommended maintenance requirements being carried out with reasonable diligence.

Sand-filled systems (Second Generation): Sand-filled carpets generally have a pile height of 10–25mm. They have been in use for pitches, designed for a variety of sports, since the early 1980s. The carpet, which is loose laid and not stuck to the layers below, is dressed with graded silica sand, which fills the interstices between the fibres to within about 3mm of the fibre tips. The weight of the sand is sufficient to keep the carpet firmly in place.

Long pile carpet systems (Third Generation): Long pile carpets were introduced in the 1990s using carpets with pile heights in excess of 35mm, and up to 65mm, for specific sports use. The carpet is similarly loose laid and relies on the weight of infill for anchorage. Long pile carpets may be filled with a combination of sand and rubber granules or only rubber granules. These systems are often referred to as 'third generation' carpets and tend to be specified where football is the primary sport. The resulting sports surface is fully permeable, hard wearing and requires a relatively modest amount of maintenance, indeed over-maintaining the surface may shorten the useful life of the carpet. This basic maintenance is, nevertheless, of vital importance if the surface is to remain good to look at, consistent in play, permeable and long lasting: the installer's guarantees will usually be conditional on the recommended maintenance requirements being carried out with reasonable diligence.

THE NEED FOR MAINTENANCE

Poor maintenance will shorten the useful life of a synthetic turf pitch surface by more than any other factor. Of course, the amount the pitch is used is directly proportional to the degree of wear and tear on the surface. But even a surface that is hardly ever used will fail prematurely if it is not maintained regularly and properly.

Maintenance procedures are designed to ensure that:

- The playing surface is kept scrupulously clean.
- The playing surface remains level and of consistent texture so that it gives a true and predictable game.
- The infill materials are evenly distributed over the surface.
- The free drainage of surface water is maintained throughout the life of the pitch.
- The facility looks attractive and well kept at all times.
- The system does not become over-compacted and hard.

Compact utility vehicle designed for maintenance of synthetic turf surfaces. (SISIS Equipment (Macclesfield) Ltd)

These objectives are achieved by:

- Sweeping leaves and other detritus from the surface.
- Grooming the surface through brushing and/or drag matting.
- Applying prophylactic treatments of moss killer and/or algicide.

Maintenance Operations
POST-CONSTRUCTION
Immediately after construction there is an initial working-in period during which the final playing surface is created. All particulate infill surfaces take time to settle and it is advisable not to test for compliance to the playing performance quality standards until the surface has been laid for at least three months. It will take up to twelve months for the infill to settle in the pile of the synthetic turf. During construction every effort should be made to ensure even distribution of infill over the whole pitch. Increasing the frequency of brushing and/or drag matting in the early weeks of use is beneficial in creating the final playing surface. If areas are found that are short of infill it should be possible to brush the infill into them from adjacent areas of ample or surplus material, provided this is done within the first few weeks.

During the first three months the surface should be watched closely for any signs of vegetation developing in the surface and appropriate actions taken. Although grass, moss and other forms of plants will germinate in the infill within the pile, this does not usually occur until the pitch has been down for a number of months. A careful watch should be kept for any signs of vegetation growing in the pile, a common occurrence when adjacent natural turf pitches have been renovated. Wind-blown seed will soon germinate, particularly where pitches are not regularly maintained and the infill material is seldom disturbed. It is essential to groom not only the areas within the playing area – all the surrounds to a pitch must be treated the

327

Brushing must be carried out regularly and thoroughly. (SISIS Equipment (Macclesfield) Ltd)

same. If vegetation does start to develop appropriate action must be taken without delay.

SURFACE CLEANLINESS

Leaves and other plant detritus should not be allowed to remain on the surface for any length of time. If this does happen, they rapidly rot down forming a drainage-inhibiting 'skin' within the surface and providing a growing-medium for algae and moss. A wide soft broom or a rubber-tined rake is ideal for removing surface vegetable matter and other rubbish. Better still, a mechanical leaf-sweeper or specialist vacuum cleaner, which does not remove the fill, will greatly speed up the operation. The equipment should be well maintained and carefully operated to avoid contamination of, or physical damage to, the surface. Both sweepers and vacuum cleaners may tend to remove rather too much infill during the first few months of the life of the surface, but thereafter this should cease to be a problem. Some disturbance of the surface of the infill will be a positive benefit.

GROOMING

Grooming the surface is a crucial operation if premature deterioration of play characteristics, appearance and drainage properties is to be prevented. Apart from improving the look of the surface, the purpose of regular and fairly vigorous brushing and/or drag matting is to prevent the formation of a compacted and impervious skin on the top of the infill bed that will inhibit drainage and encourage moss and algae. Because the bed of infill is an effective filter, it unavoidably retains any particulate matter conveyed or blown on to the pitch or carried down by rainfall. By constantly disturbing, moving and relevelling the upper layers of infill, grooming can delay, by several years, the time when problems of reduced drainage start to develop.

Brushing or drag matting should be undertaken in a number of directions. It is important that the synthetic turf pile is maintained vertically and regular brushing is an important function that must not be neglected. The surface should be brushed

Synthetic turf surfaces must be kept scrupulously clean. (SISIS Equipment (Macclesfield) Ltd)

in a number of directions, alternating the direction in consecutive activities. The type of brush or drag mat used should be determined by the condition of the surface. Drag brushes behind the power unit and drag mats tend to flatten the pile and therefore if such an implement is used the operation should be carried out twice, up and down on the same breed. The drag method is good for levelling of the infill, not cleaning or standing up the pile. Brushes that have a rotary action in a horizontal position in front of a power unit are sometimes preferred so that they flick the blades of the synthetic turf. Types of specialist 'combing' devices are recommended for pile treatment by certain manufacturers. Alternatively, brushes that rotate in a vertical direction may also be preferable to the drag type equipment. It must be borne in mind that any powered brushing will disturb the infill more, so the type of brushing

should be relevant to the end result you are trying to achieve: whether you wish, for example, to make the pile stand up and clean, or you wish to level the infill within the pile.

The recommendations of the installing company/carpet manufacturer must be followed when deciding on the type of brush to be used. Excessive brushing, particularly with a rotating action, can cause premature wear and reduce the life of the facility. The recommended frequency of grooming must depend on the amount of use the pitch receives and whether its location is open and 'clean'. Once or twice a week is a recommended norm, but it may be advisable to groom and clean more often if the pitch is heavily used, shaded or subject to pollution. It cannot be overemphasized that to neglect the grooming of this kind of pitch may have serious long-term consequences even if, in the

329

shorter term, the pitch does not appear to suffer. Grooming need not be either time-consuming or onerous, and its benefits are profound. To omit the process may result in a pitch ceasing to drain at half-life or sooner. An un-groomed pitch will look scruffy and be susceptible to moss infestation.

Moss and Algae

In certain situations, and in some seasons, algae or moss can become established on the surface. Since prevention is very much more effective than cure, it is important to treat the affected areas of the pitch with a good proprietary moss killer and algicide at least once a year. Moss is not usually found on the parts of the surface that are trafficked by play, and although it may not be essential to treat these areas it is still a wise precaution to do so. However, particular attention should be paid to the perimeter and other areas that are not trafficked, especially if they are shaded by walls or buildings, or are overhung by trees. Any good proprietary product should be satisfactory provided that it is not oil-based. The manufacturer's instructions should be closely followed. Some installers can supply specially formulated moss killers.

Where moss becomes established it should be treated immediately, the application being repeated after the dead spores are removed until eradication is complete. In the case of very severe infestation, the installer should be consulted. High air-pressure cleaning equipment is available but its use is a skilled process. Moss is only a serious problem if it is allowed to become established. An annual prophylactic application of moss killer is an easy way of preventing this. Regular grooming and regular use of the pitch render moss an even less likely problem.

Play Lines

A synthetic turf pitch will normally be supplied with permanently inlaid play lines. The number of sports to be included

and whether the lines are to be inlaid or painted on to the surface will be decided prior to construction. However, if additional lines are required for special events or changes in the sports being played, these can be painted onto the surface using proprietary line paint. Some of these are more effective than others and consultation with installers, suppliers and other users of synthetic turf pitches is recommended. Chalk lines can be applied but these tend to leave a lasting powder spread in the area of the line. Marking compounds for natural grass should not be used as these will leave a build-up forming a crust and potential trip hazard. Permanent lines require no special attention, other than, if cut-in, occasionally checking they are secure. This regular check should also be carried out on the seams in the carpet. Any breakdown of the seams at lines or in the main carpet should receive immediate attention to avoid ongoing deterioration. This should be reported to the installer if within the warranty period. If the warranty has expired, a number of specialist companies will offer seam repair services.

Stain Removal

Most stains can be removed easily with a solution of hot (not boiling) water and a household detergent such as washing-up liquid. The removal of chewing gum can be simplified by making the gum brittle with a proprietary aerosol freezing material, but great care must be taken to avoid breaking the embrittled fibres. Heavy oil marks can be removed with a cloth and white spirit.

Weeds

No matter how much care is taken, weeds may occasionally appear on the surface, usually as a result of wind-blown seeds. Small numbers of weeds can be removed by hand without damaging the surface. Localized areas of weed seedling infestation can be treated with approved herbicides without causing damage to the surface of the pitch. Oil-based herbicides should not be used.

SNOW AND ICE

Snow and ice are not harmful and can be permitted to melt through. If it is important to remove the snow to enable play to start sooner than would otherwise be the case, brushes or wooden scrapers may be used. If the area to be cleared is of full pitch size, the logistics of transporting and disposing of snow may prove prohibitive. It is not advisable to use mechanical snow removal equipment. Metal shovels or scrapers may damage the surface and should not be permitted. Rock salt and chemical de-icing agents should not be used. In certain cases vacuum-dried salt or urea have been used as effective preventatives when applied in advance of the weather deteriorating.

Provided that the foothold is adequate the pitch may be played on when frozen, but heavy use is to be discouraged because the fibre is relatively brittle at low temperatures. The degree of shock absorption will also be substantially reduced and players should be made aware of this fact. Health and Safety should be a primary consideration. If heavy rain falls immediately after a very cold spell, the pitch may become flooded for a few hours. The same thing can happen when snow or heavy frost starts to thaw. This is because the sand beneath is still frozen, but should not be a cause for concern, as the remaining ice will soon melt and the surface will then drain normally.

ROLLING

Light rolling may be required from time to time, particularly during the period of settlement. The roller must be carefully selected according to the climatic conditions and the degree of firmness in the pitch. Rolling should take place across the pitch running in the direction of the seams.

GENERAL CARE

If at all possible, wear should be spread over the entire pitch; the way a pitch is used can have a significant effect on the quality of the pitch surface, and particularly the playing characteristics. Where activities are concentrated in any one location the surface will harden off and this will in turn have an effect on ball bounce, traction, hardness and ball roll. Such areas need a higher concentration of maintenance than areas where the surface is not used to the same extent. Even when the surface is not used it still requires maintenance if it is not to deteriorate. Maintenance inputs are dependent on the extent to which a pitch is used and how effective the maintenance operations are. In certain situations, such as contamination of the particulate fill or lack of through drainage, due to such contamination, the infill may have to be replaced and therefore the extent to which it becomes contaminated is crucial to the quality of the playing surface during the life of the pitch. Testing infill materials should be carried out on a regular basis, at the very least every twelve months. If the change is noted early on, the extent of remedial works may be restricted to top-dressing. A simple operation of extracting some infill, then allowing it to settle out in a bottle or jar of water will indicate the amount of silt or fines in the pile. Comparisons from one test bottle to another can then be made, to ascertain the increase in fines.

Suitable footwear should always be used. Most shoe manufacturers produce a boot that is specifically designed for the sport played on an artificial grass surface. Some synthetic turf systems, such as long pile systems, are designed to take a normal soccer stud but, if any doubt exists, the pitch manufacturer should be consulted. The pitch should be treated as a 'no smoking' area, since a dropped cigarette can melt the fibres down to the surface leaving an unsightly mark. Chewing gum should also be banned.

IRRIGATION OF UNFILLED PITCHES

There are many existing unfilled hockey pitches for which a very important aspect of maintenance is ensuring that the pitch is properly watered during all times of activity (matches and practices). As well as short-term considerations such as playability, injury avoidance and enjoyment, improper watering has negative long-term implications for pitch maintenance and lifetime. However, on environmental and cost grounds, unnecessary overwatering should also be avoided. If not properly watered, a synthetic turf pitch loses its cleansing properties, which results in deposits of impurities, thus creating abrasion of the carpet. Furthermore, played on when dry, much greater forces are applied to the surface by player actions and they have a very detrimental effect on the turf (fibres, joints, interface with sub-base/e-layer) causing wear and more rapid deterioration (rippling, tearing, uneven stretching). This greatly decreases the longevity of the pitch – a major economic consideration. In the past, synthetic turf required extensive watering to improve the sliding properties of the surface. However, the permeability of more modern turf products is much less, which reduces the maintenance costs considerably. It is also more environmentally acceptable.

REPLACING AND/OR UPGRADING

The average life of a pitch (depending on playing intensity) is about ten years – several years more if it is well maintained, considerably less if not. Provided the sub-base has not been damaged, and irrigation/drainage systems are in good condition, at the end of this period a further ten to twelve years of life should be obtainable essentially by only having to replace the carpet.

Athletics Tracks

Athletes have been performing on synthetic track surfaces since the first tracks were developed in the mid-1960s. The improvement in athletes' performance times and the better consistency of these surfaces has generally led to the abandonment of the old cinder and grass tracks.

Maintenance Schedule

A daily log of all maintenance operations carried out on the pitch should be completed by the grounds manager.

Daily (at end of the day's play)
Check fixtures and fittings.
Check and top-up fill levels at penalty spots, short corners.
Make sure gates are shut.
Weekly
Clear leaves and rubbish from the area.
Deal with any new weeds, moss or algae.
Groom the surface of the pitch to redistribute infill and maintain vertical fibres.
Monthly
Check infill levels. Outside the fence, check and clear mowing strips and check cleanliness of access paths.
Check seams, inlaid lines and report failures to installer.
Periodically (at least every six months)
Check thoroughly for moss and algae growth, food stains and remedy as appropriate.
Top up fill as required.
Treat pitch with moss killer, algicide.
Annually
Treat pitch with moss killer/algicide,
Topdress with new infill as required.
Call in installer if any aspect is causing significant concern.

The synthetic surfacing products available in the UK marketplace can be divided into two major categories: solid polyurethane tracks for national and international level competition and porous polyurethane surfaces for club, local authority, schools and college sports competitions.

The solid polyurethane tracks are constructed on a dense asphalt base with appropriate stone foundation layers capable of bearing the loads imposed by the construction plant required for the paving operation. The final asphalt layer must be laid to very fine tolerances to ensure that a consistent thickness (usually 12mm) of the

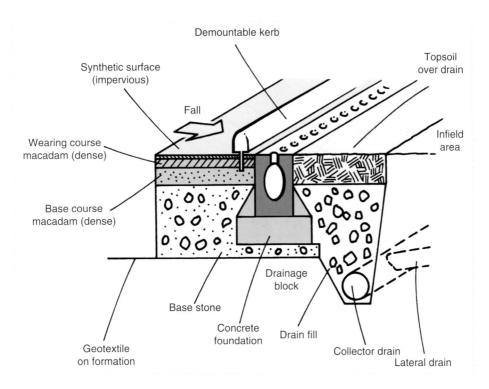

Figure 47   Cross section of a solid type athletics track.

resilient polyurethane system may be installed and that no surface water puddles remain after rainfall. To aid the surface water drainage, the athletics track needs to be laid with a crossfall on the inside lane and the surface water will be collected by an internal polyester or concrete drainage channel. The surfacing process varies with the proprietary product being used, but all polyurethane products are very susceptible to weather conditions, particularly temperature and humidity. For this reason polyurethane surfacing products are not normally installed outside the summer months in the UK.

Porous polyurethane tracks have an open-textured base construction, which would normally consist of two layers of open-textured bitmac over a suitable stone foundation layer. Again, the surface tolerance of the base layers has a critical influence

on the consistency of surface thickness although, being porous, surface water puddles should not be a feature, at least not in the early years after the track's installation. The track will again be laid with a crossfall to the inside lane where the water is collected at formation level by a subsoil drain on the inside perimeter and, if necessary, any surface water can be collected by a drainage channel as before. The normal surfacing method employed in porous track construction is to lay a black, polyurethane-bound, rubber crumb base and to apply a polyurethane structure spray-coating that includes an EPDM coloured granule. The same restrictions in ambient weather conditions apply to this process as the solid polyurethane system.

There is a third method of constructing a polymeric track surface, which is really a combination of the two systems described

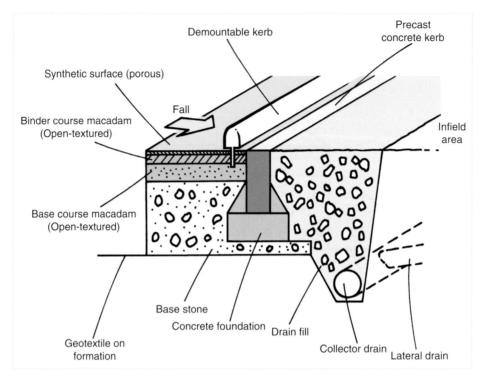

Figure 48 Cross section of a porous type athletics track.

above. Sometimes called a 'sandwich' system, this product utilizes the cast *in situ* base from the porous system, combined with the solid cast polymers from the impervious system. This produces a non-porous track, performing like a solid system but with a substantial saving in cost.

The number of lanes provided in any track design will vary with the intended use: a track intended primarily for training, for instance, may have only four or six lanes in the circuit with perhaps six or eight lanes on one straight. On the other hand, national level tracks commonly have eight-lane circuits as well as two ten-lane sprint straights.

Field events are normally provided in the same material as the main track. The high jump fan and the run-ups for javelin, long and triple jump would have an identical construction to the track system. It is

common to increase the depth of surfacing at the throwing end of the javelin and on the landing area of the water jump in order to help to absorb the additional impact in these areas.

The construction depth of the systems is normally retained by a precast concrete kerb, laid flush with the final track surface. In some cases a round-topped edging kerb is laid on the inside at 50mm above the track surface, but it is more common to have an aluminium demountable kerb acting as the running line. This kerb is fixed by plates on the track surface and is adjusted to provide the precise inside lane measurement.

Testing and Surface Standards

All reputable installers of synthetic systems for athletics will have recent test data on the surfaces they offer. These tests will have

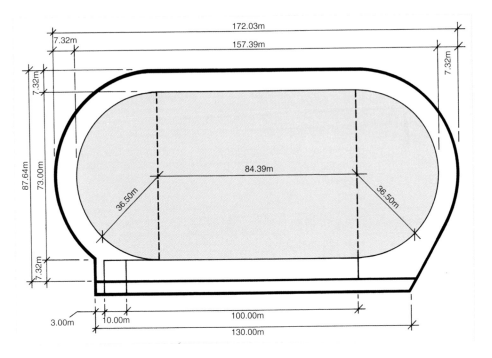

Figure 49   Dimensions for a six lane athletics track.

been carried out by an independent test laboratory on samples of the surface material or on tracks laid by the installer. These tests are designed to establish the durability of the surfacing system and its suitability, in performance terms, as a surface for athletics, over a period of time. In the UK tracks are subject to a harsh climatic environment with a wide temperature range. All track surfaces must also be designed to cope with the damage inflicted by spikes. The IAAF limits for these performance tests are included in the table on p. 337 with proposed test limits for the club/school/college standard of track in the UK.

Maintenance of Athletics Tracks

By their nature, polymeric surfaces are extremely durable, being designed to satisfy arduous performance test criteria while withstanding constant spike use in climates varying from the Arctic to the Equator. However, there is no such thing as a 'maintenance-free' sports surface, and all polymeric track surfaces will require a modest degree of maintenance. This basic maintenance is of vital importance if the surface is to remain good to look at, consistent in performance, safe for the athlete to run and jump on, and long lasting. Indeed, the installer's guarantee will usually be conditional on the recommended maintenance requirements being carried out with reasonable diligence.

SURFACE CLEANLINESS

Leaves and other detritus should not be allowed to remain on the surface for any length of time. If this does happen, they rapidly rot down, forming a contaminating 'skin' on the surface and providing a growing medium for algae and moss.

335

Tests	IAAF Limits	Proposed UK Limits
Tests carried out by inspecting the final installation		
Imperfections	No serious imperfections	No serious imperfections
Colour	One point on Methuen Handbook	Per BS 4800\5252
Drainage	No surface water after 20 mins	No surface water after 20 mins
Flatness	6mm below 4m straightedge 3mm below 1m straightedge	6mm below 3m straightedge 3mm below 1m straightedge
Thickness	Average 12mm Minimum 10mm	Average 12mm Minimum 10mm
Tests carried out on the surface material, either on site or in the lab		
Force reduction	35% to 50% between 10°C and 40°C	32% to 52% between 10°C and 30°C
Modified deformation	0.6 to 2.2mm between 10°C and 40°C	0.6 to 2.5mm between 10°C and 30°C
Friction	Not less than 0.5 when wet	Not less than 0.5 when wet
Tensile properties	Tensile strength of 0.5 MPa for solid and 0.4 MPa for porous systems Elongation at break not less than 40%	Tensile strength of 0.5 MPa for solid and 0.4 MPa for porous systems Elongation at break not less than 40%

A mechanical leaf-sweeper or vacuum cleaner is ideal for removing vegetable matter and other rubbish. Restricted areas may have to be undertaken by hand. The equipment should be well maintained and carefully operated to avoid contamination of, or physical damage to, the surface. Spillage of fuel or lubricating oil may damage the surface, so great care should be taken to ensure that the equipment remains in good mechanical order. At least once a year it is advisable to wash the surface with high-pressure jetting apparatus. There are many varieties of high-pressure washer available for purchase or hire. These can range from a simple hand-held lance through to a tractor-mounted version. The higher the capacity of the machine, the quicker the operation will be completed. Polymeric surfaces can withstand pressures up to 2000psi without suffering damage to the structure. Many commercial washers allow for carefully metered quantities of detergent and fungal inhibitors to be added to the water. These chemicals will help prevent moss and algae from invading the surface. If this is not carried out, the track will become discoloured and slippery due to a fungal growth on the surface. Budgeting for an annual treatment will keep the surface in good condition.

ACCESS OVER THE TRACK
At all track venues, both pedestrians and maintenance machinery require regular access to the central grassed area. It is good practice to provide protection for the track surface at regular pedestrian crossing points, for example from the dressing room onto a central pitch. This protection could take

Make sure any vehicles used on the track do not exceed the specified load-bearing capacity of the construction. (John Deere)

the form of roll-out matting to ensure that mud from football boots does not contaminate the track surface. It is wise to provide plywood or similar sheeting to allow access to the central area for grass-cutting machines. The load imposed by such a machine should not normally exceed 1,500kg, spread over four tyres. At some tracks, specially designated crossing points are designed to allow heavy items of plant, such as trucks and forklifts, access to the central area. This extra loading is catered for by increasing the strength of the track base works at the time of construction. Protection of the track surface will still be required in these locations.

Spreading the Wear

The inside lane of a track, along with the start areas and the long/triple jump runways, are subject to a massive amount of wear compared with the outside lanes of the circuit. For this reason, it will extend the useful life of the facility if the athletes use these areas as little as possible in training. This 'athlete management' can be achieved by measures such as coning off the inside lane. Although the polymeric materials are highly resistant to damage, point loads from sports equipment should be avoided, otherwise localized damage to the track surface will occur.

Track Repairs

Repairing polymeric tracks is a highly specialized operation best left to the experts. In the event of any damage occurring, the installer should be asked to carry out the necessary repairs as soon as possible before accidents happen or the trouble spreads.

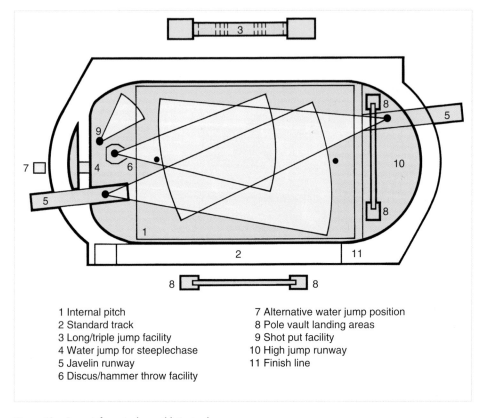

1 Internal pitch
2 Standard track
3 Long/triple jump facility
4 Water jump for steeplechase
5 Javelin runway
6 Discus/hammer throw facility

7 Alternative water jump position
8 Pole vault landing areas
9 Shot put facility
10 High jump runway
11 Finish line

Figure 50   Layout for a six lane athletics track.

PART IV

Ancillary Areas and Issues

14 Landscape Management

Many sports grounds contain areas of landscape and ornamental gardens that need to be managed and maintained. Such landscape can be made up of a combination of various features including:

- Cultivated trees and shrubs
- Ornamental grass
- Floral displays
- Parkland grass
- Hard landscape surfaces
- Walls, benches
- Wild flora
- Woodlands and forests
- Water features

All of these combine in some way to represent different landscape types, each of which will require its own management plans and maintenance programmes. The players or public users of the sports ground place different demands on land and have different perception of how it should be managed. For instance, the modern approach to amenity landscape maintenance with wildflower areas and a less intensive maintenance regime leads to complaints from those whose perception includes well-manicured grass and patterned summer bedding. Conservationists and environmentalists have their own perception of how the landscape should be maintained. This often conflicts with the wishes of those using areas for recreation activities.

Landscape Maintenance Policy

Irrespective of the organization owning the landscaped area, it is vital that a maintenance policy is prepared in order to identify and quantify various resources necessary to achieve the objectives resulting from the policy. Many businesses have detailed policy or mission statements that identify the direction in which the organization is travelling and what it is trying to achieve. In the past few years, landscape maintenance businesses/organizations have actually written out detailed policies and it is only with the introduction of competitive tendering that local authority parks departments have examined what they did, then what they should be doing, and finally prepared policy objectives for their departments and the land they maintain. A multitude of factors will influence the policy set by a particular organization for the maintenance of the landscape in its care. This basic policy statement will indicate what the organization is trying to achieve with the landscaped area and, from this, objectives can be set for the individual landscape types within an area.

Below are some examples of visual landscape features: for each is provided a stated objective for the visual requirement and a list of necessary tasks required in order to achieve that objective.

Amenity Grass Areas/Lawns

Objective: To provide an area of grass that is reasonably hard wearing, where people may walk or sit, but not play organized sports, is of even growth both in height and density, of a uniform colour, with a maximum of 5 per cent non-grass species in the sward. In order to achieve this objective, the following maintenance operations will have to be carried out.

Maintenance activities: Mowing with a cylinder mower to maintain a grass height of between 20mm and 40mm during the growing season, and between 30mm and 50mm in the winter. The clippings shall be let fly, but must be evenly distributed over the surface, and shall at no time affect the growth of the grass. All edges against buildings, footpaths, trees and so on shall be kept neat and tidy. Mowing strips may be maintained regularly using an appropriate herbicide. Border edges shall be clipped regularly, and not allowed to exceed 50mm in length. If appropriate, weeds may be controlled using a selective weed-killer in accordance with manufacturers' instructions. Fertilizer may be applied in the period March to September to maintain the colour of the sward. When necessary, the sward should be litter picked. These maintenance tasks all occur because of the original objective for that grass area. Variations in the objective would lead to variations in the activities: for instance, the objective may require the clippings to be removed, or there may be a ban on the use of any herbicides.

Shrub Borders

Objective: To maintain shrub growth to cover as much of a border area while

The 'new zero turn' rider rotary mowers are very useful for many amenity landscape areas. (Ransomes Jacobsen)

allowing the individual plants to achieve their natural form. To maintain the borders so that they are free of visible weeds and litter. To shape and prune the shrubs to avoid obstructing pathways or blocking light from windows.

Maintenance activities: Prune plants annually in the appropriate season in order to develop their desirable ornamental characteristics and to remove obstructions and remove all arisings. Prune out all damaged, dead or diseased parts and remove all arisings. Pick all litter from within the border at regular intervals. Remove any plants deemed surplus (the traditional method of planting is to plant at densities far greater than needed in order to maximize cover early and to thin out in later years). This should occur as plants touch each other. Visible surfaces may be maintained free of weeds by the use of residual herbicides in the late winter months and through the spot treatment of any emergent weeds in the summer. Alternatively, the surface of the bed can be mulched using coarse peat or pulverized bark to a depth of 75mm and again pot treat for weeds in the summer. These are general maintenance activities but it is important to note that the level and type of maintenance required will depend on the stage of maturity of each bed. As stated, it is usual to overplant new shrub beds and the first few seasons are vital for the establishment of good plants.

During the first few years, the main problem will be to reduce the competition from weeds and to maintain soil moisture during the summer months. This may be done by the use of a deep mulch that encourages the plant growth while reducing weed growth, or alternatively to use residual herbicides after the initial establishment period. In most situations, it is not cost-effective to maintain clean beds by regular hoeing. Once good cover has been achieved then the cost of maintenance reduces until major replanting is necessary after twenty years.

Ground Cover

Objective: To maintain a dense, weed-free cover of low growing plants over the whole of the planted area. To have healthy growth, the plants should be clipped or pruned to retain a neat and tidy finish throughout the year.

Maintenance activities: The area to be kept free of weeds by the application of an annual dressing of the residual herbicide and the use of spot treatments during the summer. Trim and tidy the plants once a year in winter by removing all dead and diseased material and branches that have overgrown the area. Keep the bed free of litter. As with shrub borders, ground cover beds take some time to mature, but in this case, plants are not removed, as the objective is to get a tight growth of plants across the site. The objective of this thickly planted area is the minimizing of maintenance.

Rose Borders

Objective: To maintain a free-flowering bed of healthy hybrid tea or floribunda roses by regular pruning, spraying and fertilizing. The bed to be free of weeds and tidy at all times. During the flowering season all deadheads to be removed within ten days of petal drop.

Maintenance activities: Prune the roses to approximately two-thirds of their height in the autumn and remove the cuttings from the site. Hard prune the roses according to type and vigour in late winter, leaving outward facing buds, and remove prunings from the site. Ensure all dead or diseased material is removed. Remove any plants deemed dead or diseased and replace with new plants. In the autumn, lightly cultivate the soil to a depth of 100mm, avoiding damaging the rose bush's roots. Remove all debris and weeds from the site. (Although not essential, this operation leaves the surface tidy for winter and ready for residual herbicide application in the spring.)

Apply residual herbicide to the bed in the late winter and spot treat if any weeds appear during the summer. Keep the plants free of suckers by removing all sucker growth at least twice during the growing season. Remove all dead flower heads within ten days of petal fall and remove from site. Keep the plants relatively free of fungal disease and aphids by the regular use of a multi-spray. Rose beds are rather formal and require a relatively large amount of maintenance. They do provide a mass of summer colour and last for ten to fifteen years if maintained correctly.

Herbaceous Borders

Objective: To maintain the herbaceous border in an attractive and free-flowering state throughout the summer period with a good plant cover over the area and a minimum of weeds. All plants should be free of disease, and damaged growth and dead flowers removed regularly. During the winter, after the border has died back, the bed should be kept clean and tidy.

Maintenance activities: Cut down and remove all dead and dying plant material as soon as the autumn frosts start. Lightly cultivate the soil. Dig, divide and replant in accordance with good horticultural practice to maintain a full cover of plants throughout the border. In the spring, apply a granular fertilizer and work into the soil by hoeing. Regularly hand hoe the soil to remove weed seedlings. Stake and tie those plants needing such treatment during the summer. Remove dead and unsightly flower heads within ten days of petal fall.

Hedges

Objective: To maintain a hedge in a suitable condition for it to act as a barrier of the height wanted. To keep the hedge in a uniform and tidy condition, according to the type of hedge and situation, and maintain the area at the base of the hedge clean and tidy.

Maintenance activities: Clip the top and sides of the hedge to maintain true and even levels using suitable mechanical cutters to retain the desired shape and height. All cuttings to be removed from the site. Keep the base of the hedge clean and free from weeds if appropriate. Different species require pruning at different times of the year.

Trees

Objective: To enable the development of new or recently planted trees over a period of years so that they develop the shape and size applicable to that species.

Maintenance activities: Maintain a metre diameter around the base of the tree from all other growth by hoeing or herbicide application. With young trees, ensure that no other plants are crowding out the specimen. It may be necessary to water new plantings during the summer for the first couple of years. Check stakes and ties for firmness and support, and adjust as necessary. Carry out appropriate formative pruning to remove dead or damaged growth and create a balanced form. As trees develop, they may have a period where no maintenance is necessary, and after this will require specialist treatment during maturity. Difficulties are created because of this fact when trying to write definitive specifications.

These examples show what work will have to be carried out if particular policies, aims and objectives are set. Consideration should also be taken of the fact that landscapes do not remain static. All living materials are going through a series of phases and, in the case of the landscape, those phases will influence the maintenance policy adopted at any particular time.

Phases of the Landscape Management Cycle

While all other factors are usually listed, it is often forgotten that landscapes themselves develop and have different

Ride-on rotary mowers with grass collection systems can be used effectively for leaf collection too. (John Deere)

maintenance requirements during each of the stages. These phases are as follows:

- Establishment phase: covering the time from planting through to the time when, apart from occasional special tasks, only routine maintenance is required. This phase may be as short as a couple of weeks for annual bedding plants, to five years for trees.
- Adolescent phase: during which the plantings, although established, require occasional work as well as routine maintenance.
- Maturity phase: when the landscape only requires routine maintenance and periodic rejuvenation.

- Senile phase: when the landscape is recognizably senile, and when special care is required to extend both the aesthetic and physical life. For example, special pruning or surgery may be necessary on trees.
- Death phase: when the existing vegetation is beyond saving and will have to be replaced.

There is no easy identification of these phases for any of the different types of landscape, but the life cycle will have an undoubted effect on the maintenance programme necessary and its cost. Managers should try to develop landscapes containing a variety of vegetation at different

343

stages of growth and maturity. This enables the cost of regeneration to be spread over a period of years.

Two major challenges appear:

An individual landscape component: The management task usually entails ensuring that the physical, aesthetic and other functions of the component are continued by means of at least periodic if not perpetual regeneration.

A particular landscape type: The challenge involves adopting the most effective method of perpetuating the landscape in accordance with the long-term objectives of both the designer and the client.

The amenity manager has a number of resources available. These are usually listed as the 'five Ms':

Manpower
Machinery
Materials
Methods
Management
plus
Money
Management Skills

Moreover, they represent the package a manager has to work with. Consider the 'five Ms' individually and their influence on maintenance policy.

Manpower
There are a large number of factors within manpower that influence the choice of maintenance plan to be adopted. Manpower is the most significant resource as it represents between 60 and 75 per cent of the total cost of grounds maintenance. To aid the planner, the following information is needed:

- The number of staff available.
- The horticultural expertise of each team member.
- Whether staff hold any qualifications.
- The hours during the day, and the number of days in the week, they are available to work.

Machinery
In the last decade there has been a marked increase in the number and types of machines available to the grounds maintenance team. The development of the compact tractor, the hover mower and other equipment has reduced the labour requirements for carrying out tasks, but conversely has increased the mechanical skill requirements for those staff employed. The type, number and repair policy for each category of machine will influence the grounds maintenance policy. Although machinery reduces labour costs, machines have an initial capital cost, depreciation and ongoing repair costs. The ability to do jobs faster, when they are required to be done, is also a bonus. Therefore the manager will take note of the machines owned and the availability of capital to purchase other equipment when formulating a plan.

Materials
A comprehensive list of materials could be drawn up. A few examples should suffice to show how material availability has influenced the grounds maintenance policy in recent years: the use of residual herbicides to keep down annual weeds in shrub and flower borders has reduced the labour requirement in the summer; growth retardants have reduced the number of cuts on some amenity grass areas; the acceptability of a mowing strip produced by using a total herbicide rather than the fortnightly edging of grass areas; the use of mulches as a weed control.

Methods
The methods used to carry out some grounds maintenance tasks have altered,

especially in situations where incentive bonus schemes have been in operation. Some still produce the same result, while others may not produce such a high standard. Linking method and machinery, the use of rotary mowers speeds up the mowing task, enabling units to deal with longer grass (so less mowing), but does not remove the arisings from the surface of the area. These clippings may have to be raked off, a time-consuming process. This may be justified if the saving is greater than the previous frequent mowing and boxing off.

Management Aids

The most significant aid to the amenity manager has been the introduction of computer programmes that enable the manager to plan all the grounds maintenance activities for a season and include areas and times for tasks. This will give a printout that plans the workload for both the staff and machinery, thus giving the manager a guide to work from. Because of the vagaries of the seasons, it will not give an actual plan, but enables the manager to have a start base for monthly or weekly forward plans.

The 'five Ms' will influence the manager's decision on grounds maintenance planning in many individual and combined ways, provided they fall within the remit of that manager. Planning is deciding how to achieve the policies and objectives for that business or organization. So far, the emphasis has been on setting the policy for the landscape, rather than the organization controlling that landscape. It is important to appreciate that there is a vast difference between the two in many situations. The objective of the maintenance organization will normally be written around the 'five Ms' rather than the facility. Whether it is a local authority organization, a landscape contractor, or the staff of a private sports ground, the manager will have the same problems and need to make the same sort of decisions.

Specifications for Grounds Maintenance

Traditional landscape maintenance revolved around an open style of horticultural management, rather than the ethic of commercial business management. Tasks were carried out to horticultural standards, which often required large amounts of skilled labour. During the last thirty years changes in policy standards, especially in the public sector, has led to substantial changes in maintenance requirements. Rather than operate horticultural practices of a traditional nature, situations have occurred where detailed maintenance requirements have been written out, and those carrying out the work have had to operate within these specifications.

The Object of the Documentation

Maintenance specifications are written to achieve the same result as those for landscape construction, namely the satisfactory completion of tasks for which a payment at an agreed rate will be made. In this case:

- To get the right task done
- In the right place
- In the right way
- Using the right equipment
- At the right time of year
- Producing the correct finished product
- To the satisfaction of the client
- At the right cost
- Which leaves the desired profit

This is then linked to the Bill of Quantities, where the tenderer can complete the pricing for the contract.

Writing Specifications

The specifications required for grounds maintenance programmes must be prepared very carefully and cover all aspects of grounds maintenance applicable to that contract area. The specifications are there to tell the contractor exactly what to do and how to do it. It is possible to write the specifications in two different ways, either in relation to the type of landscape area, or by the maintenance function being carried out.

- By dividing into landscape areas, there is often duplication of specifications, with only small but occasionally important changes.
- By detailing every function to be carried out, the tasks necessary to maintain each area can be identified and work programmes developed.

In order to decide exactly how specifications should be written, it is important to appreciate the differences between the two types of Function Contract suitable for grounds maintenance.

Frequency specifications: Specifies tasks to be completed at a predetermined frequency through Bills of Quantity.
Performance specifications: Specifies the performance to be achieved.

Contracts of the first type are normally based on a Bill of Quantities and a Tendered Rate. The Bill is a schedule of work to be done at each site and its frequency. (The quantities are either linear metres, square metres or numbers, and the costs are calculated by taking the unit cost and multiplying it by the total units' times the frequency.) The performance-based contract requires contractors to agree overall performance standards and to submit a lump sum bid. A Schedule of Rates for work arising from the contingencies and variations should support this, but these rates are not directly related to the lump sum bid. The following examples show the differences between the two methods.

DIFFERENCES FOR MAINTENANCE
OF AN ORNAMENTAL GRASS AREA
Frequency: Each area will be cut to a height of 25mm twenty-eight times during the season, using a six-bladed cylinder mower of 36in width.

Performance: Each area will be maintained at a height of between 25mm and 50mm throughout the season, using a six-bladed cylinder mower of 36in width.

The contractor is tied to pricing the job based on twenty-eight cuts for the frequency, but for a performance specification can decide what number of cuts may be necessary and price accordingly. If the season is dry, then the contractor gains because he will be paid for the quoted total. For a frequency specification, the client may reduce the number of cuts if the season requires it, and save money.

The client may also find performance specifications easier to monitor as there is no need to check the number of times the task has been carried out. While it is vital that the specifications include all the tasks to be carried out, authorities should be aware of unwittingly specifying higher standards or frequencies than currently applied and being embarrassed by receiving tenders with prices above those accepted.

The maintenance specification listed in the accompanying example could easily be modified to fit the requirements for a performance specification by identifying acceptable minimum and maximum levels of weeds, deadheads and so on. The critical point for the contractor is that only work specified should be carried out, although it may be necessary to write in specification details indicating when variations to specification should occur and who will authorize them. In summary, it can be seen that detailed specifications have only been written for those landscaped areas where there is a direct link between the quality of work required, the method of payment for the work and the ability to monitor quality.

Maintenance Programmes

This is the part of the process that puts the maintenance into action. These programmes are vital if the objectives or specifications are to be met. Maintenance

Sample Maintenance Specification

Bedding Maintenance (Spring and Summer)

The contractor will be required to visit the beds at a frequency in order to maintain them in a neat, tidy and attractive appearance, in accordance with the maintenance schedule set out as follows:

At each visit the contractor will carry out the following without damaging the plants:

Clear all beds of weeds, litter, remove dead flower heads, rogue plants and remove all arisings to a previously agreed tip.

Trim grass edges of each bed with long-handled shears or other mechanized means approved by the supervising officer ...... times, evenly spread throughout the growing season. Growth shall not be permitted to exceed .....mm from the edge of the grass area. Arisings from this operation to be collected and removed from site to a previously agreed tip.

Irrigate summer bedding as necessary, to ensure the plants do not wilt. At the first sign of wilting, the contractor will immediately commence irrigation. Irrigation of spring bedding will not be required unless specified by the supervising officer. The contractor will, nonetheless, ensure that the task can be undertaken when required.

The contractor will immediately report observed pests and diseases to the supervising officer. The contractor will be required to treat any pests or diseases with an approved pesticide within three working days of being notified by the supervising officer.

plans are a vital way of describing the way in which regular maintenance is going to be carried out over a specified landscape area using a particular selection of staff and machinery. The manager needs to know:

- The areas of land to be maintained.
- The landscape types to be maintained within those areas.
- The standards of maintenance required through the specifications.

With this information, the maintenance programmes can be developed. Using competitive tendering as the example again, tenderers have to prepare detailed programmes in order to be able to price the grounds maintenance jobs they are tendering for. Plans can only be developed when all the information necessary has been collected. In the example of the maintenance contract, the organization will have provided a detailed coded plan indicating where each site is, a schedule of areas by code and size, a specification and frequency information. With this and knowledge of the staff, their abilities and machinery available, the manager can then plan how the work is to be carried out both through long-term plans and short-term activity charts.

Mention has already been made of the 'five Ms'. They are important when developing programmes along with other factors.

Manpower

In this example, it will be presumed that the choice of staff to operate a specific contract is open, and the basic detail relates to a traditional local authority parks department. Traditional conditions of employment and their change is an important consideration in the contract situation. The contractor has to meet the specifications and the constraints of a thirty-nine-hour week worked between Monday and Friday will not be acceptable. Also it must be considered that with maintenance programmes there is a large difference between summer labour requirement and winter levels: no longer can the staff carry out landscaping projects in winter and spend time maintaining equipment.

To overcome these two problems, staff are being required to be available for work over six days rather than five, and a normal working week may be 46 hours in the summer, and 35 in the winter. In this way, the work can be done when appropriate and less overtime is paid. In deciding work programmes, the manager must look at the concept of a specialist workforce rather than general horticulturalists. Each has its own merits. The gang consisting of specialists requires less training: once a person is trained in the tasks they will carry out, there is no need to train them further. Against this, the staff will become bored with carrying out the same duties all the time and if those who are trained leave or are ill for a time, a gap appears in the workforce. The horticulturalist gang can divide the work to suit the group and each person, because of their width of skills, can be moved round. Knowledge of the areas and tasks enables the manager, in this situation, to develop an organization geared specifically to achieving the task. Certain skills will be required, such as qualified sprayers, or tree workers. These may form gangs responsible for all the work of that type. Consideration of the machinery to be used and the skills needed to use that machinery is also important. The management levels and spans of control are important. To compete, management structures must be very slim, perhaps with only assistant managers and supervisors between the manager and the staff. The number of ancillary staff is also important. In a local authority, most of these skills can be bought in from other authority departments. However, the cost of these skills is currently causing problems in many departments.

Machinery

The manager will need to know what level of output can be achieved from each of the machines that a particular organization owns. This is not always easy, as the manufacturers' suggested rates of work are often those achieved in ideal conditions, rather than typical environmental conditions. Other factors, such as the age of a machine and the state of maintenance, will also influence work rates. The specification requirements will affect the choice of machine for a particular task. Managers must be aware of possible alternatives that may save money and time.

Materials

In developing programmes, the manager must consider the materials available, and what they can be used for in relation to the reduction of maintenance costs. For instance, the use of growth retardants can reduce the number of cuts for a particular grass area, but requires staff with additional skills and qualifications.

Methods

The method used to carry out tasks is important. Method Study and Work Measurement techniques have been used in many situations to identify the most efficient and effective method of carrying out a task.

Management Aids

There are a large number of management aids available to the landscape manager. Computer companies have, during the past few years, developed very extensive computer software that covers all aspects of grounds maintenance from both the client and contractor's requirements.

Maintenance Standards

The standards required to be achieved for landscape maintenance activities depend on the specifications and objectives set for those activities and areas. The question must be posed: 'What is an acceptable standard of maintenance for a specific landscape situation?' As identified previously, there are many types of landscape, and even more objectives set for each one. The answer to this question will depend on a number of factors, including user expectations, owner requirements, ability of staff, finance available, aesthetic look, environmental considerations and many others.

This section examines some of the landscape features, the standards that may be set, and some of the factors influencing the achievement of those standards.

Amenity Grass Areas

In looking at the standards of maintenance of grassland areas, the traditional attitudes regarding the visual appearance must be noted. The public's perception in urban situations is that grass should be green, short and consist exclusively of grass species. For some time, grassland husbandry has been geared to producing vigorously mown grass monocultures. To achieve the perceived vision required the right grass species, fertilizers and other chemicals, aeration and irrigation, followed by frequent mowing to remove vast quantities of growth. Much grassland has in the past been over-maintained, in the sense that the cost of keeping it short does not seem to be repaid by benefits to users, except in the sports turf situation.

There are a number of options available for managing amenity grasslands more cost-effectively. These savings are accompanied by a range of consequential effects on the visual appearance of the grass as well as the overall environment. The changing of short sward management offers great scope for cost savings. Public attitudes towards cutting methods, the redesigning of areas and the substitution by other surfaces are the main factors that strongly influence the degree to which change can be introduced: initially there was public resistance to differential mowing, the infrequent cutting of roadside vegetation, and the less frequent mowing with a flail mower that left the clippings.

Some urban landscape managers have now developed a policy where there is zoning of mowing regime. Areas of long grass are left with closely mown boundaries, paths and clearings. In this way, the public can be guided where the manager wants them, and gives the idea that a more conservation-orientated policy is being implemented. The impression is not a drop in standards, but a more flexible approach to grass maintenance. Problems do occur initially, as traditional landscapes have been provided on relatively good topsoil. If the grass established in this sort of situation is left uncut, the result is long coarse growth and noxious weeds. In one local authority park, in order to change the ryegrass sward to a meadow, all the topsoil was removed and the whole area resown. This of course would not be practical on a large scale. On urban regeneration sites, this problem has not arisen as the soil is often very poor, and it cannot be expected to produce carpet-style grassland.

A problem is created by the public when mowing regimes are changed. People drop litter, fly tip and let dogs run wild: not only does the site rapidly become an eyesore but also, when it is mown, an additional job of litter picking is created. Standards are a result of policy and objectives. Many factors will, as already written, influence the achieving of these standards. There is a complex interaction between the cost of mowing and the standards set. Whatever the resulting decision, it will have a dramatic effect on whether or not the standard is achieved or maintained. As already identified, the frequencies of mowing may not only affect the visual appearance, but may actually create additional problems and costs. Trials and operating statistics identify that the most cost-effective way of keeping grass short is by frequently mowing with fast machinery that disperses the cuttings (a tractor-mounted multi-cylinder gang mower). If the cutting frequency for actively growing grass is less than every ten to fourteen days (presuming the climate and fertility are suitable), or if grass is allowed to grow longer than 10cm, then the sward outgrows the capacity of most cylinder mowers. In this case a rotary or flail mower will be needed. These are both slower and do not disperse the cuttings so well. Some tend to leave the cuttings in swathes (especially if the grass is wet), which may result in the grass beneath being killed off.

Often the result is unsightly, and at the next cut the machines have to contend with the extra burden of this undispersed debris. It may be necessary to rake the grass clippings off if they are too heavy, both to improve the visual appearance and make the next cutting easier. Therefore, in summary, flail and rotary mowers cut longer grass than cylinders, and can be used less frequently. This must be balanced against the speed of work and the appearance required. As a generalization, the mowing regime affects the visual appearance, but many other features must be considered. Other factors must be considered when deciding which mowing regime to select. The topography, both in terms of unevenness and slope, will require a different mower and maybe a different type of mowing. The landscape features affect both standards and mowing activities. Trees not only stop regular mowing runs, but the base of each tree will also require mowing, because the gangs will not reach the base of the tree. Shrub beds are usually irregular in shape, thus again creating difficulties, but also this time an additional task, that of edging, becomes necessary.

Many organizations overcome these two problems by using a herbicide such as Roundup in order to kill the grass close to the obstruction. If this operation is not carried out correctly, a rather unsightly mess can be left for some months. As mentioned earlier, wear caused by people, animals and vehicles rapidly affects the visual standard and creates additional tasks. Wear leaves compaction, bare patches and, if wet, mud, as well as uneven growth. The debris left by visitors and users reduces standards. In this instance, it is necessary to improve public attitudes and behaviour, and where possible remove problems by restricting vehicular access. Further

problems are caused through vandalism, including the removal of turf, the firing of long grass and the use of barbecues and the lighting of bonfires. The playing of ball games by children often damages lawn areas, and the practising of sports such as golf on such sites are not only dangerous but can also cause large amounts of damage through divots. Finally, the dog problem in parks has increased during the last decade as the number of parks staff has decreased. Their mess is not only very unpleasant, but also extremely dangerous to both children and adults.

The standard of grass areas can be maintained by the use of chemicals. Fertilizers both increase grass growth and help tackle fungal diseases and moss. They also enable the general or spot treatment of plants in the sward designated as weeds. Although standards may have been set requiring the production of a weed- and moss-free sward, environmental pressure has now caused those who manage the landscape to reconsider the use of chemicals. In most amenity grassland, daisies and other plants cause no real problem to the sward. Moss is indicative of poor drainage and sheltered areas. The use of fertilizers will increase the wear-resistant growth, make the grass look green, and promote growth on poor soil. Finally, growth retardants can be used to achieve the necessary standards, and at the same time save money. Inhibitors mean that the grass needs to be cut less often, but the system does mean that the grass cannot be maintained at even length for a long period.

General Plantings and Shrub Areas
Mention was made above of the life stages of landscape features. In setting and maintaining standards for these areas, consideration must be made of the stage of development. The establishment period ends when the primary stresses on individual plants are caused from companions rather than other factors. The initial mass plantings were to cover the soil and give visual pleasure immediately. As

the plants develop, it becomes necessary to remove plants in order to get the development of the acceptable specimens within the beds, or as individual specimen plants. The next stage with this type of planting will be regular pruning if the standard required is that of regular shape and size. Alternatively, the planting may be as a screening or ecological planting, which both acts as a physical barrier to people and a home for wildlife. In this case, very little maintenance may be carried out, as the appearance standard required may be very different.

In the first example, other maintenance activities may be necessary in order to achieve the whole of the standard required. Besides the pruning and thinning mentioned, it may be necessary to cultivate the soil, apply mulches or residual herbicides, or carry out regular weeding and other jobs, such as litter picking. In the more formal intensive plantings that have a strong aesthetic function, there will be a requirement for high levels of regular maintenance in order to maintain standards. Shrubs in turf areas will need pruning to stop growth over the grass or path edge. They will need to be pruned to maintain the size and shape suited to that locality. The traditional practice with shrub beds is to clip individual plants into uniform shapes, which tend to destroy the natural aesthetic formation of a closed weed-suppressing canopy. A point worth noting is that in a mature shrub bed, the death or necessary removal of an individual plant can cause a long-term imbalance unless a large replacement can be found. It is therefore vital that any disease is dealt with when it appears. Besides keeping shape and size, pruning is carried out to remove diseased wood and to improve

flowering or stem colour if cut back yearly, or bi-annually. Summer pruning will normally reduce the vigour of regrowth, while winter pruning is done to maximize regrowth in the following spring. Like all growing plants, shrubs vary in appearance depending on the stage and state of the seasons, and this must be considered when setting standards.

Climbing and Wall Plants

To consider the standards of appearance and maintenance for these plants, their purpose must be considered first. They may be grown for their floral display, their autumn leaf colour or simply to screen a poor surface. These plants may either be self-climbing or need support wires and nails. If the latter, then a suitable support must be prepared in advance. The major task needed to keep these plants to an acceptable standard usually involves pruning to remove surplus growth, which is causing the plant to become overweight and hang down, or the removal of dead flowers. Growth is rapid and failure to restrict it, especially with a self-supporting plant, may lead to severe damage to the support wall after a few years.

In most situations where there is a client-contractor situation, the monitoring of the contract to ensure that the required standards are being maintained is carried out by a client officer, who will have a copy of the specification to help identify the standard required. In some situations, the more important consideration is what happens if the standard is not maintained: for instance, the trimming of an ornamental hedge using a flail might achieve the symmetry required in the specification but would take a long time to regain the quality of appearance required.

15 Environmental Management

Sports facilities exclusively occupy and manage large areas of green space. Managers of sports grounds need to be responsive to concerns expressed by environmental groups, public authorities, academics and the media concerning the impact of their provision on the environment. It is now widely accepted within the major professional bodies that a proper understanding of environmental aspects is fundamental to good sports ground and turf management. This is not merely a reaction to external pressures from those critical of the environmental impact of sports turf. More importantly, the very basics of turfgrass management are integrally bound with ecological science. Turfgrass cultivar selection, mowing regimes, cultivation practices, fertilizer treatments, pest control, irrigation and drainage are profoundly influenced by prevailing environmental conditions. In turn, these activities can have a strong effect on the ecology of a sports ground and its immediate surroundings. In short, to be a good sports ground manager, one must also be a good environmental manager: the two are synonymous.

Sports grounds serve a broader function than simply as a particular type of sports turf. In a wider context they can provide important areas of green space in urban areas, they can be buffers between natural areas and developed land, they can provide valuable wildlife habitat in their own right, and they also have the opportunity to conserve and enhance water resources; turfgrass can be a highly effective biological filter, capable of improving water quality. No two sports grounds are identical and a whole range of site conditions and environmental influences are encountered. New facilities, new managers: old grounds, new problems through increased traffic and wear and tear: new technology, new products. Management is evolving rapidly and doing so in an age of increasing environmental awareness. Recognizing these challenges is crucial for the long-term development and sustainability of turf and sport facilities as we know them.

A Systematic Approach to Environmental Management

Real improvements in environmental management and sustainability will only be achieved through the active implementation of an Environmental Management System. Such a process and approach can be developed to include the following four components:

Environmental Policy: Sports clubs and grounds should first make a policy commitment endorsed by its membership. It should include the following points:

- Statement of intent to improve environmental performance.
- Establishment of an 'Environment team' to coordinate environmental projects within the club.

- Commitment to carry out an environmental review of the site and current management, and to implement appropriate conservation measures.

Environmental Review: This provides a picture of the current environmental management of a sports turf facility and forms the basis for developing the environmental management programme.

Environmental Management Plan: A comprehensive, integrated management plan, combining environmental and sports turf objectives appropriate to the site. It should cover the following environmental categories:

- Nature conservation
- Landscape and cultural heritage
- Water resource management
- Turfgrass management
- Waste management
- Energy efficiency and purchasing policies
- Education and the working environment
- Communications and public awareness

Audit: After a maximum of three years, progress should be evaluated to assess whether a club has achieved its initial environmental management targets.

Why Plan Your Environmental Management?

Environmental considerations are part and parcel of the operational management of sports grounds. A well-maintained sports ground requires an integrated approach to management, embracing a wide range of technical disciplines. This is important ecologically and also for practical sports turf and economic reasons. Furthermore, in accepting the fundamental link between sport and the environment, the sports turf world has a duty to strive to conserve the natural resources with which it is entrusted.

Obviously, sports grounds are primarily intended for sport. A sports ground must function adequately as a sport ground, or else it would have no purpose for existing. Any environmental programme, therefore, must be fully compatible with sporting playing surface requirements. This does not mean that environmental concerns are subordinate: it is simply a question of balance. Environmental benefits will only be sustainable if the sports turf management is sound. It is important to emphasize the benefits of an environmental approach: it is cost-effective, complementary to good ground management and enhances playing conditions. Potential benefits can be grouped into direct benefits, which have a clear link to cost, and indirect benefits, which have some other effect on overall performance.

Direct benefits of an environmental approach may include:

- Cost savings through improved efficiency: reduced water, chemical and fuel consumption due to revised irrigation, fertilizer applications and mowing regimes; introduction of Integrated Pest Management strategies to cut down on pesticide use and other controls; introduction of energy-saving policies; waste reduction, reusing and recycling; maintenance of equipment and machinery.
- Cost avoidance through compliance: environmental regulations (for example protected species, pollution controls); health and safety regulations (fewer accidents, lower insurance premiums).
- Protection of property asset value: appropriate management of trees and woodland blocks; maintenance of ponds, lakes, streams, ditches and other wetlands; general landscape management.
- Cost and time savings through accelerated approval process.
- Environmental improvement grants: grants for tree planting, hedgerow restoration, habitat management; environmental awards; local authority environmental improvement schemes.

At the same time indirect benefits may include:

- Increased employee motivation
- Membership/visitor satisfaction
- Improved aesthetic quality
- Improved local community relations
- Better public image

Despite these many possible benefits, there might still be reticence from sports clubs and others not wishing to implement what may be significant management changes. There may be worries that anticipated savings could lead to greater costs in other areas, for example where fewer chemicals may lead to more labour or more expensive equipment. High capital start-up cost is a frequently cited disincentive to adopting environmental measures, even though long-term operational benefits would accrue. However, there are many approaches here that simply involve a different way of doing things and where cost benefits will be obvious from the beginning. Among the more subjective benefits, the key consideration for most managers will be that an environmental approach to sports ground management must be compatible with the sport playing experience. There are some pitfalls to avoid. Over-enthusiastic attempts to 'naturalize' a sports ground or parts of it can backfire if club members and players perceive the changes to be 'untidy' or generally not matching their expectations of a 'well-managed' sports ground. Such problems are not automatic consequences of environmental management but they do highlight the need at all times for careful planning of conservation measures and effective communication with staff and members.

Benefits to the environment: All sports grounds, whatever their situation, have the potential for improving their environmental management. This can span a wide range of activities. Although each sports ground is a relatively small entity, the cumulative effect of many sports clubs undertaking environmental improvement measures can be significant.

Nature conservation: Sports grounds can provide different habitat conditions for a wide range of wild flora and fauna. Many of these species are known to be declining in the wider countryside, as a result of habitat loss or degradation and the effects of agricultural pesticides. Through a closer understanding of the wildlife inhabiting sports grounds, especially within the peripheral non-play areas, and the appropriate protection and management measures to take, ground managers can make an important contribution to the conservation of biodiversity.

Landscape conservation and cultural heritage: Many sports grounds, especially older ones or those in rural areas, encapsulate fragments of traditional countryside and natural landforms, such as mature trees and water bodies. In some cases historic monuments, buildings, ancient ways, boundaries and relics of former land uses can be identified on sports grounds. These features add distinctiveness and character to the site, and their conservation is an important part of preserving our cultural heritage.

Sustainable development: New sports grounds can offer many of the same environmental benefits as established grounds provided that they are sited, designed and constructed according to principles of good environmental practice and sustainable development.

Conservation of water resources: The use of water is the most critical environmental issue facing many British sports grounds and their managers today. Through an environmental management system, sports clubs will be able to demonstrate effective measures to reduce the quantities of freshwater consumed and to safeguard the quality of surface and groundwaters.

Pollution control: The Voluntary Initiative promotes the safe and appropriate usage, storage and disposal of fertilizers and pesticides. In this way, potential risks of pollution will be minimized and legal compliance with environmental protection and health and safety regulations will be highlighted.

Energy conservation and waste management: These issues have traditionally been given little attention in sports ground management. However, there is growing realization that sports grounds can make significant savings in maintenance costs and energy bills through a more rational approach to resource utilization. This applies not just to the sports ground but also to the built environment, including clubhouse and maintenance facilities.

Environmental education: A key goal is to achieve a high standard of awareness and knowledge of environmental management principles and techniques among sports ground managers and their technical advisers. Educated grounds staff can become a new force of skilled environmental managers.

Public awareness: By promoting public awareness of sports turf's role in the wider environment, sound environmental management will extend the environmental benefits to a much wider audience. In this way sports turf management can be a role model for other activities and land uses.

Implementing an Environmental Management Plan

Sports Club Policy

Environmental management is all about expressing a positive attitude towards environmental care. To participate means to believe that this is an important and worthwhile approach. In the context of a sports club this has to be a collective view. If the programme is to be effective, the membership, as well as the management team, needs to be broadly supportive and to feel involved. Environmental commitment is not a side-issue that can be left to one or two keen individuals. It is something that the club as a whole should make a conscious decision to support.

The first step, therefore, should be to secure the endorsement of the club membership and its management to work through an environmental management system. The best way to encapsulate this initial commitment is by means of a simple policy statement or charter. This is a general statement of principles. To provide more substance and a guiding framework, the policy could go on to specify the following specific commitments.

- A comprehensive Environmental Management Programme will be developed to address all aspects of sports ground management, full account being taken of the needs of players, staff and other interested parties.
- Management will conform to the most up-to-date guidelines available and will comply with relevant local, national and European regulations.
- All management personnel will be appropriately qualified and trained for the tasks they are required to perform and provision will be made for their continuing professional development.
- Details of the Environmental Management Programme and specific actions undertaken will be regularly communicated to staff, officers, club members and visitors.
- Progress in implementing the Environmental Management Programme will be monitored on a regular basis and fully reviewed every three years.

When written down, these points may seem to be a substantial commitment. In fact there is nothing here that goes beyond what any well-managed club should be aiming to do. If we are to achieve higher environmental standards, this policy framework offers a basic starting point. There are cases where ownership or management control of a sports ground is not directly in the hands of the club membership. Whatever the situation, it is important for owners, managers and users to be supportive of following an environmental approach. Different circumstances will dictate how best to present and agree an environmental policy statement.

CREATING AN 'ENVIRONMENT TEAM'

No single person within a club is realistically going to be able to fulfil the requirements across all the environmental topics unaided. This means that for any club to become properly involved in the project, a small team of contributors will be necessary. This exercise should therefore become the focus of creating a special 'Environment Team'. This will have the merit of increasing participation among staff, members and possibly outside specialists, such as environmental groups and authorities. This will give the eventual Management Plan a sounder basis.

It is surprising how often one can find people knowledgeable in different wildlife groups, or other environmental disciplines, within a sports club membership, or among the staff. The key ingredient, though, is enthusiasm. Even if there is no ecological expertise in-house, it is quite likely you may find amenable specialists in the local community. It is a good idea first to invite a local specialist to visit the sports ground, perhaps to report on the bird species or habitats on the site, and then to bring him or her into further discussions on developing a more active environmental programme. Key members of any 'Environment Team' should include as a minimum the Head Groundsman, Club Secretary or Manager and the club's Consultant Agronomist. The first task of this new group should be to evaluate the current environmental situation via an Environmental Review.

ENVIRONMENTAL REVIEW

This is the first step towards understanding the environmental condition of the sports ground. This will provide a picture of the current environmental performance and form the basis for developing future management programmes.

The Environmental Review should not be an entirely passive, recording exercise. If it is to help promote interest and participation throughout the sports club, it will need to lead on to some basic actions in the early stages of introducing active management measures. This means provoking some thoughts and discussions within the sports club on how to evaluate the information and make improvements. The first actions are likely to be ones that require minimal physical effort or investment, unless certain serious problems have been identified and need to be rectified. Generally, though, the programme should evolve at a steady pace to enable all the participants to be involved in its progress and development. The audit should also help to highlight priority areas for action. Again this should be a consultative exercise across the club membership and employees. This will be vital for achieving the necessary acceptance of the eventual Environmental Management Programme.

ENVIRONMENTAL MANAGEMENT PLAN

Once the Environmental Review has been completed one will be able to develop a comprehensive Management Plan. The Environmental Management Plan should aim to fulfil the overall environmental goals of the site in question, compatible with the normal operational management of the sports ground.

It is important to document the management programme. Written management policies, targets and records of implementation are vital to long-term, efficient management. The following provides a suggested format:

- Define overall management objectives to place environmental targets within a sports ground context.
- Define management zones around the sports ground.
- Identify appropriate practices for each Management Zone. These should include:
  - Measures to reduce any harmful environmental effects highlighted by the Environmental Review.

○ Potential environmental enhancement measures and a suitable programme for implementation.

- Define performance targets within given timescales.
- Identify personnel to be responsible for particular management operations, ensuring that they are appropriately qualified for the tasks required, or that sufficient prior training will be provided.
- Devise a regular monitoring programme, with defined baseline parameters on which to determine progress and effectiveness of management operations.
- Establish an efficient recording system. This must be simple and repeatable, so that like-for-like measurements can be taken in subsequent years to record actual progress.

AUDITING AND REVIEW

Environmental improvements do not happen overnight. If starting from scratch, you should allow three years to get the programme up and running before the first full progress review. During this period there should be regular monitoring to ensure things are kept on track. However, three years is a reasonable timescale over which to measure significant improvements in environmental performance.

Environmental Enhancement Opportunities for Sports Grounds

It is not realistic to describe all the environmental enhancement opportunities that may occur on all sports grounds. Detailed technical guidance can be found in a number of existing publications in the general environmental literature. Much of this can be applied to sports grounds. Every sports ground has its own particular circumstances and the environmental programme has to be tailored accordingly. The best approach

is likely to build up the programme in phases. Start with the categories of most immediate interest, or where most progress can be made. Once the first objectives have been attained, one can set new goals. In this way management will be committing to continual improvement. Although the following management points are presented under separate category headings, in reality there is considerable overlap. For example, a measure to improve waste management may also benefit water quality and in turn nature conservation. A truly integrated approach to sports ground management will recognize these interactions, and bind seemingly different actions into a unified programme.

Nature Conservation

There are many ways of encouraging wildlife on sports grounds. Quite often this is best done through relaxing management on certain areas, rather than engaging in complex intervention measures. Regeneration and succession are natural processes. They do not need to be designed or forced, they will occur according to the prevailing conditions. The best general conservation policy is to think first in terms of managing people rather than wildlife. Only when you have a more detailed understanding of the ecology of your sports ground should you contemplate more direct actions, such as creating new habitats or modifying existing ones.

Wildlife sanctuaries: Identify suitable out-of-play areas that can be designated as wildlife sanctuaries. These core, undisturbed areas will provide valuable sources of cover, food and nesting habitat. The priority of management should be to ensure that the habitats are adequately protected from disturbance, fire or rubbish dumping. It may also be necessary to control the spread of invasive, non-native plants if they threaten to smother the natural vegetation.

Corridors: Most of the mobile species inhabiting sanctuary areas will also utilize the sports ground proper, as well as habitats

357

on neighbouring properties. Sanctuaries are not self-contained islands. Their effectiveness can be considerably enhanced by 'support' habitats in the form of interconnecting corridors, such as a tree line, hedgerow, ditch or strip of uncut grass. It may not be practicable to establish continuous corridors but a series of small habitat 'stepping stones' can serve a useful function.

Buffer zones: The effectiveness of wildlife sanctuaries and other habitat features, such as lakes and ponds, will be improved by a protecting buffer zone. This is an intermediate area that is not of high ecological interest in itself, but is less intensively managed than the in-play areas. Buffer zones help to cushion the core area from disturbance or, in the case of rough grass strips around lake margins, they help prevent chemical run-off into water bodies.

Wetlands: Water bodies (where they exist) on sports grounds are often among the most important habitat features. Their effectiveness can be greatly improved by providing shallow, sloping edges and allowing a band of marginal vegetation to grow. If this is not suitable for the entire water's edge, try to leave at least part of the pond or lake edge in a more natural condition. It should at least be possible to establish some floating-leaved and submerged aquatic plants.

Nest boxes: On sports grounds where there are relatively few natural nesting sites, nest boxes can be a considerable benefit to several small bird species and bats. But even on grounds where more suitable habitat exists, nest boxes can serve a useful purpose in building awareness of your conservation programme among members and visitors. A few sited close to the clubhouse, perhaps complemented in winter with a feeding station, can be a point of added interest. Checking the numbers and species using nest boxes is a simple and effective means of monitoring your conservation programme over the years.

Landscape and Cultural Heritage

The environment is more than simply clean air and clean water. It is a question of

Collecting the arisings in wildflower meadows is necessary to preserve their floristic content. (John Deere)

being in harmony with nature, using natural materials such as stone, slate and wood. It is also good environmental thinking to create a harmonious visual environment and show respect for aesthetic values, good design and choice of colour and textures. Indeed, where it has been long established, sport itself can be part of the cultural heritage, and old sports grounds are an integral component of the local landscape.

Structure and pattern: Take a look at your sports ground in its wider setting. Does it blend into the local environment, or are there incongruous features that clash with the background structure and pattern of the landscape? This assessment could give you an appreciation of planting or screening requirements, or the need to remove unsightly or inappropriate features.

Colours and textures: In the selection of trees, shrubs, flowers and grasses, it is important to ensure they are as complementary as possible to the existing vegetation. Indigenous species are preferable to exotic ones. Ideally you should choose species that would naturally occur in your particular locality.

Materials: Sports ground furniture, built structures and paths can be visually jarring and add to the sense of an artificially created landscape. Wherever possible these should use natural materials and colours that blend into their setting. On open sites, try to locate signs, bins and the like so that they do not protrude above skylines or clutter long views.

Cultural heritage: Recorded archaeology represents only a fraction of the sites and features likely to exist in the countryside. Some sports grounds may contain features of historical interest. A starting point is to carry out a heritage survey to identify the precise limits and nature of archaeological sites or historic landscape features. This will provide a valuable basis for reviewing management and development options. Even below ground features can be damaged by compression from heavy machinery, or from earth moving or planting.

Water Resource Management

To have an effective water management programme should be the priority goal for all sports clubs. For most it is a question of conserving water resources and reducing quantities used. Not only is this a responsible approach to an issue of major public concern, it is also the most sensible economically and for the sport ground itself. Inefficient irrigation, especially overwatering, is probably the primary cause of poor turf management on many sports surfaces. Invasive weeds, disease problems and then reliance on chemical treatments, often stem from bad irrigation management. This can lead to risks of surface or groundwater contamination and potentially to regulatory infringements. Where water supply is not a problem, drainage often is. To manage water correctly is, therefore, vital to successful sports ground management and environmental protection. Control over water consumption is the greatest challenge facing sports ground managers.

WATER CONSERVATION
The first step should be to know how your irrigation system is set up and exactly how much water is used. Although there will be variations year on year depending on weather, you should have enough data to establish normal levels of use. This will be your baseline for checking future progress. Consider the following points:

- Are you using the best adapted turf cultivars for the climatic region in which your sports ground is situated? Advances in turfgrass breeding are producing many more drought-resistant cultivars suitable for sports grounds.
- Is irrigation confined only to crucial playing areas? Set water priority areas, to identify those requiring little or no supplementary irrigation.
- Introduce a regular checking and repair system for leaks, faulty sprinkler

heads and so on. Assess opportunities for using alternative water sources that have the least impact on local water supplies and water quality.

- Investigate possibilities for increasing water storage provision.
- Fine-tune irrigation practices to maximize efficiency: regularly monitor soil moisture levels, avoid irrigating in windy conditions or during daytime, check pump performance, use half-circle sprinklers where applicable and ensure that configuration of sprinkler heads and nozzle sizes provide uniform coverage.
- Check that products and irrigation system are suited to the locality and soil type.
- Ensure that appropriate personnel are properly trained to operate your irrigation system. Seek advice from professional, independent irrigation and drainage specialists. Use evapo-transpiration rates and weather data to adjust irrigation programme. Hand water small dry areas to prevent over-watering adjacent areas.
- Use drought-tolerant plants and mulch in landscaping areas. Create screens and windbreaks in exposed places to reduce evaporation losses.

WATER QUALITY MANAGEMENT

It is quite common to see turbid and algae-choked water bodies on sports grounds. However, with careful management these problems can be avoided and high water purity levels achieved. This is good aesthetically, for wildlife and for the wider environment. A key principle is to aim to minimize nutrient input to aquatic systems. Points to consider include:

- Create vegetative buffers around water bodies to filter run-off and reduce erosion.
- Determine no-spray zones around water bodies.
- If mowing close to the water's edge, ensure clippings do not spill onto the water body, a frequent, unnecessary source of additional nutrient input.
- Ensure that water outflow is filtered before entering off-site water grounds.
- Set up a regular water monitoring system for surface water and ground-water. This should consider sample methodology, frequency, locations and the variables to be tested.
- Monitor populations of aquatic invertebrates and amphibians inhabiting the water bodies; these serve as bio-indicators of water quality.
- Removing plugs of infected turfgrass by hand is preferable to spraying to solve localized problems.

Turfgrass Management

The essentials of turfgrass management are to maintain minimum but adequate soil fertility, apply plenty of mechanical treatments and to control soil moisture levels through good drainage, adequate irrigation and appropriate topdressing. Integrated Pest Management (IPM) is an ecologically based programme to prevent, or to limit, unacceptable levels of pest damage, using a combination of cultural, biological and chemical controls. IPM first takes a preventative approach, using sound cultural practices, regular scouting and monitoring of turf and environmental conditions, and the setting of damage thresholds. Chemical management practices are normally then used on a curative basis, and only where necessary.

Turfgrass varieties

- Select turf species appropriate for the climate and soils, and which are least demanding for water.

Cultural practices

- Employ cultural practices to increase turf health and deal with underlying problems or conditions.
- Reduce turf stress by traffic management and avoiding too low mowing heights.

Turfgrass nutrition

- Use slow release or natural-organic fertilizers.

Pest monitoring and management

- Identify local disease, insect and weed problems.
- Establish a regular scouting and monitoring programme to check turf quality, moisture levels, soil fertility and for signs of pests and diseases.
- Set threshold levels.
- Keep written records of monitoring activities, control measures used and results.
- Choose least toxic pest controls.
- Limit pesticide applications by treating affected areas only; spot treatment rather than spraying and using non-chemical methods whenever possible.
- Many sports clubs collect grass clippings, either for composting or for disposal in controlled sites.

Energy Efficiency and Procurement Policies

Energy efficiency and procurement policies are areas that may at first seem remote from sports ground management, but which have the potential to offer substantial cost benefits and environmental improvements. The clubhouse and other related buildings should also be included in the environmental programme to improve waste management and energy efficiency.

Fuel and energy consumption can be made more efficient through regular maintenance and checking of equipment and machinery, as well as heating, lighting and air-conditioning systems.

When replacing or upgrading sports ground equipment and machinery, specify models that are more fuel-efficient and run on more environmentally friendly fuels.

In all purchasing decisions, from sports ground equipment to office stationery, try to find environmentally preferred alternatives from local suppliers. It may not always appear practical or cost-effective to choose the greener option, but in most cases the medium- and long-term savings will far outweigh any additional costs. There is no harm in putting all purchasing decisions through a green filter. If nothing else it alerts suppliers to environmental issues.

Education and the Working Environment

Central to good management is to have properly trained and motivated grounds staff. All aspects of sports ground management are evolving at a rapid rate and it is imperative that grounds staffs are provided sufficient opportunities for continuing professional development.

Training: Great strides have been made in recent years in the provision of training and education facilities for the sports turf profession. There are many training options now available to sports clubs and grounds staff, including distance learning courses, as well as more structured grounds and seminar programmes. Training is an investment, vital for the industry as a whole as well as the individual employers. It is a vital component of management practice.

The working environment: Having secured higher levels of competence, it is clearly necessary to ensure that the facilities and resources back at the sports ground enable this improved expertise to be used. In many respects the quality of a sports ground will be related to the working conditions and status of the grounds staff. Poor, run-down maintenance facilities and equipment are inefficient, potentially damaging to the environment (through spillages and discharges) and a disincentive to staff.

Safety on the sports ground: Compliance with Health and Safety legislation for employees, together with adequate safeguards and awareness for public and players on the sports ground.

Communications and Public Awareness

By adopting an environmental policy statement and setting up a 'Green Team' one has taken the first important steps in communicating environmental commitment. This is a vital topic: it is essential to keep people informed and interested in your programme, to coordinate between those most closely involved and to make sure the initiative is understood both within and outside the club. There are many possible ways of building up awareness:

- Include regular features on your environmental project in the club newsletter.
- Use the notice board to announce particular management projects, or inform about recent wildlife sightings.
- Produce a poster or leaflet, or even a small book, about the natural heritage of the sports ground.
- Make 'Green Issues' a theme for a members' evening and invite local environmental specialists to talk about the findings of your sports ground environmental review.
- Inform the local press about conservation projects taking place on the sports ground.
- Commission a series of interpretative plaques to be located at strategic points around the sports ground.

- Erect signs to mark sanctuary boundaries or highlight points of interest.

It can be especially valuable to place signs or other information where public rights of way cross or abut onto the sports ground. Environmental actions should be highlighted and augmented for participants and spectators at tournaments and other special events. These extra initiatives can help raise public awareness that your sports club is actively helping to protect the environment.

Waste Management

Good sports ground management does not end with turf care. It is important to review the complete cycle of operations involved. There is an important legal dimension here, with the need for compliance with Environmental Protection and Health and Safety Regulations. Waste management is another vital topic and one that many sports grounds need to examine more closely. Poor attention to detail here can undo good work done on the turf management side. This subject is covered in depth in the next chapter.

16 Waste Management

We live in a 'disposable' society where we want to easily dispose of unwanted goods and products, often without considering the effect upon the environment. We often do not consider that our waste has taken resources and energy to create and that these are lost when we dispose of them. What is more we continue to use natural resources which are finite in nature and thus their continued depletion is not sustainable. Most of our daily work and leisure activities create waste of some sort or other.

Many millions of tonnes of solid waste are produced annually within England and Wales. Some 6 per cent of this waste arises directly from office premises, which includes sports clubs with the remainder being made up from commercial, domestic and industrial waste. It is thought that most of this 6 per cent could be eliminated at source. In recent years waste has become a major issue for both economic and environmental reasons. There are increasing populations globally and a culture of consumerism driven by technology, increases in disposable income and leisure time which are driving the production of waste ever upwards.

There is a growing movement and will however to stem this waste growth partly because of increasing legislation but also because of the recognition of the costs incurred in waste management and disposal. National government, local authorities, commercial businesses are taking responsibility for their waste and recognizing that their past practices are not sustainable in the longer term. Some now understand that waste is actually an inefficient use of resources as it can cost their business up to 6 per cent of annual turnover. Even small organizations though like our many sports clubs can play their part in the larger picture in reducing waste locally and nationally and in turn they also benefit from savings in expenditure in energy, time and materials.

A Hierarchical Approach to Waste Management

Management should consider the disposal of waste products and materials before it is actually created in operational processes. The approach advocated below will help staff to minimise waste creation and encourage proactive management of the process. Waste management can be illustrated as a pyramidal process with actual disposal being at the top of a sequence of stages designed to minimise that which cannot be used again. From top to bottom of the pyramid in sequential order would be: Eliminate, Minimize, Re-use, Recycle and finally Disposal.

1. **Eliminate:** for example by not buying products or materials in unnecessary packaging.
2. **Minimize:** for example one can service machinery regularly to prolong its life, use water sparingly.

3. **Re-use:** for example you could reuse machinery parts, 'cannibalize' old machines to keep newer ones going longer.
4. **Recycle:** compost grass clippings and tree pruning's and use as mulches on borders.
5. **Dispose**—this only applies where the first four options have not been possible.

The process of waste management should commence with an audit to measure the organizations use of consumables and the types of waste that result from their deployment. Such an audit can be used to measure waste reduction effectiveness and provide targets for the organizational staff to work towards. Savings made in waste reduction could be channelled to other more important areas such as the maintenance of the pitches. Audits should identify where the waste comes from, its type and quantity and the current disposal method including associated costs. Such an audit if conducted thoroughly should allow one to identify areas for waste reduction and thereby cost savings for the organization.

Planning for a Sustainable Operation

After the completion of a waste audit it should be apparent where and what steps can be taken to successfully reduce waste. A strategy should be formulated to reduce waste and its associated costs. The principles of the waste pyramid described earlier should be adhered to and be central to the resulting waste management plan. When formulating such a plan key considerations will often include:

Product durability and lifespan: for example the maintenance of sports ground machinery to prolong its life or the use of low energy light bulbs in work premises. These and others are important aspects to consider in waste reduction.

Procurement policies: avoid unnecessary packaging with purchased products and buy recycled products. There are many recycled products that can be used in turf and landscape management. The Waste Resources Action Programme www.wrap.org.uk is a specialist governmental group that provides advice on the purchasing of recycled products and is a very useful contact.

Staff Communication and involvement: encouraging staff to take ownership and engage in waste reduction policies is integral to success. Small steps such as electronic newsletters rather than paper based ones can be significant here.

Legislation Affecting Waste

The legal framework surrounding waste management is complex, often confusing and sometimes unclear. Outlined below are the most significant directives affecting waste management. It should be recognized, however, that this list is in no way exhaustive and that other environmental and ecological legislation could also impart controls on waste disposal if protected species or habitats could be affected. Before disposing of any substance, it is important to determine whether or not it is actually waste. Waste does have a fairly clear definition, which is not based on its usefulness to the owner or monetary worth. The Environmental Protection Act 1990 (Section 75-2) defines waste as one of the following categories:

• Products past their expiry date
• Materials spilt, lost or having undergone mishap including materials, etc. contaminated as a result
• Contaminated or soiled materials as a result of planned action
• Contaminated or soiled materials as a result of remedial action (on land)
• Unusable parts

- Substances that no longer perform satisfactorily
- Pollution abatement processes
- Machining or finishing
- Residues resulting from:
  - pollution abatement processes
  - machining or finishing
- Contaminated materials
- Any substances, products or material banned by law
- Unwanted products

Environmental Protection Act (EPA) 1990

This is the single most important piece of environmental legislation of recent times. It controls many aspects of how the environment is protected and regulated on a day-to-day basis. The EPA 1990 (amended 1995) provides the main statutory framework in relation to waste. In particular the document:

- Defines waste.
- Outlines the roles and functions of the waste collection/disposal authorities and Environment Agency.
- Establishes the criminal offences, in relation to waste.
- Lays down the waste management licensing system.
- Establishes the statutory Duty of Care in relation to waste.

The EPA makes it an offence to:

- Deposit controlled waste without a licence.
- Knowingly permit controlled waste to be deposited on site.
- Keep, treat or dispose of controlled waste.
- Knowingly cause or permit controlled waste to be kept, treated or disposed of unless a Waste Management Licence has been issued.
- It is also an offence to keep, treat or dispose of controlled waste in a manner likely to cause pollution of the environment or harm to human health.

Environmental Protection (Duty of Care) Regulations 1991

This regulation concerns the safe disposal of wastes and places responsibilities on both the manufacturer of the waste and the sports ground (company producing waste). The duties and responsibilities laid down are as much to protect the producer of the waste from disreputable waste disposal firms as they are to protect the environment. This is because the company producing the waste is still responsible for the waste even when some-one has removed it from their site. If it turns up in a ditch, the producer of the waste can also be prosecuted, not just the firm fly tipping it.

The Special Waste Regulations 1996

Special Waste is essentially any waste on a hazardous waste list that came out of the Directive. To be on the list, it must contain one or more of fourteen hazardous properties, or more than a threshold amount of a 'dangerous substance' that if simply buried in landfill would cause environmental pollution or negative health effects. The specific nature of what is special waste is detailed below. However, if in doubt, ask the manufacturer of the product from which the waste arises or the Environment Agency. The purpose of the 1996 Regulations is to provide control over special waste from the time the waste is produced to its final disposal or recovery, the so-called 'Cradle to Grave' philosophy. The Special Waste Regulations apply to persons who produce, carry, receive, keep, treat (including recovery) or dispose of special waste.

Waste is defined as 'Special' if it is any controlled waste, other than household waste, that is in the list set out in the Special Waste Regulations. It is any controlled waste (including waste not on the above lists), other than household waste, if it is:

- Highly flammable
- Irritant
- Harmful

- Toxic/carcinogenic
- Corrosive

WASTE PRODUCER'S RESPONSIBILITIES
It is the responsibility of the waste producer to:

- Describe the waste fully and accurately.
- Store waste safely on site.
- Select an appropriate treatment or disposal method.
- Ensure waste falls within the terms of the waste contractor's Waste Management Licence.
- Pack waste securely.
- Check waste carrier's registration documents.
- Make reasonable checks on the waste carrier or manager.
- Report offences to the Environment Agency.
- Complete and sign a waste transfer note of waste to another party.

You may need a Waste Carrier's Registration if you are moving waste off your site of work.

WASTE CARRIER'S RESPONSIBILITIES
If you (or a third party) wish to transport waste from the sports club to a designated disposal site you must:

- Have a Waste Carrier's Registration.
- Ensure adequacy of containment of wastes in your control.
- Ensure waste does not escape.
- Repack waste if necessary.
- Make a visual inspection to check accuracy of waste description.
- Re-describe waste that is treated or repacked.
- Ensure waste is taken to an appropriate site with a Waste Management Licence or appropriate exemption – make reasonable checks on the waste manager.
- Complete and sign transfer notes on any waste transfers to or from another party.

- Report offences to the Environment Agency.

Pollution Prevention and Control Act 1999

The Act is written so as to enable the prevention or, where not possible, the reduction of pollution by means of an integrated permitting process based on the application of Best Available Techniques (BAT). The aim is to achieve a high level of environmental protection by taking into account pollutant emissions to air, water and land; energy efficiency; consumption of raw materials; noise/vibration; heat/light; pollution prevention; waste management; and site restoration. Integrated Pollution Prevention and Control is required for all activities listed in Annex 1 of the Directive, which includes a section called 'Waste Management' that encompasses any commercial activity that produces waste.

Clean Air Act 1993

Urban air quality earlier last century was extremely poor, with frequent episodes of smog and sulphur fumes from industrial chimneys and stacks. After the 'Great Smog' settled on London in 1952, lasting for five days and contributing to more than 4,000 deaths, the Government appointed a committee to study air pollution. The eventual result was the Clean Air Act 1956, extended by the Clean Air Act 1968. These Acts constituted the operative legislation against pollution by smoke, grit and dust from domestic fires and commercial and industrial processes not covered by other legislation. They also regulated the combustion of solid, liquid and gaseous fuels and controlled the heights of new chimneys. The 1956 and 1968 Acts have now been consolidated and their provisions re-enacted in the Clean Air Act 1993.

Groundwater Regulations 1998

The Regulations complete the implementation of the obligations of the Groundwater Directive. The purpose of this Directive is to prevent the pollution of groundwater by certain named substances; these substances are on List I and List II of the Directive and are available from the Environment Agency. The Regulations prohibit discharges of List I substances to groundwater, and limit the discharge of List II substances so as to prevent pollution of groundwater. These requirements apply to all direct and indirect discharges to groundwater. They have put a limit on pollution of one part of pesticide to 10,000,000,000 parts of drinking water – equivalent to one drop in an Olympic size swimming pool! Under the Regulations it is an offence to cause or knowingly permit the disposal, or tipping for the purpose of disposal, of any List I or List II substance in circumstances that might lead to its introduction into groundwater.

The Water Framework Directive (WFD)

The EU Water Framework Directive came into force in December 2000. It is the most substantial piece of EU water legislation to date, introducing far-reaching implications for all sectors whose activities impact on, or are impacted by, the water environment. These include the water industry, agriculture, development and all businesses that have discharge consents, trade effluent licences or abstraction licences (such as sports grounds). The Directive will also be relevant to local authorities in their role as planning authorities and other agencies that have a direct or indirect role in the management of the water environment.

The primary objectives of the Directive include:

- Preventing deterioration of, and enhancing, ecological water quality.
- Ensuring reduction/prevention of groundwater pollution.
- Aiming to progressively reduce/eliminate pollution especially from priority hazardous substances.
- Promoting sustainable water use.
- Contributing to mitigation of floods and droughts.

Management of Waste Arising from Turf and Landscape Maintenance

Grass Clippings

Traditionally, grass clippings have formed an important part of compost manufacture on the sports ground and have been considered a valuable commodity. This practice, however, has largely ceased over the past thirty years, during which the disposal of this previously useful asset has become a hindrance to the sports ground manager. Indiscriminate dumping behind trees or within coarser vegetation areas around the periphery of the sports ground or in some other 'unseen' locale has become commonplace. Not only is this bad practice, leading to a nutrification of these areas, poisoning of the soil and unsightly and foul-smelling heaps on the sports ground, but it is also potentially illegal dependent on the individual circumstances. Even widespread dissemination into coarse grass areas will increase the nutrient status of the soil, thus leading to the sward becoming dominated by the broader-leaved and undesirable grass species that provide minimal ecological and aesthetic interest. The amounts of grass clippings produced on a sports ground will be determined by:

- Soil nutrient status
- Amounts of fertilizer applied
- Local climate
- Size of surfaces requiring clipping removal (greens, cricket squares and so on)

The greatest production will be between April and September, with peaks at either end of this period. As the grass decomposes, the volume of material is reduced substantially due to loss of the liquid fraction, which comprises 70–80 per cent of the leaf material. This liquid contains a concentrated potassium solution and will kill turf by scorching. Moreover, if this liquid enters waterways it is highly toxic to aquatic life.

A common but now illegal sight: washing down a machine on a hard surface without a water catchment facility. (Waste2Water Europe Ltd)

Ground contamination: the result of washing down machinery without a proper washdown facility. (Waste2Water Europe Ltd)

The best method of managing grass clippings is to adopt suitable turf management methods and reduce the amount of clippings produced and to compost any clippings that are collected. Composting of grass waste may involve the placement of a series of hard-based and bunded (embanked) temporary grass storage bays located discretely around the sports ground. Clippings can be stored for a maximum of one month before they are collected and relocated to a single composting facility. Alternatively, clippings are collected after the work is complete. This method prevents the need for storage bays where there may be no scope to introduce them. The central compost facility must be large enough to handle two or three compost piles, again on a bunded hard-standing with a fall to a collection sump. After six to eight months in one position each compost pile can be turned before the commencement of a second or third composting pile. Any leachate collected can be reapplied to the compost as a wetting agent or dealt with via dilution and spraying onto weak areas. The facility should be completely covered to prevent the addition of rainwater, which will aid the run-off of leachate while destroying the integrity of the compost. Fine turf clippings alone are poor for making good-quality compost as air cannot move within them, thus creating anaerobic decomposition and subsequently the unmistakable foul odours associated with piles of fine turf clippings. It would therefore be beneficial to the sports ground that all organic waste taken from cut rough grasslands or recently trimmed trees is collected and chipped in order to mix with fine turf clippings to create a good standard of compost. If worked correctly then usable compost should be ready for use within twelve months. This can then be applied to areas of the sports ground as a topdressing for lawn areas or in landscape plantings near the clubhouse.

Leaf Litter

The major problem with leaf litter is its perceived untidiness, particularly during leaf fall. Look on the back of many leaves that have been on the ground for a week or so and you are likely to see galls, the larvae of caterpillars, spiders and other invertebrate species. Birds require leaf litter as an important forage habitat during the winter months. Leaf litter is clearly a problem where it impacts on play – it can have a smothering effect on playing surfaces leading to water retention, which in turn could give rise to disease. It is therefore important that leaf litter is cleared from these areas and composted to provide a valuable compost or mulch for amenity plantings.

Soil Cores, Turf and Other Sand/Soil Waste

The basic problem with these organic wastes is that over time they can accumulate into large piles and become increasingly difficult to deal with. They may leach, changing the composition of the surrounding vegetation; they can have a negative visual impact and, importantly, they may be sited in areas of high ecological interest, destroying habitat quality. These wastes, however, represent quite a valuable resource that can be used to good effect in many applications. Hollow cores collected as part of routine aeration work could be stockpiled within a temporary storage area, preferably near to the main compost facility. Integrate cores into the main compost heap by layering to a maximum depth of 200mm (the proportion of soil to clippings by volume should be about 1:10). These will be generally left uncovered to allow weathering to occur before utilizing the materials within the compost process. Hollow cores can be reused for general repair work, divoting and topdressing, or in construction/landscaping project work. Turf stacks can be produced on the sports ground to aid their natural decomposition. Do not dump turves indiscriminately as this will lead to nutrient enrichment and a change in local vegetation conditions. Sand/soil materials can be stored on a temporary basis close to

Mowing often generates large amounts of grass clippings that need to be disposed of. (John Deere)

the composting facility for inclusion in the compost process. Add to the compost heap at a rate of 1:10 by volume. Sand mixed with compost at around five parts sand to one part compost would form good quality general use, divoting and top-dressing material.

Management of Waste Arising from the Sports Ground Maintenance Facility

Pesticides

Using pesticides according to the label instructions and following best practice should ensure their impact on the environment is minimized or even negated entirely; there is clear evidence, however, that poor practice when handling and mixing pesticides, cleaning up and disposing of wastes after spraying can pollute surface and groundwater. To protect the environment,

more legal controls are being introduced. Since 1999 any disposal to land of surplus spray and washings that does not take place 'in the crop' (that is, turf) requires a 'Groundwater Authorization' from the local office of the Environment Agency. Pesticides entering our freshwater matrix cause serious damage to local wildlife. Those specialist aquatic organisms that are surviving in water bodies at the very limits of their tolerance can be wiped out entirely by even a small influx of pesticides. It should be noted that it is not just the large and obvious spills that cause damage to the ecosystems but also low-level and long-term background levels.

MINIMIZE THE AMOUNT OF PESTICIDE/ CONTAINERS THAT REQUIRE DISPOSAL
- Order enough products to do the job in hand and no more.
- Buy products in the largest practical container sizes.

- Store products in good order.
- Use internal sprayer, tank-cleaning units and container rinsing devices.
- Choose products that minimize or eliminate contaminated packaging waste, such as returnable packs.
- Keep careful records of the movement of stock in and out of the agrochemical store; rotate stock on the 'first-in, first-out' principle.
- Carefully calculate required quantities needed and mix just enough to complete a task, no more.
- Ensure long-term weather forecasts are checked in advance of works in order to plan accordingly.

DISPOSAL OF SURPLUS SPRAY AND WASHINGS

- In the crop/grass area (Groundwater Authorization required). Find a suitable area of zero wildlife interest or a previously under-dosed area and spray during appropriate weather conditions.
- Fully contained washdown area with collection facility (Groundwater Authorization not required). All washings/surplus spray collected into a secure tank and collected by licensed carrier.
- Fully contained washdown area with treatment plant (Groundwater Authorization required). A treatment plant for machinery washdown can take the form of one of the commercially available 'closed loop' systems or a reedbed complex prior to discharge.

DISPOSAL OF UNWANTED CONTAINERS/OBSOLETE PESTICIDES

- Always empty and triple rinse containers before storage/disposal.
- Store clean containers upright with their lids securely on in a dedicated compound.
- Properly clean foil seals and store with containers.
- Ensure a licensed carrier is used to appropriately collect and remove unwanted containers.

- Unwanted/out-of-date products may be collected via the original seller.
- Alternatively a licensed waste handler must be brought in to dispose of the product.

SPILLAGES

- Always keep a spill kit to hand when dealing with pesticides.
- Always fill up on an appropriately bunded area.
- Crystals or other soaking materials must be disposed of via a licensed handler after use.

Tyres

More than 50 million tyres (just over 480,000 tonnes) are scrapped in the UK each year and around 80,000 tonnes are disposed of in landfill. Although sports clubs are not recognized as a major producer of tyre waste, the safe disposal of used mower, tractor or other machinery tyres is an important issue, especially given the high polluting effect of improper disposal and the new stringent legislation. Tyres use non-renewable resources in their production, cause emissions to air, land and water as fine particles are worn off during their use, and require management at the end of use (Environment Agency, 1998). It is tyres, rather than engines, that are the major source of noise pollution associated with roads. Spare tyres should be stored inside, in a secure area in order to prevent health and safety issues. Storage of used tyres prior to disposal should be indoors, on an impervious hard-standing base and safely stacked in a secure area.

If one transfers waste tyres to someone else, you must be sure they are authorized to take them. All authorized waste carriers are registered with the Environment Agency and have a certificate of registration. Ensure that your waste tyres will be reused, recycled or recovered. Extracting the maximum safe life from a tyre saves valuable resources (including oil, rubber and steel). Before the tyre can be resold it must

THE NATIONAL REGISTER OF SPRAYER OPERATORS

The NRoSO is a central register of certificated spray operators that uses Continuing Professional Development (CPD) as a means of ensuring ongoing training. The scheme is administered by the National Proficiency Testing Council (NPTC). It is an industry initiative intended to demonstrate to the Government that only responsible users apply pesticides and thereby minimize environmental risk. By registering on NRoSO, employers and operators are showing their commitment to professionalism and ongoing training. It will reinforce the responsible image of operators to the regulators and the public. (Further details of the NRoSO are available from www.nptc.org.uk.)

THE NATIONAL SPRAYER TESTING SCHEME

The NSTS is an independent, annual testing scheme supported by the Voluntary Initiative (*see* below). The scheme is open to all users of any spraying equipment within the amenity sector, including hand-held apparatus. Compliance with the scheme will ensure maximum efficiency of your sprayer,

reducing costly downtime while aiding traceability and retaining second-hand value. The cost of replacing worn jets that deliver only 5 per cent more than the recommended rate is readily recovered in chemical savings and improved efficacy resulting from better and more consistent spray quality. The tests can be carried out at the sports club by an approved technician (an up-to-date list can be found at www.nsts.org.uk). There may be a small charge, however money will soon be recovered via improved efficiency and a reduction in waste.

THE VOLUNTARY INITIATIVE

The Voluntary Initiative was accepted by the Government on 1 April 2001 in place of a proposed tax on pesticides used in agriculture and horticulture. The initiative was put forward by seven signatory organizations led by the Crop Protection Association. The Voluntary Initiative supports the National Register of Sprayer Operators (NRoSO) in order to prevent a pesticide tax and encourage best practice regarding spraying and pesticide management. (Further details of the Voluntary Initiative can be found at www.voluntaryinitiative.co.uk.)

be checked. Part-worn tyres must have a minimum of 2mm tread remaining and be marked as part-worn on both sides at the time of sale. Perhaps the most relevant recycling of tyres for the sports ground in recent years has been the reuse of ground tyres as 'rubber crumb'. This material has been used as an ameliorant to improve surface stability of natural grass playing surfaces and also as an infill material for 'third generation' (3G) synthetic turf sports pitches.

Oil

Oil takes many forms and is used in numerous tasks throughout the sports ground environment. Petrol, diesel, two-stroke oil, machinery lubricants and such are all oil-based products and, when they become surplus to requirements, must be appropriately managed. Most people in the twenty-first century are aware of the environmental devastation caused by inappropriate oil disposal and also equally aware of the potential legal implications for uncontrolled dumping. Accidental spillage and leaks of unburned fuel oils, and run-off of lubricating oils from washing maintenance machinery, are therefore the most significant oil-related pollution incidents on sports grounds. If allowed to enter the local freshwater matrix, oil will form a film above the water's surface, thus preventing oxygen from circulating and eventually leading to the death of submerged aquatic flora and fauna. Five litres of oil (or an oil-based material) is enough to cover and kill a pond measuring 1.5 hectares. Furthermore, mobile animals and birds coming into contact with oil will become coated, thus reducing their ability to move and feed within the wider countryside.

The sports ground should stock a minimum of one emergency oil spill kit in an easily accessible area close to any part of the sports ground where oil/fuel is likely to be used. Following the use of an oil spill kit, the crystals/sand used to absorb the oil must be treated as hazardous waste and removed via a licensed contractor. A contingency plan must be put into place so that every member of staff is aware of the procedure should an oil/fuel spillage occur. Detergents should never be used to clean up oil spills as they reduce the surface tension and aid dispersal. Locate an appropriate storage facility in an appropriate area of the sports ground in excess of 10m from a water body or 50m from a well or bore hole. Site the storage facility on a bunded hard-standing area leading to the waste water treatment plant. The waste oil storage facility should be constructed in exactly the same way as the virgin oil/fuel storage facility. Empty oil or fuel containers should be stored within the waste oil storage facility on an impervious base. Any water collected within an oil storage bund must be treated as hazardous waste and collected by a licensed contractor. Many oils can be recycled and will be of value to licensed collection agents. Only use contractors who will recycle the oil following collection. Small amounts of oil can be taken to a local oil recycling depot for treatment.

Batteries

It is estimated in 2000 that almost 19,000 tonnes of waste general purpose batteries and 113,000 tonnes of waste automotive batteries require disposal in the UK each year. While the exact chemical make-up varies from type to type, most batteries contain heavy metals, which are the main cause for environmental concern. When disposed of incorrectly, these heavy metals may leak into the ground when the battery casing corrodes. This can contribute to soil and water pollution and endanger wildlife. Cadmium, for example, can be toxic to aquatic invertebrates and can bio-accumulate in fish, which damages ecosystems and makes them unfit for human consumption. Some batteries, such as button cell batteries, also contain mercury which has similarly hazardous properties. Mercury is no longer being used in the manufacture of non-rechargeable batteries, except button cells where it is a functional component; the major European battery suppliers have been offering mercury-free disposable batteries since 1994. Currently, only a very small percentage of consumer disposable batteries are recycled (less than 2 per cent) and most waste batteries are disposed of in landfill sites. The rate for recycling of consumer rechargeable batteries is estimated to be 5 per cent. Automotive batteries, on the other hand, are more routinely recycled in the UK, with a current recycling rate of approximately 90 per cent. They are collected at garages, scrap metal facilities and many civic amenity and recycling centres.

- Use the mains when possible.
- Use rechargeable batteries and a battery charger. This saves energy because the energy needed to manufacture a battery is on average fifty times greater than the energy it gives out. However, rechargeable batteries are not suitable for smoke alarms as they tend to run out suddenly, preventing the alarm from warning when battery power is low.

- Opt for appliances that can use power derived from the sun via solar panels or from a winding mechanism.
- Participate in local authority battery collection schemes where they are available.
- Seek guidance on how to dispose or recycle batteries from either the distributor who originally supplied the battery, the battery manufacturer or the appliance manufacturer.
- Send batteries back to manufacturers for recycling or reprocessing where such a scheme is available.

End of Life Machinery

There were around 30 million motor vehicles in use within the UK in 2002. Every year approximately 2 million new vehicles are registered; the average lifespan of a car is 13.5 years. More than 2 million vehicles also reach the end of their useful lives every year, either because of old age or due to an accident. In the sports ground scenario, we not only have cars and vans but also more specialist machinery including the likes of mowers, tractors and flails. All of these machines must be dealt with when they no longer become useful to their owners. Given the complexity of a vehicle, they are obviously difficult to recycle and dispose of without an effect on the environment and therefore extending the useful life of such products is crucial. Efficient maintenance of machinery is essential in ensuring sustainability. Waste is not only generated by the physical disposal of parts but also in the inefficient running of the engine. Higher levels of waste materials such as nitrogen oxides, carbons, sulphur dioxide, lead and even water are emitted from a poorly maintained engine and are all harmful pollutants (water vapour is a significant contributor to the greenhouse effect). Therefore regular servicing of machinery and sharpening of mower blades are crucial elements of waste management. Investigate the possibility of conversion to a cost- and emission-saving fuel such as LPG, bio-diesel or electric.

INDIVIDUAL COMPONENTS

Oil filters: These are predominantly steel and are therefore easily recycled. Remove the filter from the engine to 'hot drain' it while the engine is still warm. Hot draining is defined as draining the oil filter at or near engine operating temperature. Using a tool such as a screwdriver, carefully puncture the dome end of the filter. Then turn the filter upside down, so it can drain completely into your container for used oil recycling. Allow the filter to drain overnight (or a minimum of twelve hours) to remove all the oil. Recycle used oil and drained oil filters at your local garage or special waste recycling centre. Check with your local authority for information about collection centres. Some auto parts stores also accept drained filters for recycling.

Air filters and water filters: These are made from a variety of materials. After removal filters should be stored in a covered area. Contact your local authority for the location of your nearest licensed recycling facility. Some auto parts stores also accept filters for recycling.

Engine breakdown: This is usually the fault of only one or two parts, leaving the remainder in good working order. Many parts of a broken down engine can be salvaged for spares in other machines or sold on to salvage merchants. Repairing broken machinery is far more cost-effective than buying new. When cleaning any oily machine parts, ensure run-off is treated as 'special waste' and is passed through a water treatment area.

Waste Water Following Machinery Washdown

Appropriate treatment of waste water following the washdown of sports ground maintenance machinery has been a long-standing and debatable topic within the sports turf industry. The legality surrounding discharge to the local freshwater matrix has been considered a 'grey area' with incorrect and even biased information being issued in a number of trade publications. The legal complications aside,

Engines and Fuel

ENGINE EMISSIONS

During the combustion process, internal combustion engines of all types generally produce, in varying quantities, the following substances:

- Oxides of nitrogen, a contributor to photochemical smog and to ozone layer damage
- Carbon monoxide, a toxic gas (harmful to humans, animals and plants)
- Carbon dioxide, the most significant cumulative 'greenhouse gas'
- Hydrocarbons, a constituent of photochemical smog
- Sulphur dioxide, an element in acid rain formation
- Lead, a toxic heavy metal
- Particulate matter, a potential carcinogen and inhibitor of photosynthesis in plants.
- Water, an important contributor to the 'greenhouse effect'

TYPES OF ENGINES

The vast majority of maintenance machinery use one of the following engine types:

- Two-stroke engine fuelled by a petrol/oil mix or converted to propane
- Four-stroke engine fuelled by petrol, diesel or propane

ALTERNATIVE FUELS

A number of machinery manufacturers are now taking their environmental responsibilities very seriously and pioneering the use of less environmentally damaging fuels. The main alternatives to traditional fossil fuels at the time of writing include bio-diesel, liquid petroleum gas (LPG) and electric motors.

Bio-diesel is a fuel made from animal or vegetable fats that performs identically to petrol/diesel but produces less exhaust gases. It is also bio-degradable and less damaging to the environment if spilt.

LPG is one of the fastest growing commercial fuels in the UK. It is a byproduct of North Sea oil production and is a mixture of butane and propane. Almost any vehicle can be converted to run on LPG and many cars, vans and maintenance machines are now constructed with the option of LPG. Its use within an engine gives no discernible difference to traditional fuels and emits up to 99.8 per cent less pollutant.

Electric motors have come a long way over the past few years with 'hybrid' cars now becoming commonplace on our roads. The use of an electrically powered mower or sports cart may at first seem environmentally sound but we must consider how the energy is produced in the first instance. If the machine is charged up from mains electricity then we are simply moving the pollution to a different source (the power station). Far more desirable than this is the use of small-scale generators in-house. Wind turbines and solar panels are now available commercially and the technology is now becoming such that they are economically viable.

it is the moral responsibility of every sports ground to appropriately manage washdown water before it is released into the surrounding environment in order to reduce impact on groundwater and associated ecology, and also to provide a healthier and more aesthetically pleasant environment in which to play sports. If best practice is followed for the disposal of surplus pesticides and fertilizers, then the likely potentially damaging pollutants arising from discharge of untreated washdown water is moderate to low. However, undoubtedly the most problematic waste arising from this operation is the large amounts of fine turf clippings that readily stick to turf maintenance machinery, particularly in wet weather. Grass clippings

Environmentally 'friendly' washdown area and waste water treatment plant. (Waste2Water Europe Ltd)

Grass clippings separated from the washdown water in the catchments bay and treatment plant. Such clippings can now be composted. (Waste2Water Europe Ltd)

contain a significant amount of nitrogen, phosphorus and potassium (equivalent to approximately 2.5 per cent nitrogen, 0.7 per cent phosphorus and 2 per cent potassium in dry leaf material). This equates to approximately 24g/kg nitrogen, 8g/kg phosphorus and 20g/kg potassium being released following thirty days' breakdown of grass clippings.

- Reduce the amount of water to be discharged via appropriate planning for machinery usage and subsequent washdown on a phased and structured basis.
- The use of air hoses where applicable and collection of waste arising is a more controlled method of machinery cleaning that gives rise to zero effluent.
- Install some form of interceptor/recycler/collection unit.

- Following grass cutting, use a return maintenance track, which will allow the majority of green waste to dissipate away from machinery wheels (such as over a hard-standing).
- Ensure all green waste is collected following machinery washdown in some form of grass trap and appropriately managed by composting.

The release of organic waste through machinery washdown water into the surrounding freshwater matrix will not only raise the biological oxygen demand (BOD) of the water body, thus reducing the likelihood of aquatic life, but can also result in the retention of partially fermented clippings resulting in high levels of potassium leaching into water bodies, thus actively killing invertebrates and other aquatic flora and fauna.

Useful UK Contacts

Institute of Groundsmanship
28 Stratford Office Village
Walker Avenue
Wolverton Mill East
Milton Keynes
MK12 5TW
Tel: 01908 312511
Fax: 01908 311140
http://www.iog.org

**The Sports and Play
Construction Association**
Federation House
Stoneleigh Park
Warwickshire
CV8 2RF
Tel: 024 7641 6316
Fax: 024 7641 4773
http://www.sapca.org.uk

**Land Drainage Contractors
Association**
NAC Stoneleigh Park
Stoneleigh
Kenilworth
Warwickshire
CV8 2LG
Tel: 01327 263264
Fax: 01327 263265
http://www.ldca.org

Environment Agency
National Customer Contact Centre
PO Box 544
Rotherham
S60 1BY
Tel: 08708 506 506
http://www.environment-agency.
gov.uk

The Health and Safety Executive
Rose Court
2 Southwark Bridge
London
SE1 9HS
Tel: 0845 345 0055
http://www.hse.gov.uk

**British Association of
Landscape Industries**
Landscape House
National Agricultural Centre
Stoneleigh Park
Warwickshire
CV8 2LG

Tel: 024 7669 0333
Fax: 024 7669 0077
http://www.bali.co.uk

J Mallinson (Ormskirk) Ltd
Landscape and Sports
Ground Contractors
Firtree Nurseries
Old Engine Lane
Skelmersdale
Lancashire
WN8 8UZ
Tel: 01695 723414
Fax: 01695 724514

**SISIS Equipment
(Macclesfield) Ltd**
Hurdsfield
Macclesfield
Cheshire
SK10 2LZ
Tel: 01625 503030
Fax: 01625 427426
http://www.sisis.com

Autoguide Equipment Ltd
Stockley Road
Heddington
Nr Calne
Wiltshire
SN11 0PS
Telephone: 01380 850885
Fax: 01380 850010
http://www.autoguide.co.uk/
groundcare/index.html

John Deere Ltd
Harby Road
Langar
Nottingham
NG13 9HT
Tel: 01949 860491
Fax: 01949 860490
http://www.deere.com/en_GB/
index.html

Ransomes Jacobsen Ltd
West Road
Ransomes Europark
Ipswich
Suffolk
IP3 9TT
Tel: 01473 270000
Fax: 01473 276300
http://www.ransomesjacobsen.com

Bernhard and Company Ltd
Bilton Road
Rugby
CV22 7DT
Tel: 01788 811600
Fax: 01788 812640
http://www.bernhard.co.uk

Lely (UK) Limited
1 Station Road
St Neots
Cambridgeshire
PE19 1QH
Tel: 01480 226800
Fax: 01480 226801
http://www.lely.com

Waste2Water Europe
102A Longton Road
Barlaston
Staffordshire
ST12 9AU
Tel: 01782 373878
Fax: 01782 373763
http://waste2water.com

Fleet Line Markers Ltd
Fleet House
Spring Lane
Malvern
Worcestershire
WR14 1AT
Tel: 01684 573535
Fax: 01684 892784
http://www.fleetlinemarkers.co.uk

Harrod UK Limited
Pinbush Road
Lowestoft
Suffolk
NR33 7NL
Tel: 01502 583515
Fax: 01502 582456
http://www.harrod.uk.com

Dennis Mowers
Ashbourne Road
Kirk Langley
Derbyshire
DE6 4NJ
Tel: 01332 824777
Fax: 01332 824525
http://www.dennisuk.com

Index